CATHOLIC THEOLOGICAL FORMATION SERIES

General Editor: Christopher J. Thompson

The Catholic Theological Formation Series is sponsored by The Saint Paul Seminary School of Divinity, the graduate school of theological formation for both Roman Catholic seminarians and laity enrolled at the University of St. Thomas in Saint Paul, MN. As a premier institution of theological formation for the region and beyond, The Saint Paul Seminary School of Divinity seeks to form both men and women for the task of fulfilling the specific call God has for them grounded in their common baptismal vocation to serve one another in Christ.

As an institution of the Archdiocese of Saint Paul and Minneapolis, the school is intentional in its commitment to priestly formation for the archdiocese and the broader region. As an institution of graduate theological education, the school prepares the laity for the equally compelling task of making Christ known and loved in the world. Though distinct in their various ministries, the common goal of intense theological formation is shared across the curriculum.

It is precisely this challenge of theological formation, faithfully informing one's understanding, that serves as the focus of this series, with special attention given to the task of preparing priests, teachers, and leaders within the Roman Catholic tradition. While academic in its tenor, the aim is intellectual — that is, we seek to promote a form of discourse that is not only professional in its conduct but spiritual in its outcomes. Theological formation is more than an exercise in academic technique. Rather, it is about the perfecting of a spiritual capacity: the capacity on the part of the human person to discern what is true and good. This series, then, aims to develop the habits of mind required of a sound intellect, that spiritual aptitude for the truth of God's living Word and His Church. Most often the series will draw from the more traditional specializations of historical, systematic, moral, and biblical scholarship. Homiletics and pastoral ministry are anticipated venues as well. There will be occasions, however, when a theme is examined across disciplines and periods, for the purposes of bringing to our common consideration a thesis yet undeveloped.

Despite the variety of methodologies and topics explored, the aim of the series remains constant: to provide a sustained reflection upon the mission and ministry of Catholic theological formation of both priests and laity alike.

The General Editor of the Catholic Theological Formation Series, Christopher J. Thompson, serves as the Academic Dean of the Saint Paul Seminary School of Divinity.

On Earth as It Is in Heaven

Cultivating a Contemporary Theology of Creation

Edited by

David Vincent Meconi, SJ

WILLIAM B. EERDMANS PUBLISHING COMPANY
GRAND RAPIDS, MICHIGAN

Published 2016 by
Wm. B. Eerdmans Publishing Co.
2140 Oak Industrial Drive N.E., Grand Rapids, Michigan 49505

Printed in the United States of America

22 21 20 19 18 17 16   7 6 5 4 3 2 1

Library of Congress Cataloging-in-Publication Data

Names: Meconi, David Vincent, editor.
Title: On earth as it is in heaven : cultivating a contemporary theology of creation /
    edited by David Vincent Meconi, SJ.
Description: Grand Rapids, Michigan : Eerdmans Publishing Company, 2016. |
    Series: Catholic theological formation series
Includes bibliographical references and index
Identifiers: LCCN 2015045475 | ISBN 9780802873507 (pbk. : alk. paper)
Subjects: LCSH: Creation. | Catholic Church — Doctrines.
Classification: LCC BT695 .O57 2016 | DDC 231.7/65 — dc23
LC record available at http://lccn.loc.gov/2015045475

www.eerdmans.com

Contents

Introduction

Leading up to the 2015 release of *Laudato Si'*, Pope Francis's groundbreaking encyclical on the environment, a group of scholars gathered at the Saint Paul Seminary on the campus of the University of St. Thomas in St. Paul, Minnesota, to spend long summer days discussing what the ancient Christian tradition might have to say about ecological stewardship and a faithful theology of solidarity with all of creation. These discussions occurred as Pope Francis was preparing *Laudato Si'*, and it was too early for any of us to draw from the vision he was about to promulgate. As rich as that convergence may have been, what is fascinating about the following fifteen essays is how closely they all parallel the major concerns, themes, and figures put forth by the Holy Father. Francis's care is exact, and his call is encouraging. Christians of good will must resist the contemporary dangers of mindless acquisition and the consequent squandering of the earth's rich resources. These and other concerns explain the timing of Francis's promulgation of *Laudato Si'*: to teach everyone today about "the intimate relationship between the poor and the fragility of the planet, the conviction that everything in the world is connected, the critique of new paradigms and forms of power derived from technology, the call to seek other ways of understanding the economy and progress, the value proper to each creature, the human meaning of ecology, the need for forthright and honest debate, the serious responsibility of international and local policy, the throwaway culture and the proposal of a new lifestyle" (*Laudato Si'*, hereafter LS, §16).

The theses of the following essays inevitably fall between two extremes. On the one hand, any contemporary care of creation must resist sacralizing subhuman creatures; on the other, we must refuse to reduce creatures to merely natural objects to be manipulated and exploited for human gain only. Pope Francis himself captured this balancing act well throughout LS, teaching that an ecological spirituality "is not to put all living beings on the same level nor to deprive human beings of their unique worth and the tremendous responsibility it entails. Nor does it imply a divinization of the earth which would prevent us from working on it and protecting it in its fragility" (§90). Thus, the best of the Christian tradition may perhaps call creatures holy, but only God is absolutely and inherently sacred. He alone is the holiness in which all creatures participate, and with whom they can never be identified. So even though the goodness of creation is the litany through the opening pages of the book of Genesis, the Jewish people refused to follow their Mesopotamian neighbors in apotheosizing the visible order as a sacred entity apart from the author of its being. All things proclaim the greatness of God, but no one thing is God. Yet, today the tendency perhaps lies on the other extreme, wherein we all too glibly dismiss natural phenomena as raw data, able to be preyed upon and discarded as we humans find convenient. This functional reduction of creation to mere utility has occurred with an ever-increasing dismissal of the true nature of creation, especially of the human person, who stands as the frontier being, representing all levels of the visible order while still maintaining a supreme dignity over all that can be seen.

In Francis's maneuvering between the Scylla of false divinization and the Charybdis of selfish exploitation, he is inevitably drawing from the theology of creation found most recently in the *Compendium of the Social Doctrine of the Church,* which rightly teaches, "*A correct understanding of the environment prevents the utilitarian reduction of nature to a mere object to be manipulated and exploited. At the same time, it must not absolutize nature and place it above the dignity of the human person himself.* In this latter case, one can go so far as to divinize nature or the earth, as can readily be seen in certain ecological movements."[1] Accordingly, a Catholic approach to creation means honoring God by tending to his works with reverence and honest stewardship. Integrity is no longer only a human category. The Church is now calling all persons of good will to see that regard for the wholeness of the human person involves, to some degree, regard for the flourishing of nonhuman creation as well. Even though the human person may be the only

---

1. *Compendium of the Social Doctrine of the Church* (Washington, DC: USCCB; Vatican City: Libreria Editrice Vaticana, 2004), 202, §463.

visible *imago Dei,* the *vestigia Dei* (traces of God) that surround each of us are to be tended to with God's own solicitude and sympathy.

In the second-century *Letter to Diognetus,* Christians heard that they were to be to this world what the human soul is to the body.[2] Just as the soul collects and unifies otherwise disparate matter into a purposeful and powerful body, the Christian faithful are to immerse themselves in the created order so as not only to give it purpose but to consecrate it and make it ever and everywhere easier for God's glory to be known through his created works. This care and Christianization of creation is something the Church is only now beginning to recover from her ancient treasury. For today we are more aware than ever that we live in a very interdependent world in an even more fragile ecosystem. Accordingly, Vatican II (1962-65) taught all people of good will that "the expectation of a new earth should not weaken, but rather stimulate, the resolve to cultivate this earth where the body of the new human family is increasing and can even now constitute a foreshadowing of the new age. Although earthly progress must be carefully distinguished from the growth of Christ's kingdom, nevertheless its capacity to contribute to a better ordering of human society makes it highly relevant to the kingdom of God."[3] No longer can Christians dismiss this earth; no longer can they talk merely of heavenly realities.

The Christian God is a Father who knows every sparrow that flies on earth and who takes care of every lily of the field (Matt 6:28; Luke 12:26-27); God is a Son who assumes created matter to himself, learned life at a carpenter's bench, and used seeds, wheat, and weeds to speak of the kingdom of God (Matt 13:1-9, 18-30); God is a Spirit who labors to free all of creation from its "slavery to corruption" (Rom 8:21) into the same glorious freedom of the children of God. The manner in which the incarnate Son chose to teach us is primarily a discourse on the theophoric nature of creation itself, as "the sense of the divineness of the natural order is the major premise of all the parables."[4] The Christian creed affirms that this world was divinely willed by God (not wrestled from its original chaos into something manageable); this world is where God himself assumes the very elements of matter and humanity, and this created world is the place where his final consummation will occur, when all bodies will be resurrected forever. By creating, the God

2. Cf. *Letter to Diognetus,* in *Early Christian Writings,* trans. Maxwell Staniforth (New York: Penguin Classics, 1987), 145, §6.

3. *Gaudium et spes,* §39, as found in *Decrees of the Ecumenical Councils,* ed. Norman Tanner, SJ, et al. (Washington, DC: Georgetown University Press, 1990), 1092-93.

4. C. H. Dodd, *The Parables of the Kingdom* (Glasgow: Collins Press, 1935), 21.

of Genesis has chosen not to be everything but to be "all in all" (1 Cor 15:28), desirous to be known in lesser beings, refracting his own perfections.

This is a story that has tremendous significance today. For who has not awoken to the various ecological crises of our world? Men and women today cannot help but look for solutions to the environmental destruction they both experience and hear reported daily. Likewise, many scholars are becoming more sensitive to the world's vulnerability amid so many ecological threats and concerns. These thoughtful men and women enjoy a renewed boldness, unwilling to apologize for seeking ways to connect the central tenets of orthodox Christianity with a secular call to care for creation. It is the Christian's job to remind the modern citizen that the earth deserves our care, paraphrasing G. K. Chesterton, *not* because she is our mother but because she is our sister.[5] Many theologians and philosophers have thus begun to bring timeless principles to a rather recent conversation. They know that this new consciousness of the environment's needs is best addressed, not through more politicized pleas, but through the great tradition of the great Church. In fact, *Laudato Si'* marks a new beginning, with the Church now "officially" speaking out in defense of environmental responsibility and even in favor of an ecological spirituality (LS §216), rightly understood. The Church is now poised to comment on this kaleidoscopic relationship between God, creation, and the human person in a way not possible even a generation ago. The world's fragility has ushered in a new awareness, allowing us to draw from ancient tools that have for far too long been sheathed.

To respond to this new awareness, the scholars that gathered in the summer of 2014 to examine what the great Christian tradition might have to say about caring for creation were led by Robert Louis Wilken, the William R. Kenan, Jr., Professor of the History of Christianity Emeritus at the University of Virginia, the keynote speaker of our days together. Setting the tone for the present volume, Wilken presents "The Beauty of Centipedes and Toads," a provocative title introducing many important themes (and books) when looking at a contemporary Christian care of creation.

Drawing mainly from the Cappadocian Fathers, Wilken shows that a truly human person manifests the proper natural piety for all of God's works, the lowliest of bugs and beings included. In fact, this was one of the major ways Augustine broke from the Manichaean deprecation of matter. When

5. In following St. Francis of Assisi, Pope Francis does open *Laudato Si'* by quoting the great saint's canticle and calling the earth both our sister and our mother (LS §1) but then quickly calls creation our sister (§2) only.

members of this overly spiritualized gnostic sect mocked God for having created mice and frogs, Augustine chides them for acting like ignorant children in a master's workshop, making fun of things whose purpose and beauty they cannot fathom.[6] In the same way, Wilken likewise uses the foundations of the Catholic tradition to show that, simply because the human person is the crown of creation, he or she is not all of creation. There is an entire world below and around us teeming with God's own life.

Consequently, each species of nonhuman creation has a particular purpose and thus role to play in God's overall economy. For this reason pivotal thinkers like the brothers Basil of Caesarea (d. 379) and Gregory of Nyssa (d. ca. 395) both composed a Hexaemeron, a lengthy commentary on the days of creation. Basil and Gregory turned to the six days of Genesis in both sermons and treatises to show not only the goodness of a God willing to share his existence and life with ontologically inferior beings — "centipedes and toads" — but also to extend his own solicitude for others. Those persons made in God's image and likeness can therefore imitate God by tending to his creation (cf. LS §77). This is how both Basil and Gregory root their moral vision of the world in the wild complexity and individuality of all that God has brought out of nothing. Wilken thus concludes his inaugural essay by asking about the compassionate heart — to see all of creation as God does, to love all creatures as their Creator does.

In "The Place of Faith in the Geography of Hope," Dean Christopher J. Thompson, our host at the Saint Paul Seminary, aims to ensure that no creature whatsoever is reduced to a "resource" solely in order to be "used." The exploitation of ecosystems, the transgenetic modification of creatures, as well as the whimsical destruction of life, are areas where Thompson sees we might be ever more vigilant with (and as) creatures. His essay develops six major areas. The first is his analysis of our fallen tendency to flee *natura* and thereby treat all creation as a lower substrate necessarily in need of human resistance and domination. Thompson appeals to Aquinas's engagement with the Albigensian movement and this group's heretical deprecation of the created order. Preaching and prayer happily now have a place in the Christian care for creation. Thompson then considers the role of *natura* in leading the rational soul to one common Creator (cf. LS §12); Thompson thus cleverly returns his readers to the neglected appreciation that the natural law reflects the divine law. Now care for creation also receives a moral element. The third area is a movement from what Thompson calls the stan-

6. Cf. Augustine, *On Genesis: A Refutation of the Manichees* 1.16.25.

dard "theology of the body" to a "theology of embodiment." What contemporary Catholicism should be concerned about, he argues, is not simply what happens with and in the human body but, rather, what happens when embodiment itself is factored in to theological discourse. What does it mean to be members in a community with other enfleshed beings? What does it mean to inhabit a particular location? What does it mean to be the kind of being who, as embodied, occupies the earth and yet, as intellectual, enjoys an interior life known to God alone?

This shift in emphasis brings about Thompson's fourth concern, namely, to combat an encroaching "angelism" that has reduced the rational, human knower to a mind only. Here Thompson draws from contemporary thinkers who criticize the Magisterium for not being physicalist enough. Whereas the world thinks Christianity should content itself with discoursing on the things of heaven exclusively, Thompson desires to see more appreciation for what it means to be both soul and body.

The fifth area Thompson raises pertains to Catholic education (cf. LS §§ 209-32). Thompson wonders why more schools do not offer courses (and thus a vision) in agriculture and basic theologies of creation. Finally, he exhorts the reader to consider how we choose to interact with nonhuman creatures. What modifications and greater awareness of our role as stewards might we make when considering our habits and default tendencies toward the grandeur of the world around us?

In "The Teleological Grammar of the Created Order in Catholic Moral Discourse," Steven A. Long utilizes his expertise in the thought of St. Thomas Aquinas to show that all Christian discussions about the natural order must rediscover the theonomic character of creation. Long shows that, because divine governance reaches to all things, to understand the creation rightly is to understand created order as a participation in the eternal law. Natural law is nothing other than a rational participation in the eternal law, but this rational participation presupposes a prior divine ordering of creation, a "passive participation" in the eternal law that extends to all things.

There is a certain limited participation of the eternal law proportionate to the creature: "Thus since all things subject to divine providence are ruled and measured by eternal law . . . it is evident that all things participate somewhat in the eternal law, insofar as from its being imprinted on them they have their inclinations to their proper acts and ends."[7] The passive participation in the eternal law, from which all things have their inclinations to their acts

---

7. Thomas Aquinas, *Summa theologiae* I-II, q. 91, art. 2.

and ends, is shared by all creatures (including the human person, who does not cause the unified order that defines him, and whose rational appropriation provides the content for natural law). Such passively participated order presupposes the human person's rational participation, which is the natural law. When this transcendent character of passively participated order is grasped, we begin to appreciate the wonder of the world (cf. LS §199n141), as Thomas's insights rightly invite. The created order is an imprint of the eternal law, and this "imprint" (as Long names this teleological order, which is an impress of the divine wisdom) is precisely how all creatures enjoy and manifest their agency and purpose. In the divine providence, this participation in the eternal law conditions from within even the gift of revelation and our contemplation of it.

Long shows why this is a crucial move to make, for creation is humanity's point of contact with our Creator. It is the place where we first learn of divine generosity, participation, and purpose (cf. LS §79). As he beautifully writes, creation is "the home of our poetry, the stuff of wonder and beauty, the primal beginning of our science." Moreover, to know ourselves fully and to understand the higher causality of grace, we must know creation as well. We enfleshed souls cannot truly come to appreciate the depths and wonder of our own existence until we open ourselves up to the movements and meaning of matter. Insofar as the human person is thus the apex of all creation, a microcosm of existence, life, vegetation, sensation, and reason — all of creation is recapitulated in the human. Furthermore, the common good of the created universe — the divinely instilled order of creation — is a primordial divine gift that conditions from within man's contemplation of God and man's elevation and transfiguration in the life of grace. The prime significance for man of the divine ordering of the cosmos is thus its role in fecundating and perfecting our contemplation, which continues even within the pedagogy of grace. While lower created good is indeed ordained to the service of man, it together with man is part of a divinely ordained order defining the common good of the universe. This is an order that is not merely one of potential use or technical transformation — as important as these are — but of divine instruction and beauty. The importance of human stewardship of lower goods is thus manifested as extending beyond simple allocation or technical transformation of lower goods and is tied to the honoring of divine wisdom in creation and to its contemplation in nature and in grace.

Marie George is professor of philosophy at St. John's University, New York, where she teaches environmental ethics. Recipient of several awards from the John Templeton Foundation for her work in science and religion (including an interdisciplinary grant on the evolution of sympathy) and author of *Stewards of Creation: What Catholics Need to Know about Church Teaching concerning the Environment* (St. Catherine of Siena Press, 2009), she brings unique insights to this volume. While many writings on the environment focus on Genesis naming the human a "steward" or "servant" of creation, George's essay, "Kingship and Kinship: Opposing or Complementary Ways of Envisaging Our Relationship to Material Creation?," makes the much-needed point that men and women's care of creation requires the exercise of their God-given sovereignty.

George opens her essay with a rare description of human stewardship found in the tradition, namely, the office of kingship. Quoting John Paul II, the *Compendium of the Social Doctrine of the Church* teaches that "God willed that man be the king of creation" (§460). A king is not a tyrant; dominion is not ruthless domination. We have been charged with caring for the totality of earthly creatures, which individually and as parts of a greater whole give glory to God. In George's mind, such kingship evokes a simultaneous sense of kinship: we are only parts of creation and, with other creatures, share God as our common source and end (cf. LS §116). Our kingship also consists in what George calls "intellectual mastery," that is, in understanding the natures of various creatures, an understanding that ultimately leads us to knowledge of the Creator. Here we are brought into the world of St. Francis and St. Pope John Paul II, men who saw the divine life sustaining and reflected in all that is. In this way, the human person is motivated to join the rest of creation in giving glory to God.

Hearkening back to God's first commandment to his creatures, Matthew Levering looks at the pressing and very politicized question of human population and sustainability. Levering, the James N. and Mary D. Perry Family Foundation Professor of Theology at Mundelein Seminary in the Archdiocese of Chicago, is a most prolific author, with numerous scholarly essays and sixteen monographs, including *Engaging the Doctrine of Revelation* (Baker Academic, 2014) and *Mary's Bodily Assumption* (University of Notre Dame Press, 2014). Included here is his "'Be Fruitful and Multiply, and Fill the Earth': Was and Is This a Good Idea?" wherein Levering keeps a very influential work firmly in his crosshairs. In dialogue throughout, mainly with Bill McKibben's *Maybe One: A Case for Smaller Families,* Levering cheekily asks whether God's commandment to "be fruitful and multiply" really was a good idea. Maybe we somehow misread the signs; maybe today's food shortages, incessant wars, climate changes, and other ecological disasters only show that the human race can no longer be trusted to increase as it wills.

As Levering builds his case, he never dismisses the global threats of our easily broken ecosystem, nor does he brush aside the call to responsible parenthood; instead, he brings us through these problems to uphold even more brilliantly the intrinsic good of every human life. While Levering also calls for many forms of ecological conversion, he is never willing to follow McKibben and question the inherent beauty of every human birth (cf. LS §50). The panic many people feel when watching the nightly reports of global warming and overly populated cities will be overcome not by eradicating human life but by embracing all humans anew. In this way Levering helps us understand how God's incessant command to "be fruitful and multiply" still stands as the foundational call to those willing to listen truly. The good Lord has deigned to rely on creatures to advance his kingdom, which will be done not by eradicating humans but only by receiving them rightly.

No Catholic volume on creation would be complete without an essay from a follower of the beloved St. Francis of Assisi. Sr. Dawn M. Nothwehr, OSF, PhD, is professor of theological ethics at Catholic Theological Union and holder of the Erica and Harry John Family Endowed Chair in Catholic Ethics. Her recent book *Ecological Footprints: An Essential Franciscan Guide to Sustainable Living* (Liturgical Press, 2012) has earned the acclaim of many. Like Pope Francis, Nothwehr too relies on what she refers to as a clear brown thread in turning to the treasures of Franciscan spirituality. In her essay here, "Bonaventure of Bagnoregio's *imitatio Christi* as an Agapistic Virtue Ethics," Nothwehr uses the Seraphic Doctor to resituate creation not in fallen humanity's utilitarianism, but in the Christ-event. With Bonaventure's Christology guiding her thoughts, Sr. Nothwehr holds up the Father's call to imitate his Son *(imitatio Christi)* as the remedy for anthropogenic global warming (cf. LS §§23-25).

Nothwehr's central argument involves snatching creation out of the hands of those who see matter as nothing more than that which can be manipulated for personal convenience and putting it back in the pierced hands of the Incarnate Word. It is Bonaventure's Franciscan Christology, then, that provides future generations with hope (cf. LS §§11, 66). The deleterious effects of climate change need not have the last word, for in resituating the world in Christ, we can sacramentally behold the world again rightly, replacing (in the words of Nothwehr) a "mathematical objectivity" with a "sacramental sensitivity." By separating the use of creation from its Creator's intentions, fallen humanity unwittingly separated the human from the divine realm. A christological and Franciscan moral vision therefore seeks to reunite the two by placing the world firmly back in the divine person who became human for love of the very same world.

John A. Cuddeback is professor and chairman of the Philosophy Department at Christendom College. His book *True Friendship: Where Virtue Becomes Happiness* was republished in 2010, and his essays and reviews have appeared in *Nova et Vetera, Thomist,* and *Review of Metaphysics,* as well as in several volumes published by the American Maritain Association. His website www.baconfromacorns.com is dedicated to the philosophy of the household and would prove valuable to the readers of these pages. His "Restoring Land Stewardship through Household Prudence" examines the truest sense of economy, as its etymology denotes — rule *(nomos)* of the household *(oikos)*. In his chapter he looks at the household and what the great minds of our tradition have thought about its proper functioning, and he finds therein the first principles of the right practice of land stewardship.

Cuddeback begins with Aristotle's understanding of the household as a natural society that is ordered through domestic prudence, not to the amassing of domestic comforts, but to the true flourishing of the family and the wider *polis:* "Thus it is clear that household management attends more to men than to the acquisition of inanimate things, and to human excellence more than to the excellence of property which we call wealth."[8] Central to Aristotle's and Aquinas's view of the household is the notion that the pursuit of wealth is given limit and order by the vision and intention of the good human life (cf. LS §80n52). However, as Cuddeback argues, dominant Western economic models tend to up-end the order of the household, abandoning the disposition of land, labor, and other human goods to the logic of market forces.

With the industrial revolution, land, like labor, tended to be reduced to a commodity, more and more removing it from the proper purview of the prudence of the householder. True environmental stewardship, Cuddeback argues, will seek to approach the land differently, reestablishing the priority of prudence over the market and thereby participating in God's own care for the earth (cf. LS §§28-32). Aquinas's understanding of economy, household, and human prudence points to a stewardship of the land that can be practiced by all people — a stewardship that begins in the home and, by God's providential design, bears great fruit for generations to come.

Faith Pawl teaches philosophy at the University of St. Thomas in St. Paul, Minnesota. She received her doctorate in philosophy from St. Louis

8. Aristotle, *Politics* 1.13, 1259b18-20.

University, where she concentrated on animal suffering as an evidential challenge to the rationality of traditional theism. Included here is Pawl's "Flourishing and Suffering in Social Creatures," where she continues this interest. Pawl contends that human care of nonhuman animals is essential to all of creation because if we recognize that animals can actually enjoy certain goods (which most do), we should also recognize and try to make sense of suffering in order to alleviate animal pain (cf. LS §§34-37). Doing so requires a more complete understanding of what constitutes animal flourishing. According to Pawl, a deeper understanding of animal flourishing serves an apologetic rationale as well: Christians are better equipped to respond to challenges to the rationality of theism that appeal to the suffering of animals as evidence against God's existence.

As Pawl sees it, for human theists, the relationship with God and with one another constitutes their greatness. If relationship and connectedness is what characterizes human well-being, might it not be the same with many of the nonhuman animals similar to us? This is why Pawl turns to the savannah baboon and the incredible interrelationality this creature clearly exhibits. If so, should those who claim to have a special vocation to care for God's creation also hear within that call the duty to care not only about alleviating animal pain but also restoring right relationships among those creatures whose good life is constituted by social harmony? This is not so much a theodicy trying to make sense of animal suffering but, rather, a mandate: both to recognize where humans deprive many animals of their God-given nature to be in concord with one another and to strive to restore order to creation in a way that promotes animal social flourishing. In this way humans come, once again, to realize their own distinct purpose on earth by serving, while also realizing a shared conscious experience with other creatures who, like ourselves, are also made for communion with others.

Paul M. Blowers is the Dean E. Walker Professor of Church History at Emmanuel Christian Seminary in Johnson City, Tennessee. His primary specialization is early and Byzantine Christianity, and he recently published a gloriously comprehensive study, *Drama of the Divine Economy: Creator and Creation in Early Christian Theology and Piety* (Oxford University Press, 2012). His essay here, "Unfinished Creative Business: Maximus the Confessor, Evolutionary Theodicy, and Human Stewardship in Creation," draws from Maximus (d. 662) to speculate how Christ's promise of full restoration to all of creation might affect our discussions on evolutionary theories, where death, tragic loss, and waste appear necessary.

The traditional Christian narrative proceeds with the belief that decay, destruction, and death are all the result of human disobedience. Yet, contemporary evolutionary theories realize that biological growth demands constant cosmic change and thus the inevitable cessation and genesis of new forms of life. As such, "animal pain" (in the words of C. S. Lewis) seems to be part and parcel of the world's natural trajectory. A seventh-century Byzantine monk may not have answers directly pertaining to contemporary evolutionary theories, but in Blowers's hands, Maximus is able to speak to these insights (drawn mainly from Christopher Southgate's 2008 monograph *The Groaning of Creation: God, Evolution, and the Problem of Evil*). Approaching Maximus through a Balthasarian lens of "theo-drama," Blowers thus sees in Maximus's "cosmic Christ" a love divested of self for the sake of creatures (cf. LS §236). This kenotic love not only affects all of creation but effects a union with all suffering and death. Accordingly, the "new heaven and new earth" promised in the Christ-event is extended to all creation, especially for those beings that were deprived in this life.

Christopher A. Franks teaches in the Department of Religion and Philosophy at High Point University in High Point, North Carolina, and is also a clergy member of the Western North Carolina Conference of the United Methodist Church. Among his recent publications is *He Became Poor: The Poverty of Christ and Aquinas's Economic Teachings* (Eerdmans, 2009). In "Knowing Our Place: Poverty and Providence" Franks uses the image of suffering Job to ask what a "gentle life" might look like. Like Job, each of us can persevere faithfully among the trials of this world only if we first trust in the providence of God in the very concrete circumstances in which each person finds himself or herself circumscribed. As long as we question whether God is laboring in creation on our behalf, we will never allow ourselves to love or be loved because we will always remain suspicious and defensively aloof (cf. LS §§79-80). Franks thus shows that "knowing our place" does not mean being apathetically content with the status quo, but being more readily grateful and reliant upon God for and in all things.

Adopting a posture of gratitude and dependence can lead to a particularly Christian care of our world because only then can we see how God is patient with the countless processes of creation. Even Job's Leviathan is a delight to God because God alone knows perfectly that he and not some creature — however menacing — has the final word over what is. Environmental problems should therefore not frighten the human race into defensiveness and a desire to trample natural threats underfoot, but to acknowledge God's care in and through all creation. This is what Franks sees as "a trajectory drawing toward God-likeness, a trajectory whose contours are best glimpsed in terms of the defenseless poverty of Christ." The poor and pierced Christ thus emerges from this essay as the way we make sense of this world in all its diversity and even depletions. Only in Christ and Christ's own are our current torments transfigured into our eternal ornaments (cf. LS §241). For the humanity of God in Christ invites all of us to embrace, not eradicate, our creatureliness. Here we can trust the providence of the Father and enter his creation more trusting, less self-protective, and more charitable.

When Jonathan J. Sanford delivered his excellent essay, he was professor of philosophy and the associate vice president for academic affairs at Franciscan University of Steubenville; now he is dean of the Constantin College of Liberal Arts at the University of Dallas. He received his doctorate from SUNY Buffalo under Jorge J. E. Gracia and is the founding director of the Franciscan University Press and the author of the recently published *Before Virtue: Assessing Contemporary Virtue Ethics* (Catholic University of America Press, 2015). In his "Nature and the Common Good: Aristotle and Maritain on the Environment," Sanford enlists the Philosopher, alongside the great French Thomist Jacques Maritain (d. 1973), to ask why it is important that we care for creation. The command to care for the environment is of course embedded in the first pages of Scripture, but human disobedience has brought blight upon God's good creation. Abel the farmer is brutally murdered by his brother Cain, who, as Scripture tells us, is the founder of cities.

Is this to suggest that those who cultivate the land are closer to God than those who choose to dwell in cities? Sanford enlists the help of Aristotle and Maritain to arrive at an understanding of our obligation to discern this question. The obligation to be good stewards, Sanford argues, is grounded in our nature, and our nature, properly understood, is political (cf. LS §231). Following Maritain, Sanford argues that the deeper roots of our political nature, and thus our reasons for caring for the earth, find their "richest soil" in God. Whereas some environmentalists argue that civilization is a threat to the earth, Sanford argues that, by means of civilization, we can acknowledge and exercise our responsibility to care for our environs and all those other environs to which they are connected.

Paige E. Hochschild appears next, introducing many of us to the Canadian social critic George Grant (d. 1988). Hochschild is currently assistant professor of theology at Mount St. Mary's University in Emmitsburg, Maryland, where she teaches historical and systematic theology, as well courses in philosophical anthropology. She publishes widely, in *Studia Patristica, Nova et Vetera,* and *Thomist,* and her outstanding *Memory in Augustine's Theological Anthropology* was published in 2012 by Oxford University Press; she is currently engaged in research on Augustinian influences in modern Catholic theology (especially Daniélou and Congar). Hochschild continues this approach in "Knowing the Good of Nature: St. Augustine and George Grant," where she argues that central Augustinian themes regarding creation can be helpful in understanding Grant's own call to contemplate and not dominate nature. That is, if we are ever going to grow in study and in true wisdom, we need to return to a unified vision of the sciences and to a deeper appreciation for the inherent glory of every creature.

Enlisting a long line of significant scholars, Hochschild builds her case for a metaphysical defense of nature. She first draws from Augustine's lengthy commentary *De Genesi ad litteram* to showcase an approach to natural philosophy that refuses to reject the Trinity's continual creation. As he writes and thinks, Augustine clearly delights in the "distinctions and complexity" of creation, relishing not only each word of Scripture but each created thing as a participated instantiation of God's own goodness. Onto this stage, Hochschild ushers in George Grant and his desire to restore the environmental and ecological issues within a broader question of justice. From Grant we are challenged out of our complacency (cf. LS §59); the critique is even harsher for smug individuals who today expect nothing more from self and neighbor than technological efficiency and moral vacuity. It is a matter of social justice that we cease now reducing the human person to a consumer and the rest of creation to an enemy to be defeated (cf. LS §109).

Chris Killheffer is a writer and activist based in New Haven, Connecticut. His many essays exploring the relationship between Christianity and agriculture have appeared in such journals as *Touchstone: A Journal of Mere Christianity* and *Pilgrim: A Journal of Catholic Experience*. Killheffer has worked on small organic farms in Connecticut and Ireland, and for many years he served on the board of the Northeast Organic Farming Association of Connecticut, an organization that promotes sustainable growing practices and food systems. In "Rethinking Gluttony and Its Remedies," Killheffer draws from ancient monastic sources to show how modern insights into the nature and need for proper eating have their roots in the first few centuries of Christian reflection on food. And why not? Was it not a piece of fruit that separated us creatures from our Creator? Is it not bread and wine that the Lord uses to continue his incarnation throughout all the earth?

Killheffer very cleverly shows that today's "foodies" and the concerns we see glamorously written about and aired on various cable stations dedicated to eating smartly can be traced back to early Christian, especially monastic, literature. Eating the needed amount and not too much or too little, eating in community ("with the brethren") when available, eating at a table and not on the go, and consuming foods and drinks in a way that respects the movements of nature as well as distributive justice for others — all are gustable concerns traceable back to many fathers of the Church. Drawing mainly from John Cassian (d. 435), as well as Pope Gregory the Great (d. 604), Killheffer makes his case in a helpful and convincing way, teaching us that gluttony was never understood simply as overeating but eating wrongly. In contrast stands the Word made flesh, who longs to nourish his Church with his own body and blood (cf. LS §236).

In my "Establishing an I-Thou Relationship between Creator and Creature," I explore the beautiful exchanges with inanimate and nonhuman creation among those who live on a different level than most people enjoy. I am aiming in these pages for a certain thaumatography, writing in order to elicit a wonder at the awe-filled way creatures and their Creator interact on seemingly personalistic terms (cf. LS §81). The psalms are replete with creatures praising their God, singing out to him and moving back in pious fear. Similarly, so many scenes in the New Testament reveal a God who not only speaks to his followers through the lilies of the field and the birds of the air, but also addresses fevers directly (Luke 4:39) and curses fruit trees (Mark 11:25), thereby engaging such creatures with a second-person "I-Thou" familiarity.

I accordingly argue that, the more one grows in godliness, the more one becomes able to "speak" to all creatures and, in turn, hear their own response. When I was a young boy, I remember walking into our kitchen only to see my Italian-born grandmother, Avelia Meconi, kiss a piece of stale bread before throwing it away. I quizzically inquired why she would do such an odd thing. "That is the food Jesus became," was her response. This scene taught me early on that there is a type of person who appreciates God's presence in things more powerfully and personally than most. Mia Nonna proved to be quite the Catholic intellectual, as I came to learn that both Augustine and Aquinas also argue that the ultimate ground of all reality is not just impersonal *esse* but the eternal triune relationship between persons, Father, Son, and Holy Spirit (cf. LS §§238-40). This is what the theologian knows, this is what the poet senses — that underneath all creatures is found a Trinity, who acts in time and space in order to bring all things into personal communion with him.

Like all of creation, the final essay concludes in liturgy. Sr. Esther Mary Nickel, RSM, PhD, SLD, is an associate professor and teaches sacred liturgy and sacramental theology at St. John Vianney Theological Seminary, Denver, Colorado. She completed her doctorate in agronomy and plant genetics at the University of Minnesota and until 1994 was engaged in farming and research in Minnesota. Her studies continued in Rome, where she completed a baccalaureate in sacred theology at the Angelicum (STB). She then continued graduate work at the Pontifical Institute at St. Anselm's, where she completed a pontifical license and doctorate in sacred liturgy. She serves on various governing boards for both liturgical and rural concerns. A recent publication entitled "Rogation Days, Ember Days, and the New Evangelization" (*Antiphon* 16, no. 1 [2012]: 21-36) includes her interest in rural life, agriculture, and liturgy.

Nickel's essay "The Liturgical Theology of the Participation of Creation in the Sacred Triduum" concludes this volume by showing how the Church's rituals depend on the movement of the seasons, the fruits of the earth, and the awareness that the entire Christian creed is one of making supernatural what would otherwise be simply ordinary, beginning in the womb of Mary. Nickel telescopes this story into the three days of the Sacred Triduum in order to show succinctly the centrality of sacramentality (cf. LS §§233-37). During this time the oils are blessed, the feet are washed; the wood of the cross is venerated, and the fasting commences once again. The Blessed Sacrament is reserved in darkness until the candle (and the bees that made it) is exalted as the sun prepares to rise. Now the baptismal waters make new those who approach, the bread and the wine are again consecrated and consumed, and the stone is rolled away, speaking to us of eternally new life.

At the heart of *Laudato Si'* lies Pope Francis's revolutionary vision of a world cared for by faithful stewards who, at every turn, realize that the cosmos they inhabit is first a gift to them from a God who loves them in and through all things (cf. LS §100). The following fifteen essays foreshadow Francis's call to treat God's gifts rightly in smart and sensitive ways, furthering Catholic social teaching by helping the Church see how the divine dwells not in the saints and the sanctuary alone. Thoughtful Christians thus realize that the Creator is present to them in the land they trod, the food they eat, and the air they breathe. Reconciling all of creation to this God is the work of Jesus Christ, but a work in which he calls all his faithful to participate. Caring for our common heaven and earth therefore proves to be an eschatological exercise. It is how we fundamentally show forth not only our filial gratitude but responsible dominion and Christian charity as well. No creature is ultimately separate from any other. How we treat this world the Father has given us for a time may just be how we are treated in eternity.

DAVID VINCENT MECONI, SJ
Feast of St. Isidore the Farmer, 2015

CHAPTER 1

The Beauty of Centipedes and Toads

Robert Louis Wilken

After the publication of Lynn White's article "The Historical Roots of Our Ecological Crisis" in the journal *Science* in 1967, a noisy chorus arose of criticism of the presumed responsibility Christianity bears for despoiling the environment. White's way of putting things resonated among those disposed to blame Christianity. Formerly man had been part of nature, wrote White, but "now he was the exploiter of nature." Christianity made it possible "to exploit nature in a mood of indifference to the feeling of natural objects."[1]

White was a Christian, and in defense of Christian tradition he held up the figure of St. Francis of Assisi. The medieval saint, according to White, demonstrated by his life "the virtue of humility — not merely for the individual but for man as a species. Francis tried to depose man from his monarchy over creation and set up a democracy of all God's creatures." Francis was, however, a singular and solitary figure and can hardly serve as exemplar of the tradition as a whole. Nor does he offer a theological understanding of the natural world.

White's article unleashed decades of ill-informed and superficial writing on Christianity and the environment that fit in with the spirit of the time. It was published five years after Rachel Carson's best-selling *Silent Spring*, a book that was prompted in part by the dying of birds because of pesticides. I remember well Tom Paxton's song from the late 1960s, "Whose Garden Was This?" which caught the mood with lines such as "Whose garden was

---

1. Lynn White, "The Historical Roots of Our Ecological Crisis," *Science*, March 10, 1967, 1203-7.

this? / It must have been lovely" and "The oceans were blue and birds really flew, / Can you swear that was true?"

Predictably, in the decades after White's article, some Christian thinkers joined the ecological choir. Gordon Kaufman, a Harvard theologian, charged that the Christian theological tradition was overwhelmingly anthropocentric. The vocabulary of Christian theology, he wrote, is littered with words such as sin, salvation, forgiveness, repentance, hope, faith, love, righteousness. Creation, he argued, "never became the subject of any technical theological vocabulary or doctrines." Because of the belief that human beings were created "in the image of God," the natural world is "of an ontologically different order from man."[2]

One biblical text cited in support of this view was Psalm 8:

When I look at thy heavens, the work of thy fingers,
   the moon and the stars which thou hast established;
what is man that thou art mindful of him,
   and the son of man that thou dost care for him?
Yet thou has made him little less than God,
   and dost crown him with glory and honor.
Thou hast given him dominion over the works of thy hands;
   thou has put all things under his feet,
all sheep and oxen,
   and also the beasts of the field,
the birds of the air, and the fish of the sea,
   whatever passes along the paths of the sea. (vv. 3-8)

Had the environmentalists been more conscientious students of Western intellectual history, they would have recalled the words of the ancient Greek dramatist Sophocles, in his *Antigone*, lines 366-81:

Wonders are many on earth, and the greatest of these
Is man, who rides the ocean and makes his way
Through the deeps, through wind-swept valleys of perilous seas
That surge and sway.
He is master of ageless Earth, to his own will bending
The immortal mother of gods by the sweat of his brow,
As year succeeds to year, with toil unending

2. Gordon Kaufman, "A Problem for Theology: The Concept of Nature," *Harvard Theological Review* 65 (1972): 350.

Of mule and plough.
He is lord of all things living; birds of the air
Beasts of the field, all creatures on sea and land
He takes, cunning to capture and ensnare
With sleight of hand;
Hunting the savage beast from the upland rocks,
Taming the mountain monarch in his lair,
Training the wild horse and the roaming ox
His yoke to bear.

So much for facile pronouncements about Christianity and man's dominion over nature.

More sober voices have made the obvious point that all forms of life modify their environment. Many different attitudes toward nature have existed, and other cultures have been as responsible as Christianity in changing the world in which we live. A few years ago J. R. McNeil, an environmental historian, observed that the "environmentally rapacious culture of the west" was invidiously compared with East Asian traditions (e.g., Buddhism) or the indigenous peoples of the Americas or Oceania. The judgment is based on quotations from scriptural texts, not by an actual comparison of different environments.[3]

None of this, wrote McNeil, "is terribly convincing, because environmental change and ruin is and long has been widely dispersed around the world." Whether Buddhist, Chinese Communist, American, or Polynesian, all manner of ideas were at work using nature "to achieve what comfort and security they could." How "disruptive" their behavior was, was determined more by their technologies and the size of the population and available natural resources than by religious beliefs. Intellectual and cultural factors make their strongest contribution in midlevel ideas about specific projects (e.g., water management, building of dams, or methods of agriculture). McNeil's article was a wholesome reminder that theology's role in effecting environmental change is minimal.

For Christians, however, theology has a place in thinking about the environment. In Christian tradition the world in which we live did not come about randomly. The psalmist sings: "O LORD, how manifold are thy works! In wisdom hast thou made them all" (Ps 104:24). There is purpose and order

---

3. J. R. McNeil, "Observations on the Nature and Culture of Environmental History," *History and Theory* 42 (2003): 7-8.

in all things. As Origen of Alexandria wrote in the third century, citing Psalm 8: "God causes the grass to grow for the cattle and herbs for the service of men; that he may bring forth fruit out of the earth, and that wine may gladden man's heart and that his face may shine with oil, and that bread may strengthen man's heart."[4]

What does it mean to say that all things are made in wisdom? One place to begin is a simple phrase that occurs in the account of the third day of creation in Genesis 1. There we read: "And God said, 'Let the earth put forth vegetation, plants yielding seed, and fruit trees bearing fruit in which is their seed, each according to its kind, upon the earth.'" The phrase "according to its kind" is repeated on the fifth day, when "swarms of living creatures" in the sea are created, as well as "birds that fly above the earth." And then in the interim between the fifth and sixth days, when human beings are created, it is used again of "living creatures . . . cattle and creeping things and beasts of the earth according to their kind."

The church fathers were fascinated by the account of creation in Genesis, what in Greek was called the Hexaemeron, the six days. One of the most polished and elegant writings from Christian antiquity is a series of nine homilies on the six days preached by Basil the Great, the bishop of Caesarea in Asia Minor (modern-day Kayseri, in central Turkey).[5] His homilies quickly won many admirers. Ambrose drew on them while preparing his sermons on the six days, and Augustine consulted them before writing his "literal interpretation" of Genesis.

Basil was a man of many parts. As a bishop he took an active role in the defense of the faith of Nicaea, and as a theologian he wrote the first treatise on the Holy Spirit. As pastor he built hospitals for the sick and hostels for the poor. He came from a large Christian family; two of his brothers became bishops, and his sister was renowned for her strength of character, holy life, and learning. As a preacher he brought to the text of Genesis the accumulated wisdom of Christian learning.

Basil's brother Gregory of Nyssa said that Basil's homilies were preached "before a crowded church" filled not only with educated folk but also with workers and artisans, housewives, and a noisy group of young people. It is an improbable scene, the old bishop speaking on cosmogony, a topic more

---

4. Origen, *Contra Celsum* 4.75.

5. For the text of the homilies, see Basil of Caesarea, *Sulla Genesi: Omelie sull'Esamerone*, ed. and trans. Mario Naldini (Milan: Fondazione Lorenzo Valla: Arnoldo Mondadori Editore, 1990); English trans. in *A Select Library of Nicene and Post-Nicene Fathers* (Grand Rapids: Eerdmans, n.d.)

suited to the classroom than the pulpit, to a congregation more interested in being entertained than instructed, or getting on with the day's work. Not surprisingly, there were moments when the minds of the congregation wandered and were unable, says Gregory, "to follow the penetrating subtlety of [Basil's] thoughts."[6] In plain English: Basil had difficulty holding his audience.

The first several homilies deal with the creation of the heavens and the earth and address questions that arose in response to ancient philosophers who taught that the world exists eternally. But in many ways the later homilies are more interesting and surprising. For they treat, in staggering detail, the world of plants, animals, fish, and birds.

At one point Basil asks: "How can I offer an exact review of all the distinctive characteristics of birds?" Much to the astonishment of his hearers, no doubt, as well as to readers today, he then proceeds to treat in exquisite detail the unique features of different kinds of birds. He surveys the behavior of cranes, storks, kingfishers, turtle doves, ospreys, and crows. Kingfishers, he says, live near the sea and lay their eggs in the sand along the shore. He admires the intelligence of storks, which makes it possible for them to migrate over long distances. He is fascinated by bats and owls, which are able to "live by night in the midst of darkness." He even includes bees and wasps in his catalog of "winged creatures."[7]

Genesis has only a few short syllables about birds, notes Basil: "Let birds fly above the earth across the firmament of the heavens" (Gen 1:20). It is only when we look at the great wonder before our eyes that we understand their meaning. In other words, the text of Genesis is to be interpreted in light of what we observe. "What we see today," says Basil, is a "sign" of what was done at creation. Basil had traveled widely in Greece, Asia Minor, Syria, and Egypt, and his delight in the natural world is unconcealed. His language is suffused with the fragrances and colors of nature.

Basil thought his hearers were expecting a flight into allegory to explain the creation account. But that was not his way. I know the laws of allegory, he says, but those who use it too often will not "admit the plain sense of the Scripture," and "they see in a plant, in a fish what their fancy wishes." "For

---

6. Gregory of Nyssa, *Apologia in Hexaemeron,* in *Gregorii Nysseni in Hexaemeron: Opera exegetica in Genesim, Pars* 1, ed. Hubertus R. Drobner (Leiden: Brill, 2009), 10.

7. Basil, *Homily* 8.5ff.

me," says Basil, "grass is grass; plant, fish, wild beast, domestic animal, I take everything as it is written."[8]

Besides his own actual observations, Basil's information about the natural world comes from ancient scientific accounts, for example, Aristotle's *History of Animals*. Of course, some of what he reports is not confirmed by later scientific investigation. But in his magisterial *Traces on the Rhodian Shore*, Clarence Glacken asserted that Basil's account of the natural world "is the best of its kind until the works of Ray and Derham in the late seventeenth and early eighteenth centuries before the heady discoveries of Galileo, Descartes, and Newton."[9]

The abundance of details in the homilies commands one's attention. But as one looks more closely at his language, it is evident that Basil's account of the great diversity of winged creatures has a point that springs directly from the text. It is not simply that God said, "Let birds fly above the earth across the firmament of heaven." God also said: "Let the earth bring forth living creatures *according to their kind*." This means, says Basil, that, in creating winged creatures, God "divided them into unique species," each different from the other, each with "its own distinctive characteristics." In other words, amid all the variety among living things, something precious is given at creation that sets each species apart from others. In the taxonomy of nature, species is the lowest rank designating particularity; one species cannot be replaced by another.

Birds are only a part of what Basil has to say about the world of living things. Just as the words of Genesis "let birds fly above the earth" prompted him to embark on a catalog of winged creatures, so the words "let the water bring forth swarms of living creatures" launched him on an account of creatures of the sea.

Basil explains that fish have gills, which allow them to live in water. As with birds, God created a great variety of things, each unique. Besides fish there are scallops, sea snails, mussels, conches, and the "infinite variety of oysters." Then there are crustaceans, crabs, and lobsters; lampreys and eels; dolphins and swordfish. Each has its own name, even the tiniest fish, and all are subdivided "into innumerable classes." Basil is impressed by the cleverness of the squid, which attaches itself to a rock to escape detection.

---

8. Basil, *Homily* 9.1.

9. Clarence J. Glacken, *Traces on the Rhodian Shore: Nature and Culture in Western Thought from Ancient Times to the End of the Eighteenth Century* (Berkeley: University of California Press, 1963), 194.

Some fish migrate from rivers to the sea and back. They lack the reason of human beings, but they have the "law of nature firmly seated within them to show them what they have to do"; God "gave to each being the means of preservation."[10]

Basil died shortly after delivering the homilies on the Hexaemeron. Some were dissatisfied with his effort to explain the opening chapters of Genesis, and his younger brother Gregory of Nyssa wrote a companion treatise entitled *Apology on the Hexaemeron.* In this work Gregory sought to address certain of the philosophical and cosmological questions in greater depth. No doubt he was pleased to address the topic without having Basil looking over his shoulder, and he seizes the opportunity to move out from behind the imposing figure of his older brother. Had Basil been alive, it is unlikely he would have countenanced his little brother discoursing on a subject he had treated only a few months earlier.

Gregory, a more penetrating thinker than Basil, gave greater attention to philosophical difficulties posed by the biblical narrative. He thought Basil had not adequately dealt with the central problem presented by the account in Genesis, namely, that creation is depicted as having taken place over a series of days. What needs to be explained, says Gregory, is how one can make sense of a narrative of the coming into being of the natural world that is sequential. For we know by observation and experience that all the individual parts of the world are interconnected. Just as there cannot be life without warmth and water, and birds cannot fly without air, so there cannot be day and night without the light of the sun. The idea of a sequential creation is unintelligible to reasoned inquiry, whether the inquirer be a Christian bishop or a Greek philosopher. The church fathers knew that the account in Genesis could not be taken literally.

To deal with this conundrum, Gregory begins with the first words in Genesis. The Greek translation used in the churches, the Septuagint, translates the opening words "in the beginning." But the translation of Aquila, a convert to Judaism, rendered the sentence, "God made the heavens and the earth summarily." Gregory takes "summarily" to mean simultaneously or at once. In his words, "Everything was created together."[11]

If the world came into being in a single moment, what does one make of the narrative in the first chapter of Genesis? Gregory suggests that the succession of days, with the creation of the sun and moon on one day, plants

---

10. Basil, *Homily* 7.1-3.
11. Gregory of Nyssa, ed. Drobner, 16-17.

on another, and animals after that, is to be understood to signify the connectedness of things, or as we might say, the ecological structure of the natural world. By presenting the creation of all things in a sequence of actions, Moses wished to display the interdependence of the natural order. In other words, Moses presents in a narrative what are in fact necessary natural interrelations. "The nature of beings proceeds by a sequence which necessarily is effected by what precedes them."[12]

As Gregory moves through the text of Genesis, he comes to the sixth day. After each thing was created, Genesis says, "And God saw that it was good." But when the narrative reaches its end, the text reads: "And God saw everything that he had made, and behold, it was *very* good. And there was evening and there was morning, a sixth day." Gregory is intrigued by the addition of the word "very" or "exceedingly." In Greek the term for "good" also means "beautiful." Because Genesis says "very good," or "very beautiful," says Gregory, we should examine what is meant by the "perfection of beauty with respect to created things." By adding the word "exceedingly," Moses shows that nothing is lacking in "perfection."[13]

The natural world, says Gregory, is made up of countless kinds of creatures of different types. Yet, says Gregory, it goes against our experience to say that every species is very beautiful. For example, it takes imagination to see that "the centipede or the toad" is "exceedingly beautiful." Certainly in appearance they are not very beautiful. But that is because we are looking only at what our eyes can see. God has a different perspective: "The divine eye does not look at the elegance of the things that have come to be and does not have an eye for beautiful color or form. Rather each thing in and of itself has a perfect nature. A horse is clearly not a cow. The nature of each is maintained and its unique properties are conserved and has within itself the power to maintain its uniqueness." Though the elements differ from each other, yet each is "exceedingly" good by itself; they are all perfectly good by reason of their "own properties."[14]

The Gospel of John says that everything came into being by God's "word." The term for "word" — *logos,* or reason — means, says Gregory, that no living thing was made "without reason" *(alogos),* "randomly," or "by chance." "God made all things in wisdom," says the psalmist (Ps 104:24). Therefore it is right to believe that each living thing has a reason and pur-

12. Gregory of Nyssa, ed. Drobner, 18.
13. Gregory of Nyssa, ed. Drobner, 44.
14. Gregory of Nyssa, ed. Drobner, 44.

pose. Because wisdom brought into being all visible things, even the lowliest creature is precious. When we look at plants, we wonder at the form, character, and individuality of each one.[15]

Of course in discussing creation, the church fathers spoke not only of the natural world. After writing his *Apology on the Hexaemeron,* Gregory wrote another treatise, *On the Making of Man,* to deal with the famous passage in Genesis "Let us make man in our image, after our likeness." His ostensible reason for writing the essay was that Basil's homilies had reached only verse 26 and had not provided "an investigation of man."

As he develops this theme, one has the impression that Gregory was as much interested in pleasing his readers with the felicity of his prose as he was in persuading them of the cogency of his arguments. So he introduces the topic of the creation of man with an extended simile explaining why the natural world was created before human beings:

> It is not right that the ruler should appear before his subjects. Hence his kingdom was first prepared and only afterward did the ruler appear. After the maker of all had prepared a royal dwelling place (the earth and islands and sea and the heavens covering everything like a roof) for the king and a great horde of wealth was stored in the palace (and by wealth I mean the whole creation, the plants and trees, everything that has sense and breath and life . . .), only then does he bring man into the world to behold its wonders.[16]

It is true that, in Christian tradition, man is the crown of creation, but this affirmation must be set within the context of the uniqueness of even the meanest things that live on this globe. Man's place is singular, but each species of birds, fish, plants, and animals has its own reason for being and its own end. The great teachers of Christian antiquity unmask the caricature of the twentieth century that nature was created only to serve man. The natural world in all its multifarious particularity has its own integrity, purpose, and beauty.

The Syriac writer Isaac of Nineveh was once asked, What is a compassionate heart? He replied:

> It is a heart on fire for the whole of creation, for humanity, for the birds, for the animals, for demons, and for all that exists. At the recollection and

15. Gregory of Nyssa, ed. Drobner, 21.
16. *Patrologia Graeca* 44.133d-134a.

at the sight of them such a person's eyes overflow with tears owing to the vehemence of the compassion which grips his heart; as a result of his deep mercy his heart shrinks and cannot bear to hear or look on any injury or the slightest suffering of anything in creation. . . . This is why he constantly offers up prayer full of tears, even for the irrational animals . . . even for those who harm him, so that they may be protected and find mercy. He even prays for the reptiles as a result of the great compassion which is poured out beyond measure — after the likeness of God — in his heart.[17]

17. Translated by Sebastian Brock in *Heart of Compassion: Daily Readings with Isaac the Syrian,* ed. A. M. Allchin (London: Darton, Longman & Todd, 1989), 29.

CHAPTER 2

The Place of Faith in the Geography of Hope

Christopher J. Thompson

> *i thank You God for most this amazing*
> *day: for the leaping greenly spirits of trees*
> *and a blue true dream of sky; and for everything*
> *which is natural which is infinite which is yes . . .*
>
> E. E. CUMMINGS

The year 2014 marked the fiftieth anniversary of the Wilderness Act. Signed into law by Lyndon Johnson, the act was the first piece of federal legislation to forever designate some 9 million acres of land as "wilderness places," putting them under the protection of the newly created National Wilderness Preservation System. Today, that system includes more than 110 million acres, and for many people the passage of the Wilderness Act marked one of America's greatest achievements concerning the protection of our heritage and the promotion of the common good.

There is a simple text at its core: "A wilderness, in contrast with those areas where man and his own works dominate the landscape, is hereby recognized as an area where the earth and its community of life are untrammeled by man, where man himself is a visitor who does not remain." The act goes on to state that such land is to be understood to retain its "primeval character and influence," to have been "shaped primarily by the forces of nature," and to have outstanding opportunities for such things as "solitude."[1]

1. Wilderness Act, Public Law 88-577 (16 USC, §§1131-36), 88th Congress, Second Session, September 3, 1964.

The language is succinct, even poetic, and stands in sharp contrast to the often more plodding prose typical of government legislation. More important, the language points to underlying claims, implicit convictions about the meaning of nature, its place in our lives, and the role and significance of nature in the development of one's own character and the common good of the country. Commenting on the importance of wilderness in our collective imagination, the advocate and novelist Wallace Stegner says that, even if some of us are never able to enter wild spaces, we can still contemplate the *idea of wilderness;* we can "take pleasure in the fact that such a timeless and uncontrolled part of earth is still there. For it can be a means," he says, "of reassuring ourselves of our sanity as creatures, a part of the geography of hope."[2]

Such a seamless identification of wilderness with sanity and hope could have emerged only from a posture toward the world as *kosmos,* an ordered whole brought into existence by a God who is good. To put my thesis in its simplest terms: the legislation of the Wilderness Act and the overall movement of environmental concern out of which it came are fundamentally rooted in the often unexpressed but nonetheless unequivocal affirmation that the created order is good and that it has intrinsic values to be shared, that nature in its vastness[3] offers us something worthy to behold. The opportunity to behold it, moreover, to stand before its veiled splendor, is an essential aspect of our human, our religious, our national flourishing. Ours will forever remain a religious nation as long as our natural piety is preserved and the porticoes of the sacred — that is, our wilderness spaces — remain open to its citizens.

The Wilderness Act is a miraculous achievement on the part of the American people that put into "concrete" practice the theological conviction that creation is good — indeed, very good. As the Lord employed Cyrus in order to achieve his aims in restoring Jerusalem (as noted by the prophet Isaiah), so he used the Johnson administration in a kind of modern-day equivalent. For through him (and others engaged in similar efforts) the foundations were laid for the rebuilding of a new Jerusalem, a Catholic culture that can be built only upon the pillars of the earth, can be built only from the ground up.

And so mine is not a call to some kind of back-to-nature movement or an altar call to some nature cult. My remarks should be taken as a foreword

2. Wallace Stegner, "Wilderness Idea," in *The Sound of Mountain Water* (New York: Penguin Books, 1997), 115.

3. The act stipulates that portions to be designated as wilderness must be "at least five thousand acres of land or is of sufficient size as to make practicable its preservation and use in an unimpaired condition" (sec. 2[c][3]).

(really, a plea and a prayer) for a much deeper and profound revolution: to set in motion the conditions in which a renewed, authentic Catholic culture can emerge. For there and only there, squarely within the temple of creation, a Catholic culture takes root, the good news of Jesus Christ moves from its conceptual power to its cultural expression, heaven and earth are wed in the *physical body* of the believer, the *mystical body* of believers, and the *plan of the incarnation* takes root in history.

There is always a geography to our hope, in other words, because there is always a place in our faith. Christianity is not an idea, an abstraction nurtured in the intricacies of some curriculum, nor is it an insight, an ego marooned on an island of self-preoccupation, nor, finally, is it woven within a political agenda, a labyrinth of like-minded citizens united to a cause. Christianity is, rather, the extraordinary invitation of one enfleshed person to another, the bold exchange of an eternal friendship between the embodied being of the human person and the divine person enfleshed in Jesus Christ.

Christ, the Logos made flesh, *is* the one through whom all flesh, all things, are made. Made visible in the person of Jesus Christ, one and the same Logos remains veiled in his creation. The book of the Holy Scriptures and the book of nature are one because God is the serial editor. Catholics cannot be indifferent to this *preambula fidei* writ large that is our wilderness, because we are not indifferent to the Word of which it speaks. Christ, the Logos made flesh; Christ, the Logos of creation. There is always a geography to our hope because there is always a place in our faith.

The native habitat of the human person is as an embodied being among embodied beings, an enfleshed creature in the material cosmos of enfleshed creatures, intelligently arranged by God and intelligibly pondered by man, a nexus of which constitutes the natural environment of the human person as such. The human person, whose dignity lies within his spiritual destiny, is nonetheless a creature of the earth, a living, organic being among living, organic beings, whose immortal soul by nature transcends material creation and yet by grace permeates it with eternal significance.

The entire hierarchy of being, from the lowliest creature up to man (and, beyond, to angels), is permeated by a Provident intelligence that supplies the necessary connections between lower creation and its grace-filled care. Contemplation, conservation, or cultivation — each vocation unfolds within this milieu; every vocation unfolds in a location.

Take one example, the vocation of the farmer: bent low in respect of the soil, he enters into a relationship with an order of creation that is itself already ordered and whose wisdom becomes his norm. His practical wisdom must submit to a logos that lies hidden in the order of things. For this reason his labor was understood for centuries to be an *ars cooperativa,* a co-operative art, because his achievements are yoked to the intelligible forces at work in creation itself.[4] Like the teacher who guides the natural desire to know on the part of the student, or the doctor who capitalizes on the natural desire to live, or the husband and wife who enact the natural desire for communion, the prudent farmer labors with nature's creative forces and coaxes from the earth the fruits it is destined by Providence to yield.

The farmer's practical craft is to be distinguished from that of the craftsman, who works to create what is first only in the human mind. The farmer, by contrast, becomes a master in his craft only through the long and laborious tutorial in the fields. Agriculture is a unique human enterprise, for it is through this labor, perhaps more than any other, that one learns of the grammar of the Creator.[5] There is always a geography to our hope, because the earth *(geo)* is written *(graph)* by God.

St. Thomas teaches us as much. Notwithstanding the dignity of the human being as the *imago Dei,* the human person nonetheless occupies the lowest order of intellectual creatures, because the human being is utterly dependent upon organic substances in order to engage in any intellectual acts. Thomas's portrait of the person is premised upon the notion that human knowing is dependent upon *things,* things already thick with meaning, immersed in light, pregnant with intelligence. Blinded before the brilliance of beings, I am an apprentice in the Braille of all learning. I feel my way across the texts of the world, discerning through its impressions the message of creation, the message of the Creator. Deaf to its vocation, I listen in solitude, for as the author of Job says, "Ask the animals, and they will teach you; the

4. "Man, who discovers his capacity to transform and in a certain sense create the world through his own work, forgets that this is always based on God's prior and original gift of the things that are. Man thinks that he can make arbitrary use of the earth, subjecting it without restraint to his will, as though it did not have its own requisites and a prior God-given purpose, which man can indeed develop but must not betray. Instead of carrying out his role as a co-operator with God in the work of creation, man sets himself up in place of God and thus ends up provoking a rebellion on the part of nature, which is more tyrannized than governed by him" (John Paul II, *Centesimus annus,* encyclical letter, May 1, 1991, §37).

5. See chapter 3, "Agriculture and Personal Values," in *The Importance of Rural Life according to the Philosophy of St. Thomas Aquinas: A Study in Economic Philosophy,* by George H. Speltz (Washington, DC: Catholic University of America Press, 1945). Also Emerson Hynes, "Consider the Person," *Catholic Rural Life Bulletin* 2, no. 2 (1939): 16. The integral nature of agricultural labor, as well as, more generally, the family farm was a constant theme of Catholic rural social teaching throughout the 1930s, 40s, and 50s in the United States.

birds of the air, and they will tell you; ask the plants of the earth, and they will teach you; and the fish of the sea will declare to you. Who among all these does not know that the hand of the LORD has done this?" (Job 12:7-9).

For the "poetry of the earth is never dead";[6] divine wisdom speaks in things. The coherence of living organisms, as well as the community toward which they naturally tend, is objectively given in reality and expresses "a design of love and truth. It is prior to us and it has been given to us by God as the setting of our life."[7] It is not contrived from a set of clear and distinct ideas of some disembodied cogito; it is not the projection of a transcendental ego; nor is it the remnant of some human habit or social custom. Wisdom is intrinsic to things, and its apprehension by reason is an exercise in objective knowing.[8]

This wisdom, moreover, written into the very order of things, is not directly implicated in the fall. The punishment of original sin, the loss of original justice, does not directly affect the lower orders of creation, specifically the animals, the plants, and inorganic matter. Rather, it is our grasp of the logos of creation that is now fleeting and fraught with error because of original sin. Already limited by its dependence upon organic experience, the human mind is further wounded by a disordered will. As Christopher Franks so aptly put it, "We resent our nature, and we resent nature in general. We struggle against it, and we seek ways to triumph over it through technology. Ours is a pathological ingratitude, a special sort of ingratitude, because it amounts to being resentful of who we are."[9]

But for their part, Aquinas says, "all natural things were produced by the divine art, and so may be called God's works of art."[10] Divine providence continues to extend to the communities of creatures, even in this postlapsar-

---

6. John Keats, "On the Grasshopper and the Cricket."

7. Benedict XVI, *Caritas in veritate,* encyclical letter, June 29, 2009, §48.

8. "The first act of the intellect is to know, not its own action, not the ego, not phenomena, but objective and intelligible being" (Reginald Garrigou-Lagrange, OP, *Reality: A Synthesis of Thomistic Thought,* trans. Patrick Cummins, OSB [St. Louis: Herder, 1950], 388). Cf. Thomas Aquinas, *Summa theologiae* I, q. 84, art. 7: "The proper object of the human intellect, which is united to a body, is a quiddity or nature existing in corporeal matter; and through such natures of visible things it rises to a certain knowledge of things invisible." For a recent discussion of the practical implications of this priority of being for moral theology, especially medical ethics, see Edward J. Furton, "Ethics without Metaphysics: A Review of the Lysaught Analysis," *National Catholic Bioethics Quarterly* 11, no. 1 (Spring 2011): 53-62.

9. Christopher Franks, *He Became Poor: The Poverty of Christ and Aquinas's Economic Teachings* (Grand Rapids: Eerdmans, 2009), 10.

10. *Summa theologiae* I, q. 91, art. 1.

ian state, for the nature of animals, he explicitly states, was not changed by man's sin (I.96.1). Their habits of being are precisely now what they would have been prior to the fall, for it is only the intellectual creatures, the angelic and the human, which are immediately caught up in the drama of rebellion. In contrast to our checkered history, each creature of lower creation has always borne the *vestigia Dei* — indeed, the *vestigia Trinitas*. The universe of things placed before us this very day, "the gay great happening illimitably earth," continues to reflect the beneficent wisdom of God.

The thesis that the integrity of lower creation remains intact throughout the drama of our salvation history is one of the most important aspects of our Catholic theological tradition and seems to be increasingly beclouded in Catholic intellectual circles. The loss of confidence in integral *natura*-as-given, as the medium through which divine wisdom is discerned, hobbles our capacity to build a vibrant Catholic culture.

In the first place, in matters of preaching the gospel in contemporary times, the flight from *natura* impedes the potential convergence between our living Catholic doctrine and the environmental movement more broadly. For seen in its best light, the movement is at the core the unthematic revolt of conscience among those generations of modernity who intuit that something is deeply flawed in our posture before the natural order, that our habits of treating nature as a mere raw datum of purposeless matter is not consonant with the facts on the ground.

This would not be the first time the Church could be called upon to correct a widely held but alien vision of material creation and our place within it. The Albigensian heresy of the twelfth century (itself an ancestor of a still-earlier heresy: Manichaeanism) was, somewhat anachronistically, an environmental philosophy that endorsed a vision of material creation as utterly corrupted, and the human person as an abomination in a disordered world. Thomas, of course, was among the Order of Preachers who responded, and he can still supply us with the necessary tools to address the meaning of the environment and our place within it. Of course, it will not be enough to merely repeat the insights of the thirteenth-century mendicant; Thomism is never a matter of learning by rote. But we would be very well served if we would renew our efforts to consider how the Church's affirmation of creation, and Thomism in particular, can address some of the fundamental questions surrounding environmental stewardship.

Second, in matters of moral theology, the loss of *natura* makes difficult a proper appropriation of the natural law as the rational creature's participation in the eternal law. Increasingly cast as an ethic set within a cosmos devoid of a natural teleology, the characterization of our participation becomes conceptual, idealist, epistemic, or, as Steven Long says, logicist.[11] But the "affirmation or a transgression of the Eternal Divine Law," according to the Dominican Mislaw Krapiec, "does not take place in an abstraction nor directly in relation to God Himself. Rather, it takes place through the composition of things . . . with which we either do or do not reckon in our conduct."[12]

In other words, our rational participation in the eternal law unfolds in a distinctively human manner, that is to say, as an embodied creature of the earth. And thus our participation, our inclinations are inescapably woven within the fabric of relations that makes our living human. The natural law, at its core, asks the question, How do I as an organic, albeit rational, being flourish within this theonomic cosmos?

Third, the adumbration of *natura* makes it that much more difficult for the theology of the body to blossom into a full-fledged theology of embodiment, of an enfleshed, organic creature among organic creatures, in which the body is not merely the medium by which the person expresses a gift of self but is the welcoming threshold by which one receives the originative gift of being in all its splendor. Its recovery may create the conditions for the further development of the theology of the body from the skin outward, if you will, and thus a theology of embodiment within a community of organic bodies. It may allow the philosophical anthropology of the human person to take root once again in its native soil, namely, cosmology, and resist the temptation to cast the analysis of the human person within the horizon of interiority.

Fourth, overcoming the encroaching angelism that besets our intellectual endeavors, the recovery of the body may inspire a reevaluation of what constitutes "bioethics" in Catholic circles, perhaps to include the "nonrational 99 percent" in its considerations. It may inspire from its practitioners

---

11. Steven A. Long, *Natura pura: On the Recovery of Nature in the Doctrine of Grace* (New York: Fordham University Press, 2010).

12. Mieczylaw A. Krapiec, OP, *I-Man: An Outline of Philosophical Anthropology,* trans. Marie Lescoe, Andrew Woznicki, and Theresa Sandok et al. (New Britain, CT: Mariel Publications, 1983), 229-30. His emphasis here pertains to the human person, but the general insight applies more broadly. See also Bernard Quelquejeu, OP, "'Naturalia manent integra': Contribution à l'étude de la portée, méthodologique et doctrinale, de l'axiome théologique 'gratia praesupponit naturam,'" *Revue des sciences philosophique et théologique* 49 (1965): 640-55; see also Jan Aertsen, *Nature and Creature: Thomas Aquinas's Way of Thought,* Studien und Texte zur Geistesgeschichte des Mittelalters (Leiden: Brill, 1988), 386.

an equally detailed analysis of the first command given to Adam: to till and to keep the earth (remarkably passed over in silence), as well as the prohibitions regarding food and what we are permitted to eat.

The problem, William French notes,

> is not that recent Popes have been too physicalist in their reasoning, but rather quite the opposite. I would submit that they have been insufficiently physicalist. If you want to see physicalism, read Medieval theologians on the doctrines of the Incarnation and Creation. Read in Thomas about how God sustains each existent entity and living being in each moment. Read in Francis's Canticles and other writings how he names a wolf and the sun "Brothers" and the moon, water, and "Mother Earth" as "Sisters." If ecology [and the tradition] has taught us anything, it is that there is nothing wrong with physicalism.[13]

Fifth, advancing a conception of the human person as the substantial union of soil and soul is the only thing I can think of that might address the remarkable gap in our own Catholic educational mission, namely, that of the 244 Catholic colleges and universities here in the United States, not a single one offers a program of instruction in agriculture. It is difficult to know what accounts for our collective loss of appetite for acknowledging the fact that we eat and that our food comes from — dare I say it? — dirt. But it might be related to the broader neuralgia concerning the natural teleology of the human body, or embodiment in particular.

And finally, retrieving a Catholic theology of creation may at last give us grounds for hope in some of the most vexing matters facing us today. For it follows that, if it is we who are caught up in the drama of sin and creatures are not, a certain docility to their intelligibility would be the only prudent measure to take. Before we propose to modify creatures to suit our expectations, it would be wise to consider how our own ways of acting may be in need of modification. Before we ignore the form and finality of living things, the distinctive principles of organic life, we might pause to consider how our modern biases have lent themselves to reducing the creature to an artifact of our productions. The deliberate, genetic modification of a naturally occurring creature is not just an exercise in human ingenuity; it is a recasting of the divine creature as a mere product of human making. If unchecked by habits of humility, natural piety, and the norms of pru-

---

13. William C. French, "Natural Law and Ecological Responsibility: Drawing upon the Thomistic Tradition," *University of St. Thomas Law Journal* 5, no. 1 (2008): 39.

dence,[14] such practices run the risk of deforming creation, whose original wisdom is our norm, of transforming the creature into a "resource" whose value is to be merely to be "used."

When our "use" of creation involves the manipulation of its very structures and natural purposes, as in the case of the transgenetic modification of creatures, such an enterprise cannot be undertaken except in deliberate deference to the order and wisdom of creation, of which the creature is a part, with utmost care and prudent circumspection, when proportionate goods are clearly identified and reasonably expected, and all other reasonable alternatives have been considered, including the modification of one's lifestyle.[15] It is not a question of using creatures for the benefit of man and the glory of God. It is rather a question of the norms for such use, norms that are not only written in the human heart but written into creation itself from the beginning.[16]

In conclusion, my insistence on the ontic priority given to things, a kind of preferential option for the creature, emerges from a conviction — in truth, an inexpressible joy — about the character of the eternal law as manifest in this cosmos of which I find myself a part.[17] In all humility, I suggest that cre-

---

14. Because I appeal to the exercise of prudence, it precludes the notion that the deliberate, genetic modification of lower creatures is, strictly speaking, intrinsically disordered. At the same time, prudence would demand the greatest circumspection in such an instance. Because "we are not yet in a position to assess the biological disturbance that could result from indiscriminate genetic manipulation and from the unscrupulous development of new forms of plant and animal life, to say nothing of unacceptable experimentation regarding the origins of human life itself" (*Compendium of the Social Doctrine of the Church*, §459), it is only wise to counsel against such practices.

15. "Thomas understood that by resisting some practices of a developing profit economy, he was defending the very notion that reality is penetrated by divine reason" (Franks, *He Became Poor*, 184).

16. *Compendium of the Social Doctrine of the Church*, §§458-59. Also, "Science and technology must be put in the service of the divine design for the whole of creation and for all creatures. This design gives meaning to the universe and to human enterprise as well. Human stewardship of the created world is precisely a stewardship exercised by way of participation in the divine rule and is always subject to it. Human beings exercise this stewardship by gaining scientific understanding of the universe, by caring responsibly for the natural world (including animals and the environment) and by guarding their own biological integrity" (International Theological Commission, *Communion and Stewardship: Human Persons Created in the Image of God* [2004], §61, at www.vatican.va/roman_curia/congregations/cfaith/cti_documents/rc_con_cfaith_doc_20040723_communion-stewardship_en.html).

17. Elsewhere I have called for a "green Thomism" to emerge as an apt response to the challenges identified here. See my "Perennial Wisdom: Notes toward a Green Thomism," *Nova et Vetera* 10, no. 1 (Winter 2012): 67-80.

ation's integrity in this present age, its capacity to disclose the divine wisdom at work, is a matter of received Catholic doctrine and needs to be reasserted and celebrated in every corner of theology, for the eclipse of *natura* makes the vision of a Catholic culture impossible and is contributing to a kind of theological somnambulance from which we will have to wake up.

At the conclusion of *After Virtue,* Alasdair MacIntyre famously comments that we have to await a new Benedict. I will be waiting somewhere along the Green Mountain Trail, where the Big Meadows meet along Lower Tonahutu at the southern edge of Rocky Mountain National Park. Or maybe our paths will cross somewhere in the back country of the Quetico Superior Region, or sauntering in the native prairies of western Wisconsin. Wherever I meet him, I suspect he will keep a steady pace because he respects the rules of the wilderness and knows that man is a mere visitor and cannot remain. A rosary in his pocket, a *Te Deum* on his lips, he will be fixing his eyes on a point on the horizon — a spire stands in contrast among the cathedral of the pines, a still point in the geography of hope, where a table is set with bread and wine, where all creation rightly gives him praise, saying, I thank you, God, for most this amazing day.

CHAPTER 3

The Teleological Grammar of the Created Order in Catholic Moral Discourse

Steven A. Long

The Role of Natural Teleology within Moral Theology

The central and normative role of natural teleology within the Catholic moral tradition receives its most conspicuous and definitive articulation in the work of St. Thomas Aquinas. Thomas's account of natural law is thoroughly theocentric, emphasizing that natural law is nothing other than a rational participation in the eternal law, which is the idea, or type, or *ratio,* in God of the governance of things, and which itself presupposes, and is a modality of, divine providence. Yet according to St. Thomas, the rational participation in eternal law, which is the natural law, itself depends upon an ontologically prior and distinct created participation of divine governance that it shares with all creatures whatsoever. It is this ontologically prior participation of the eternal law — upon which the rational participation depends — that has become the object of much dissent and confusion in the understanding both of Catholic moral teaching and of the teaching of St. Thomas Aquinas in the years immediately before and after the Second Vatican Council. This ontologically prior participation is described by St. Thomas in question 91, article 2 of the prima secundae of the *Summa theologiae,* when he writes, "Thus since all things subject to divine providence are ruled and measured by eternal law, as was stated above, it is evident that all things participate somewhat in the eternal law, insofar as from its being imprinted on them they have their inclinations to their proper acts and ends."[1] This participation

---

1. *Summa theologiae* (hereafter *STh*) I-II, q. 91, art. 2, resp.: "Unde cum omnia quae

of all things in the eternal law, which is not yet in and of itself properly natural law according to Aquinas, is often referred to as "passive participation in the eternal law" — because all creatures whatsoever have this participation. It is ineradicably teleological. In the lower creation this participation is not itself properly denominated a law, because as Thomas notes in his response to the third objection of this same article, "The participation of the eternal law in the rational creature is properly called a law, since a law is something pertaining to reason." Lower creation participates in the eternal law only "by way of similitude" (*per similitudinem* — that is to say, it is "law-like"). Because law in its proper sense proceeds from the mind of the legislator to the mind of the recipient, one sees that the participation of the rational creature in the eternal law occurs in an objectively higher mode than that of mere passive participation, because the rational creature partakes of "a share of providence, by being provident both for itself and for others."[2] Inasmuch as Thomas says that natural law is "nothing other" than this higher rational participation (and refers to the passive participation *in the lower creation* as merely a similitude of law), it has been frequently supposed that, for Thomas, the passive participation *as such* is of no very great importance in the understanding of natural law. First, it is supposed that such participation is exclusively that of lower creation, "nonrational" creation. Yet *all creatures* receive their being, nature, powers, and the order of these to acts, objects, and the hierarchy of ends, *passively from divine providence*. Not alone lower things devoid of reason then, but as Thomas expressly states, "all things" receive this imprint of the eternal law from which they receive the inclinations for their proper acts and ends. While not yet natural law, this imprint of the eternal law on the creature is a passively participated teleological order from which *all creatures* receive their inclinations to their acts and ends. For example, the natural motion of the will toward the good, or of the intellect toward the true, is *derived from* this imprint of the eternal law, which is the passively participated order.

Most destructively, passive participation is often mistakenly taken to be merely a neutral physical precondition — a necessary condition for natural law, to be sure — but nonetheless merely an *extrinsic physical condition of*

---

divinae providentiae subduntur, a lege aeterna regulentur et mensurentur, ut ex dictis patet; manifestum est quod omnia participant aliqualiter legem aeternam, inquantum scilicet ex impressione eius habent inclinationes in proprios actus et fines."

2. *STh* I-II, q. 91, art. 2, resp.: "Inter cetera autem rationalis creatura excellentiori quodam modo divinae providentiae subiacet, inquantum et ipsa fit providentiae particeps, sibi ipsi et aliis providens."

lower nature, contributing no normative character or content to the natural law. Just as from a person's latitude and longitude alone one cannot deduce the order of law to which that person may be subject, so it is thought that, from the mere "is" of natural "fact," there is no path to the "ought" of normatively prescriptive moral governance. As a result, the sum total of the natural law is read as though the rational participation in the eternal law was freestanding and, in its normative character, independent of the passive participation of creation in the divine government of the cosmos. This is simply to imply what some authors are happy to affirm: that from propositions about nature, one cannot derive conclusions that contain reasons for action, because natural propositions *do not and cannot contain reasons for action.* While it is true that from propositions lacking reasons for action one cannot derive propositions containing reasons for action, one might think it an inadequate and false account of nature to deny that nature *contains reasons for action,* precisely inasmuch as final causality is real. Accordingly, certain natural propositions may indeed contain reasons for action, and so conclusions regarding reasons for action may be drawn from them.

Of course, there are complete negations of natural teleology that deny its pertinence throughout the physical world as such. But the truth that action *as* action — as distinct from action taken abstractively merely in terms of quantity or quality — can only be, or be known, in relation to *end,* manifests the deficiency of such negations. As Thomas puts it in the *Summa contra gentiles,*[3] without an end, either action would never begin (because there would be nothing for the sake of which it would occur), or it would never be fulfilled or terminated (because there would be no such fulfillment or termination) and so would need to pass through an actual infinitude, which is impossible. Accordingly, to argue that being ordered to an end is not a reason for action because value cannot be derived from fact is either (1) to abstract from the nature of "end" and imagine that this is enough to conjure it out of existence or else (2) to contradict the very meaning of "end."

The stress upon a superior and freestanding rationality with respect to

---

3. *Summa contra gentiles* III, ch. 2: for example, "Sed in actione cuiuslibet agentis est invenire aliquid ultra quod agens non quaerit aliquid: alias enim actiones in infinitum tenderent; quod quidem est impossibile, quia, cum infinita non sit pertransire, agens agere non inciperet; nihil enim movetur ad id ad quod impossibile est pervenire. Omne igitur agens agit propter finem." — "But, in the action of all agents, one may find something beyond which the agent seeks nothing further. Otherwise, actions would tend to infinity, which is impossible: since it is impossible to proceed to infinity, the agent could not begin to act, because nothing is moved toward what cannot be reached. Therefore every agent acts for an end."

passive participation in eternal law that some interpreters take to be constitutive of the natural law manifests itself in many ways, but in moral thought
involves three pivotal negations:

1. The negation of the normativity of natural teleology for natural law.
2. The negation — deriving from a logicist account of the object of the
   moral act — of the integral nature and per se effects of action (its natural
   teleology) from the object of the moral act, thereby reducing it merely
   to what makes a particular act appetible or choiceworthy to the agent.
3. The negation of any morally significant hierarchy of goods or ends prior
   to choice, implying most crucially the denial of the supordinate character of *common good* in relation to individual good, and negating the
   hierarchy of common goods reaching finally to God, who is the extrinsic
   common good of the entire universe.

These negations affect not only our understanding of the moral life but
also our understanding and appreciation of the created order as participating
in the divine providential government and further ordered in grace. Such
errors necessarily affect *sacra doctrina* and Catholic moral thought. Because
— as St. Thomas notes in *STh* I, q. 1, art. 7, ad 1 — the Christian *in via* to the
beatific vision does not possess a quidditative or essential vision of God, the
theologian must make use of all the effects of God in nature and grace to
stand in for the lack of such a definition. In particular, the judgment that the
most universal and proper effect of God is *being* — a judgment that is both
metaphysically conspicuous and actually implicit in the doctrine of creation
— necessarily enters constitutively into *sacra doctrina*. As Thomas puts it:

> It sufficiently appears at the first glance, according to what precedes, that
> to create cannot be the action of any but God alone. For the more univer-
> sal effects must be reduced to the more universal and prior causes. Now
> among all effects the most universal is being itself: and hence it must be
> the proper effect of the first and most universal cause, and that is God.
> Hence also it is said (*De Causis prop.,* iii) that "neither intelligence nor
> the soul gives us being, except inasmuch as it works by divine operation."
> Now to produce being absolutely, not as this or that being, belongs to
> creation. Hence it is manifest that creation is the proper act of God alone.[4]

4. *STh* I, q. 45, art. 5, resp.: "Respondeo dicendum quod satis apparet in primo aspectu,
secundum praemissa, quod creare non potest esse propria actio nisi solius Dei. Oportet
enim universaliores effectus in universaliores et priores causas reducere. Inter omnes autem

Thus is the privileged instrumentality of metaphysics within theology observed by St. Thomas.

Thus all creation — including, in particular, the proportionate order that Aquinas holds to *define* natural law as distinct from the divine law, which rules and measures our motion toward the transcendent supernatural end — is included within *sacra doctrina*. The theologian *in via* toward ultimate supernatural beatitude cannot help at every juncture leaning upon the created order of being and nature, which is the proper effect of God, and without which no other effect could obtain. Even the effect of createdness, as Thomas makes clear in his *Commentary on the Sentences,* is a quasi-accident consisting in "having being from another."[5] But the real relation of having being from another presupposes having being, since nonexistent things do not have real relations. Being and nature are everywhere presupposed within *sacra doctrina,* and accordingly the account of being and nature cannot help but condition it from within. This is why the *Summa theologiae* is written as it is written.

---

effectus, universalissimum est ipsum esse. Unde oportet quod sit proprius effectus primae et universalissimae causae, quae est Deus. Unde etiam dicitur libro de causis, quod neque intelligentia vel anima nobilis dat esse, nisi inquantum operatur operatione divina. Producere autem esse absolute, non inquantum est hoc vel tale, pertinet ad rationem creationis. Unde manifestum est quod creatio est propria actio ipsius Dei."

5. *Commentary on the Sentences,* book II, dist, I, q. 1, art. 2, ad 4, where he speaks of creation passively (because taken *actively,* creation signifies merely the divine essence with a conceptual relation to the creature): "If, however, it [i.e., creation] is taken passively, then it is a certain accident in the creature and it signifies a certain reality which is not in the category of being passive properly speaking, but is in the category of relation. Creation is a certain relation of having being from another following upon the divine operation. In the same way, sonship is in Peter insofar as he receives human nature from his father, but it is not prior to Peter himself, but rather follows upon the action and motion which are prior. The relation of creation, however, does not follow upon motion, but only upon the divine action, which is prior to the creature." (Si autem sumatur passive, sic est quoddam accidens in creatura, et sic significat quamdam rem, non quae sit in praedicamento passionis, proprie loquendo, sed quae est in genere relationis, et est quaedam habitudo habentis esse ab alio consequens operationem divinam: et sic non est inconveniens quod sit in ipso creato quod educitur per creationem, sicut in subjecto; sicut filiatio in Petro, inquantum recipit naturam humanam a patre suo, non est prior ipso Petro; sed sequitur actionem et motum, quae sunt priora. Habitudo autem creationis non sequitur motum, sed actionem divinam tantum, quae est prior quam creatura.)

Rational Participation in the Eternal Law

And so we return to the question of rational participation in eternal law, a participation that often is construed as one rationally deracinated and independent of the passively participated teleological order. We understand this question best if we ask, "In virtue of *what* is the rational creature able to participate in a ratio that is analogically identical with God himself?" As Thomas reminds us in *STh* I, q. 28, art. 2, ad 1: "Nothing that exists in God can have any relation to that wherein it exists or of whom it is spoken, except the relation of identity; and this by reason of God's supreme simplicity." Eternal law is the type or idea or *ratio* in God himself of the government of things. How *can* the mind of man, apart from grace, be thought to participate in this divine idea? There are in history several different types of answers to this question, each with implications for the understanding not alone of moral theology but of *sacra doctrina.*

At least some authors seem to have held an ontologism according to which the human mind by its very nature is not only tending to be aware of God but has intuitive and direct knowledge of God himself. Neither Aquinas himself nor the Catholic Church has ever embraced this answer. Indeed, when the *monitum* on the work of Rosmini was removed, it was removed, not because ontologism was considered permissible or reconcilable with Catholic doctrine, but solely because many of the ontologistic propositions earlier condemned by the Holy See were only posthumously made public and lacked a sufficient critical apparatus provided by the author to identify the precise sense of many of the critical expressions used. The Congregation for the Doctrine of the Faith held that Rosmini's work did not need to be read as propounding idealism or ontologism, while admitting that it could be read as insufficiently safeguarded from erroneous interpretation. But it also reaffirmed the condemnation of ontologism in its statement of July 1, 2001: "At the same time the objective validity of the Decree *Post obitum* referring to the previously condemned propositions, remains for whoever reads them, outside of the Rosminian system, in an idealist, ontologist point of view and with a meaning contrary to Catholic faith and doctrine."[6] The view, then, according to which the human intellect is by its very nature "up

---

6. Congregation for the Doctrine of the Faith, "Note on the Force of the Doctrinal Decrees concerning the Thought and Work of Fr. Antonio Rosmini Serbati," July 1, 2001, www .vatican.va/roman_curia/congregations/cfaith/documents/rc_con_cfaith_doc_20010701 _rosmini_en.html.

periscope" in the divine essence, is a possible Catholic understanding neither of rational participation in the eternal law nor of *sacra doctrina*. The
human cognitive gaze does not behold the divine essence in itself because
God infinitely transcends all creatures, and because there is nothing in the
intellect that is not first in sense.

Yet another mode of interpretation of the rational participation in eternal
law — with implications for *sacra doctrina* — is found in nineteenth-century
Catholic attempts to utilize basically idealist or rationalist notions of an a
priori content given to the human mind prior to any particular achievement
of knowledge and conditioning all cognitive achievements. Two extremely
prominent illustrations of this idealist tendency might be found in George
Hermes (1775-1831) and Anton Günther (1783-1863). For a time, Hermes was
perhaps the most influential Catholic thinker in Germany, as he attempted
to develop a Christian apologetic wholly based on premises derived from
Kant. Günther was a Christian Hegelian critic of Hegel. The major works of
these authors were finally placed on the Catholic index. For our purposes, a
more recent illustration with a happier ending would be Giorgio Del Vecchio
(1878-1970), a Catholic ethicist and legal scholar. He attempted to minimize
the metaphysical silhouette of moral philosophy precisely for the sake of not
being indefinitely impeded by philosophic wrangles in the effort to address
practical moral questions, essentially treating "ideal reason" as a stand-in
for "metaphysical objectivity" without, however, expressly concurring in
Kant's negations.[7] Yet, any teaching according to which the human mind
does not derive its objects from the things to be known, but instead has a
prior content conditioning all possible understanding and judgment, negates
genuine objectivity in knowledge, even if it is capable of sustaining a certain
intersubjectivity of judgment.

Finally, there is an account of rational participation in the eternal law
that is directly illuminationist. This account — indebted to certain readings
of Augustine — most certainly does have an authentically Catholic prov-
enance. It does deny, however, a proportionate active cognitive principle
in man. On the side of the object, such a doctrine does exhibit a realism of
intention, because it seeks to affirm that it is reality itself of which divine illumination makes the rational creature aware. Yet, it is difficult to understand

---

7. Cf., for example, Giorgio del Vecchio, *The Philosophy of Law*, trans. Thomas Owen
Martin (Washington, DC: Catholic University of America Press, 1953), whose reference to
Kant focuses upon the issue of an ethical norm prior to the state — but in terms of "ideal
reason," which is not quite the same thing as authentic "objectivity."

how a natural act of the intellect could realize this conformity of rational awareness and reality, lacking as it does direct knowledge of the divine essence and so achieving only conformity to an extrinsic principle surpassing our capacity to judge. Any account of divine illumination that denies any active cognitive principle in man ends by reducing natural knowledge to a species of faith, since the verific character of the divine light cannot be "seen" — there is no natural vision of the divine essence — and the putative conformity of mind illumined by God with the real does not terminate directly in God (it is neither the beatific vision nor the act of supernatural faith) or in the real, but in a cognitive act whose bona fides are neither available to, nor native to, the human mind. Thus it is not a promising account of natural law.

Natural knowledge of truth requires of the knower the capacity to compare what he conceives and judges with what is the case. This does not mean that there are not truths incapable of resolution into evident principles (faith vouchsafes us such truths). But natural knowledge is distinct from — even if related to — the act of faith. And the act of faith, while principally founded in the intellect (as moved by the will under the influence of grace), yet does not achieve direct knowledge of the divine essence.

On the side of the subject, such a view of knowledge seems closer to the mode of direct inspiration through the gifts of the Holy Spirit than to natural law. As an epistemological doctrine, strong illuminationism seems wholly to supplant the proportion of knower and known with the veracity of the divine Mind in relation to creation, thus rendering genuine knowledge incommunicable to man (who lacks all active power proportionate to the potentially intelligible created object to be known).

While acknowledging that all created knowledge is indeed a created participation in the divine light, St. Thomas affirms a true but mediated divine illumination. It is mediated in two ways. First, for Thomas, it is the divinely created agent intellect of the human person — and also, as is too often forgotten, the divinely *applied* agent intellect, since for St. Thomas every power is first and principally applied to act by God[8] — that constitutes the rational creature's natural participation in the divine light. Thomas's account of the light of natural reason discerning good from evil is indeed properly understood as an account of "an imprint on us of the divine light" *(impressio divini luminis in nobis)*. Second, the human intellect is enabled by its proportionate light, and within the divine motion, to achieve conformity with created reality.

Precisely because the passively participated teleological order — the order

---

8. Cf. *Summa contra gentiles* III, ch. 67.

*from which all things derive their inclinations to their proper acts and ends —
is an impress of the eternal law, it is when the rational creature intellectually
receives this order as giving normatively authoritative reasons for action that
the mind rationally participates in eternal law.* The selfsame order that, prior
to rational reception, is *not* natural law, consequent upon rational reception
is natural law: but the normative content remains *the same*. Likewise, no
literary activity is "going on" in a book until it is read; a traffic light blinking
away after some species of apocalypse communicates no legal admonition;
but when a mind reads the book or receives the signal of the light as convey-
ing a legal admonition, *now* the legal direction *is occurring.* As the mind of
an author is in some measure participated in through his writing, so likewise
when the mind receives the divine impress "written" — imprinted — on
nature as providing authoritative reasons for action, it participates in the
eternal law. *The rational reception of this order to which we are subject prior to
any choice, and of which we are aware because we are subject to it, is the natural
law.* We enjoy both connatural awareness of this order and a more detached
consideration. We do not choose to be beings who need food and water to
drink lest they die of hunger and thirst; nor to be beings who need friends
lest they be alienated and lonely; nor to be beings who must achieve some
knowledge of the world and their place in it lest they be confused, ignorant,
and without stable judgment. We simply are such beings, as these simply are
ends that specify natural human inclinations.

The passively participated teleological order — the order very commonly
derided as "physicalist" and "subhuman," and contemned as the realm of
valueless facticity — comprises the whole of created nature. It comprises not
merely the lower creation, but even the ordering of intellect toward universal
truth, and of will toward universal good (an ordering that manifests the foundational level of the *imago Dei* in man, and constitutes both man's obediential
potency for grace and glory and man's openness to the relational dynamism
of the *imago Dei* toward the *imago Christi* and the *imago gloriae*). *All* things
are subject to the eternal law insofar as, from its being *impressed on them* from
creation, they derive their inclinations to their proper acts and ends.[9] When

---

9. *STh* I-II, q. 91, art. 2, resp.: "Unde cum omnia quae divinae providentiae subduntur,
a lege aeterna regulentur et mensurentur, ut ex dictis patet; manifestum est quod omnia
participant aliqualiter legem aeternam, inquantum scilicet ex impressione eius habent inclinationes in proprios actum et finem." And again, from *Summa theologiae* I-II, q. 109, art. 1,
resp.: "Non solum autem a Deo est omnis motio sicut a primo movente; sed etiam ab ipso
est omnis formalis perfectio sicut a primo actu. Sic igitur actio intellectus, et cuiuscumque
entis creati, dependet a Deo quantum ad duo, uno modo, inquantum ab ipso habet formam

we intellectually receive this very passively participated order in a *preceptive* and rational manner, as giving us normatively authoritative *reasons to do, and reasons not to do,* we have natural law. The passively participated order is a *teleological order,* and because *final causality* signifies a real causality in the universe, *it is not the case that propositions regarding nature necessarily exclude reasons for action.* Indeed, the practical order begins with intention or perhaps — *in potentia* — with desire; but prior to either of these there must be knowledge. While it may be accidental to the good or end known that we desire it, it is not thereby accidental in relation to human nature, which is essentially ordained to it as perfectible to perfect or potency to act.

As has been seen, our rational participation in the eternal law presupposes a passive participation that consists in the impress of the divine wisdom on all creatures, from which as St. Thomas argues (in *Summa theologiae* I-II, q. 91, art. 2) they derive their inclinations to their proper acts and ends. This impress of the divine wisdom on all creatures is a teleological ordering, and it is when we rationally receive this ordering in a preceptive manner — as giving authoritative reasons to do or not to do — that we have natural law. This knowing of the order impressed on our nature — an order to which we are subject prior to choice — is itself a divine illumination mediated by our natural mode of cognition. Thus, God, who is the first and principal cause of the application of every power to act,[10] applies our agent intellect so that we may come (via the possible intellect) directly to conceive and understand some aspect of the

---

per quam agit; alio modo, inquantum ab ipso movetur ad agendum" (But not only does every motion depend on God as first mover; but all formal perfection is from Him as the first act. *Thus the act of the intellect and of any created being whatsoever depends on God in two respects, in one way, inasmuch as from Him it has the form through which it acts; in another way, inasmuch as it is moved by Him to act* [emphasis added]). *Every created being whatsoever is moved to its act by God.* And again, from the same q. 109, art. 1, resp.: "Sic igitur dicendum est quod ad cognitionem cuiuscumque veri, homo indiget auxilio divino ut intellectus a Deo moveatur ad suum actum" (Thus it should be said that for the knowledge of any truth whatsoever, man needs divine aid that the intellect may be moved to its act).

10. Cf. *Summa contra gentiles* III, ch. 67: "Sed omnis applicatio virtutis ad operationem est principaliter et primo a Deo" (But every application of power to operation is principally and first from God). Thus "Similiter etiam omnis motus voluntatis quo applicantur aliquae virtutes ad operandum, reducitur in Deum sicut in primum appetibile et in primum volentem. Omnis igitur operatio debet attribui Deo sicut primo et principali agenti" (Likewise, every motion of the will whereby powers are applied to operation, is reduced to God as the first appetible and the first willer. Thus every operation should be attributed to God as to the first and principal agent). For this reason this consideration could also be undertaken from a different aspect in terms of the divine efficient causality (which is always implicit in teleology); and alike in terms of the divine exemplar causality (in terms of the external formal cause of degrees of perfection).

order of things. This knowledge of the divinely impressed order is both connatural, because we are aware of it simply by being subject to it, and conceptual, because we have a certain understanding of it. This secondary causality of our intellect is genuinely a mediated divine illumination — *impressio diuini lumini in nobis* — because it conforms our intellect to the ordering wisdom of God as impressed in the passively participated teleological order of creation; and it is God who applies our cognitive power to act, enabling us to achieve this.

The Baneful Effects of the Negation of the Normative Role of the Passively Participated Teleological Order

As noted at the start, three principal destructive effects have been drawn from the rationalist/logicist view of natural law as a wholly *freestanding* rational participation in eternal law. The first is the denuding of moral law of any normative indebtedness to the divine ordering of nature, an ordering that is reduced to merest facticity. This denial that the normativity of the natural law derives from the divine impress upon nature has further direct implications in the denial that the natural teleology of what we choose must — when the choice is conscious and deliberate — be included in the object of our action, even if we act for some other reason. To illustrate: The action of a man who is in line for life-saving therapy and whose prognosis is such that he will not survive to receive treatment unless he moves ahead in line, may try to persuade others to get out of line ahead of him. If he cannot persuade them and accordingly kills those ahead of him in the queue, his action cannot properly be described as merely "removing impediments to life-saving therapy." It is murder, even if the one committing the act finds it horrible and chooses the act solely to attain life-saving therapy. Likewise, spouses who use contraceptives principally to avoid communicating the AIDS virus nonetheless both contracept and fail to achieve a one-flesh union. The action of a woman who aborts a child to address dangerous pulmonary hypertension — as occurred in the famous St. Joseph's Hospital case in Phoenix, Arizona, over which a hospital lost its Catholic status — cannot be said to constitute merely a medical treatment for pulmonary hypertension, contrary to some very widespread accounts. And so on.

Of course, there is also the teleology that relates what we choose to what we intend — the order of object to end determining whether the species from the end contains the species from the object, or not. Yet, both choice of object and intention of end are subject to possible deprivation and defect. And so when we know the order of object to end and the number and kind of moral species involved in an action, these are still judged as good or evil in relation to the normative order of ends (the passively participated teleological order).

A further principal effect of the negation of passively participated teleological order with its essential hierarchy of ends, which defines the *ratio boni,* is the negation of the order of common goods that rises as high as the natural love of God above all things (a love that must be restored by grace after the fall) and that defines true natural rectitude. The understanding of *common good* in itself — today so commonly taken to be exclusively a political matter or even a merely instrumental good — is in its roots metaphysical and drawn from contemplation of the normative hierarchy of ends. In St. Thomas's teaching, the dignity of man consists in the intellective and volitional ordering to progressively nobler and more universal ends that are common goods. This order is essential to the Christian life that rises above, rather than sinks below, the proportionate natural good. The *ratio boni* for man, which is twofold, is defined both by the proportionate, proximate end from which the human species is derived and by the supernatural end of the beatific vision, to which we are ordered in grace.[11] (As Charles De Koninck so controversially put the matter, the sin of Lucifer was that of preferring a private good of the person to the ultimate common good of supernatural beatitude.)[12]

The *imago Dei,* which chiefly consists in the rational nature, constitutes an analogically specific image of God and affords the basis — in the universality of intellect and will — of the possibility for man's elevation to grace and glory. Thus the passively participated order — which embraces more than the lower creation, but includes it — takes us back to the truth that *as a condition of man being created in grace and for God from the beginning,* human nature must first and proximately be ordered to the common good of the universe. Only because of this order can man exist within the universe, and can have been — from the beginning — subject to divine elevation to the divine friendship in grace. Furthermore, it is from this ordering that the natural intelligibility of theism derives.

11. Cf. *STh* I, q. 75, art. 7, ad 1.

12. For one illustration of this teaching in his writing, see Charles De Koninck, *The Primacy of the Common Good: Against the Personalists,* in *The Writings of Charles De Koninck,* vol. 2, ed. and trans. Ralph McInerny (Notre Dame, IN: University of Notre Dame Press, 2009), 73: "The sin of the angels was a practically personalist error: they preferred the dignity of their proper person to the dignity that would have come to them in the subordination to a superior good, but one common in its very superiority."

Eternal Law and the Lower Creation

This chapter has chiefly engaged the teleological grammar of the created moral order as constituting the imprint of the ordering wisdom of God. Yet, while the passively participated teleological order is not merely the order of the lower creation, it does *include* this lower order, which is not barren of moral significance. The passively participated order — inclusive of, but not reducible to, the lower order of creation — is not merely a neutral factual precondition for the natural law but provides the essential normative content for the law. It is neither separated from nor opposed to God but is the impress of the ordering wisdom of God in creation. When this passively participated order — principally that of man's own nature, but also of the cosmos as such within which and to which one is naturally ordered — is received by the rational creature *preceptively,* as giving authoritative direction for action, then this very order specifies our *rational* participation in the eternal law known as natural law.

While the chief element in this reception is the divine ordering of *our own* nature, this reception extends to discerning the divine ordering of the lower creation, thus informing our moral agency as stewards of creation, who, while ordering the sensible to the intelligible, *even more profoundly discern in the lower order — and seek to preserve in this order — the intact mystery and variety of the created manifestation of God.*

Precisely because the passively participated teleological order is not the subhuman and merely physical facticity that Cartesian and modern thought generally supposes; because it includes the teleology of every natural power, including immaterial powers of intellect and will; because, for example, this order is not the bifurcated world of Wittgenstein, for whom the speakable is reduced to empirical science, and for whom reality in its metaphysical subjectivity and depth is the domain solely of a gnostic poetry of the ineffable; precisely for this reason, the passively participated teleological order that transcends the order of the lower creation *nonetheless includes the lower creation.* And because it includes the order of the lower creation without being reducible to it, this divine ordering *even of lower nature* is necessarily of moral significance and subject to a certain piety that places constraints on our habitudes toward the lower creation, and on our right treatment and use of it. Whether one formulates the truth of this proposition in terms of the ordering of the lower creation to the common good of the universe, or simply in terms of the passive participation in the eternal law — the former being in a sense an effect of the latter — the lower creation is more than merely the staging ground for, and an aid to, human survival.

It is important to understand the proposition at stake.[13] We do not worship lower creation, nor, precisely, venerate it. But we *may* venerate (although certainly *not* worship) the ordering wisdom of God impressed upon creation. Eternal law *is* God. Created things — including *created grace* — are *not* God. Likewise, the signate ring of the king is not the king. But one honors the king by honoring his seal, because his seal participates in his authority in a distinctive fashion (and dishonoring it merits distinctive penalty). *The action of the agent is in the patient.* If we are called to honor what God *does*, this is *to honor the creature as manifesting, in some way and to some degree, its divine cause.* It is, after all, from the existential indigence of real sensible effects that we naturally become aware of the dependence of all creatures upon God; but it is also from the *perfection* of act, even as limited by potency in creatures, that we become aware that act as such is not self-limiting, and that we have a positive foundation — in the actual effects wrought by God — for affirming that God not only *causes* being but *is ipsum esse subsistens per se,* not only causes "good" but is "Good." St. Thomas insists that we call God "good" not merely as its cause but because God is indeed Good.[14]

The order that permeates all things, and so likewise permeates the lower creation, is *real in things.* Just as we honor God through the honoring of the *real sanctity of his saints,* so we honor God through honoring the true wisdom that orders — and is imprinted upon — all things, including the lower creation. Thomas himself tells us that God's knowledge is to be compared to the things themselves "as the knowledge of art to the objects of art."[15] But as we

13. I am indebted to Prof. Marie George of St. John's University, New York, for the perception of the danger that my remarks might erroneously be construed as an incipient "Gaia-ism," were they to be interpreted as implying that man is ordered to the lower creation simply and as such rather than (1) being ordered to the common good of the universe and to God in a *sense* "alongside" the lower creation, while (2) existing within an *order* within which *sensible being is ordered to intelligible being, and the lower creation ordered to the nobler creation.* The account that follows seeks, among other things, to argue that to honor the eternal law impressed upon all things in the passively participated teleological order — to honor the immanent common good of the universe (the right ordering of the universe to God) and to honor God as ultimate extrinsic common good of the universe — is neither to subordinate man to the subhuman nor to deny that the lower creation exists *for the sake of* the nobler creation. The *ordering* of the lower creation to man is itself part of the passively participated teleological order.

14. *STh* I, q. 13, art. 2, resp.

15. *STh* I, q. 22, art. 2, resp.

honor the supereminent genius of the artist in honoring his work — without necessarily implying that the work exhausts his gifts — so we honor God in venerating *the wise order* he imprints upon all his effects, while realizing that he infinitely transcends these effects.

Furthermore, in the preceding article in which he compares God's knowledge to created things as the knowledge of art to the objects of art, Thomas insists that two things pertain to providence: the reason of order called "providence," and the execution of order called "government." But "the first is eternal, the second, temporal."[16] So the execution of providence over temporal creatures is temporal, is in temporal things themselves. But we rightly honor God not alone for the plan of divine providence *but for the divinely ordained execution of providence in things.* As a court would hold one guilty of dishonoring its authority if one did not honor its writ, so to fail to honor the impressed order, even in the lower creation, constitutes a species of impiety.

A fuller consideration of providence would manifest that not only *what* occurs, but even the *manner in which it occurs* — whether necessarily or contingently — is *infallibly* governed by providence. Hence — not because all things are grace in the sense of being sanctifying grace, but because all perfection and all determinate actuality or order to it lie entirely within God's providential causality — we can speak of creation as such as the "first grace" in the sense of "first unmerited gift." We can also speak of creation in the sense that "everything is grace," because the divine wisdom and love without flaw "write straight with crooked lines," bringing forth the very perfection of holiness in the saints unto final glory, even amid deprivation and defect (e.g., even from the very sorrows of his saints).

It would be very odd if the font of our cognitive life in the richness of sensation were in itself to be thought — as in differing ways both Descartes and Hume seem to have supposed — to be singularly empty of intelligible order or necessity. Granted that God has no real relation to the creature, while the creature has a real relation to God; nonetheless, God is the true cause for every perfection of the creature, and these perfections *are real.* In honoring the order impressed by God even upon the lower creation, we honor God himself. This is not worship or even veneration of lower creation, properly speaking, but worship of God and veneration of the wise

---

16. *STh* I, q. 22, art. 1, ad 2: "Ad secundum dicendum quod ad curam duo pertinent, scilicet ratio ordinis, quae dicitur providentia et dispositio; et executio ordinis, quae dicitur gubernatio. Quorum primum est aeternum, secundum temporale."

order he imprints upon all created things. Piety for this order, which God has himself placed in the things themselves, is owed to God. After all, the good of religion flows forth from the natural virtue of justice, inasmuch as we realize that God is the author of all good, and so that we owe him public and private thanks and praise. But just this *goodness* — without implying a servile subjection of the intelligible to the sensible or of the more noble to the less noble — must be honored precisely in the mode in which dominion is exercised, recognizing that lower good is not a pure utility but participates in the common good of the universe and manifests the divine wisdom. The book of nature must not be viewed merely as firewood to be burned, but likewise man must not freeze for fear of upsetting the gods in the trees: the wood is for man. But it is *for* man *first* and *principally* in the lower creation's nourishing of contemplative wonder and instigating our science and poetry. This truth does not prevent the multiplex use of nature but is in a profound and vital way — reaching even into how we deem it fitting to use nature for human good — prior to such use.

What does "honoring the order" *mean?* Surely it minimally suggests that we see the order as a divine gift; and that we reject the idea of arbitrary destruction.

If one sees the need to honor the passively participated teleological order in moral action itself, where the normative order of ends is a principle of judgment, and where the per se natural teleology of chosen action cannot be excluded from the object of moral action, it is similarly manifest in the piety owed to the divine governance of the lower creation. Even the licit subjection of the lower creation to serve man's needs is wholly a function of the normative hierarchy of ends, and of the relation of sensible to intelligible good — which is part of the passively participated order. Recognition of this makes even of the reasonable *use* of nature an obedience to nature as norm. That which principally accounts for the dignity of the lower creation — its participation in the eternal law and in the indwelling common good of the universe (the right order of the universe with respect to God) — is also that which determines the hierarchic subordination of the lower creation itself to the good of man, insofar as lower goods are divinely ordained for the sake of nobler goods.

The chief service of the lower creation, however, is *first and foremost* a contemplative exigency, inasmuch as sense contact with the lower order is the point of origination for our understanding of the natural world, the home of our poetry, the stuff of wonder and beauty, the primal beginning of our science. Here the order of lower to nobler good is manifest. Second, our own being not only in part materially derives from the elements of the lower created order but is in its own way subjected to these and proximately ordered to them for the sake of the terrestrial whole. In creating the universe, God intends principally the common good of the universe as a necessary condition for the further ordering of man to the *finis ultimus* of supernatural beatitude. Thus the whole material creation is also represented by man, and the whole creation *indirectly* but *truly* is affected by the incarnation.

The lower creation with its own subjectivity in being does participate passively in the eternal law, participates in the common good of the terrestrial cosmos, and also *indirectly, through the elevation of man in grace,* participates in the common good of the new heaven and new earth. It manifests the ordering wisdom of God and provides the primordial evidence from which we infer the reality and transcendence of the First Cause. Accordingly, regard for the variety, mystery, beauty, intelligibility, and splendor of the lower creation is necessarily implied by the virtue of piety, insofar as this order is an impress of the divine wisdom. For example, surely we ought to honor the truth, for if we do not begin to honor truth in "small t" truths, how should we ever properly honor and worship the First Truth? This is analogous with the proposition that, if we do not love our neighbor whom we can see, how should we love God, whom we cannot see?

What we are honoring is the wise order impressed, and not merely that in which the impress is received — although it would be churlish to suggest that joy and piety with respect to creation are out of place. As the seal of the king in the wax commands a certain honor — an honor that is not paid to the wax as such — so the order divinely impressed upon nature commands honor as the impress of the divine wisdom, without implying nature worship. Creation as such is not *in God* but *in the creature,* as "createdness" for Thomas designates a "quasi-accident" of "having being from another." But having being from another presupposes *habens esse,* presupposes *having being.* Our footing in the divine gift of being — and in the passively participated order — is part of our inheritance. Nonetheless, the passively participated order *itself* is the ground for the judgment that lower goods are ordered toward nobler ones, so that one does not suppose that a hypostasized good of "the environment" licenses sacrificing human lives exclusively for sub-human good.

These remarks have not addressed the rightful limitations to technical superventions upon, and alterations of, nature. Such questions demand treatment at the appropriate level of complexity. With respect to the distinction between correcting defect and attempting to proliferate new and artificial species, the argumentation is not simple. For example, one might think that the created order has "gaps" that suggest, and so even divinely *invite,* limited creativity. Yet, granted that the external effects of human intelligence themselves thoroughly presuppose and depend upon natural order, there is a prior debt of piety with respect to the divinely decreed antecedent order, whose contemplative dimensions outstrip any innovation in technical mimicry. This major premise is essential for any adequate analysis, which cannot be wholly submerged in considerations of utility or technical capacity. A certain prudential reserve and fear of hubris should check adolescent inclination simply to do everything we can possibly do, which is no more a good here than it is anywhere else in life.

The passively participated teleological order includes the order of the lower creation, which cannot simply be separated off from this unified order and discarded as though lacking all subjectivity in being and reducible to a pure utility, or as though it distinctively lacked any participation in the indwelling common good of the cosmos or impress of the divine wisdom. The lower creation is neither a Cartesian residuum nor independent of the wider order. The divine ordering of creation is a normative principle for man prior to any choice whatsoever — indeed, even for *technē,* as Aristotle observed, in noting that we can only make something either as nature *does make it* or as nature *would make it* if it did make it. Furthermore, and more crucially, the passively participated teleological order defines natural moral rectitude, determining the specifications of the regard due to the lower order, the contemplative rectitude specified by that order, and the due subjection of that order to human goods.

Because the lower nature shares in the common good of the order indwelling the cosmos as such, the rational creature can perceive the normativity of this ordering and — following the telos connatural to the rational soul — honor it. But this honor paid to the divinely imprinted order of the cosmos as participated in by lower nature is not a replacement for the rational nature's own teleology but rather an essential instruction and aid for it, for we are not mere physical natures, and nature is an essentially analogical principle that rises beyond the lower creation. It is in the *dramatis personae* of redeemed humanity that the lower creation can enter within the hymn of praise to God.

Lower terrestrial nature should be neither opposed to technical development nor disdained as mere matter before technical form but should be regarded, precisely in its participation in cosmic and divine order, as a good to be preserved. Such preservation will to some degree occur in enclaves apart from technical civilization, where by reason of its beauty, its variety, and its manifestation of an order that is not merely that imposed by *technē* and that stands in analogical relation to all the other goods of human nature, it is kept pristine. But the virtualities of nature are preserved in a different manner when they are cultivated and brought to fruition by human ingenuity in the service of human life and elevated to a greater analogical participation in the good of human nature.

The lower creation is the womb of science, the home of poetry and beauty, and the primal evidentiary foundation for the causal ascent of human reasoning to God.[17] One must recollect, however, that it is the order inscribed upon *our nature* that provides the content for natural moral wisdom — as we both need the lower creation to subsist, but need it all the more to contemplate. The teleology of man as a composite being of rational soul and matter thus in grace indirectly but really betokens the new heaven and the new earth, in which the final obedience of all terrestrial things to God is perfected in man's worship — alongside the angels[18] — and transfigured in the glory of the achievement of beatitude.

---

17. Steven A. Long, "Thomistic Reflections on the Cosmos, Man, and Stewardship," *Nova et Vetera* (Eng. ed.) 10, no. 1 (2012): 212-13.

18. I say "alongside," not because the angels are not more perfect than man (for the *imago Dei* is more perfect in the angels than in man) but because, nonetheless in the order of charity, we are not precisely subordinated to the angels, even while being committed to their care by divine providence as sojourners.

CHAPTER 4

Kingship and Kinship: Opposing or Complementary Ways of Envisaging Our Relationship to Material Creation?

Marie George

Church documents do not often use the word "king" to name our relationship to the rest of nature; the word "steward" is much more common.[1] However, the *Compendium of the Social Doctrine of the Church,* quoting John Paul II, affirms: "God willed that man be the king of creation."[2] And *Gaudium et spes* speaks of humans as rulers of creation: "Man was created in God's image and was commanded to conquer the earth and to rule the world in justice and holiness."[3]

Another way of envisaging the relationship of humans to material creation is that of kinship. Thus, for example, the Jesuit authors of "Healing a Broken World" tell us:

1. The *Catechism of the Catholic Church,* the *Compendium of the Catechism of the Catholic Church,* Pope John Paul II, and Pope Benedict XVI all speak of us as stewards of creation. The idea central to stewardship is that the earth first and foremost is the Lord's and he has delegated to us the responsibility of tending it in keeping with his purposes. ("The Lord God then took man and put him in the garden of Eden to work it and to take care of it," Gen 2:15.)

2. *Compendium of the Social Doctrine of the Church* (Washington, DC: USCCB, 2004) (hereafter *CompSDC*), §460, quoting John Paul II, "Address to the Thirty-Fifth General Assembly of the World Medical Association" (October 29, 1983), *L'Osservatore Romano,* Eng. ed., December 5, 1986, 11. The *CompSDC* also speaks in terms of kingship at §255.

3. *Gaudium et spes,* §34, in *Vatican Council II: The Conciliar and Post Conciliar Documents,* ed. Austin Flannery (Northport, NY: Costello Publishing Company, 1992). See St. John Damascene, *An Exact Exposition of the Orthodox Faith,* www.orthodox.net/fathers/exactidx.html, 2.11: "Now when God was about to fashion man out of the visible and invisible creation in His own image and likeness to reign as king and ruler over all the earth and all that it contains, He first made for him, so to speak, a kingdom in which he should live a life of happiness and prosperity."

The meditations on the Incarnation (Spiritual Exercises, 101-9) and the Nativity (110-17) emphasize that the created world is the place to experience God. By being born in a concrete place (Nazareth), Jesus Christ shares with us a deep relationship with creation, with life, nature and the air we breathe. From the Trinitarian perspective underpinning this contemplation, we are called to live in kinship and communication with creation.[4]

And the authors of *Care for Creation: A Franciscan Spirituality of the Earth* assert that Francis "did not view the elements or animals as something for which he was responsible but rather as brothers and sisters to which he was related. . . . Francis lived out of a horizontal, not a vertical, relationship with the earth. He manifested a familial or kinship ethic. He did not speak of stewardship, of being in charge, of being responsible, or of managing creation."[5]

Characterizing our relationship to creation as one of kingship or kinship is doubtless different. The question, though, is whether they are incompatible or complementary. This depends on how kinship and kingship are understood.

Commonly Held Views of Kinship That Conflict with Kingship

Sometimes kinship is understood as entailing a denial of human superiority to the rest of creation, and of our consequent kingship over the earth, as do the authors of *Care for Creation:*

> But his [Francis's] example reminds us that our first calling, our first responsibility, as human beings is to be creatures of God, living in relationship to Creator and creation. Our fundamental ethic is to love God and the rest of creation, and our stewardship responsibilities flow from that. For too long, modern society has emphasized the special privileges of humans, and so Francis' example reminds us of our essential creaturehood. He reminds us of our identity as human beings, members of and co-participants in creation.

4. "Healing a Broken World: Task Force on Ecology," *Promotio Justitiae* 106, no. 2 (2011): 34.

5. Ilia Delio, OSF, Keith Douglass Warner, OFM, and Pamela Wood, *Care for Creation: A Franciscan Spirituality of the Earth* (Cincinnati: St. Anthony Messenger Press, 2008), 75.

At its deepest root, our ecological crises derive from our belief that humans are somehow above or fundamentally distinct from — indeed absolutely superior to — the rest of creation. This conceit is incompatible with a Franciscan worldview.[6]

Such an understanding of kinship is contrary to Church teaching to the extent that it denies the superiority of humans to the rest of earthly creatures. The *Catechism of the Catholic Church* affirms:

The *hierarchy of creatures* is expressed by the order of the "six days," from the less perfect to the more perfect. God loves all his creatures and takes care of each one, even the sparrow. Nevertheless, Jesus said: "You are of more value than many sparrows," or again: "Of how much more value is a man than a sheep!"

Man is the summit of the Creator's work, as the inspired account expresses by clearly distinguishing the creation of man from that of the other creatures.[7]

What puts us at the summit of earthly creation is that we alone are created in the image of God. These truths are repeatedly affirmed in Church documents: "Of all visible creatures only man is 'able to know and love his creator.' He is 'the only creature on earth that God has willed for its own sake,' and he alone is called to share, by knowledge and love, in God's own life.... Being in the image of God the human individual possesses the dignity of a person, who is not just something, but someone."[8]

While we, like other earthly creatures, clearly have a body, unlike them, we have a spiritual soul, and because of it we are fundamentally different from them. Some of the partisans of the kinship model deny this radical difference between humans and other living things, in some cases claiming that the human soul is simply a manifestation of matter, and in other cases affirming that other creatures are to be treated in an I-Thou manner instead of an I-It manner. For example, Elizabeth Johnson, CSJ, maintains:

The human race along with all living creatures is physically made of the dust of the earth which is the fallout of stardust. But, one might argue, what about intelligence and freedom which so distinguish the human

6. Delio, Warner, and Wood, *Care for Creation*, 77-78.

7. *Catechism of the Catholic Church*, 2nd ed. (Washington, DC: United States Catholic Conference, 1997) (hereafter *CCC*), §§342-43.

8. *CCC*, §§356-57; quoted is *Gaudium et spes*, §12 and §24. See also *CompCCC*, §66.

species? Does this not break the kinship that humanity shares with the rest of creation? Not at all. Human consciousness is in continuity with the energy of matter stretching back through galactic ages to the Big Bang, being a special, intense form of this energy. . . . Matter, alive with energy, evolves to spirit. While distinctive, human intelligence and creativity rise out of the very nature of the universe which is itself intelligent and creative.[9]

And the authors of *Care for Creation: A Franciscan Spirituality of the Earth* tell us:

With our common understanding of a separate self comes the perception that the earth is "out there" and thus our human attempt to protect it is defined as an altruistic duty. However, if our sense of self becomes rooted in our kinship with creation, as Francis' was, we will naturally be moved to protect our home, because we must protect that which we love and to which we belong. For us contemporary Christians, moving from an "I-It" relationship with the created world to an "I-Thou" relationship can transform our way of being in the world. Francis models how to live in right relationship with the world.[10]

To the contrary, the *CCC* teaches that "every spiritual soul is created immediately by God";[11] it is not the product of natural causes. And Vatican II affirms: "Man, as sharing in the light of the divine mind, rightfully affirms that by his intellect he surpasses the world of mere things."[12] Accordingly, the *CCC* asserts: "One can love animals; one should not direct to them the affection due only to persons." Animals and other nonhuman material creatures are "its," not persons. Again, we, being in the image of God, possess "the dignity of a person, who is not just something, but someone."[13]

---

9. Elizabeth A. Johnson, *Women, Earth, and Creator Spirit* (Mahwah, NJ: Paulist Press, 1993), 37. Thomas Berry also fails to recognize that the rational soul, though the form of a material body, is not a material form and so cannot arise through natural processes but must be directly produced by God; see *Evening Thoughts,* ed. Mary Evelyn Tucker (San Francisco: Sierra Club Books, 2006), 55: "Thought itself and the highest of human spiritual achievements are attained through the activation of the inner capacities of carbon in its alliance with the other elements of the universe. Thus carbon has varied modes of expression, from inorganic to organic to conscious self-awareness in humans."

10. Delio, Warner, and Wood, *Care for Creation,* 60.

11. *CCC,* §366.

12. *Gaudium et spes,* §15. See also *CompCCC,* §358.

13. *CCC,* §§2418, 357.

Our dominion or kingship over other earthly creatures follows from
the superiority we have to them in virtue of our being created by God in his
image: "At the summit of this creation, which 'was very good' (Gen 1:31),
God placed man. Only man and woman, among all creatures, were made
by God 'in his own image' (Gen 1:27). The Lord entrusted all of creation
to their responsibility, charging them to care for its harmony and development (cf. Gen 1:26-30). This special bond with God explains the privileged
position of the first human couple in the order of creation."[14] There is no
doubt, then, that our responsibilities vis-à-vis creation flow from the special status that we have as the only earthly creatures created in the image
of God. Any version of the kinship paradigm that denies this is out of step
with Church teaching.

A Systematic Look at the Meanings of Kinship

The *CCC* and liturgy indicate that there is another way of understanding kinship that does not entail a rejection of human superiority or of the kingship
that is rooted in that superiority, but instead provides a complementary way
of understanding our relationship to the environment, which understanding
is at the basis of how we should treat it. St. Thomas Aquinas can help us in
fleshing out the Church's teaching on this matter.

In order to determine whether kinship taken in any sense provides a
reason that should motivate a Christian to care for creation, we need to
consider the different senses of kinship. The first and most obvious sense
is "Connection by blood, marriage, or adoption; family relationship."[15] A
second sense is "the state of having common characteristics or a common
origin."[16] A final sense is "a close connection marked by community of
interests."[17]

14. *CompSDC*, §451. See Gen 1:26: "Then God said, 'Let us make man in our image,
after our likeness; and let them have dominion over the fish of the sea, and over the birds of
the air and over the cattle, and over all the earth, and over every creeping thing that creeps
upon the earth.'"

15. *The American Heritage Dictionary of the English Language,* 4th ed. (Boston: Houghton Mifflin, 2000).

16. *Collins English Dictionary — Complete and Unabridged,* 9th ed. (New York: HarperCollins, 2003).

17. Thesaurus based on WordNet 3.0, Farlex clipart collection (Princeton University:
Farlex Inc., 2003-12), www.thefreedictionary.com/kinship.

Kinship as Family Relationship

Aquinas explains clearly why nonrational creatures are not our kin in the sense of members belonging to the same family:[18]

> It belongs to the notion of filiation that a son is produced in the likeness of the species of the generator itself. Man, however, insofar as he is produced through creation in a participation of intellect is produced as it were in a likeness of the species of God himself: for the ultimate of those things according to which created nature shares in the likeness of uncreated nature is intellectuality; and therefore only the rational creature is said to be to the image [of God] . . . whence only the rational creature through creation obtains the name of filiation. But adoption . . . requires that a right [*ius*] is acquired by the adopted in the inheritance of the one adopting. The inheritance, however, of God himself is his very beatitude, of which none except the rational creature is capable: nor is it acquired by its very creation, but from the gift of the Holy Spirit. . . . And therefore it is manifest that creation does not give to nonrational creatures either filiation or adoption; however, to rational creatures it gives a certain filiation, but not adoption.[19]

18. According to Aquinas, *Scriptum super Sententiis* (Paris: Lethielleux, 1956), bk. 3, d. 10, q. 2, a. 2, qc. 2, s.c. 2: "Angels are called our brothers and consorts." This thought fits with the *CCC*'s affirmation that "in her liturgy, the Church joins with the angels to adore the thrice-holy God" (§335). All translations of Aquinas are my own.

19. Aquinas, *Scriptum super Sententiis*, bk. 3, d. 10, q. 2, a. 2, q. la 1, sol. 1. See *Summa theologiae*, ed. Instituti Studiorum Medievalium Ottaviensis (Ottawa: Commissio Piana, 1953) (hereafter *STh*), I, q. 33, art. 3: "A name is said first and foremost [*per prius*] of that in which the whole notion of the name is perfectly preserved rather than in that in which it is preserved according to something; for about the latter it is said as through a likeness to that in which it is perfected preserved. . . . And whence it is that the name 'lion' is said first and foremost of an animal in which the whole notion of lion is preserved, than about some man in which something of the notion of lion is found, such as audacity . . . for this is said by way of likeness. . . . The perfect notion of paternity and filiation are found in God the Father and God the Son, for there is one nature and glory of Father and Son. But in creatures, filiation in respect to God is not found according to the complete notion, but only according to a likeness of some sort, since there is not one nature of Creator and creature. To the extent that the likeness is more perfect, to that extent it draws closer to the true notion of filiation. For God is called Father of any creature on account of the likeness alone of a vestige, as is the case of nonrational creatures; according to Job 38:28: 'Who is Father of the rain? Or who begets the dewdrops?' [God is Father of] some creature, namely, the rational, according to the likeness of an image; according to Deut 32:6: 'Is he not your Father who possesses you and made you and created you?'" Although the whole Trinity is Father of creation according to some

Aquinas is restating the Church teachings we have seen above. Other material creatures on earth are not persons. Our common origin does not justify calling nonrational creatures by family names such as brother, sister, mother, taking these words in their proper sense, contrary to what the authors of *Care for Creation* maintain: "The Canticle discloses Francis' view of nature as a sacramental expression of God's generous love.[20] This love binds us together in a family of relationships that are rightly termed 'brother' and 'sister.'"[21]

Of course, we may call creatures by family names by way of poetic metaphor based on some distant likeness. "Mother earth," by providing humans with nourishment, bears a similarity to a mother feeding her child. Other creatures can be regarded as sisters insofar as they are associated with us in a various ways, for example, insofar as we share God as our origin.[22]

A further consequence of filiation with God being unique to humans

---

distant likeness, the use of "Father" rather than "Creator" borders on being metaphorical, as one would not say that a rock or frog was a son or daughter of God; Aquinas often refers to them as vestiges, or "footprints," of God *(vestigia Dei)*. Consequently, I do not think that this passage contradicts what Aquinas says in the *Commentary on the Sentences*. The situation parallels how we call dogs "man's best friend," even though, strictly speaking, animals cannot be friends with humans because "we cannot properly want the good for an irrational creature because it does not belong to it to properly possess the good, but this belongs only to the rational creature who is a master using the good through free will. . . . Secondly, all friendship is founded upon some sharing of life . . . irrational creatures, however, are not able to have a share in human life which is according to reason" (*STh* II-II, q. 25, art. 3).

20. It is correct to regard nature as sacramental in the sense that it is something perceptible that indicates God's presence. Thus the American bishops write: "For many people, the environmental movement has reawakened appreciation of the truth that, through the created gifts of nature, men and women encounter their Creator. The Christian vision of a sacramental universe — a world that discloses the Creator's presence by visible and tangible signs — can contribute to making the earth a home for the human family once again. Pope John Paul II has called for Christians to respect and protect the environment, so that through nature people can 'contemplate the mystery of the greatness and love of God'" ("Renewing the Earth: An Invitation to Reflection and Action on Environment in Light of Catholic Social Teaching" [Washington, DC: USCCB, 1991], 6).

21. *Care for Creation,* 84.

22. Note how John Paul II put "fraternity" in scare quotes: "It is my hope that the inspiration of Saint Francis will help us to keep ever alive a sense of 'fraternity' with all those good and beautiful things which Almighty God has created. And may he remind us of our serious obligation to respect and watch over them with care, in light of that greater and higher fraternity that exists within the human family" ("Peace with God the Creator, Peace with all of Creation," www.vatican.va/holy_father/john_paul_ii/messages/peace/documents/hf_jp-ii_mes_19891208_xxiii-world-day-for-peace_en.html).

among earthly creatures is that both the gift of piety and the moral virtue of piety by which we show reverence and honor to God is to be extended to other humans, but not to nonrational creatures, apart from those specially consecrated to the service of God.[23] Any sort of talk of the earth or any earthly creature as such as being sacred or being owed honor or reverence entails a failure to respect the hierarchy God himself established in things: *"The Christian vision of creation makes a positive judgment on the acceptability of human intervention in nature, which also includes other living beings, and at the same time makes a strong appeal for responsibility.* In effect, nature is not a sacred or divine reality that man must leave alone."[24]

Certainly we are to use things in a responsible manner and not just in any manner we please. However, we are not to treat nature with reverence. Recall how Christ allowed the demons to enter the herd of pigs, resulting in the pigs' destruction. He did not treat these pigs with reverence; rather, he used them as instruments to teach us our worth. Yet, many of those who advocate the kinship model tell us that earthly creatures are sacred,[25] and that we should reverence them.[26] This is not surprising, given that they fail to recognize the fundamental difference between humans and nonhuman creatures. On earth, human life alone is sacred.[27]

---

23. See *STh* II-II, q. 121, art. 1, ad 3: "Just as through piety which is a virtue man shows service and respect [*cultum*] not only to one's corporeal father, but also to all joined by blood insofar as they belong to the father; so also piety, according as it is a gift, not only shows reverence [*cultum*] and service to God, but to all men insofar as they belong to God."

24. *CompSDC*, §473.

25. See Johnson, *Women, Earth, and Creator Spirit*, 21: "Our eyes have been blinded to the sacredness of the earth, which is linked to the exclusion of women from the sphere of the sacred." See Delio, Warner, and Wood, *Care for Creation*, 62: "Are there times you forget your true identity and live out of a more narrow sense of self? Can you think of times when you have lived out of a sense of self that was more connected to God and the world as sacred?"

26. See Delio, Warner, and Wood, *Care for Creation*, 36: "Francis of Assisi was at home in the cosmos. We know this because at the end of his life he composed the Canticle of the Creatures in which he sang of the brotherhood and sisterhood in the family of creation. . . . The cosmos became home to Francis because this is where he discovered love, the overflowing goodness of God. The brothers who lived with Francis remember him as one who reverenced the earth." See also 100: "Am I caring toward my larger family of creation? Have I shown fidelity, humility, reverence and love to my Sister Mother Earth and all my brother and sister species?"

27. See *CompCCC*, §466: "Human life must be respected because it is *sacred*. From its beginning human life involves the creative action of God and it remains forever in a special relationship with the Creator, who is its sole end." See also John Paul II, *Evange-*

Kinship as Having Common Characteristics or a Common Origin

Let us consider a second meaning of kinship: "the state of having common characteristics or a common origin." This is certainly true of us and other creatures. The *Compendium of the Catechism of the Catholic Church* gives the following response to the question "What kind of bond exists between created things?" "There exist an interdependence and a hierarchy among creatures as willed by God. At the same time, there is also a unity and solidarity among creatures since all have the same Creator, are loved by him and are ordered to his glory."[28] The *Compendium* states that humans have kinship with creation in three ways: we and they are both loved by God, and we and they have him as origin and as end. Let us consider these three one by one.

There is no doubt that God has brought all created things into existence from nothing, and he sustains them in existence: "I believe in God, the Father Almighty, Creator of heaven and earth."[29] There is a difference, though, between how humans and other earthly creatures *come into* existence. God specially creates the soul of each human being,[30] for since the human soul is a self-subsisting substantial form, it cannot come to be through natural processes.[31] The substantial forms of other earthly beings come to be through natural processes of change (or were concreated in the original creation).[32]

---

lium vitae, §39. See Marie I. George, "Thomistic Considerations on whether We Ought to Revere Non-rational Natural Beings," *Nova et Vetera,* Eng. ed., 11, no. 3 (2013): 751-78, for a discussion of why reverence is owed to all rational creatures (except the damned), but not to nonrational ones.

28. *CompCCC,* §64.

29. See *CCC,* §338: "*Nothing exists that does not owe its existence to God the Creator.* The world began when God's word drew it out of nothingness; all existent beings, all of nature, and all human history are rooted in this primordial event, the very genesis by which the world was constituted and time begun." See also §301: "With creation, God does not abandon his creatures to themselves. He not only gives them being and existence, but also, and at every moment, upholds and sustains them in being, enables them to act and brings them to their final end."

30. See *CCC,* §366: "The Church teaches that every spiritual soul is created immediately by God — it is not 'produced' by the parents — and also that it is immortal: it does not perish when it separates from the body at death."

31. See *STh* I, q. 90, art. 2: "The rational soul is a subsistent form . . . and because it cannot come to be from an underlying matter, neither from a corporeal one, for thus it would be of a bodily nature, nor of a spiritual one, for thus spiritual substances would be transmuted into one another, it is necessary to say that it does not come to be except through creation."

32. *STh* I, q. 45, art. 8: "But this happened to them from their ignorance of form. For they were not considering that the form of a natural body is not subsistent, but is that by

While the coming into being of the human soul differs from that of nonsub-
sisting substantial forms, the being of both depends on God's creative action:
"The Lord is good to all, and His mercies are over all His works" (Ps 145:9).[33]

Let us next consider how God is the end common to us and other earthly
creatures. Aquinas provides us with a clearly articulated answer. He first
notes that, given that humans and other creatures share the same beginning,
it seems the two should share the same end. He continues:

> End is said in two ways . . . the thing itself in which the notion of the good
> is found and the use or obtaining of that thing. As if we say that . . . the
> end of the miser is money as a thing, or the possession and use of money.
> If therefore we speak of the ultimate end of man as to the thing itself
> which is the end, in this manner all other things unite [with man] in the
> ultimate end of man, because God is the ultimate end of man and of all
> other things. If, however, we speak about the ultimate end of man as to
> the attainment of the end, in this manner nonrational creatures do not
> share in this end of man. For man and other rational creatures attain the
> ultimate end by knowing and loving God which does not belong to other
> creatures that attain the ultimate end insofar as they share some likeness
> of God, according as they are, or are alive, or even are knowing.[34]

Thus, while in one way we share the same end with other earthly creatures,
in another way we do not.[35]

---

which something is, and therefore, since to become and to be created do not properly belong
except to a subsistent thing . . . there is neither coming to be nor creation of [these] forms,
but they are concreated."

33. See Aquinas, *Scriptum super Sententiis,* bk. 4, d. 46, q. 2, a. 2, qc. 2, ad 1: "Similarly,
mercy is said in two ways. In one way, according as it repels a preceding misery not out of
debt; and in the work of creation mercy cannot be in this manner. In another way mercy
is said in a common manner, according as any defect is destroyed without debt; and in this
way there is mercy in the work of creation: for God by creating removes the greatest defect,
namely, nonbeing; and he did this by his gratuitous will, unconstrained by any debt." See
also *CCC,* §295.

34. *STh* I-II, q. 1, art. 8.

35. Just as we and other creatures are all ordered to God, but not in the same manner,
we and other material creatures accordingly all love God, but not in the same manner.
See *STh* I, q. 6, art. 1: "All things in seeking [*appetendo*] their proper perfections seek God
himself, insofar as the perfections of all things are certain likenesses of the divine being. . . .
And thus of those that seek God, certain know him according to himself, which is proper to
the rational creature. Certain know some participations of his goodness, which is extended
even to sensible knowledge. Certain have a natural appetite without cognition, as inclined

At the root of the commonality and difference between humans and other earthly creatures as to origin and end is the love that God has toward each. God's love creates goodness in things. As Aquinas explains:

> God loves all existing things. For all existing things, insofar as they are, are good; the being itself of every thing is a certain good, and similarly any perfection whatsoever of it. It was shown above, however, that the will of God is the cause of all things, and thus it is necessary that the extent to which something has being or any good whatsoever is the extent to which it is willed by God. Therefore, God wants for every existing thing something good. Whence, since to love is nothing other than to want the good for something/someone, it is manifest that God loves all the things which are. . . . The love of God pours in and creates goodness in things.[36]

All things share in common being a product of God's love, and as a result all created things have their own inherent goodness. As the *CCC* notes: "*Each creature possesses its own particular goodness and perfection.* For each one of the works of the 'six days' it is said: 'And God saw that it was good.' 'By the very nature of creation, material being is endowed with its own stability, truth and excellence, its own order and laws.' Each of the various creatures, willed in its own being, reflects in its own way a ray of God's infinite wisdom and goodness."[37] A right understanding of kinship embraces the truths that all creatures are loved by God and have intrinsic goodness.[38] Nonrational creatures are not merely instruments at our service.

---

to their ends by another superior knowing being." See also *STh* I-II, q. 26, art. 1: "In each of these appetites [natural, sensitive, and rational], however, love is said to be that which is the principle of motion tending to the end loved. In the natural appetite, however, the principle of this sort of motion is the connaturality of the one seeking to that to which it tends, which can be called natural love. . . . And similarly the suited-ness [*aptatio*] of the sense appetite or of the will to some good, i.e., the very being pleased with the good [*ipsa complacentia boni*], is called sensitive love or, in the intellectual appetite, intellectual love."

36. *STh* I, q. 20, art. 2.

37. *CCC*, §339.

38. A complementary truth is that God's providence extends to every creature, but not in the same manner. See *Summa contra gentiles*, ed. C. Pera, OP, et al. (Turin: Marietti, 1961), III, ch. 90: "The governance of providence proceeds from the divine love by which God loves the things created by him: for love chiefly consists in this that the one loving wants the good to the loved. Therefore to the extent that God loves certain things more, they fall more under his providence." Thus, it is true both that God "provides for all living creatures, for his love is everlasting" (Ps 136:25), and that "he has put all things under our feet" (Ps 8:6) and "disposes us with reverence" (Wis 12:18). See also chs. 111–14, concerning God's

At the same time, a right understanding of kinship does not level the differences in goodness God wants for creatures. The view that all creatures are of the same goodness or value is censured in the *Compendium of the Social Doctrine of the Church*:

> *The Magisterium finds the motivation for its opposition to a concept of the environment based on ecocentrism and on biocentrism* in the fact that "it is being proposed that the ontological and axiological difference between men and other living beings be eliminated, since the biosphere is considered a biotic unity of undifferentiated value. Thus man's superior responsibility can be eliminated in favour of an egalitarian consideration of the 'dignity' of all living beings."[39]

The notion of kinship proves useful in preventing people from making the opposite error, namely, looking to the superior goodness of humans to the point that they fail to recognize the inherent goodness of other earthly creatures. The notion of kingship does not exclude the notion that other creatures have intrinsic goodness, but it does not call attention to it, as does kinship. Consider the following psalm that is regularly cited in Church documents when speaking of the notion of human dominion:

> What are human beings that you are mindful of them,
>   mortals that you care for them?
> Yet you have made them a little lower than God,
>   and crowned them with glory and honor.
> You have given them dominion over the works of your hands;
>   you have put all things under their feet. (Ps 8:4-6)[40]

Read too hastily and in isolation from other scriptural passages, this passage gives the impression that all material creatures are simply there for our use.[41]

---

special providence of humans, and *CCC*, §§302-3, concerning God's general providence over all creatures.

39. *CompSDC*, §363.

40. *The New Oxford Annotated Bible*, ed. Bruce M. Metzger and Roland E. Murphy (New York: Oxford University Press, 1991).

41. Johnson criticizes the kingship paradigm, or rather a caricature of the kingship paradigm: "The kingship model is the position I have been criticizing in this lecture. It is based on hierarchical dualism that sees humanity separated from the earth and placed in a position of absolute dominion over all other creatures who are made for us. . . . In the progression from the pebble to the peach to the poodle to the person, with women somewhere between the

Whereas the notion of kinship is that we and other creatures are all loved by God and consequently all possess intrinsic goodness that reflects God's glory, which is not to deny that human goodness is superior in a way that allows us to share in God's own life and that legitimates our use of other creatures.

A sign that the notion of kinship more than that of kingship helps us keep in mind that all material creatures have intrinsic goodness and are not pure instruments is that Aquinas, who emphasizes the dominion of man over creation, fails to recognize that one reason why mistreatment of animals is wrong is because it needlessly harms creatures that have intrinsic goodness:

> The affect of man is twofold: one according to reason, another according to emotion. Therefore, according to the affect of reason it does not matter what man does in regard to animals, for all things are subject to his power by God, according to Ps. 8: "you have put all things under his feet." And according to this, the apostle says that God has no concern for cattle, for God does not require from man that he act a certain way concerning cattle and other animals. As to the affect of emotion, the affect of man is moved even in regard to other animals, for since the passion of mercy arises from the afflictions of others, and it happens that brute animals also sense punishments, the affect of mercy can also arise in man concerning the afflictions of animals. It is characteristic that the one who exercises the affect of mercy concerning animals is from this more disposed to the affect of mercy concerning humans, whence it is said in Prov. 12: "the just man recognizes the souls of his beasts; the hearts of the impious, however, are cruel." And therefore in order for the Lord to call the Jewish people, prone to cruelty, back to mercy, he wanted them to exercise mercy also towards brute animals, prohibiting certain things to be done to the animals which seem to pertain to a certain cruelty.[42]

---

latter two, the higher order of creatures has the right to use and control the latter" (Johnson, *Women, Earth, and Creator Spirit,* 29). Contrast this view with dominion as characterized by *CompSDC,* §255: "The dominion exercised by man over other living creatures, however, is not to be despotic or reckless; on the contrary he is to 'cultivate and care for' (Gen 2:15) the goods created by God. These goods were not created by man, but have been received by him as a precious gift that the Creator has placed under his responsibility. Cultivating the earth means not abandoning it to itself; exercising dominion over it means taking care of it, as a wise king cares for his people and a shepherd his sheep."

42. *STh* I-II, q. 102, art. 6, ad 8. He expresses the same view in the response to the first objection and in *Summa contra gentiles* III, ch. 112. Although in the response to the fourth

The reason Aquinas offers for not being cruel to animals is because people are then more prone to be cruel to other people; from the standpoint of reason, he does not think there are restrictions as to what we can do to animals. In contrast, the *CCC* has the following to say about the right treatment of animals: "Animals are God's creatures. He surrounds them with his providential care. By their mere existence they bless him and give him glory. Thus men owe them kindness. We should recall the gentleness with which saints like St. Francis of Assisi or St. Philip Neri treated animals."[43] The *CCC* invokes the inherent goodness of these creatures as a reason to treat them gently. It seems the kinship notion helps us keep this in mind. In the words of the *Compendium of the Social Doctrine of the Church:* "Benedictine and Franciscan spirituality in particular has witnessed to this sort of kinship of man with his creaturely environment, fostering in him an attitude of respect for every reality of the surrounding world."[44]

Kinship as a Close Connection Marked by Community of Interests

Earlier the kinship of rational and nonrational creatures was spoken of in terms of having God as their common end. This is true of them taken individually. However, it is also true of them insofar as they are parts of a greater whole that gives glory to God. Here the third meaning of kinship — having a close connection marked by community of interests — comes into play. As the American bishops explain in "Renewing the Earth":

> The diversity of life manifests God's glory. Every creature shares a bit of
> the divine beauty. Because the divine goodness could not be represented
> by one creature alone, Aquinas tells us, God "produced many and diverse

---

objection he says that the proscription of cooking a kid in its mother's milk was because it "seems to pertain to a certain cruelty," it is not clear that he sees this as problematic, apart from its potentially leading to cruel treatment of humans.

43. *CCC*, §2416. At the same time, the kindness we owe animals does not mean that we cannot kill or experiment on them; we must nonetheless do so in a humane manner: "God trusted animals to the stewardship of those whom he created in his own image. Hence it is legitimate to use animals for food and clothing. They may be domesticated to help man for his work and leisure. Medical and scientific experimentation on animals is a morally acceptable practice if it remains within reasonable limits and contributes to caring for or saving human lives. It is contrary to human dignity to cause animals to suffer or die needlessly" (*CCC*, §§2417-18).

44. *CompSDC*, §464.

creatures, so that what was wanting to one in representation of the divine goodness might be supplied by another . . . hence the whole universe together participates in the divine goodness more perfectly, and represents it better than any single creature whatever" (*Summa Theologica,* Prima Pars, question 48, ad 2).[45] The wonderful variety of the natural world is, therefore, part of the divine plan and, as such, invites our respect. Accordingly, it is appropriate that we treat other creatures and the natural world not just as means to human fulfillment but also as God's creatures, possessing an independent value, worthy of our respect and care.

The notions both of kingship and of kinship, when rightly understood, elicit the recognition that humans are parts of a greater whole ordered to the glory of God. Kinship highlights the fact that, collectively with other earthly creatures, we are ordered to God's glory. Accordingly, the *CCC* affirms: "There is a solidarity among all creatures arising from the fact that . . . all [are] ordered to his [i.e., God's] glory."[46] And Johnson, an advocate of the kinship paradigm, quotes the above passage from Aquinas and goes on to comment: "Realizing this, the religious kinship attitude cherishes and seeks to preserve biodiversity, for when a species goes extinct we have lost a manifestation of the goodness of God."[47] Kingship, on the other hand, highlights our responsibility in guiding creation to its goal of giving glory to God.

Our Kingly Responsibilities

People who reject the kingship paradigm seem to do so because they confuse king and tyrant. A tyrant rules solely for his or her own benefit. A tyrannical rule of nature regards nature as "stuff" for us to use in any way we please. A king, in contrast, looks to the common good of the ruled. A kingly rule of nature respects the intrinsic goodness of creatures and orders it in a way that is in keeping with God's purposes for creation, which are the sustenance of the entire human family and the glory of God. A kingly rule entails ensuring human well-being by prudent and just management of earthly goods and by the technological development of creation. It entails caring for the diversity of creatures that makes up a universe giving glory to God. It also entails a

45. "Renewing the Earth," 7. The quoted text from Aquinas is actually *STh* I, q. 47, art. 1.
46. *CCC,* §344.
47. Johnson, *Women, Earth, and Creator Spirit,* 39.

mastery of creation through understanding it. Finally, it includes enabling creation to fully praise God through our voices. Let us consider each aspect in more detail.

Kingly Rule Ensures a Just Use of Creation

God's command to subdue the earth is an order to make the earth a more suitable home for all of humanity:

> "God destined the earth and all it contains for all men and all peoples so that all created things would be shared fairly by all mankind under the guidance of justice tempered by charity." This principle is based on the fact that "the original source of all that is good is the very act of God, who created both the earth and man, and who gave the earth to man so that he might have dominion over it by his work and enjoy its fruits (Gen 1:28-29). God gave the earth to the whole human race for the sustenance of all its members, without excluding or favouring anyone. . . ." . . .
>
> By his work and industriousness, man — who has a share in the divine art and wisdom — makes creation, the cosmos already ordered by the Father, more beautiful. He summons the social and community energies that increase the common good, above all to the benefit of those who are neediest.[48]

Kingly rule of creation is incompatible with hoarding resources, for "the injustice of hoarding resources: greediness, be it individual or collective, is contrary to the order of creation."[49]

Such rule is also incompatible with destroying the balance of nature:

> *Man, then, must never forget that "his capacity to transform and in a certain sense create the world through his own work . . . is always based on God's prior and original gift of the things that are."* He must not "make arbitrary use of the earth, subjecting it without restraint to his will, as though it did not have its own requisites and a prior God-given purpose, which man can indeed develop but must not betray." When he acts in this way, "instead of carrying out his role as a co-operator with God in the work of creation, man sets himself up in place of God and thus ends up provoking

---

48. *CompSDC,* §§171, 266.
49. *CompSDC,* §481.

a rebellion on the part of nature, which is more tyrannized than governed by him."[50]

Kingly Rule Conserves the Order of Nonrational Creation

Another aspect of our kingly rule is to protect biodiversity insofar as species individually and as parts of an interactive whole are ordered to God's glory. As the *Compendium of the CCC* affirms, "The seventh commandment . . . requires respect for the *integrity of creation* by the prudent and moderate use of the mineral, vegetable, and animal resources of the universe with special attention to those species that are in danger of extinction."[51] Certainly, if the choice is between a human life and the extinction of a species, the human life takes precedence.[52] However, we were put in charge by God because of our intelligence, and we need to use it to prevent such conflicts. One might ask: Does kingly rule extend to the well-being of individual nonrational creatures as such, or does it extend to them only as representatives of species, whose diversity makes the universe a more suitable reflection of the divine nature? It is proper to a king to look after what is essential to the common good, rather than to what is derivative of it. Individuals of different species come into existence and go out of existence, and although each individual as individual reflects a ray of God's wisdom and goodness, it does so more by maintaining a species in existence, which contributes to the representation of God's goodness.[53] A king is not directly devoted to any given citizen's

---

50. *CompSDC,* §460. Kingly rule of creation includes the prudent and just development of technology. Also, the *CompSDC* affirms that the *"results of science and technology are, in themselves, positive"* and that "as people who believe in God, who saw that nature which he had created was 'good', we rejoice in the technological and economic progress which people, using their intelligence, have managed to make" (*CompSDC,* §457, quoting from John Paul II, "Meeting with Employees of the Olivetti Workshops in Ivrea, Italy" [March 19, 1990]). At the same time, it also insists: "A central point of reference for every scientific and technological application is respect for men and women, which must also be accompanied by a necessary attitude of respect for other living creatures" (§459).

51. *CompCCC,* §506.

52. See Pontifical Council for Justice and Peace, "A Contribution of the Delegation of the Holy See on the Occasion of the Third World Water Forum" (Kyoto, March 16-23, 2003), 3: "While never overlooking the need to protect our eco-systems, it is the critical or basic needs of humanity that must be operative in an appropriate prioritization of water access."

53. See *Summa contra gentiles* II, ch. 45: "The good of the species exceeds the good

well-being, but to the common good of society in which that citizen shares, and nonrational creatures are not even citizens, strictly speaking.[54] Kinship, more than kingship, evokes concern for the individual creature as such.

Kingly Rule Entails Intellectual Mastery of Creation

Our kingly rule over creation also consists in understanding the universe. Thus, the *CCC* affirms: "Basic scientific research . . . is a significant expression of man's dominion over creation."[55] As we come to understand the different beings in the universe, we assimilate them by way of cognitive likeness; and thus they serve us by contributing to the perfection of our intellect.[56]

This knowledge of creation further serves us by leading to knowledge of the Creator. As Aquinas notes: "All corporeal beings are believed to be made

---

of the individual, as what is formal to what is material. Therefore, a multitude of species adds more to the goodness of the universe than a multitude of individuals belonging to one species." See also II, ch. 84: "The perfection of the universe is attendant upon species and not upon individuals, since in the universe many individuals are continually added to pre-existing species."

54. See *Quaestiones disputatae de potentia* in *Quaestiones disputatae*, vol. 2, ed. P. Bazzi et al. (Turin: Marietti, 1965), q. 5, a. 5: "It can happen that something of lesser value [*vilior*] is the term of the operation of something nobler; not, however, that it be the end of the latter's intention. Just as the security of a peasant is a certain term to which the operation of the governing king terminates; nevertheless, it is not that the rule of the king is ordered to this peasant's security as to an end, but to something better, namely, the common good." See also *Scriptum super Sententiis*, bk. 2, d. 1, q. 2, a. 3, ad 3. Thus, the International Theological Commission document "Communion and Stewardship: Human Persons Created in the Image of God" is not entirely right in affirming that "Christian theology uses both domestic and royal imagery to describe this special role. Employing royal imagery, it is said that human beings are called to rule in the sense of holding an ascendancy over the whole of visible creation, in the manner of a king. But the inner meaning of this kingship is, as Jesus reminds his disciples, one of service: only by willingly suffering as a sacrificial victim does Christ become the king of the universe." Human lives and genuine human fulfillment are not to be sacrificed for the well-being of nonrational creatures; see *CCC*, §2418: "It is likewise unworthy to spend money on them [i.e., animals] that should as a priority go to the relief of human misery." See also *STh* I-II, q. 113, art. 9, ad 2: "The good of the grace of one individual is greater than the good of nature of the entire universe."

55. *CCC*, §2293.

56. It is also noteworthy that, while Aquinas acknowledges that Adam and Eve in paradise did not need animals either to meet their corporal needs or to know God, he still affirms that "they needed them in order to gain experimental knowledge of natures of these beings" (*STh* I, q. 96, art. 1, ad 3).

for the sake of man; whence even all things are said to be 'subject' to him. However, they serve man in two ways: in one way, to the end of sustaining his corporeal life; in another way, to advance his knowledge of what is divine, insofar as man 'perceives the invisible things of God through the things that are made,' as is said in Rom. 1:20."[57] Through knowledge we in some sense subject creation to us, and this subjection of creation can lead us further to natural knowledge of God.[58]

Kingly Rule Leads All to Praise God

Our natural knowledge of God is conducive to another kingly task, that of praising God.[59] In the words of Aquinas:

> From the meditation of what he [God] has made, we are able in a certain manner to admire and consider divine wisdom. For those things which are made by art are representative of the art itself, as being made to the likeness of art. God, however, produces things in being by his wisdom. . . . Whence, from a consideration of divine works, we are able to gather what divine wisdom is, as in things made through a certain impressed communication of his likeness; for it is said: "He pours out his wisdom over all his works."

57. *Scriptum super Sententiis,* bk. 4, d. 48, q. 2, a. 1. There are arguments for God's existence based on the order observed in nature (both ordering to an end and the hierarchical ordering of being) and the beauty that accompanies it; see *STh* I, q. 2, art. 3. This position accords with what is said in *CompCCC,* §3: "Starting from creation, that is, from the world and from the human person, through reason alone one can know God with certainty as the origin and end of the universe, as the highest good and as infinite truth and beauty."

58. See Michael Baur, quoted in J. J. Ziegler, "Catholics, the Environment, and the 'Culture of Waste,'" www.catholicworldreport.com/Item/2575/catholics_the_environment _and_a_culture_of_waste.aspx: "Benedict XVI's 'natural law' vision allows him to assert that the human being — by virtue of its unique intellectual nature — is able to apprehend the immanent orderliness and goodness of any aspect of the natural world, and thus is more capable than any other terrestrial being of reflecting God's wisdom and goodness. Since the perfection of the created universe requires the manifestation or reflection of God's wisdom and goodness, it follows for Benedict XVI that the perfection of the created universe is made possible uniquely through the intelligent activity of human beings."

59. Many of the psalms attributed to King David praise God, e.g., Ps 30: "High praise, Yahweh, I give you, for you have helped me up"; see also 2 Sam 22:1-51. In the Old Testament the kings played a crucial role as to whether the Jewish people praised and worshiped the one true God or false gods; see, e.g., 2 Kgs 18:3-5 and 21:2-4.

Secondly, this consideration leads to admiration of the highest power of God, and as a result it gives birth to reverence of God in the human soul. For, it is necessary that the power of the maker be understood as more eminent than the things that are made.

Praise is a way of expressing admiration and reverence. Indeed, all creatures in some way praise and give glory to God; in the words of the *CCC:* "By their mere existence they [i.e., animals] bless him [God] and give him glory."[60] The Third Eucharistic Prayer also affirms this: "Father, you are holy indeed, and all creation rightly gives you praise,"[61] as does the *Sanctus:* "Heaven and earth are full of your glory." Nonrational creatures, by their inherent order and goodness, bear silent witness to their Creator: "The heavens declare the glory of the God, the vault of heaven proclaims his handiwork. . . . No utterance at all, no speech . . . yet their voice goes out through all the earth" (Ps 19:1, 3-4).

In the strict sense of praise, however, only a rational creature can praise someone. For praise, strictly speaking, requires that one has some understanding of what another's excellence consists in. (The same is true for blessing and giving glory; strictly speaking, only beings endowed with understanding can do these things.) For this reason, Aquinas maintains that passages in Scripture that speak of nonrational creatures praising God are to be understood in the following manner: "According to the Damascene, the heavens are said to proclaim the glory of God, to praise [him], to exult [him], in a material manner, insofar as they are matter for men to praise or proclaim or exult [God]. Similar things are found in Scripture concerning mountains and hills and other inanimate creatures."[62]

In reflecting on what it means to say that the world was made for the glory of God, the *CCC* notes that "St. Bonaventure explains that God created all things 'not to increase his glory, but to show it forth and to communicate

---

60. *CCC,* §2416. See *Summa contra gentiles* III, ch. 65: "Things are said to be ruled or governed according to this that are ordered to an end. Things are ordered to the ultimate end that God intends, namely, divine goodness, not only through this that they operate, but even through this that they exist: for insofar as they are, they bear a likeness of divine goodness, which is the end of things. . . . Therefore that things are conserved in being pertains to divine providence."

61. The Latin text reads: "Vere Sanctus es, Domine, et merito te laudat omnis a te condita creatura."

62. *Quaestio disputata de spiritualibus creaturis,* in *Quaestiones disputatae,* vol. 2, ed. P. Bazzi et al. (Turin: Marietti, 1965), unicus, a. 6, ad 14.

it.'"[63] To show it forth to whom? To the rational creature who is capable of appreciating creation as a divine work. In the words of Aquinas:

> Of what sort are these waters [i.e., those mentioned in Genesis as being above the firmament] is not described in the same manner by all. For Origen says that those waters above the heavens are spiritual substances, whence in Ps. 148 it is said "waters above the heavens, praise the name of the Lord"; and Dan. c. 3: "bless the Lord all the waters which are above the heavens." But to this Basil, in III *Hexaem.*, responds that this is not said because those waters which are above the heavens are rational creatures; but because the "consideration of them, when contemplated prudently by those having sense, perfects the glorification of the creator." Whence, in the same place, the same is said about fire and ice and things of this sort which surely are not rational creatures.[64]

We are able to articulate creation's silent praise. This is professed in the Fourth Eucharistic Prayer: "With them [the angels] we, too, confess your name in exultation, giving voice to every creature under heaven, as we acclaim, Holy, Holy, Holy." It is also affirmed by Bl. Dom Columba Marmion:

> We can lend our lips to sing the canticle of all creation which takes its life in the Word, so that all the things which were made by the Word . . . may sing, in Him and by Him, to the glory of God. . . . The soul leads all creation to the feet of its God and its Lord, that He may receive homage from every creature. . . . "All ye works of the Lord, bless the Lord: praise and exalt Him above all for ever. . . . Sun and moon, stars of heaven, bless the Lord."[65]

We also lead creation to the praise of God by offering the bread and wine that become the sacrifice of praise, the Eucharist. As the *CCC* notes: "The signs of bread and wine become, in a way surpassing understanding, the Body and Blood of Christ; they continue also to signify the goodness of creation. Thus in the Offertory we give thanks to the Creator for bread and wine, fruit of the 'work of human hands,' but above all as 'fruit of the earth' and 'of the vine' — gifts of the Creator."[66]

---

63. *CCC,* §293.

64. *STh* I, q. 68, art. 2.

65. Bl. Dom Columba Marmion, *Christ, the Life of the Soul* (St. Louis: B. Herder Book Co., 1925), 279-80. Marmion goes on to paraphrase the rest of the canticle found in Dan 3:51-90.

66. *CCC,* §1333; see also §1149: "The liturgy of the Church presupposes, integrates and

In a somewhat different way the *Compendium of the Social Doctrine of the Church* speaks of nonrational creatures praising God through us: "*Through his corporeality man unites in himself elements of the material world;* these 'reach their summit through him, and through him raise their voice in free praise of the Creator.'"[67]

Our kingly concern, then, for material creatures, and especially for their diversity, is both because they give glory to God in the broad sense and also because they lead us to give glory to God in the fullest sense of the word. We fail in our kingly rule when we allow creation's beauty to be needlessly defaced, as by doing so, we are destroying a conduit to people's natural knowledge of God.[68] This is a constant and valid theme among those who favor the kinship paradigm, although sometimes they go too far in what they say.[69] Nature is a "book" through which God communicates with us.[70]

---

sanctifies elements from creation and human culture, conferring on them the dignity of signs of grace, of the new creation in Jesus Christ."

67. *CompSDC,* §128; it quotes *Gaudium et spes,* §14.

68. Augustine notes how the beauty of creation naturally leads us to recognize its Creator: "Question the beauty of the earth, question the beauty of the sea, question the beauty of the air distending and diffusing itself, question the beauty of the sky . . . question all these realities. All respond: 'See, we are beautiful.' Their beauty is a profession [*confessio*]. These beauties are subject to change. Who made them if not the Beautiful One [*Pulcher*] who is not subject to change?" (*CCC,* §32, quoting Augustine, *Sermo,* 241.2).

69. See Delio, Warner, and Wood, *Care for Creation,* 44: "In his small 'handbook of theology' the *Breviloquium,* Bonaventure wrote: 'From all we have said, we may gather that the created world is a kind of book reflecting, representing, and describing its maker, the Trinity, at three different levels of expression: as a vestige, as an image, and as a likeness.'" Immediately after, however, the authors make the ambiguous assertion that, "since every creature has its foundation in the Word, each is equally close to God (although the mode of relationship differs)," seemingly ignoring Bonaventure's distinction of three levels. As Aquinas notes, while God's love does not differ in intensity in the case of different creatures, it does differ in the good that he wants for different creatures (see *Summa contra gentiles* I, ch. 91); those to whom he wants the greater good of rationality are closer to him as being created in his image. *Care of Creation* affirms of creatures: "And it is in being themselves that they are Christ — words of God incarnate" (47); and it maintains: "Bonaventure, too, realized that the Body of Christ (which includes the Earth) is incomplete and can only be completed by those who live in relation to this Body as a living Body" (203). While human beings who belong to the Church are rightly considered Christ insofar as they are parts of his mystical body, material creatures, aside from the human body the Word assumed, are in nowise Christ or parts of his mystical body, for this depends on being capable of grace.

70. See "The Columbia River Watershed: Caring for Creation and the Common Good; An International Pastoral Letter by the Catholic Bishops of the Region," January 2001, www .seattlearch.org/NR/rdonlyres/A7B1C149-481D-41DA-B701-273D9B4983E9/0/english.pdf,

Conclusion

In sum, when we envisage our relationship with creation in terms of kinship, our minds are directed to the intrinsic goodness of creatures, all of which are loved by God. Doing so also directs our attention to other earthly creatures as sharing with us God as source and as final end. When we think in terms of kinship, we do not focus on the utility creatures have for us. Rather, we view each creature in its individuality as something whose goodness we should respect and in some cases even foster.[71] In the light of kinship, we also readily view creatures as collaborators in an interconnected universe that gives glory to God.

In contrast, when we envisage our relationship with creatures in terms of kingship, our minds are directed to our roles in ensuring the ends to which God destined creation, namely, that of serving the entire human family and of giving glory to God. The right use of creatures as ordered to human well-being is an indispensable part of this vision. This vision also embraces care for creation in the sense of species protection, with the result that we preserve the diverse interconnected parts of a whole that gives glory to God. Finally, our rule of creation embraces our intellectual mastery of it, which leads ultimately to the glory of God in its fullest expression.

A proper understanding of kinship does not deny that the material creation is meant to serve human well-being or that humans are to care for material creation because we are created in the image of God (and thus are superior to material creatures). Nor does it deny our central role in giving praise and glory to God. A proper understanding of kingship does not deny that material creatures have intrinsic goodness, nor does it deny that individual creatures in some manner praise God. Each notion comes together

---

9: "Creation is a 'book of nature' in whose living pages people can see signs of the Spirit of God present in the universe, yet separate from it." See also Aquinas's sermon "Puer Jesus," ed. Enrique Alarcón, www.corpusthomisticum.org/iopera.html: "But where ought you to seek wisdom? . . . You ought to reflect upon your examination of creatures; for as is said in Eccl. 1: 'God pours out his wisdom over all of his works.' The works of God are witnesses of his wisdom; just as we are able to conjecture many things about the wisdom of a master builder in his artifact. Whence [the words of] Job 12: 'ask the beasts and they will teach you, the birds of the air and they will speak to you.'" Johnson, who advocates the kinship paradigm, quotes this same passage from Job and comments: "To the contemplative spirit, the vivifying power of God flashes out from the simplest natural phenomenon, the smallest seed" (Johnson, *Woman, Earth, and Creator Spirit,* 64).

71. See *CCC,* §2457: "Animals are entrusted to man's stewardship; he must show them kindness."

in its own way to affirm that we and other creatures are parts of a whole ordered to God's glory.

Both kingship and kinship, when rightly understood, make an important contribution to understanding our role vis-à-vis earthly creation. For this reason, John Paul II's proclamation of St. Francis of Assisi as the patron of those who promote ecology stands side by side with Vatican II's affirmation of the human rule of creation:

> He [St. Francis] offers Christians an example of genuine and deep respect for the integrity of creation. As a friend of the poor who was loved by God's creatures, Saint Francis invited all of creation — animals, plants, natural forces, even Brother Sun and Sister Moon — to give honour and praise to the Lord.[72]

> Man was created in God's image and was commanded to conquer the earth and to rule the world in justice and holiness: he was to acknowledge God as maker of all things and relate himself and the totality of creation to Him, so that through the dominion of all things by man the name of God would be majestic in all the earth.[73]

72. John Paul II, "Peace with God the Creator, Peace with All of Creation," message for the celebration of the World Day of Peace, January 1, 1990. Note that *CCC*, §344, reads the Canticle as expressing the solidarity that exists among creatures as having the same Creator and being ordered to God's glory.

73. *Gaudium et spes*, §34.

CHAPTER 5

"Be Fruitful and Multiply, and Fill the Earth":
Was and Is This a Good Idea?

Matthew Levering

The universe did not have to include human beings. Indeed, for all but the tiniest fraction of the universe's nearly 14-billion-year history, dating back to the Big Bang, the universe has contained no humans. But 4.5 billion years ago, the sun and solar system came to be, perhaps because of the explosion of a supernova. During its formative period, the earth first became so hot that its inner core became molten, after which its gradual cooling produced millions of years of torrential rain, forming the oceans.[1] The simplest forms of life emerged 3.5 billion years ago, followed by multicellular animals roughly 550 million years ago. Hominids broke away from primates about 7 million years ago. Brendan Purcell notes, however, that "we don't find among Neanderthal or other late hominids indications of self-awareness, or any of the other qualities we regard as central to adult human existence."[2] Among late hominids, points, pigment, grindstones, and blades are already present beginning 240-270 thousand years ago. Barbed points, bone tools, mining, and fishing can be found 100-110 thousand years ago. Burial of the dead appears no later than 95 thousand years ago.[3] Purcell argues that *Homo sapiens* evolved in Africa around 165 thousand years ago, although he adds that fully symbolic behavior, and the full emergence of *Homo sapiens*,

1. See Robert N. Bellah, *Religion in Human Evolution: From the Paleolithic to the Axial Age* (Cambridge, MA: Harvard University Press, 2011), 52-53.
2. Brendan Purcell, *From Big Bang to Big Mystery: Human Evolutions in the Light of Creation and Evolution* (Hyde Park, NY: New City Press, 2012), 171.
3. In addition to Purcell, see Edward O. Wilson, *The Social Conquest of Earth* (New York: W. W. Norton, 2012), 278.

dates to about 80 thousand years ago. Some 90-135 thousand years ago, however, tropical Africa endured a severe drought, with the result that, as Edward O. Wilson states, "The size of the total *Homo sapiens* population on the African continent descended into the thousands, and for a long while the future conqueror species risked complete extinction." Only when the drought lifted did the human population expand again and move out of Africa, through "a corridor of continuous habitable terrain up the Nile to Sinai and beyond."[4]

This "breakout from Africa" led to a "vast overall increase in population size," as well as to beneficial cognitive mutations and innovations. Cultural change began to occur rapidly around 50,000 years ago. Humans arrived in Europe "no later than 42,000 years before the present," entirely displacing the native Neanderthals within 12,000 years.[5] Since Wilson denies the existence of God and the spiritual soul, he sees the emergence of human beings as dependent entirely upon evolutionary adaptation and brain size (despite the difference in kind, not merely degree, between animal cognition and human cognition).[6] In his view, the reason there are no other hominids pos-

4. Wilson, *The Social Conquest of Earth*, 82.

5. Wilson, *The Social Conquest of Earth*, 88; on the cultural explosion, including the development of agriculture, see 91-93. Later in the book Wilson observes, "The beginnings of the creative arts as they are practiced today may stay forever hidden. Yet they were sufficiently established by genetic and cultural evolution for the 'creative explosion' that began approximately 35,000 years ago in Europe. From this time on until the Late Paleolithic period over 20,000 years later, cave art flourished. Thousands of figures, mostly of large game animals, have been found in more than two hundred caves distributed through southwestern France and northeastern Spain, on both sides of the Pyrenees. Along with Cliffside drawings in other parts of the world, they present a stunning snapshot of life just before the dawn of civilization" (278-79).

6. Wilson does not argue for, but simply assumes, this position in his *The Social Conquest of Earth*. He does briefly argue that humans began with "just-so" stories, around which have built up the elaborate "myths and gods of organized religions," myths and gods that "are stultifying and divisive" and that "encourage ignorance, distract people from recognizing problems of the real world, and often lead them in wrong directions into disastrous actions" (292). While religion is divisive and occult, science is empirical and open to everyone. For Wilson, therefore, "The conflict between scientific knowledge and the teachings of organized religions is irreconcilable. The chasm will continue to widen and cause no end of trouble as long as religious leaders go on making unsupportable claims about supernatural causes of reality" (295). For a profound defense of the arguments for God's existence and for the existence of the spiritual soul, see David Bentley Hart, *The Experience of God: Being, Consciousness, Bliss* (New Haven, CT: Yale University Press, 2013). On the spiritual soul, see also Edward Feser, *Philosophy of Mind: A Beginner's Guide* (Oxford: OneWorld, 2006), and W. Norris Clarke, SJ, "The Immediate Creation of the

sessed of human intelligence is "the extreme improbability" of each of the "preadaptations" occurring at precisely the right time, so as to enable each of the necessary evolutionary adaptations. As a species, humans "have made every one of the required lucky turns in the evolutionary maze."[7]

The emergence of human beings has had a significant impact upon the earth, especially beginning ten thousand years ago, when "the Neolithic revolution began to yield vastly larger amounts of food from cultivated crops and livestock, along with rapid growth in human populations." This impact has increased dramatically in the past few centuries, since for thousands of years there were less than ten million people on earth (and even in 1650 there were only five hundred million). Thanks to much lower mortality rates and numerous technological/agricultural improvements, there are now more than seven billion people on the planet. The vastly increased presence of human populations could have been predicted, Wilson notes, because "region by region, recent studies show, the populations have approached a limit set by the supply of food and water" — human multiplication simply does not stop until such limits are reached.[8] The impact on the earth has thus become enormous.

Has the impact been a good one? Or should we conclude, with Wilson, that the rise and spread of humans means that "Darwin's dice have rolled badly for Earth"?[9] Purcell celebrates how "the range of our feeling and imagination, of our understanding and our effective freedom, while still rooted in incarnate finitude, opens out to a transfinite horizon of beauty, truth and goodness."[10] But Purcell certainly is no romantic; he fills out his portrait of human beings with examples taken from the Nazi period, including among

Human Soul by God and Some Contemporary Challenges," in *The Creative Retrieval of St. Thomas Aquinas: Essays in Thomistic Philosophy, New and Old* (New York: Fordham University Press, 2009), 173-90.

7. Wilson, *The Social Conquest of Earth*, 45.

8. Wilson, *The Social Conquest of Earth*, 76.

9. Edward O. Wilson, "Is Humanity Suicidal?" *The New York Times Magazine*, May 30, 1993, 24, cited in Thomas Sieger Derr, "Environmental Ethics and Christian Humanism," in *Environmental Ethics and Christian Humanism*, by Thomas Sieger Derr, with James A. Nash and Richard John Neuhaus (Nashville, TN: Abingdon Press, 1996), 96. Derr critiques the leading voices of the environmentalist movement for being overly negative and alarmist about the numbers of humans on earth. Derr gives approval to the drop in fertility rates brought about by the use of contraception (74-76). Yet Derr strongly opposes organized "birth control campaigns" (75), coerced birth control and abortion, and the tendency to blame the ecological crisis upon population.

10. Purcell, *From Big Bang to Big Mystery*, 271.

his examples not only the heroic death of Sophie Scholl but also the evil actions of Albert Speer. The Nazi reign of terror has given way to an era in which humans seem to be on the verge of destroying the earth's ecosystem, whether by nuclear conflagration or by carbon emissions or simply by eventual overpopulation that crowds out and extinguishes other species.

In this context, I wish to reflect upon God's command in Genesis 1:28 to "be fruitful and multiply, and fill the earth," a command that God repeats elsewhere in Genesis. What should we make of this command today? Randall Smith, Hava Tirosh-Samuelson, and others have rightly contested the view that Genesis 1 is negative toward the environment.[11] While agreeing with their position, I think that the command to "be fruitful and multiply, and fill the earth" requires more attention, especially in light of the growing consensus expressed by the Protestant theologian Michael Northcott that "reductions in population in both North and South are highly desirable in the light of the environmental crisis."[12]

In the first section of this essay, therefore, I examine God's command to

---

11. See Randall Smith, "Creation and the Environment in the Hebrew Scriptures: A Transvaluation of Values," in *Green Discipleship: Catholic Theological Ethics and the Environment,* ed. Tobias Winright (Winona, MN: Anselm Academic, 2011), 74-90; in the same volume, see Hava Tirosh-Samuelson, "Judaism and the Care for God's Creation," 286-318. See also such works as Ellen Davis, *Scripture, Culture, and Agriculture: An Agrarian Reading of the Bible* (Cambridge: Cambridge University Press, 2009), and Elijah Shochet, *Animal Life in Jewish Tradition: Attitudes and Relationships* (New York: KTAV, 1984). Critiques of Genesis 1 are generally focused upon God's command to "subdue" the earth and "have dominion over the fish of the sea and over the birds of the air and over every living thing that moves upon the earth" (Gen 1:28).

12. Michael S. Northcott, *The Environment and Christian Ethics* (Cambridge: Cambridge University Press, 1996), 28; cf. 300-301 for strategies to accomplish this reduction, indebted to Herman Daly and John B. Cobb, *For the Common Good: Redirecting the Economy towards Community, the Environment, and a Sustainable Future* (London: Green Print, 1990). Northcott observes, "The United Nations Population Fund estimates that world food production can sustainably (that is, without soil erosion, desertification, ground-water depletion etc.) feed around 5.5 billion people with an adequate calorific intake if everyone was on a vegetarian diet. If, however, the population derives 25 per cent of calorie intake from meat products, as North Americans and West Europeans do, then the number which can be sustainably fed reduces to around 2.8 billion" (Northcott, *The Environment and Christian Ethics,* 27). Does this number assume that soil erosion, desertification, and so forth are impossible to address in ways that do not reduce food production? For a theology of the Holy Spirit in light of climate change, emphasizing the work of the Spirit in "the restoration of creation and of human and creaturely relations," see Northcott's "Holy Spirit," in *Systematic Theology and Climate Change: Ecumenical Perspectives,* ed. Michael S. Northcott and Peter M. Scott (London: Routledge, 2014), 58.

"be fruitful and multiply, and fill the earth." I emphasize that God reaffirms this command, even after fallen humans have exhibited their destructive tendencies, including destructive ecological tendencies. God strongly promotes human multiplication even after it has led to the near-annihilation of life on earth, as it does in the flood narratives. My second section then explores the quite different perspective on human multiplication that is found in the Christian environmentalist Bill McKibben's *Maybe One: A Case for Smaller Families*. McKibben argues that Americans need to limit family size to one child or else face imminent, catastrophic ecological disaster. He would surely agree with the biblical scholar Richard Bauckham that, in Genesis 1:28-30, God shows humans "that the produce of the earth is not intended to feed them alone, but also all the living species of the earth. Humans are not to fill the earth and subdue it to the extent of leaving no room and no sustenance for the other creatures who share the earth with them."[13]

Having set forth this tension, I seek in my third section to develop a theological framework for approaching the command to "be fruitful and multiply" in a manner open to concerns about population growth while mindful, in light of the divine pattern I identified in Genesis, that "the Church stands for life: in each human life she sees the splendor of that 'Yes,' that 'Amen,' who is Christ Himself."[14] My fourth and final section, then, seeks to draw some conclusions, in dialogue with contemporary theologians, about whether the Church should now encourage couples to have small families or should continue to recognize the value of large families, even in an ecologically strained world of more than seven billion people.

13. Richard Bauckham, *Living with Other Creatures: Green Exegesis and Theology* (Waco, TX: Baylor University Press, 2011), 227. See also, for a related emphasis on the "sacred trust" that humans have received to be "preservers and conservers of all life," Douglas John Hall, *Imaging God: Dominion as Stewardship* (Grand Rapids: Eerdmans, 1986), 200. In my view, the extinction of other species can sometimes be an acceptable cost of the expansion of human interpersonal communion. For example, I do not consider the massive loss of species that came about because of the populating of America by nonnative peoples to be a tragedy, since these humans could not have survived in large numbers without extensive clear-cutting of forests for agricultural use of the land. Likewise, I do not mourn the first arrival of humans in the Americas (which took place when "a single Siberian population reached the Bering land bridge no sooner than 30,000 years ago, and possibly as recently as 22,000 years"), despite "its catastrophic impact on the virgin fauna and flora" (Wilson, *The Social Conquest of Earth*, 83).

14. Pope John Paul II, *Familiaris consortio*, Vatican translation (Boston: St. Paul Books & Media, 1981), §30.

"Be Fruitful and Multiply, and Fill the Earth"

According to the first chapter of Genesis, after creating human beings male and female, "God blessed them, and God said to them, 'Be fruitful and multiply, and fill the earth'" (Gen 1:28). In a brief note on this passage in his recent *Commentary on the Torah,* the Jewish exegete Richard Elliott Friedman states simply, "This commandment has now been fulfilled."[15] From an evangelical Christian perspective, Bill T. Arnold's commentary on Genesis treats Genesis 1:28 with similar brevity, remarking simply that God's blessing consists in his favorable disposition toward humankind and his desire that they "fill up and inhabit that portion of the cosmos set apart especially for them."[16] Likewise, Walter Brueggemann connects the passage with other texts of "blessing" and observes that the point is that God's creative activity is intended to flow through "the generative power of life, fertility, and well-being that God has ordained within the normal flow and mystery of life."[17] Among the recent commentaries on Genesis that I have read, R. R. Reno has the most to say on Genesis 1:28. Reno focuses on the fact that procreation "gives us a future" and "realizes the capacity of creation to have time and history."[18] He points to Scripture's later connection of idolatry with immoral sexual practices, and he observes that the ultimate goal of fruitful procreation consists in a blessing that we cannot give to ourselves or to our children, namely, Christ's gift of eternal life. For Reno, human parenthood is a paradigmatic act of self-surrendering trust in the goodness of God.

Yet, was God's command to humans to "be fruitful and multiply, and fill the earth" a good idea? Does the earth really need to be filled by humans, and even if so, what about the risk of overfilling it? It would seem that God's command, even if one granted that it is good for the earth to become full of humans, unwisely leaves out what happens when the earth is filled with humans. Since humans breed more humans, an earth filled with humans is at severe risk of becoming overfilled with humans. In his seemingly rather blithe command, God does not appear to take this risk into account.

---

15. Richard Elliott Friedman, *Commentary on the Torah* (New York: HarperCollins, 2001), 13. Robert Alter's *Genesis* (New York: W. W. Norton, 1996) does not comment on this verse.

16. Bill T. Arnold, *Genesis* (Cambridge: Cambridge University Press, 2009), 47.

17. Walter Brueggemann, *Genesis* (Louisville, KY: Westminster John Knox Press, 2010), 37. Brueggemann cites Claude Westermann's *Blessing in the Bible and the Life of the Church* (Philadelphia: Fortress Press, 1978).

18. R. R. Reno, *Genesis* (Grand Rapids: Brazos Press, 2010), 56.

Various responses might be given from the text or from the text's reconstructed historical context. Perhaps filling the earth is a good command and a good idea, so long as humans remain without sin.[19] After all, in Genesis 1:28 there is as yet no mention of human sin. On the contrary, created in the royal image of God, humans are part of the whole creation that, far from being marred by sin, God has reason to deem "very good" (Gen 1:31). After the first humans sin, therefore, does God rescind his command to be fruitful and multiply, and fill the earth?

The answer is no. Instead, after Adam and Eve's fall and their alienation from God and each other, God foretells that humankind's relationship to the earth will be marked by conflict and pain. He tells Adam, "Cursed is the ground because of you; in toil you shall eat of it all the days of your life; thorns and thistles it shall bring forth to you; and you shall eat the plants of the field" (Gen 3:17-18). There is a sense here that Adam and the ecosystem will be opposed to each other, that the ecosystem has been "cursed" because of Adam, and that its well-being (the well-being of the "plants of the field") is now set in opposition to Adam's ("thorns and thistles it shall bring forth to you").[20] Given this conflictual relationship, it seems that Adam's sin has

19. John Hart, for instance, argues that "environmental crises do not result when human activity is natural. Crises result when humans deny their place in creation as its integrating consciousness reflecting on itself and as its complexity evolving beyond itself. When humans lose their sense of place — their setting and their role — they lose a sense of the sacred, they reject intrinsic value in abiotic nature and in species and individuals of the biotic community, they deny natural rights to nature, and they reject humanity's situation in creation as one of the uncounted numbers of all species who have complementary roles in the community of life, and are related to each other as the common offspring of cosmic becoming" (Hart, *Sacramental Commons: Christian Ecological Ethics* [Lanham, MD: Rowman & Littlefield, 2006], 203). Hart defines a "natural" human action as one that "is integrated with human biological-personal-social-psychological-spiritual identity and aspirations; is consonant with the integration of humans within the biotic community and with abiotic nature; is compatible with Earth's evolutionary flow of time, energies, elements, and events; and represents or complements generally accepted social values and conduct. Humans are most natural when they are social beings who live in and with nature, and relate to nature while they work to ensure the commons good and the common good through an equitable distribution of commons goods as common goods" (202). The goal of human natural action is "to bear fruit not only for itself but for the extended biotic community and for Earth for generations to come" (202). For this goal to succeed, the number of fallen humans in the world would likely need to be quite small.

20. For a somewhat contrasting (agrarian) vision, see Fred Bahnson and Norman Wirzba's argument that "ecological amnesia" has been produced by the separation of most modern people from food production. Bahnson and Wirzba state rather romantically that,

permanently marred the ecosystem and that Adam's efforts to obtain food will cause the ecosystem pain. Yet, despite God's foretelling of this conflictual relationship between Adam and the ecosystem, God proceeds to help Adam and Eve have children — and thus to help Adam and Eve "be fruitful and multiply, and fill the earth." When Eve conceives a child, she rejoices, saying, "I have gotten a man with the help of the LORD" (Gen 4:1).

What joy is there, however, in conceiving Cain, murderer of his brother Abel and the first builder of a city? Should God have helped Adam and Eve introduce urban life to the world? Furthermore, Cain's descendant Tubal-cain became the first "forger of all instruments of bronze and iron" (Gen 4:22). The God who commanded that humans be fruitful and fill the earth, the same God who helped the fallen Adam and Eve have a child (Cain!) and who thereby set in motion the multiplication and filling of the earth, is thus responsible in a certain sense for the rise of the technology that, to some degree at least, has harmed the earth's ecosystem: "instruments of bronze and iron." That such instruments are made by the descendants of Cain is of course significant: we already have a sense that such instruments, in addition to being unnecessary before the fall, are going to wreak a good deal of havoc. But my point is simply that God does not take back his commandment to multiply and fill the earth; in fact, according to Eve, God helps her have a child and thereby helps to set the whole thing rolling, despite God surely foreknowing the result of such events. Having failed to rescind the command

---

"whether as hunters and gatherers or, more likely, as peasants and farmers, people understood that in order to eat, they had to understand and respect the soil, climate, plants and animals. . . . Although it did not guarantee a fully satisfied or comfortable life, such work refined and reinforced the understanding that survival was deeply implicated in the lives of other creatures. It taught humans that the basis for health and well-being was thoroughly bound up with the health and well-being of the fields, waters and animals that warmed and fed them. In short, this was an understanding of humans as embodied beings in multiple, unfathomably complex relationships with nonhuman bodies" (Bahnson and Wirzba, *Making Peace with the Land: God's Call to Reconcile with Creation,* with a foreword by Bill McKibben [Downers Grove, IL: InterVarsity Press, 2012], 35). Bahnson and Wirzba suggest that the meaning of God's Sabbath blessing is that "no creature, no body whatsoever, should be neglected, despised or abused. Each body is God's love made visible, touchable, smellable, hearable and delectable" (40). I agree with this position, although it needs to be emphasized that human (ensouled) bodies in particular are "God's love made visible" and that human interpersonal communion, even if it displaces or in some way causes harm to other nonhuman bodies (e.g., building cities or more concretely fallen human actions), is the supreme instance of "God's love made visible." I do not think that Bahnson and Wirzba would disagree with this latter point, not least since (as they indicate in the acknowledgments) they have three and four children, respectively.

to be fruitful and multiply, God sets up the situation in which human sinners build cities and forge iron and bronze tools, which inevitably are going to threaten the ecosystem, in accord with God's foretelling that Adam and his descendants would be in a conflictual relationship with the ecosystem.

For those who might like to see a victory of the ecosystem over the steadily multiplying human sinners, things improve somewhat in the next few chapters of Genesis. The line of Seth emerges as a counterpoint to the city-building, tool-forging Cainites. Seth has good descendants, including Enoch, who "walked with God" (Gen 5:24). From this line, Noah is born. God also perceives that the multiplication of human beings, their filling of the earth, has corrupted the earth. We read, "Now the earth was corrupt in God's sight, and the earth was filled with violence. And God saw the earth, and behold, it was corrupt; for all flesh had corrupted their way upon the earth" (Gen 6:11-12). According to the narrative, God's solution is to flood the entire earth, thereby destroying all animals and trees, as well as humans. This solution leaves intact the ocean's ecosystem, even if it does temporarily destroy all land-based animals and plants. Had God stuck to his original plan to wipe out all humans, the life-sustaining beauty of the earth would not today be threatened by nuclear holocaust or by the turning of the entire habitable earth into a polluted pavement.[21]

Noah, however, is found to be righteous, and so God decides not to follow through on his earlier decision to "blot out man whom I have created from the face of the ground, man and beast and creeping things and birds of the air" (Gen 6:7). Instead, God commands Noah to make an ark, so that Noah and his family can survive the catastrophic flood that God has decided

---

21. As Bahnson and Wirzba point out, "The nightmare is not over. God promised to never again destroy the world, but we humans just might. The findings of ecologists and environmental historians show that people have yet to learn what is required to live harmoniously on and with the earth. God's soil and water are daily being poisoned and wasted. God's forests and glaciers are quickly disappearing. God's animals, particularly the agricultural animals that we have domesticated, are systematically being abused. And perhaps worst of all, we are causing the 'dome in the midst of the waters,' that protective mantle we call the *atmosphere,* to rupture (Gen 1:6). Polar ice is melting, hurricanes and droughts are becoming more frequent and severe, sea levels are rising, and the tropics have expanded by two degrees latitude" (Bahnson and Wirzba, *Making Peace with the Land,* 17). Nuclear war also remains a real possibility, as more and more countries gain nuclear weapons. Although Bahnson and Wirzba do not raise the issue of population, and in fact suggest that their solutions will serve "the world's poor" (17), it seems that the growth of the world's population to more than seven billion fallen humans is a factor in many of the ecological problems that Bahnson and Wirzba recount.

to unleash. Noah is to be the means of survival for many animals and plants as well. God commands Noah, "Of every living thing of all flesh, you shall bring two of every sort into the ark, to keep them alive with you; they shall be male and female. Of the birds according to their kinds, and of the animals according to their kinds, of every creeping thing of the ground according to its kind, two of every sort shall come in to you, to keep them alive" (Gen 6:19). Noah also brings into the ark a sample of every edible plant. In a second version of the story, Noah goes so far as to bring seven pairs of each clean animal, along with one pair of each unclean animal — the Mosaic law here being explicitly introduced into the creation stories (thus reminding us not to misread these accounts as modern historiography).

According to Genesis, God goes ahead with the worldwide flood and blots out, surely, quite a number of species — somewhat as modern science tells us that catastrophic events have indeed damaged and radically altered the earth's ecosystem in ages past.[22] Yet God does not learn what seems to be the lesson of the multiplication of sinful human city-builders and tool-users. On the contrary, once the floodwaters recede and Noah and his family, together with all the animals, return to the land, God gives to Noah and his family the *very same blessing* that God had given to Adam and Eve before the fall. Rather than preserving the earth's ecosystem from the corruption that human sinners inevitably carry with them, "God blessed Noah and his sons, and said to them, 'Be fruitful and multiply, and fill the earth. The fear of you and the dread of you shall be upon every beast of the earth, and upon every bird of the air, upon everything that creeps on the ground and all the fish of the sea; into your hand they are delivered'" (Gen 9:1-2).[23] This hardly sounds

22. Bahnson and Wirzba describe the flood in evocatively agrarian terms: "Human disobedience, arrogance and violence — to which the soil constantly bears witness — had so degraded and destroyed creation's order. What began as a garden of 'delight' (which is what *Eden* really means) quickly became a nightmare of drowning and death" (Bahnson and Wirzba, *Making Peace with the Land,* 17). They urge us to cultivate our own food as much as possible, by cultivating our own gardens (18). They remark, "When we garden well, we do not only grow food for our bodies and flowers for our tables; we share in and extend God's feeding, healing and sustaining ways with the world. With more honesty and practical discipline than our words can convey, we demonstrate an appreciation for the divine love that forever cherishes the earth" (18).

23. Rachel Muers observes that "the core biblical images of peaceable relationships between humanity and nonhuman creatures are eschatological as much as, or more than, protological" (Muers, "Creatures," in *Systematic Theology and Climate Change,* ed. Michael S. Northcott and Peter M. Scott [London: Routledge, 2014], 101). She notes that, in the eschatological covenant renewal described in Hosea 2:18-23, "God is represented as instituting a

like a wise plan! Why deliver the ecosystem once more into the hands of humans? Why encourage humans, once again, to "fill the earth"?

Perhaps, at this stage of the story, we might imagine that Noah is righteous and that paradise has been restored.[24] But such a reading would be

---

new covenant between humanity and nonhuman animals — particularly the animals that are *not* humanity's immediate 'neighbours' — in order to restore both human security and the fertility of the land, in the context of a restored relationship between 'the heavens' and 'the earth' (2:21). In the context of Hosea, the cause of the disruption is human wrongdoing. . . . The promised covenant amounts, on one possible reading, to a *re*-creation that reaches back before the flood; hence it draws attention, in any particular context of reading, to present failures and problems of co-creaturely existence, and to the impossibility of a final peace. At the same time, it draws attention to the everyday lived needs of humanity and the other creatures for one another, and to the ongoing reshaping of creaturely life by their interactions (for example, in the reference to crops bred and grown for food, Hosea 2.22)" (101-2). Muers concludes that Hosea and other such texts underscore "the urgent need for interim and local forms of peace-making to enable creaturely life to continue" (102). See also the discussion of Hosea 2:18-23 in Ellen F. Davis, *Biblical Prophecy: Perspectives for Christian Theology, Discipleship, and Ministry* (Louisville, KY: Westminster John Knox Press, 2014), 84-89 (cf. 104-8); as well as Christopher J. H. Wright, *Old Testament Ethics for the People of God* (Downers Grove, IL: InterVarsity Press, 2004), 184-86.

24. The idea that it might be possible to retrieve or renew a paradise on earth has parallels in contemporary ecological theology. Thus, in his *A Political Theology of Climate Change* (Grand Rapids: Eerdmans, 2013), Michael Northcott holds not simply that, "for the early Christians, salvation was an ecological as well as a political and spiritual reality in which the earth and all its creatures, as well as human society, were being redeemed through the worship and the witness of the saints and under the kingly rule of Christ," but also that "the restoration of Paradise on earth was for more than a thousand years understood to be the work of the Christian Church" (199). I would note, however, that the fathers of the Church understood that the new creation (not a "restoration of paradise") is the work of the triune God, not of the Church, even though the Church certainly is the inaugurated kingdom and the triune God works through the Church to transform the world and to prepare for the gift of the new creation. Northcott suggests that medieval monks, in their desire to restore "paradise on earth," were moved "to create gardens and herbariums and to develop crafts and workshop techniques and technologies which were labour saving while also increasing the fertility and productiveness of the earth" (199). Northcott relies here upon a work whose scholarly value seems to me to be minimal: Rita Nakashima Brock and Rebecca Parker, *Saving Paradise: How Christianity Traded Love of This World for Crucifixion and Empire* (Boston: Beacon Press, 2008). Northcott advances a similar argument in his "Holy Spirit," 58-60; here Northcott cites Elspeth Whitney, *Paradise Restored: The Mechanical Arts from Antiquity through the Thirteenth Century* (Philadelphia: Temple University Press, 1989), and George Ovitt Jr., *The Restoration of Perfection: Labor and Technology in Medieval Culture* (New Brunswick, NJ: Rutgers University Press, 1987). Indebted to Jacob Taubes's *Occidental Eschatology*, trans. David Ratmoko (Stanford, CA: Stanford University Press, 2009), as well as to William Blake, Northcott reflects at length upon the eschatologies of Augustine and

contrary to God's recognition, after Noah's disembarking from the ark and before God's words of blessing, that "the imagination of man's heart is evil from his youth" (Gen 8:21). And in fact, after receiving God's covenant of blessing as symbolized by the rainbow, Noah starts a farm, plants a vineyard, and then gets drunk. As Noah lies naked on the ground stone drunk, his son Ham "saw the nakedness of his father" (Gen 9:22). After awakening, Noah responds by cursing the son of Ham, Canaan.

Hardly a chapter later, we find that the expansion of humans across the earth has begun — with predictably dire consequences. At this time the human population is still so small that "the whole earth had one language and few words" (Gen 11:1). A group of migrating humans builds a city and a tower whose purpose is to "make a name for ourselves" (Gen 11:4).[25] This is

---

Joachim of Fiore, with the latter (along with Paul) as the revolutionary hero; see Northcott, *A Political Theology of Climate Change,* 271-305. Northcott is sympathetic to distributivist "Transition" movements, but he warns that "Transition" will work only if its advocates can persuade the nation-states to undertake radical change: "Only the nations acting together in a concerted fashion can restrain large multinational fossil fuel corporations, power companies, and advertising and marketing corporations from producing ongoing streams of fossil fuels into global markets and enticing consumers to ongoing growth in fossil fuel consumption and use" (312). I fear that a Green Revolution of a radical, relatively quick, and global kind would be devastating in its impact upon agriculture, local and national economies, education, and medical care, and it would result in a mass death of a few billion of the poor and weak around the world by returning us essentially to conditions prior to the industrial revolution. For Northcott, by contrast, the Green Revolution is the only way to stave off such a tragedy. For positions similar to Northcott's, see Christoph Stueckelberger, "Who Dies First? Who Is Sacrificed First? Ethical Aspects of Climate Justice," and George Zachariah, "Discerning the Times: A Spirituality of Resistance and Alternatives," both in *God, Creation, and Climate Change: Spiritual and Ethical Perspectives,* ed. Karen L. Bloomquist (Minneapolis, MN: Lutheran University Press, 2009), 47-62 and 75-91. Stueckelberger assures us, all too blithely, "A new lifestyle and society, not based on fossil energy and carbon emission, are possible. To leave existing lifestyles and to look for new ones is an inner journey, involving psychological and spiritual processes of mourning and reorientation. . . . Not only all sectors of societies, but also all religions are challenged to find answers to the burning spiritual questions climate change has given rise to" ("Who Dies First? Who Is Sacrificed First?" 59).

25. See also the concerns regarding "anthropocentrism" in Norman Wirzba's *The Paradise of God: Renewing Religion in an Ecological Age* (Oxford: Oxford University Press, 2003). Wirzba connects "anthropocentrism" with the view that "we are the only species that really matters" and also with "the vast scope of our manipulation of the earth" (95). Rather than demonizing the human race, Wirzba states, "We are a species that, far from being an alien or cancerous presence, must learn to take up its proper place and role" (192). He is aware, too, that "traditional agrarian societies" can be criticized, just as our modern urban society can be (192). From his agrarian perspective, he proposes the following solutions to the ecological crisis: become gardeners, support local economies, rethink energy use, unplug

an act of pride, and the punishment that God delivers is to multiply human languages and to scatter the people "abroad over the face of all the earth" (Gen 11:9). For the earth's ecosystem, it would seem, a worse solution could hardly be found. When humans were small in numbers and contained in one city, their sinfully destructive capabilities could be contained; but when humans are spread "over the face of all the earth," they are liable to multiply, build new cities, and generally run amok. And this is precisely what they do as the narrative continues.

Prior to blessing Noah and his family and fatefully commanding them once again to multiply and "fill the earth," God had promised: "I will never again curse the ground because of man . . . neither will I ever again destroy every living creature as I have done" (Gen 8:21). The destructive power of humans, however, is not thereby minimized. Thus, during the time of Abraham, with whom God makes a covenant, according to which, by Abraham, "all the families of the earth shall bless themselves" (Gen 12:3), we find a new cause of devastation: war.[26] The kings of the various cities make war on each other. We read, "In the days of Amraphel king of Shinar, Arioch king of Ellasar, Chedorlaomer king of Elam, and Tidal king of Goiim, these kings made war with Bera king of Sodom, Birsha king of Gomorrah, Shinab king of Admah, Shemeber king of Zeboiim, and the king of Bela (that is, Zoar)" (Gen 14:1-2). As if this kind of destruction were not enough, the citizens of Sodom and Gomorrah turn out to be so sinful that God brings upon them utter destruction as the punishment for their sins. This does nothing good for the ecosystem, although as yet the destruction involves only a small portion of land. After the destruction of Sodom and Gomorrah, Abraham "looked down toward Sodom and Gomorrah and toward all the land of the valley, and beheld, and lo, the smoke of the land went up like the smoke of a furnace" (Gen 19:28).

---

the media, design a generous household economy, and develop Sabbath rituals. He explains his viewpoint: "There are limits to what we can and should do, limits set by the integrity of the land. The way to show that we respect those limits is to make ourselves the students and servants of the land, for in being servants we relinquish our own will and desire for the sake of the creation's well-being. Anthropocentrism is replaced not by ecocentrism but by theocentrism, a vision that is focused on God's intention together with the sweep of God's creative work" (139).

26. Matthew A. Shadle points out that, although military leaders have always wreaked destruction upon the environment, modern warfare's technological advances mean that its "potential to harm the natural environment has increased exponentially" (Shadle, "No Peace on Earth: War and the Environment," in *Green Discipleship*, ed. Tobias Winright [Winona, MN: Anselm Academic, 2011], 407).

The proliferation of flocks and herds that ensues hardly benefits the ecosystem. During this time, too, the human population continues to grow and to seek new land upon which to live. Indeed, the history of the people of Israel is a history of struggle for land upon which to survive, in competition with many other peoples who want to control the same land. In two ways, the Bible recounts the people's entrance into the land after their escape from generations of Egyptian slavery: first the entrance under Joshua, in which the people of Israel win decisive victories over the peoples of the land; then the stories of the book of Judges, which reveals a time of petty chieftains and constant warfare, culminating in a long territorial war with the Philistines. During the time of Saul and David, civil warfare is added to the struggles against the Philistines, and the briefly united twelve tribes divide again during the reign of David's grandson Rehoboam. The people of Israel in both the Northern and Southern Kingdoms soon find themselves pinched between Egypt on the one side and various empires — Assyrian, Babylonian, Persian, Greek, and eventually Roman — on the other. If the endless territorial wars and frequent periods of famine are any indication, the land hardly suffices for its population.

Nonetheless, in the midst of the formative period of the people of Israel, we consistently find God blessing his favored ones by promising them many descendants and by encouraging them to have children. Thus God promises Abraham, "I will multiply you exceedingly," and "I will make you exceedingly fruitful; and I will make nations of you, and kings shall come forth from you" (Gen 17:2, 6-7). Nor does God bless only his favored people in this way. God says of Ishmael, whom Abraham expelled from his home: "I will bless him and make him fruitful and multiply him exceedingly; he shall be the father of twelve princes" (Gen 17:20). Again, in the very midst of the terrible strife caused by the rape of Jacob's daughter and the brutal attack upon the city of Shechem by Jacob's sons, God gives Jacob the new name Israel and promises: "I am God Almighty: be fruitful and multiply; a nation and a company of nations shall come from you, and kings shall spring from you" (Gen 35:11). God intends not only for the Israelites to flourish and spread, but also for Abraham and Jacob (and Ishmael) to father many nations, many peoples. In fact, God tells Abraham that "I will multiply your descendants as the stars of heaven and as the sand which is on the seashore" (Gen 22:17). Even granted that this statement is hyperbole, it remains the case that God has no worry whatsoever about overpopulation, notwithstanding that the land of Canaan itself already seems overcrowded, with wars and brutal violence of all kinds.

Can this promotion of human multiplication really be a wise decision on God's part? Why does God repeatedly command humans — both before and after the fall — to "be fruitful and multiply, and fill the earth"? It is not that God is unaware that cities, wars, famines, and ecological disasters are the inevitable result of ever-increasing human population. On the contrary, the book of Genesis testifies to all of these, and to God's concern about them. In the book of Genesis, however, God nonetheless presses forward with his command regarding human multiplication and with his promise that the central biblical figures will have an enormous number of descendants. In the Mosaic law, too, God forbids sexual intercourse during a woman's period and thereby focuses sexual intercourse upon the fertile time of the female cycle. One could interpret these commands and blessings as simply the human authors' desire to aggrandize their own nation, or as simply the result of an agrarian mentality marked by the presence of a high mortality rate. But even if this reductive interpretation were partly true, it cannot explain — at least for those for whom the Torah is Scripture and mediates divine revelation — why the same God who knows full well what terrible troubles are caused by humans nonetheless encourages humans to spread around the entire earth.[27]

Bill McKibben's *Maybe One*

Bill McKibben is a contemporary environmentalist and an active Methodist Christian. In the acknowledgments of his 1989 book *The End of Nature,* he thanks "the men and women of the Johnsburg United Methodist Church and our pastor, Rev. Lucy B. Hathaway." Even more clearly, he dedicated his 1998 book *Maybe One* to his three godchildren and to "the many, many children of the Johnsburg and Mill Creek United Methodist Church Sunday School."[28] In the latter book, he specifies that he regularly teaches Sunday school at Mill Creek United Methodist Church.

From his perspective as a Christian environmentalist, McKibben argues in *Maybe One* that couples should have no more than one child.[29] He

27. For appreciation of "human dominion over creation" as *service,* of our intrinsic "relatedness and interdependence," and of the need for showing "gratitude for the gift of life that we and the creation as a whole are," see Wirzba, *The Paradise of God,* 137.

28. See Bill McKibben, *The End of Nature* (New York: Random House, 1989), ix; Bill McKibben, *Maybe One: A Case for Smaller Families* (New York: Penguin, 1998).

29. McKibben is strongly joined by most environmental activists in his concern about human population. See, for example, Eric Kaufmann, *Shall the Religious Inherit the Earth?*

reaches this conclusion on the grounds that the heavy carbon footprint of contemporary Americans is producing devastating effects upon the ecology of the planet. He makes clear that he does not intend to imply that couples who have more than one child are guilty of a sin, since he considers that children "are magnificent."[30] Nor is he proposing that government, as in China, should mandate a family size limit.[31] Rather, he is simply trying to address what he considers to be humankind's biggest problem: our consumption habits and use of fossil fuels, especially in rich countries such as America, are literally causing the destruction of the planet. Once Americans realize this damaging course of action, Americans will be able to "develop new social norms" that address the problem, without needing to coerce people or make anyone feel guilty. McKibben grants that limiting families to one child would

Demography and Politics in the Twenty-First Century (London: Profile Books, 2010), 263: "The earth's growing population is combining with economic development to produce unsustainable levels of carbon emissions. In the present climate, a falling global population may be exactly what the doctor ordered — at least until we find the technological fix required to meet our energy needs while cooling the planet. . . . According to Andrew Watkinson of the Tyndall Centre for Climate Change Research, three-quarters of climate change is caused by population growth. This was recently recognised by the UN Population Fund in its 2009 report, *The State of World Population*. Coming just a month before the Copenhagen conference on climate change, the report broke fresh ground in challenging its decades-long reticence about broaching the population-environment link. . . . The UN report also hints that family planning could be the most effective green policy of all. UN projections suggest that world population will rise from 6.8 billion today to between 8 and 10.5 billion at mid-century. If fertility cuts reduce world population by a billion in 2050, this would achieve the same effect as the daunting task of constructing all new buildings to the highest energy-efficiency standards or replacing all coal-fired power plants with wind turbines."

30. McKibben, *Maybe One,* 12. In Elizabeth A. Johnson's *Ask the Beasts: Darwin and the God of Love* (London: Bloomsbury, 2014), she asserts that "not all levels of human birth are morally correct" (245). Thus, with regard to having a large family, the question of sin is a live one in some Catholic circles, even if Vatican II's *Gaudium et spes* strongly approves of married couples "who after prudent reflection and common decision courageously undertake the proper upbringing of a large number of children" (*Gaudium et spes,* §50, in *Vatican Council II,* vol. 1, *The Conciliar and Post Conciliar Documents,* rev. ed., ed. Austin Flannery, OP [Northport, NY: Costello, 1996], 954).

31. Other scholars consider this a serious option. See, for example, the remark of Dave Foreman that "to say that women have the right to have as many children as they want is much the same as saying that men have the right to as many gas-guzzling, land-ripping SUVs as they want. Except it is worse. Either way, it says that it is okay for anyone to act on selfish whims that ransack wild things. As in so many things, we scramble rights with irresponsibility. Freedom becomes no better than a two-year-old's temper tantrum" (Foreman, "The Great Backtrack," in *Life on the Brink: Environmentalists Confront Overpopulation,* ed. Philip Cafaro and Eileen Crist [Athens: University of Georgia Press, 2012], 63).

eventually "yield populations smaller than almost anyone would want."[32] But if the United States can get its birthrate down to 1.5 and can simultaneously cut immigration, there could be only 230 million Americans in the year 2050, which would be millions less than we have now.[33] If the birthrate remains the same and immigration goes unchecked, there will be 400 million Americans by the year 2050, with a devastating environmental effect.

McKibben tells us that he and his wife thought for a long time that they might have no children, but they eventually decided to have one — after which they surgically ensured that they would not have another child. As he points out, the spread of birth control around the world may mean that the world's population will not go much beyond 10 billion. But were birthrates not to continue to go down worldwide, the world's population would reach 296 billion by 2150, assuming hypothetically that so many humans could be fed. Indeed, if worldwide birthrates fell only to 2.5 children per woman, this would mean a world population of 28 billion by 2150. Of course, a significant factor here is life expectancy: in the United States, for example, if the mortality rate were the same as it was in 1900, the population would be half of what it presently is.

These numbers, McKibben observes, will get us off track if we fail to realize that the most pressing problem today is the human appetite for consumption — the amount of timber, pasture, precious metals, and oil that our lifestyle requires. If humans were willing and able to stay on small farms and used little or no electricity, oil, chemicals, or manufactured products, then population growth would be less of a problem than in fact it is. McKibben runs quickly through the list of population doomsayers: Thomas Malthus, William Vogt, Fairfield Osborn, William and Paul Paddock, and Paul Ehrlich.[34] So far, they have all been wrong, but McKibben points out

32. McKibben, *Maybe One*, 13.

33. For an essay on immigration congenial to McKibben's position, see Philip Cafaro and Winthrop Staples III, "The Environmental Argument for Reducing Immigration into the United States," in *Life on the Brink*, 172-88.

34. In a book published in 1971, when he occupied a prominent position in left-wing politics (but was an opponent of Ehrlich), Richard John Neuhaus offers a telling sketch of the 1970 Earth Day protest in New York City, in which a university scientist spoke of the earth having only ten years left to (forcibly) reduce human population before mass starvation would become unavoidable. See Neuhaus's *In Defense of People: Ecology and the Seduction of Radicalism* (New York: Macmillan, 1971), 23. The stories that Neuhaus tells from the period remind us that the environmental activism of the 2010s was already fully present in the elite culture of 1971, though the scientific warnings then were based not on global warming but on resource scarcity. For further background to the period, see Meredith Veldman, *Fantasy,*

that there must be some population number that will prove to be unsustainable.[35] Against those who might wish to ignore the problem of population growth, McKibben cites evidence that the earth's environment is *already* buckling under the strain of providing for so many eaters.

McKibben also cites evidence that the earth is being crippled by the gases that our consumption habits pour daily into the atmosphere. During the industrial revolution, cities discovered that their air became unlivable if too much pollution was poured into it. But it now appears that the atmosphere itself, and not just the air of a few cities, is reaching an unlivable amount of pollution, including nitrous oxide, carbon dioxide, and methane. McKibben warns especially against pollution-caused global warming, which he argues will produce environmental catastrophes of various kinds, including a rise in temperatures in the twenty-first century alone by 3-6 degrees.[36]

---

the Bomb, and the Greening of Britain: Romantic Protest, 1945-1980 (Cambridge: Cambridge University Press, 1994). For a vigorous defense of the fundamental accuracy of Paul Ehrlich's warnings, see Alan Weisman, *Countdown: Our Last, Best Hope for a Future on Earth?* (New York: Little, Brown, 2013), 399-406.

35. Alan Weisman suggests that the number is in fact 7 billion (our present number). He states that "there are other, simpler ways that nature will halt our unimpeded growth if we don't take the reins ourselves. The most basic is the world's oldest: cutting off our sustenance. The bottom line of the twenty-first century is that we will have less food — not more as we did, only briefly, during the Green Revolution. That is what an odds maker would bet on: We will not be able to grow, hunt, or harvest enough for the 7 billion we already are, let alone the 10.9 billion we're racing toward" (Weisman, *Countdown,* 383; cf. 384-85; although on 424-27 he suggests that it might theoretically be possible to feed 8-10 billion people for a short time). Weisman blames global warming and the end of the Green Revolution for this approaching food scarcity. Just prior to this discussion, however, Weisman warns about fertility problems linked to "endocrine disruptors found not just in agro-chemistry, but in pharmaceuticals, household cleaners, detergents, plastics, and even cosmetics and sunscreens. . . . From animals to us, fertility is dropping not by choice, but by exposure to molecules that never existed before. The term we've invented to describe them, *gender-benders,* is precisely accurate, but unfortunately too snappy to be taken as seriously as it truly is. This is a tragedy — and it is also nature rejecting an unnatural act, making life inhospitable for the actors" (382). This line of thought would suggest that population is going to drop, no matter what we might wish. In making the case for the urgent need to expand the use of contraception, Weisman suggests focusing on male contraception, and he also devotes an extensive section to promoting abortion, not least because the existence of billions of young males in poor countries is generating violence. From a similar population-control perspective, see also Albert Bartlett, "Reflections on Sustainability and Population Growth," in *Life on the Brink,* 29-40; as well as the essays in *The Future of Sustainability,* ed. Marco Keiner (Dordrecht: Springer, 2006).

36. For a recent summary of climate data and prediction of the grave consequences of

The only practicable solution is to try immediately to limit this damage by limiting our population growth.

McKibben is aware that some population-control advocates blame the countries of the so-called Third World and focus upon increasing the use of contraception in those countries. But McKibben focuses instead upon wealthy countries such as the United States because of their tremendously elevated carbon footprint. Each member of the richest tenth of Americans causes the emission of twenty-two times the amount of carbon dioxide as does each person in the poorer countries of the world. Some might suppose that this problem can be solved solely by Americans living more simply and with technology that is more energy-efficient. But McKibben points out that reducing our number of children will be much easier than changing

---

global warming caused by man-made carbon emissions, see Northcott, *A Political Theology of Climate Change*. Citing Richard A. Betts, Matthew Collins, Deborah L. Hemming et al., "When Could Global Warming Reach 4° C?" *Philosophical Transactions of the Royal Society* 369 (2011): 67-84, Northcott observes that the "current best scientific guess for the timing of a four degree temperature rise is 2070. The world has not been that warm for three million years, and never in the time of *Homo sapiens*. According to climate scientist Kevin Anderson, a four degree warmer world is 'incompatible with organised global community, is likely to be beyond "adaptation," is devastating to the majority of ecosystems, and has a high probability of not being stable (i.e., 4° C would be an interim temperature on the way to a much higher equilibrium level)'" (Northcott, *A Political Theology of Climate Change*, 164; the interior quotation is from Anderson, "Going beyond Dangerous Climate Change: Exploring the Void between Rhetoric and Reality in Reducing Carbon Emissions" [public lecture, London School of Economics, October 21, 2011]). Civil debate about climate data is now nearly impossible, as was already apparent in the response to Bjørn Lomborg's *The Skeptical Environmentalist: Measuring the Real State of the World* (Cambridge: Cambridge University Press, 2001). See also Lomborg's *Cool It: The Skeptical Environmentalist's Guide to Global Warming* (London: Cyan-Marschall Cavendish, 2007). Skepticism about the extent to which global warming is being caused by humans is also expressed by Roger Scruton, *Green Philosophy: How to Think Seriously about the Planet* (London: Atlantic Books, 2012). Warning against "climate denialists," Northcott points out that "predictions of climate catastrophe . . . represent a *politics* because climate science indicates that, absent a *leveling* of unequal uses of fossil fuels between rich and poor and between developed and developing countries, the earth itself will enforce a leveling on the presently disequalising tendencies of fossil-fuelled industrial capitalism through climate catastrophe. Unmitigated climate change by the end of the century will flood the rich cities of the powerful and disrupt their global resource extraction and wealth accumulation systems, as well as turning the lands of the poor into deserts" (Northcott, *A Political Theology of Climate Change*, 16-17). I cannot share Northcott's certitude about the extent of man-made global warming and about its sole possible solutions, but I grant that he (and McKibben, along with numerous others whom Northcott cites) may be right.

our consumption and energy-usage patterns in the radical ways that will also soon be necessary.[37] As he states, "If we can cut the birthrate, that's 50 or 100 million fewer cars and furnaces; 50 or 100 million fewer dinners to serve and thermostats to set each day; 50 or 100 million fewer giant balloons [of energy-use pollution] hovering above the landscape."[38] Speaking practically, McKibben points out that humans are not going to easily give up the cars, air travel, computers, technology, spacious houses, healthcare, television, heating, air conditioning, and so forth that many now enjoy in the developed West. Given the imminence of the ecological threat, therefore, it is fortunate that the evidence shows that people gladly accept contraception and sterilization. He argues that, since this crisis will reach its peak during the next fifty years, now is the time to have one or fewer children, if we care about the environment.

Describing his own vasectomy, McKibben admits that "it felt sad" and even "a little *shameful*," feelings that he attributes to his biologically inbuilt urge to reproduce. In this context, he addresses God's injunctions in Genesis to "be fruitful and multiply, and fill the earth." He rejects as "canards" the commonplace attacks upon the pope (or upon Hasidic Jews and Mormons), and he seeks to take seriously the religious critique of contraception. He first explores Jewish understandings of the passages in Genesis. Indebted to the work of David Feldman, he notes that the most relevant religious duty in this regard is not procreation but marriage, which "is good in its own right"; since sexual intercourse aids marriage, it too "is considered a great good." According to Jewish teaching, each married couple can obey the commandment to be fruitful and multiply simply by having a boy and a girl, "but the Talmud urges that parents keep going, if only to make sure that their children are not sterile, or don't die before reproducing *themselves*." The Jewish teaching seems straightforward enough: it involves the survival of the people of Israel. McKibben comments, "It celebrates sex but not self-indulgence, and it has helped assure growth from a tiny band and survival against odds more daunting than any other race has ever faced."[39]

Christianity, however, does not require the survival of a particular na-

---

37. McKibben adds that this is so, especially given that consumption and energy use are on the rise in China, India, and other developing countries. Similarly, Weisman observes that, since no one really has "a solution for overconsumption," the main plan for addressing the ecological crisis must in fact be "lowering the number of consumers" (Weisman, *Countdown*, 418).

38. McKibben, *Maybe One*, 125.

39. McKibben, *Maybe One*, 184-87.

tion, and Jesus makes "scant comment on birth control or marriage or re-production."[40] In his discussion of Christianity, McKibben is particularly indebted to John T. Noonan. Early Christians rejected what they considered to be the hedonism of Roman culture, and they adopted certain ascetic ideas current at the time. Given his expectation of the imminent end of the world, Paul favored celibacy and said little about procreation. The early church fathers likewise favored celibacy and did not encourage procreation, and Tertullian even praised natural disasters for reducing population in overcrowded nations. Yet from the third century onward, the Church has condemned contraception. Why so, given that the Church has encouraged celibacy and has not made a big deal out of the command to "be fruitful and multiply"?

McKibben argues that the historical reason for the Church's teaching against contraception is to be found, not in God's commands in the book of Genesis, but in the Church's controversies against metaphysically dualistic splinter groups. On this view, Augustine's fight against the Manichaeans, who believed matter was evil and practiced birth control, was especially significant. Reacting against the extreme position of the Manichaeans, Augustine arrived at the other extreme. He forbade all contraception and held that sexual intercourse is good only when its purpose is procreation. Augustine's position won the day, although during the Renaissance the Church began to allow for the value of pleasure and companionship (and not just procreation) with regard to marriage and sex.[41] During the French Revolution, McKibben observes, a twenty percent reduction in the birthrate indicated changing social mores, and the late nineteenth century introduced widespread birth control movements, culminating in the Anglican Church's decision in 1930 to allow contraception. Even the Catholic Church now allows for the rhythm method, and almost all Catholics ignore the Church's formal teaching against contraception.

McKibben grants that the Church's teaching, while rooted in an Augustinian extreme, nonetheless identifies a real danger: selfishness. Not having children can be an excuse for American couples to give way even more fully to consumerism and self-indulgence. Positively citing contemporary theologians such as Gilbert Meilaender and John Berkman, McKibben praises

40. McKibben, *Maybe One,* 187.

41. For a better-instructed view of medieval understandings of marriage, against such caricatures, see Stan Parmisano, OP, *The Craft of Love: Love and Intimacy in Christian Marriage* (Antioch, CA: Solas Press, 2009).

John Ryan, a Catholic priest and moral theologian of the New Deal era, for arguing in favor of large families on the grounds that living a self-sacrificial life is good for the parents, as well as for the children. McKibben agrees that, in order to lead Christian lives, we need to be trained in self-sacrifice. He accepts that parenting does often instill self-sacrificial habits in people, and he also accepts that parenting large families can do this particularly well. But as he points out, "The problem, of course, is that now we live in an era — maybe only a brief one, maybe only for a few generations — when parenting a bunch of kids clashes with the good of the planet."[42] How, then, to become people who focus on others, who are willing to sacrifice rather than indulge? McKibben suggests that the statements of Pope John Paul II in preparation for the 1994 Cairo Conference on population rightly emphasize both the need to avoid selfishness and the need to make informed, responsible decisions about procreation. But in McKibben's view, the current environmental situation and the fact that world population is going to balloon to ten billion (even if birthrates continue to go down) mean that responsible decisions about procreation now mean having no more than one child.[43] Indeed, it would be selfish and irresponsible to sacrifice the earth's ecosystem by insisting on having many children. As it stands, we have already reached the point where "huge swaths of God's creation are being wiped out by the one species told to tend this particular garden."[44]

42. McKibben, *Maybe One,* 196.

43. In a hopeful moment, Weisman points out that if "the entire world adopted a one-child policy tomorrow," then "by the end of this century, we would be back to 1.6 billion, our population in 1900. . . . That would reduce our numbers by three-quarters, freeing billions of acres for other species, on whose existence a functioning ecosystem — including our place in it — depends" (Weisman, *Countdown,* 415). He points out that women in developed countries freely and radically limit their fertility, without need for a government edict. In this context, he raises a line of thought quite similar to McKibben's, but with more governmental involvement: "'There is not a single problem on Earth that wouldn't be easier if there were fewer people,' said a woman in Salt Lake City, and surprisingly, no one objected. That made me wonder: Was there something in the histories or holy books of the rest of the world's cultures and religions that might embrace the idea of, so to speak, refraining from embracing as much during the next two or three generations, limiting our progeny to bring us back into balance with the rest of nature — at which point, having reached an optimum number, we could resume averaging two children per family? . . . Might we benefit *right now* if everyone agreed to bring population down in the twenty-first century, much as the world's nations came together during the last century to sign a protocol to save our flickering ozone layer?" (417).

44. McKibben, *Maybe One,* 197-98. On this point, from a population-control perspective, see the following essays in *Life on the Brink:* Leon Kolankiewicz, "Overpopulation

Part of an unselfish, sacrificial life today involves using contraception so as to keep our number of children low.

Has McKibben thereby rejected or devalued God's command to be fruitful and multiply? He argues that humans have already succeeded in amply fulfilling this commandment of God. The entire earth has been marked and refashioned by human presence. On the negative side, we have corrupted the environment; but on the positive side, we have "spread wondrous and diverse cultures, full of love and song."[45] Now that we have fulfilled this first commandment of God, we should focus our attention on fulfilling the other commandments, rather than on having large families. We can lead self-sacrificial lives by helping to ensure that people around the globe have food, clothing, and comfort. We can also lead self-sacrificial lives by ensuring that the earth remains environmentally able to sustain life. This means ensuring clean water and the survival of species, and it also means strengthening parenthood and freeing societies from violence. The energy that we would have spent raising large families, we can now spend on these crucial communal, environmental, and societal goals — goals that answer to God's

---

versus Biodiversity: How a Plethora of People Produces a Paucity of Wildlife," 75-90; Jeffrey McKee, "The Human Population Footprint on Global Biodiversity," 91-97; and Winthrop Staples III and Philip Cafaro, "For a Species Right to Exist," 283-300. From this perspective, see also Dave Foreman, *Man Swarm and the Killing of Wildlife* (Durango, CO: Raven's Eye Press, 2011); E. O. Wilson, *The Future of Life* (New York: Knopf, 2002); and Bill McKibben, *Deep Economy: The Wealth of Communities and the Durable Future* (New York: Henry Holt, 2007). Citing McKibben's *Deep Economy,* Staples and Cafaro point out that "ever more people and ever more human economic activity are impossible to square with sustaining the resources and ecosystem services necessary for *people* to lead comfortable and enjoyable lives in the future. That is the clear, if largely unacknowledged, lesson of climate change and other examples of planetwide environmental degradation" ("For a Species Right to Exist," 297). Staples and Cafaro look forward to a much less populated world (they estimate 2-3 billion) "where people are less likely to suffer hunger, sickness, resource wars, and other ills stemming from the overuse and collapse of ecosystems. It would be a world where the human right to experience and celebrate wild nature is more widely ensured" (297).

45. McKibben, *Maybe One,* 198. Weisman evocatively underscores the negative side of population growth, namely the paving of many green spaces: "No matter where people are from, or whatever age or politics or faith, everyone remembers a place where they used to go to escape the clamor and congestion of their lives. A place not too far away, where they could hike, or picnic, or ride a dirt bike. Where they could watch birds — or if they like to hunt, kill birds. Where they could hug trees, or cut them for firewood, or just fall asleep beneath one. But now, that favorite place is gone, vanished beneath strip malls or industrial parks or condominia. Everyone remembers a world that was better. Less crowded. Lovelier. Where they felt freer" (Weisman, *Countdown,* 420).

other commandments. He concludes that the call to have only one child and to use birth control to avoid large families accords with the pope's focus on self-sacrifice in a way that fits with "the signs of the times" regarding the need to care for the environment.[46]

Even so, what about people who, in their quest to live simply and naturally, who rule out birth control (and abortion) as a further instance of the failed modern desire to control nature by means of technology? He cites the example of a group of "conservative" (or radical) Quakers who, like the Amish, have large families. In response to this subset of the environmentalist movement, McKibben argues that, precisely in order to preserve God's earth, we now need to plan, since "there are so many of us, and we have done such a poor job of planning for our numbers."[47] On this view, if today we refuse any technological intrusion in our reproductive lives, we will simply be facilitating the ongoing destruction of the earth by uncontrolled human technologies.

Reading Genesis and McKibben: God's Blessings and Human Procreation

Thus far, I have advanced two contrasting views. First, I noted that the God of Israel, in commanding humans to "be fruitful and multiply, and fill the earth," does not seem to include the prudential limitations that we might

---

46. Weisman, too, reaches out in a certain way to Christian leaders. He describes his meeting "with Reverend Richard Cizik, a former Washington lobbyist for the National Association of Evangelicals. In 2008 he left them and founded the New Evangelical Partnership for the Common Good, a Christian organization with an environmental mission he calls 'Creation Care.' For the past three years, he told me, 'I've been laying theological groundwork for interpreting how the mandate to be fruitful and multiply applies to today, in light of the current crisis of the planet.' A thin, intense man with straight, receding blond hair, he'd just come out publicly in support of family-planning funding a few weeks earlier in a piece for the *Washington Post*'s faith blog. 'Family planning is not only moral: it's what we should be doing. Be fruitful and multiply was superseded by a post-flood mandate to live peacefully with all of God's creatures.' He was undaunted by the pushback from conservative evangelicals, he said, and encouraged by the response of a new generation of concerned young Christians. '*Thy will be done on Earth as it is in heaven,* Jesus says in the Lord's Prayer. If that's the case, then we should bring the values of heaven to Earth. In heaven things don't go extinct. Sustainability means you don't make things go extinct. Yet that's what we're doing, to entire species'" (Weisman, *Countdown,* 428).

47. McKibben, *Maybe One,* 203.

expect. God seems to be well aware of the damaging results (including ecologically damaging results) of increasing human population, and yet God
continues to promote such increase. Furthermore, God does not qualify the
commandment prudentially, even by suggesting that, once the world (or
the land of Israel) is full, the commandment can be set aside. Second, I sur-
veyed Bill McKibben's proposal that Americans should have no more than
one child because of the ecological crisis that he perceives to be present, a
crisis stemming largely from global warming. For McKibben, promoting
the widespread use of contraception and sterilization is now necessary, not
only because of his view of the current ecological crisis, but also because
otherwise world human population would quickly jump beyond ten billion. Such a vast human population, if it did not result in mass starvation
and devastating conflict over scarce resources, would certainly result in the
extinction of numerous plant and animal species and would turn much of
the earth into pavement and apartment buildings.[48]

The purpose of this third section is to provide a broader context for
evaluating the messages of Genesis and McKibben. In this regard, it is noteworthy that in Genesis 1:1–2:4, blessing is attributed three times to God.
The first blessing has to do with the fish and the birds: "And God blessed
them, saying, 'Be fruitful and multiply and fill the waters and the seas, and
let birds multiply on the earth'" (Gen 1:22). The second blessing has to do
with humans: "And God blessed them, and God said to them, 'Be fruitful

48. See also the alarm expressed by Eric Kaufmann about the fact that religious couples have more children than secular couples in his *Shall the Religious Inherit the Earth?*,
though he distinguishes between liberal churches and more conservative or fundamentalist ones. Kaufmann remarks rather disturbingly: "Liberals are aware that tolerating
illiberal groups is risky. . . . The problem arises when illiberal groups such as religious
fundamentalists demographically increase to the point where they are able to threaten
the freedom of others" (*Shall the Religious Inherit the Earth?* 262). With fundamentalist
Muslims and Christians in view, he goes on to state, "what [Alex] Renton and the UNFPA
[United Nations Population Fund] report deliberately fail to mention are the taboos of immigration and religious fertility. Without (largely religious) immigration and the impact of
religious fertility, the American population would be closer to 300 million in 2050 instead
of its projected 400-500 million. Western Europe's population would be falling instead of
soaring. . . . Seculars and moderates can encourage the fastest-growing fundamentalists to
integrate, pointing out that high fertility is a political act which, for the sake of harmony,
should be moderated. All the same, we must be prepared for the possibility that religious
demography cannot be killed with kindness" (264). The implication is that political coer-
cion will be necessary, although Kaufmann — who describes himself as a libertarian who
hopes for a world freed from religious superstition and who rejects such things as "free
will and the Self" (267) — avoids drawing this conclusion.

and multiply, and fill the earth and subdue it; and have dominion over the fish of the sea and over the birds of the air and over every living thing that moves upon the earth'" (Gen 1:28).[49] Finally and most important, the third blessing involves the completion of all things: "So God blessed the seventh day and hallowed it, because on it God rested from all his work which he had done in creation" (Gen 2:3).

Is there a relationship of these three blessings to each other? John Walton and others have suggested that "we should think of Genesis 1 in relation to a cosmic temple."[50] In Genesis 1:1–2:4, Walton observes, we find "a seven-day inauguration of the cosmic temple, setting up its functions for the benefit of humanity, with God dwelling in relationship with his creatures."[51] If this is so, then the three blessings express, not merely God's approval of procreation, but also the goal of human existence, namely, to share in God's Sabbath. The second blessing (of humans) is intimately related not only to the first blessing (of living creatures), but also most fundamentally to the third (of the Sabbath). Human life is at its fullness in giving temple-praise to God, thereby lifting up all creation into worship of the Creator. R. R. Reno rightly remarks, "The created order is organized so as to prepare for the ascending logic of fellowship with God."[52] Similarly, Abraham Joshua Heschel comments, "The Sabbath is not for the sake of the weekdays; the weekdays are for the sake of the Sabbath. It is not an interlude but the climax of living."[53]

---

49. Bill Arnold comments that "God's blessing of all living creatures [Gen 1:22] here anticipates his blessing of humankind in v. 28, and with similar effect. In both cases the divine blessing is articulated as a command to 'be fruitful and multiply,' and fill those reaches of the universe intended for them. Indeed, the blessing to procreate distinguishes 'living creatures,' animals and humans alike, from sun, moon, stars and other parts of the universe. The capacity to reproduce is the fundamental definition of what it means to be a 'living creature.' The command 'be fruitful and multiply' is a verbal play *(pĕrû ûrĕbû),* which may be intended to bring to mind the nominal hendiadys 'formless void' of v. 2 *(tōhû wābōhû).* In this case, the living creatures of God's creation are hereby empowered to perpetuate God's life-giving creativity by bringing still more life into the world, by filling up and inhabiting that which was previously empty and uninhabitable" (Arnold, *Genesis,* 43).

50. John H. Walton, *The Lost World of Genesis One: Ancient Cosmology and the Origins Debate* (Downers Grove, IL: IVP Academic, 2009), 87.

51. Walton, *The Lost World of Genesis One,* 163. See also Arnold, *Genesis,* 50-51; Bernhard W. Anderson, *Creation versus Chaos: The Reinterpretation of Mythical Symbolism in the Bible* (Philadelphia: Fortress Press, 1987).

52. Reno, *Genesis,* 56.

53. Abraham Joshua Heschel, *The Sabbath: Its Meaning for Modern Man* (New York: Farrar, Straus & Giroux, 1951), 14.

If sharing in God's Sabbath is the purpose of human existence, what does this purpose mean for being fruitful and multiplying? Most important, the people that come to be in the process of human multiplication have an everlasting vocation. Thus, Paul remarks that we were created so as not only to be the "image of God" (Gen 1:27) but "to be conformed to the image of his Son, in order that he might be the first-born among many brethren" (Rom 8:29). The resurrection of Jesus shows that people are called to fellowship with God not only here and now, but also for eternity. As Paul states, "Though our outer nature is wasting away, our inner nature is being renewed every day. For this slight momentary affliction is preparing for us an eternal weight of glory beyond all comparison, because we look not to the things that are seen but to the things that are unseen" (2 Cor 4:16-18).

Do such appeals to life beyond the grave involve, for Paul, a lack of care about the earth's ecosystem? On the contrary, Paul appreciates the unity of the whole cosmos. He observes in Romans 8:21 that "the creation itself will be set free from its bondage to decay and obtain the glorious liberty of the children of God," and he is quite sure that we and the whole creation are united in our purposeful striving toward God. At the same time, however, the whole creation strives toward an interpersonal communion, a "royal priesthood, a holy nation, God's own people" (1 Pet 2:9). This is the purpose of creation, in the plan that God made "before the foundation of the world," "a plan for the fulness of time, to unite all things in him [Jesus Christ]" (Eph 1:4, 10).[54] It is this purpose — the blessing of eternal sharing in the life of the Trinity (the Sabbath blessing) — that makes human life so extraordinarily meaningful and valuable.

Does this mean, then, that humans must have all the children that we can physically have, so as to give as many people as possible the opportu-

---

54. For reflection on this theme in relation to ecology, see Richard John Neuhaus, "Christ and Creation's Longing," in *Environmental Ethics and Christian Humanism*, 128-37. Neuhaus remarks, "The creation has, in Christ, been incorporated into the very Godhead. . . . Citing, and affirming, the wisdom of the Athenians, St. Paul declares, 'In him we live and move and have our being' (Acts 17:28). And what is true of us human beings is true of all that is, the macrocosmic and microcosmic, the galaxies beyond numbering and the subatomic particles beyond discernment. In creation and redemption, God's covenantal faithfulness holds all that is, was, and ever will be to himself. In the dynamic of creation, even the millions of species that have disappeared are not finally lost. This, I believe, is the sensibility that is consonant with Jesus' words about every hair being counted and every fallen sparrow taken into Divine account. It is in this context, a context decisively shaped by God's redemptive purposes in Christ, that we can join with St. Francis of Assisi in hymns of familial and filial piety toward nature" (135).

nity of eternal life with God?[55] On the contrary, the commandment that Jesus gives us is not to have all the children that we can possibly have but, rather, to "love one another as I have loved you" (John 15:12). Not all will be called to married life. The bearing of children is neither the "pearl of great price" (Matt 13:46) nor the "new commandment" (John 13:34). Jesus tells a parable about a wedding banquet — an image of the eschatological consummation — and, among those invited to the banquet, one refuses to come on the grounds that he has "married a wife, and therefore cannot come" (Luke 14:20). This excuse is not accepted as a good one by the Lord of the banquet. Furthermore, Jesus approves of renouncing marriage for the sake of bearing witness to the kingdom that he has inaugurated: "There are eunuchs who have made themselves eunuchs for the kingdom of heaven" (Matt 19:12). Paul, too, argues that the ability to focus upon the Lord is hampered by marriage and children, good though the latter are. Paul states, "He who marries his betrothed does well; and he who refrains from marriage will do better" (1 Cor 7:38).

Nonetheless, far from rejecting marriage or children, Jesus affirms both quite strongly. With regard to marriage, he explains to the Pharisees who seek to test him by questioning him on the lawfulness of divorce for any cause: "Have you not heard that he who made them from the beginning made them male and female, and said, 'For this reason a man shall leave his father and mother and be joined to his wife, and the two shall become one'? So they are no longer two but one" (Matt 19:4-6). In the same context, Jesus underlines the importance of children. The disciples had sought to keep people from bringing their children to Jesus for his blessing. Jesus rebukes his disciples and commands, "Let the children come to me, and do not hinder them; for to such belongs the kingdom of heaven" (Matt 19:14). Elsewhere Jesus tells his disciples that they must become like children in order to enter the kingdom of heaven. Calling a child to himself, he instructs his disciples, "Whoever receives one such child in my name receives me" (Matt 18:5). When we welcome "children" (whether literal

---

55. This view is held by the groups that Kathryn Joyce chronicles in her *Quiverfull: Inside the Christian Patriarchy Movement* (Boston: Beacon Press, 2009). See Rick Hess and Jan Hess, *A Full Quiver: Family Planning and the Lordship of Christ* (Brentwood, TN: Wolgemuth & Hyatt, 1990); Charles Provan, *The Bible and Birth Control* (Monongahela, PA: Zimmer Printing, 1989). For more recent works in this direction, see Craig Houghton, *Family UNplanning: A Guide for Christian Couples Seeking God's Truth on Having Children* (Longwood, FL: Xulon Press, 2006); Nancy Campbell, *Be Fruitful and Multiply: What the Bible Says about Having Children* (San Antonio, TX: Vision Forum, 2003).

children or disciples of Christ) in Christ's name, we welcome unique new humans whom Christ has called to become adopted sons and daughters of God in the eternal kingdom.

How, then, should Christians balance these two aspects: Jesus' affirmation of the choice not to marry and have children, on the one hand, and, on the other, Jesus' affirmation of the importance of welcoming children? Should we envision, as McKibben does, a world in which some become eunuchs for the kingdom of heaven, and others (married couples) become somewhat like eunuchs — via contraception, sterilization, and perhaps even direct abortion (McKibben leaves this point ambiguous) — for the planet's long-term sustainability?

Here we can note that Jesus, in his discussion of "eunuchs" in Matthew 19:12, does not offer this option for married couples, as opposed to single persons who wish to dedicate their lives to him. Indeed, the nature of marriage itself excludes, morally speaking, the possibility of deliberately sterilizing the act of marital intercourse.[56] It is not possible here for me to give a full account of the reasons why contraception distorts the meaning of sexual intercourse, but the fundamental point is that contraception turns it inward upon lesser goods rather than allowing it to be what God created it to be, namely, the embodied enactment of the couple's spiritual gift of self in a manner that opens the couple to welcoming a new human life, rather than focusing their love solely on each other.[57] McKibben recognizes the connection of contraception with the danger of selfishness, but he underestimates the way in which the bodily constitution of marital intercourse matters spiritually.

Yet, in McKibben's view, as we saw, the loss of contraception — when combined with the better healthcare that has resulted in such gains in life

56. By contrast, Weisman rejoices in the power of soap operas to popularize contraception. As he notes, the 1970s Mexican soap opera "*Acompáñame* is widely credited for the 34 percent drop in Mexico's fertility rate during the decade the series aired. [Miguel] Sabido's method inspired the work of the Population Media Center in Burlington, Vermont, which today produces soap operas that promote family planning in twenty-two languages: electronic analogs of the family-planning street theater I witnessed in Pakistan" (Weisman, *Countdown*, 432).

57. For a fuller account, see Alexander Pruss, *One Body: An Essay in Christian Sexual Ethics* (Notre Dame, IN: University of Notre Dame Press, 2013); Jaroslaw Kupczak, OP, *Gift and Communion: John Paul II's Theology of the Body*, trans. Agata Rottkamp, Justyna Pawlak, and Orest Pawlak (Washington, DC: Catholic University of America Press, 2014). See also the Pontifical Council for Justice and Peace's *Compendium of the Social Doctrine of the Church* (Vatican City: Libreria Editrice Vaticana, 2004), §§217-21, 230-34, 237.

expectancy — would produce a catastrophic ecological event as population quickly moved to more than ten billion. Even if the Church cannot promote contraception, should the Church therefore urge believers in Christ not to "be fruitful and multiply," at least for a generation or two, so as to keep the earth going longer and to respect the place of other species? Given that Christians surely "have an obligation to take future generations into account" by caring for the earth, should the Church today generally promote increased use of natural family planning (to avoid conception) and a new emphasis upon adopting unwanted children rather than begetting new children?[58]

In this regard, Thomas Aquinas offers some helpful principles. He remarks that God's command "be fruitful and multiply, and fill the earth" should be obeyed not blindly but with attention to "the good of the species."[59] He thus finds that "the precept of procreation regards the whole multitude of men, which needs not only to multiply in body, but also to advance spiritually." He does not hold that Christians should have as many

58. The quotation is from Thomas Derr, "Environmental Ethics and Christian Humanism," 88. Derr observes: "It is common sense to say that if we engage in wasteful and destructive behavior, but escape the consequences of our actions by passing them off on future generations, we have done something morally wrong. We know we would be guilty, even if we were not alive to face our victims. Nor can we hide behind ignorance of the needs of coming centuries. Biological similarity assures their comparable need for air, food, water, space, and shelter; and we know enough ecology to admit that what we do now will affect our descendants' ability to satisfy those needs. Thus even if we do not know the details, we do know we have an obligation to take future generations into account. . . . Biblical theology appeals explicitly to this general insight with its assumption of intergenerational solidarity, the obligation to pass on to subsequent generations the divine blessing given 'to [our] descendants forever.' Christians appeal to it also in the doctrine of the communion of saints, where all the faithful, living, departed, and yet to come, are bound together in Christ, virtually present to each other in living relationship. Christian love is not limited to the near and familiar, but is given to all the household of God, to all people in all time" (88). Derr rightly adds that, although "our policies must keep the far future in mind," nonetheless "in cases of genuine conflict between present and future peoples I would prefer the present, whose needs we know, to the future with its uncertainties" (88-89). Derr is not here speaking about how many children the human race should optimally beget in this generation. He goes on to warn strongly against programs of population control that target poor countries, holding (without, however, criticizing contraception per se) that "a lower birth rate depends a good deal on a *prior* improvement in socio-economic conditions. Otherwise women will have more children because they want them, because they need them for security, because they have to have many to make sure that some will live past infancy" (91-92).

59. *Summa theologiae* (hereafter *STh*) II-II, q. 152, art. 2, obj. 1.

children as possible so as to build up the kingdom of God. Instead, he considers that "sufficient provision is made for the human multitude, if some betake themselves to carnal procreation, while others abstaining from this betake themselves to the contemplation of divine things, for the beauty and welfare of the whole human race."[60] He thinks of this as a division of labor for the common good, as in an army some are sentries and others fight. As important as bearing and raising children is, "virginity that is consecrated to God is preferable."[61] Although he certainly does not foresee the ecological crisis that McKibben argues is now taking hold, Aquinas's emphasis on the common good seems to tell in the direction of less marriage and many fewer children among Christians today.

Yet, Aquinas also thinks of God's perfect goodness as self-diffusive, and the purpose of human life is to imitate God's goodness in Christ Jesus. Aquinas states that "what belongs to the essence of goodness befits God. But it belongs to the essence of goodness to communicate itself to others."[62] God communicates himself to us supremely by becoming incarnate as one of us, in the womb of Mary. We, too, seek to share our goodness, the goodness of human life. Thus we have a natural inclination toward the procreation and raising of children, and, far from bemoaning human multiplication per se, we should love all humans as created to be members of Christ's mystical body. The Holy Spirit "communicates the goods of one member to another," and so we all benefit from each expansion of the circle of interpersonal communion.[63] Aquinas comments that "what we ought to love in our neighbor is that he may be in God," since this is the greatest good, and the good for which humans are made.[64]

Regarding the diversity of creation, Aquinas recognizes that "the multitude and distinction of things is from God" and is good. As he puts it, "The divine wisdom is the cause of the distinction of things for the sake of the perfection of the universe," since "the universe would not be perfect if only one grade of goodness were found in things." He remarks further that God "brought things into being in order that his goodness might be communicated to creatures and be represented by them; and because his goodness could not be adequately represented by one creature alone, he produced

---

60. *STh* II-II, q. 152, art. 2, ad 1.
61. *STh* II-II, q. 152, art. 4, ad 3.
62. *STh* III, q. 1, art. 1.
63. *STh* III, q. 68, art. 9, ad 2.
64. *STh* II-II, q. 25, art. 1. For discussion, see my *The Betrayal of Charity: The Sins That Sabotage Divine Love* (Waco, TX: Baylor University Press, 2011).

many and diverse creatures."[65] Aquinas finds a "trace" of the Trinity in all creatures, and an "image" of the Trinity in rational creatures. The final perfection of all things will be a glorious reflection of the divine goodness.[66] In this final perfection — the "kingdom of God," or the "new creation" — humans will have a special place, even though certainly not the sole place. Aquinas states that "of all creatures the rational creature is chiefly ordained for the good of the universe," since the blessed attain to the highest possible participation in God's happiness.[67] The universe is created for the saints, not in the sense that the universe is a discardable shell, but in the sense that the new creation, the goal for which God makes all things, will have as its pinnacle the unfathomable intimacy of glorified humans and angels with God in Christ and the Holy Spirit.

Simply as created, then, humans participate in the ontological goodness of God: it is good to be. Wondrously, God also calls humans to share in his own happiness, to be God's friends and to know him as he knows us. This extraordinary union with God is the friendship to which we and any children that we have are called. Already, "parents love their children as being part of themselves."[68] In charity, we also love our children in light of God's supreme self-diffusion in the incarnation, as "heirs of God and fellow heirs with Christ" (Rom 8:17). The begetting and raising of children involves the self-diffusion of goodness in a way that participates deeply in the divine gifting. For Christians, the begetting and raising of children displays, not

---

65. *STh* I, q. 47, art. 1, 2. In her *Ask the Beasts,* Elizabeth Johnson comments that "if the diversity of creatures is meant to show forth the goodness of God which cannot be well represented by one creature alone, as Aquinas saw, then extinction of species is rapidly erasing testimony to divine goodness in the world now and for the foreseeable future" (*Ask the Beasts,* 255). Given that almost all species that have ever existed have long been extinct, and also given the still vast numbers of species that exist today, I think that ample testimony to the divine goodness remains present. Yet it is evident that the extinction of a species, let alone many species, is not something that humans would wish to bring about. Edward O. Wilson predicts, "If global changes caused by HIPPO (Habitat destruction, Invasive species, Pollution, Overpopulation, and Overharvesting, in that order of importance) are not abated, half the species of plants and animals could be extinct or at least among the 'living dead' — about to become extinct — by the end of the century" (*The Social Conquest of Earth,* 294).

66. See *STh* I, q. 44, art. 4. For an excellent discussion of Aquinas's view, see Oliva Blanchette, *The Perfection of the Universe according to Aquinas: A Teleological Cosmology* (University Park: Penn State University Press, 1992). See also chapter 7 of my *Jesus and the Demise of Death: Resurrection, the Afterlife, and the Fate of the Christian* (Waco, TX: Baylor University Press, 2012).

67. *STh* I, q. 23, art. 7.

68. *STh* II-II, q. 26, art. 9.

only a natural desire to share the good of human life, but also the desire for extending the fellowship of God with humanity in the mystical body of Christ. Since the Church is ignorant of the time of the second coming and the final judgment,[69] we cannot put off doing good today solely because the presence of fewer people might allow the earth to sustain life for more generations than otherwise would have been the case.

The charitable married person, then, will be loath not to share the gift of existence. Yet, for the sake of the common good (including the common good of the ecosystem of the earth), a married couple may rightly abstain from procreation by abstaining from marital intercourse during fertile times. The married couple must intend to try to have a child whenever it becomes prudently possible. Given the greatness of the potential good involved — a child of God — there must be an important good that abstinence aims to achieve. The blessing of life is the greatest blessing that a married couple can share, and so having children is the charitable norm.

Concluding Reflections:
Should the Church Advocate Small Families?

Where fallen humans are, there will be exploitation, violence, and disease, as well as the joy of interpersonal communion. Human cities and trade will be marked by both the positive and the negative aspects of the human condition, but the negative aspects can easily gain the upper hand. Thus, the book of Revelation condemns "Babylon the great" (Rev 18:2), representing all human empires with their pride, idolatry, and violence. The kings and tradesmen, the wealthy and powerful of the earth, weep and wail at the destruction of Babylon, whereas the blessed rejoice that its idolatrous and violent power has been removed.[70] Is it better, then, to do without many people?

The book of Revelation does not answer this question, but it does seem significant that the kingdom of God takes the form of a city.[71] The Seer re-

---

69. See *STh* III, q. 10, art. 2, ad 1.

70. For discussion from an ecological perspective, see Davis, *Biblical Prophecy*, 115-19, 127-39. Davis points out that "the Romans, like the Greeks before them, vigorously and radically transformed the Mediterranean landscape. . . . They devoured forests for fuel, agriculture, shipbuilding, and other construction, including siege works" (131).

71. Richard Bauckham has demonstrated the ecological significance of the symbolism of the four living creatures of Rev 4; see Bauckham, *Living with Other Creatures*, ch. 8.

ports that "I saw a new heaven and a new earth; for the first heaven and the first earth had passed away, and the sea was no more. And I saw the holy city, the new Jerusalem, coming down out of heaven from God, prepared as a bride adorned for her husband" (Rev 21:1-2). This city is represented as being large and wealthy. Into this city will stream "the glory and the honor of the nations" (Rev 21:26). Far from being poorly populated, the city will glory in a vast population. In a vision of the heavenly liturgy, the Seer finds angels to the number of "myriads of myriads and thousands of thousands" (Rev 5:11), and the number of redeemed humans is symbolic of perfect plenitude: "a hundred and forty-four thousand" (Rev 7:4). Indeed, the number of humans in the new Jerusalem is literally innumerable. The Seer states, "After this I looked, and behold, a great multitude which no man could number, from every nation, from all tribes and peoples and tongues, standing before the throne and before the Lamb, clothed in white robes, with palm branches in their hands" (Rev 7:9). This innumerable multitude sings the praises of God and the Lamb, Jesus Christ. Overcrowding is not going to be a problem, although vast numbers will be there, thanks to God's grace working through the generations of humans who have obeyed God's command to "be fruitful and multiply, and fill the earth."

Similarly, the letter to the Hebrews says that we are "strangers and exiles on the earth," and our homeland is "a better country, that is, a heavenly one" (Heb 11:13, 16). God is preparing "a city" for us (Heb 11:16). At the same time, however, we are called to be good stewards of the earth, since all creation is linked together. Indeed, Genesis itself shows that the earth's ecosystem can rise up against those who perpetrate violence upon the land; this is surely one of the meanings of the flood story. Sodom and Gomorrah become a wasteland, and drought and famine afflict the peoples of Egypt and Israel. Yet, as we saw, the living God of Israel repeatedly insists upon, and commands, the goodness of human multiplication, which expands the circle of human interpersonal communion.

Once Jesus Christ has inaugurated the kingdom of God, he introduces new energies of charity into the world through the Spirit-filled proclamation of the gospel. In self-giving service to others, Christians seek to imitate our crucified Lord, who, "though he was in the form of God, did not count equality with God a thing to be grasped, but emptied himself, taking the form of a servant" (Phil 2:6-7). The Holy Spirit's configuration of humans to the image of Jesus' self-giving love is the task of kingdom of God, and this task goes on in the world not least through the sacrament of the Eucharist. As we have seen, in the Church generous self-giving must be the norm, including with regard to the welcoming of children. Whenever possible, Christians need to seek solutions that expand the circle of human interpersonal communion rather than narrowing this circle.[72]

According to Catholic social teaching, although governments must not interfere in a married couple's decision-making with respect to family size, nonetheless, "Granted that rapid population growth may at times impede the development process, governments have rights and duties, within the limits of their own competence, to try to ameliorate the population problem."[73] In this regard, James McHugh takes heart from the United Nations'

72. For a recent book addressed to an evangelical popular readership, suggesting that man-made climate change is real, even though the human costs of various proposed solutions are not yet clear, see Jonathan Merritt, *Green like God: Unlocking the Divine Plan for Our Planet* (New York: FaithWords, 2010). Merritt approvingly cites the actor Sidney Poitier's observation that, whereas in previous generations the environment "was so massive, so pure, and so thunderously healthy that we had no need to worry for generations upon generations whether it would be able to sustain itself on our behalf. In its infinite beauty, it has done that, but now things are different. We are 6.4 or 6.5 billion human beings on the planet. The water supply is shortening. The amount of topsoil to produce food is dwindling. The remaining clean, fresh, unpolluted air for breathing and for nurturing all living things is being poisoned by substances incompatible to its health" (Poitier, *Life beyond Measure: Letters to My Great-Granddaughter* [San Francisco: HarperOne, 2008], page number not given, cited in Merritt, *Green like God,* 138). By contrast, another evangelical author argues that "Christians above all should resist the green agenda which puts six billion people in second place to some narrow, idealised concept of 'the environment'" (Ian Hore-Lacy, *Responsible Dominion: A Christian Approach to Sustainable Development* [Vancouver: Regent College Publishing, 2006], 8). At the same time, Hore-Lacy recognizes that "there is a clear stream of Western culture which is detached from any Christian sensitivity or constraints and which has approached the natural world exploitively, carelessly and unconscionably and which has consequently caused much environmental damage and waste of resources" (13).

73. James T. McHugh, "A Catholic Perspective on Population," in *The Challenge of Global Stewardship: Roman Catholic Responses,* ed. Maura A. Ryan and Todd David Whitmore (Notre Dame, IN: University of Notre Dame Press, 1997), 88. See Pope Paul VI, *Populorum progressio* (Boston: St. Paul's Books & Media, 1967), §37: "It is true that too frequently an accelerated demographic increase adds its own difficulties to the problems of development: the size of the population increases more rapidly than available resources, and things are found to have reached apparently an impasse. From that moment the temptation is great to check the demographic increase by means of radical measures. It is certain that public authorities can intervene, within the limit of their competence, by favouring the availability of appropriate information and by adopting suitable measures, provided that these be in conformity with the moral law and that they respect the rightful freedom of married couples. Where the inalienable right to marriage and procreation is lacking, human dignity has ceased to exist. Finally, it is for the parents to decide, with full knowledge of the matter, on the number of their children, taking into account their responsibilities towards God, them-

demographic estimate that world population will likely not go much beyond ten billion — although admittedly this figure depends upon continued growth in the use of birth control.[74] For McHugh, reflecting the position of the Church's magisterial teaching on this topic, the real problem is not population but development. Namely, rich countries' consumption of resources results in environmental devastation in poor countries because of developmental imbalances.[75]

By contrast, John Schwarz has argued that the Catholic Church errs when it tries to sideline or ignore the role of population in the ecological crisis. Schwarz states, "Excessive population as well as excessive consumption and abuse of resources damages the environment."[76] Because of his concern

---

selves, the children they have already brought into the world, and the community to which they belong. In all this they must follow the demands of their own conscience enlightened by God's law authentically interpreted, and sustained by confidence in Him."

74. For diverse sociological responses to the current striking decline in fertility in developed countries, see Ben Wattenberg, *Fewer: How the New Demography of Depopulation Will Shape Our Future* (Chicago: Ivan R. Dee, 2004); Elizabeth L. Krause, *A Crisis of Births: Population Politics and Family-Making in Italy* (Belmont, CA: Wadsworth/Thomson Learning, 2005); and Susan Greenhalgh, ed., *Situating Fertility: Anthropology and Demographic Inquiry* (Cambridge: Cambridge University Press, 1995).

75. See also Maura A. Ryan, "Introduction," in *The Challenge of Global Stewardship*, 1-16. Ryan argues that something is deeply wrong with our current choices, which can be seen in what she calls the "deepening poverty for many of the world's people, depletion of natural resources, and persistent conflict around the world. We need not agree on the question of contraception to agree that 'something must be done'" (8).

76. John C. Schwarz, *Global Population from a Catholic Perspective* (Mystic, CT: Twenty-Third Publications, 1998), 173. For this position, see also Amartya Sen, "Population: Delusion and Reality," in *The Nine Lives of Population Control*, ed. Michael Cromartie (Grand Rapids: Eerdmans, 1995), 101-27. Contemporary Catholic theologians writing on ecology tend to avoid the issue of population, while circling around it nervously because of questions about the status of nonhuman species, land use, and so forth. See, for example, Christopher P. Vogt, "Catholic Social Teaching and Creation," in *Green Discipleship*, 220-40; in the same volume, Marcus Mescher, "Neighbor to Nature," 200-216; Daniel K. Finn, "Theology and Sustainable Economics," in *God, Creation, and Climate Change: A Catholic Response to the Environmental Crisis*, ed. Richard W. Miller (Maryknoll, NY: Orbis Books, 2010), 95-111, especially 109. For an exception, see Elizabeth Johnson's *Ask the Beasts*, which confronts "the problematic impact of population growth on the world of other species" and affirms population control, although without explicitly coming out in favor of contraception: "While the question of *how* to control population growth does indeed divide interested parties at the global and national level, it is important to note that in recent decades the Roman Catholic Church has endorsed the basic idea that it is legitimate to limit human births" (244). Citing Pope John Paul II's general audience of September 5, 1984, Johnson states, "If the good of future children, the material conditions of the times, and the interests of society are factors

for the way in which increasing population damages the environment, he rejects the Church's teaching against birth control.[77] He gives the example of China's population of 1.2 billion; surely without birth control the population growth in China would destroy the ecosystem (both China's and the world's) even more rapidly than the already over-high population is presently doing. Schwarz cites approvingly John Haught's argument that a truly pro-life ethic today "cannot turn away from the global population problem and the additional pressures placed on the earth's systems by the sheer force of human numbers."[78] This comment fits with an urgent warning issued in 2012 by

in weighing the ethical rightness of reproductive activity [as John Paul II's general audience address suggests], then the good of the ecological world that sustains human society must also be relevant" (244-45). Johnson warns of the unsustainable environmental destruction (especially species extinction) caused by current human population levels and "rapacious habits" (253; see also 245-59). She concludes that "Christians personally and as church are called by the power of the Spirit to enter into solidarity with suffering creation and exercise responsibility for a new project of ecojustice. . . . The long-term goal is a socially just and environmentally sustainable society in which the needs of all people are met and diverse species can prosper, onward to an evolutionary future that will still surprise" (284-86). For an evangelical work that bemoans "the ecological realities caused by too many people, too many cars, the proliferation of invasive (nonnative) species and the global effects of climate change," see Edward R. Brown, *Our Father's World: Mobilizing the Church to Care for Creation,* 2nd ed. (Downers Grove, IL: InterVarsity Press, 2008), 97.

77. Schwarz does not discuss global warming, no doubt because he was not yet aware of it at the time of writing. For recent Catholic and Protestant theological responses to global warming, see Richard W. Miller, "Global Climate Disruption and Social Justice: The State of the Problem," in *God, Creation, and Climate Change,* 1-34. Miller argues that the world is facing an "unimaginable tragedy" and that "people need to start demonstrating en masse in the streets all across the globe, especially in the United States" ("Global Climate Disruption and Social Justice," 22, 25). Miller focuses upon cutting carbon emissions rapidly via renewable energy sources. He does not speak about trying to solve global warming by reducing population; rather, he warns that global warming itself will produce a huge loss of population: "While the planet's population is projected to reach 9 billion by 2050, Hans Joachim Schellenhuber, one of the leading climate scientists in the world, carefully argued at a major international climate conference that, if global temperatures increase from pre-industrial temperatures by five degrees Celsius (= nine degrees Fahrenheit), which is where we are headed on our current path, the planet could probably support only about 1 billion people" (18).

78. John Haught, *Science and Religion* (Mahwah, NJ: Paulist Press, 1995), 200, cited in Schwarz, *Global Population from a Catholic Perspective,* 198. Ian Hore-Lacy makes the same point but with a greater recognition of human ability to overcome apparent limits; see Hore-Lacy, *Responsible Dominion,* 41-42; cf. 84-100. Against Steven Bouma-Prediger's *For the Beauty of the Earth: A Christian Vision for Creation Care* (Grand Rapids: Baker Academic, 2001), which he suggests suffers from romanticism, Hore-Lacy makes clear the

more than one hundred science academies worldwide regarding not only overconsumption but also population growth.[79]

Whereas Schwarz, Haught, McKibben, and most contemporary scientists consider preventing human population from growing much beyond its current level to be a positive good, I think that the unique greatness of each human existence and the value of expanding the human interpersonal communion still make increasing human population to be justifiable today. The risk of my position has been succinctly stated by Alan Weisman in relation to global warming: "Only over time, scientists caution, can we know if mounting weather events add up to a trend that means the climate has entered a phase shift. But if we wait to act until all the numbers are in, we'll have waited too long."[80] Not only global warming, but scarcity of resources, destruction of species and green spaces, and other possible threats follow upon increased population. Why, then, do I propose further waiting? I do so because each new human life that today enters the world is such a treasured addition to the interpersonal communion that God is building up, and because I am hoping that we will find other, less radical ways to adapt. I take heart from the seeming recklessness of the Creator God, who, despite the destruction caused by fallen humans and despite the overpopulation of the land of Israel and its environs, commands his people to be fruitful and multiply. Thus, at present, the generous welcoming of children seems to me to be the path that charitable married couples, with due prudence, should pursue.

I find inspiration in Pope Emeritus Benedict XVI's message for the 2010 World Day of Peace, "If You Want to Cultivate Peace, Protect Creation." In this message, Benedict does not include population among the causes of ecological degradation; in fact, he never mentions population.[81] From one

---

need to understand "the world of agriculture, mining and forestry" as *part of* care for the environment (45).

79. See Weisman, *Countdown*, 404.

80. Weisman, *Countdown*, 422-23.

81. For strong criticism of positions such as this, see Martha Campbell, "Why the Silence on Population?" in *Life on the Brink*, 41-55; in the same volume, Dave Foreman, "The Great Backtrack," 56-71. Foreman is particularly negative. While admitting that "social justice Leftists felt that talk about overpopulation blamed the world's poor for the 'environmental' plight," Foreman blames the Catholic Church and its "gruesome belief that contraception is a sin": "The old men of the Catholic hierarchy swore that those worried about overpopulation were anti-Catholic. Moreover, the church set out 'to disprove that rising population size had anything to do with deterioration of natural or human environments or the ability of poor countries with rapidly growing populations to develop economically.' Unlike [Richard] Nixon, the popes and cardinals have been shortsighted old men, deaf to

perspective, this seems rather simplistic, because surely the more (fallen) humans we have, the more resources will be strained and the more the natural habitats of other species will be supplanted. But Pope Emeritus Benedict's approach makes sense if his goal is to encourage the development of ways of living that will allow for more humans to live and thrive, while at the same time enhancing environmental stewardship. Citing paragraph 36 of Pope John Paul II's *Centesimus annus,* Pope Emeritus Benedict states, "We can no longer do without a real change of outlook which will result in *new life-styles,* 'in which the quest for truth, beauty, goodness and communion with others for the sake of common growth are the factors which determine consumer choices, savings and investments.'"[82] Benedict associates these "new life-styles" with a new "model of development" that has human interpersonal communion at its heart.[83]

In his "Message to Mr. Jacques Diouf, Director General of FAO, on the Occasion of World Food Day 2008," Pope Emeritus Benedict XVI comments upon the theme of the 2008 World Food Day, namely, "World Food Security: The Challenges of Climate Change and Bioenergy."[84] Surely the topic of

---

the whimpering of millions of hungry babies headed for slow deaths or crippled lives" ("The Great Backtrack," 61, 63).

82. Pope Benedict XVI, "If You Want to Cultivate Peace, Protect Creation: Message for the 2010 World Day of Peace," in *Green Discipleship,* 69. Quite rightly, Vogt states: "Catholic social teaching does not provide the most radical vision of green discipleship. When placed on a spectrum alongside other approaches to environmental ethics, Catholic social teaching might appear to some to be timid. However, if one places the understanding of authentic human development found in Catholic social teaching alongside the typical American lifestyle of superabundance, Catholic social teaching looks challenging or even radical. By providing a clear explanation for why people should aim for lives of simplicity and strive to be in solidarity with one another and the rest of creation, Catholic social teaching can contribute substantially to contemporary conversations about ecological ethics" (Vogt, "Catholic Social Teaching and Creation," 239-40).

83. Pope Benedict XVI, "If You Want to Cultivate Peace, Protect Creation," 63. In his advocacy for new lifestyles, I do not think that Pope Benedict means entirely abandoning agricultural and industrial technologies. As Hore-Lacy points out, "It is agriculture, at increasing intensity and productivity, which enables six billion to be fed" (Hore-Lacy, *Responsible Dominion,* 48), and he gives particular credit to crop breeding and genetic modification, mechanization, and fertilizers. I assume that forestry and mining, along with power plants (including, where appropriate, nuclear ones), industry, "aquaculture," and sewage plants (increasingly for the recycling of water and nutrients) will have some role in these new lifestyles.

84. See George Wuerthner's observation that, although modern agriculture feeds more than seven billion people, in the process agriculture (including livestock production, which Wuerthner singles out for particular blame) "is the largest single contributor to many

population must arise here, and indeed it does. He grants that today "climate change contributes to endangering the survival of millions of men, women, and children, forced to leave their country in search of food."[85] In this context, he engages the topic of population. He notes that increasing population is often blamed for the poverty of poor countries, with the result that "there are international campaigns afoot to reduce birthrates." With considerable understatement, since he is speaking of contraception, he remarks that these campaigns "sometimes" use "methods that respect neither the dignity of the woman, nor the right of parents to choose responsibly how many children to have; graver still, these methods often fail to respect even the right to life." Since 1981, he points out, population has increased, yet the rate of "absolute poverty" has been cut in half.[86] Population size has also been correlated

environmental ills, including soil erosion, deforestation, species' extirpations and range contractions, and ground and surface water pollution. It is also a major contributor to the greenhouse gases responsible for global climate change" (Wuerthner, "Population, Fossil Fuels, and Agriculture," in *Life on the Brink*, 124).

85. Pope Benedict XVI, excerpt from "Message to Mr. Jacques Diouf, Director General of FAO, on the Occasion of World Food Day 2008," in Pope Benedict XVI, *The Garden of God: Toward a Human Ecology,* ed. Maria Milvia Morciano (Washington, DC: Catholic University of America Press, 2014), 157-58. The "FAO" is the UN Food and Agriculture Organization. For the prediction of a "swelling flow of environmental refugees" because of global warming (108), see Lester Brown, "Environmental Refugees: The Rising Tide," 108-22. See also Brown, *World on the Edge: How to Prevent Environmental and Economic Collapse* (New York: W. W. Norton, 2011); Brown, *Outgrowing the Earth: The Food Security Challenge in the Age of Falling Water Tables and Rising Temperatures* (New York: W. W. Norton, 2004); Environmental Justice Foundation, *No Place like Home: Where Next for Climate Refugees?* (London: Environmental Justice Foundation, 2009). It is unclear that much such migration has actually occurred.

86. Pope Benedict XVI, "Message to Mr. Jacques Diouf," 162-63. Pope Benedict goes on to say, against the mere rejection of capitalism, that "it cannot be denied that policies which place too much emphasis on assistance underlie many of the failures in providing aid to poor countries. Investing in the formation of people and developing a specific and well-integrated culture of enterprise would seem at present to be the right approach in the medium and long term. If economic activities require a favorable context in order to develop, this must not distract attention from the need to generate revenue. While it has been rightly emphasized that increasing per capita income cannot be the ultimate goal of political and economic activity, it is still an important means of attaining the objective of the fight against hunger and absolute poverty. Hence, the illusion that a policy of mere redistribution of existing wealth can definitively resolve the problem must be set aside. In a modern economy, the value of assets is utterly dependent on the capacity to generate revenue in the present and the future. Wealth creation therefore becomes an inescapable duty, which must be kept in mind if the fight against material poverty is to be effective in the long term" (169-70).

with economic development. He observes that, "since the end of the Second World War, the world's population has grown by four billion, largely because of certain countries that have recently emerged on the international scene as new economic powers, and have experienced rapid development specifically because of the large number of their inhabitants." Among developed countries, furthermore, those that have higher birthrates have greater economic development. He is persuaded, in other words, that efforts to reduce population should instead focus upon cultivating "a true 'human ecology.'"[87]

In sum, while I think that the threats posed by population growth are real, I share Pope Emeritus Benedict's sense that the population-control movement needs to attend further to the irreplaceable good that each and every new human life adds to God's world.[88] As Pope John Paul II observed some years ago, even in the midst of our present ecological crisis — with its corresponding need for "ecological conversion" — we should not fall uncritically into a "panic deriving from the studies of ecologists and futurologists on population growth," since these studies may be insufficiently attuned to the fact "that human life . . . is always a splendid gift of God's goodness."[89]

87. Pope Benedict XVI, "Message to Mr. Jacques Diouf," 162-63. For similar reflection on these themes, see Pope Benedict XVI, *Caritas in veritate* (Vatican City: Libreria Editrice Vaticana, 2009), §44; *Compendium of the Social Doctrine of the Church*, §483. See also, on *Caritas in veritate*, J. Brian Benestad, "Three Themes in Pope Benedict XVI's *Caritas in Veritate*," *Nova et Vetera* 8 (2010): 723-44; Douglas Farrow, "Baking Bricks for Babel?" *Nova et Vetera* 8 (2010): 745-62; Stratford Caldecott, *Not as the World Gives: The Way of Creative Justice* (Kettering, OH: Angelico Press, 2014), 60-74, 91-93; and Daniel K. Finn, ed., *The Moral Dynamics of Economic Life: An Extension and Critique of* Caritas in Veritate (Oxford: Oxford University Press, 2013). Pope John Paul II coined the term "human ecology": see *Centesimus annus*, §38, and *Evangelium vitae*, §42 (available at www.vatican.va).

88. Pope Benedict also warns against "the risk humanity runs in the face of a technology seen as a more efficient 'response' than political voluntarism or the patient effort of education in cultivating morals" (excerpt from "Address to Six New Ambassadors Accredited to the Holy See," in *The Garden of God*, 75). Along these lines, Pope Benedict states, "Technology must help nature blossom according to the will of the Creator. Working in this way the researcher and the scientist adhere to the design of God, who willed that man be the summit and steward of creation. Solutions with this as its foundation will protect human life and human vulnerability, as well as the rights of present generations and those to come. And humanity will be able to continue to benefit from the progress that man, with his intelligence, succeeds in achieving" (75). See also another recent compendium of Pope Benedict's environmental statements: Pope Benedict XVI, *The Environment*, ed. Jacquelyn Lindsey (Huntington, IN: Our Sunday Visitor, 2012).

89. See Pope John Paul II, message for the 1990 World Day of Peace, "Peace with God the Creator, Peace with All of Creation," §15, at www.vatican.va; Pope John Paul II, *Familiaris consortio*, §30. Pope John Paul II's message for the 1990 World Day of Peace is

This is not to say that the ecological situation could never reach the point where married couples should try to have no more than one or two children (indeed, as Weisman makes clear, the ecological situation could mean that human procreation unavoidably becomes far rarer in the near future, due to "gender-bending" pollutants).[90] It is simply that I hold that before sacrificing such a great good as the sharing of the gift of human life today, other nonnecessary goods should first be sacrificed.

Put another way, even though the earth today is certainly not lacking in humans, God's command to "be fruitful and multiply, and fill the earth" remains at the heart of the human vocation. Expanding the human communion pertains to the common good for which God has created us. After all, the ultimate goal of God's command is not populating Israel or the world. Rather, the goal is the new Jerusalem, and each new human who comes into the world today enriches, with a uniqueness that can never be replicated by any potential future person, this glorious city that God is bringing about. Indeed, as *Gaudium et spes* states, "True married love and the whole structure of family life which results from it is directed to disposing the spouses

---

quite similar to Pope Benedict XVI's message for the 2010 World Day of Peace, in both tone and content. For a critique of Pope John Paul II's "Peace with God the Creator, Peace with All of Creation," as well as his moral encyclicals (including *Sollicitudo rei socialis, Veritatis splendor,* and *Evangelium vitae*), see Northcott, *The Environment and Christian Ethics,* 134-37. Northcott rejects John Paul II's "humanocentrism," especially as it plays out in John Paul II's condemnation of contraception, which "has tremendous implications for human population growth, especially in majority Catholic countries in the Third World" (135-36). In his most recent monograph, however, Northcott leaves out any reference to population control and instead focuses his criticisms upon "economic neoliberalism" (*A Political Theology of Climate Change,* 238). He emphasizes that local practices such as "using less energy, using wherever possible energy that is not derived from fossil fuels, and living more lightly on the earth by eating less meat, consuming less 'stuff,' flying and driving less, and turning down the heating and air conditioning, particularly when they are powered by fossil fuels" (263), are not enough. Instead, what is required is "more concerted global action to address the continued extraction of fossil fuels and the corporate media marketing of fossil fuel-intensive goods and lifestyles" (264). See also Ecumenical Patriarch Bartholomew's "Encyclical of His All-Holiness for the Church New Year," September 1, 2012.

90. Caldecott observes about Pope Benedict XVI: "Like his predecessor he was at loggerheads with environmentalists who see human populations as a plague upon the planet. . . . There are many possible ways to reduce a population, ranging from genocide to migration, and to reduce the number of births per household, from natural family planning to abortion. The Church teaches 'responsible parenthood,' encouraging parents to judge carefully how many children they might reasonably seek to have in their particular circumstances, only using morally licit methods, such as abstaining from sexual relations at times when conception is likely" (Caldecott, *Not as the World Gives,* 82).

to cooperate valiantly with the love of the Creator and Saviour, who through them will increase and enrich his family from day to day."[91] It is this goal — and certainly not Edward O. Wilson's goal of turning "earth, by the twenty-second century . . . into a permanent paradise for human beings, or at least the strong beginnings of one" — that we should pursue.[92]

91. *Gaudium et spes,* §50, in *Vatican Council II,* 953.

92. Wilson, *The Social Conquest of Earth,* 297. For a goal quite similar to Wilson's — a goal that immanentizes Christian eschatology — see Elizabeth Johnson's concluding paragraph of *Ask the Beasts:* "A flourishing humanity on a thriving planet rich in species in an evolving universe, all together filled with the glory of God: such is the vision that must guide us at this critical time of Earth's distress, to practical and critical effect. Ignoring this view keeps people of faith and their churches locked into irrelevance while a terrible drama of life and death is being played out in the real world. By contrast, living the ecological vocation in the power of the Spirit sets us off on a great adventure of mind and heart, expanding the repertoire of our love. The beasts ask of us no less" (*Ask the Beasts,* 286). As Johnson has earlier made clear, this work of "expanding the repertoire of our love" in fact requires significantly reducing the number of humans whom today we welcome into the communion of God's love. Far from "irrelevance," the Church today is caught up in the "drama of life and death" that plays out when new human lovers enter the world. Although the Church's eschatological vision must not be reduced to "a flourishing humanity on a thriving planet rich in species in an evolving universe," since the Church looks forward to a new creation in which all the blessed will know and love God and each other eternally, nonetheless the "ecological vocation," properly understood, certainly belongs to the Church's mission.

CHAPTER 6

Bonaventure of Bagnoregio's *imitatio Christi* as an Agapistic Virtue Ethics

Dawn M. Nothwehr, OSF

Following the release of the Fifth Assessment Report (AR5) of the Intergovernmental Panel on Climate Change, the US government published its Third National Climate Assessment (NCA) on May 6, 2014.[1] Distinctive about the NCA was that (1) it followed unprecedented natural disasters — heat waves, droughts, hurricanes, wildfires, and flooding — which left no section of the United States unscathed, and (2) it outlined in great detail, but distilled in a "Fact Sheet," how local conditions in all of its eight regions of the country would be affected by increasingly more extreme weather and other events that would change the climate.

The NCA confirmed that climate change is already affecting the entire United States and key sectors of its economy and society. The need to tackle the causes of climate change and to increase community preparedness and resilience is immediate and urgent as this excerpt indicates:

- extreme weather and climate events have increased in recent decades, some of which are related to human activities;
- human-induced climate change is projected to continue and will accelerate significantly if global emissions keep increasing;

---

1. See Intergovernmental Panel on Climate Change, Fifth Assessment Report (AR5), www.ipcc.ch. Also see the March 2014 issue of *New Theology Review* at http://newtheology review.com/index.php/ntr/article/view/1013. Find the full report, regional reports, highlights, and educational and interactive resources at "National Climate Assessment," http://nca2014.globalchange.gov.

- climate change threatens human health and well-being, including through extreme weather events and wildfires, decreased air quality, and diseases transmitted by insects, food, and water;
- climate change is jeopardizing water quality and water supply reliability, which is affecting ecosystems and livelihoods;
- climate disruptions to agriculture have been increasing, and their severity is projected to increase;
- the capacity of ecosystems to withstand the impacts of extreme events, such as fires, floods, and severe storms, is being overburdened;
- oceans are warming and increasing in acidity, which is affecting ocean circulation, chemistry, ecosystems, and marine life; and
- while adaptation and mitigation planning is increasing, implementation efforts are inadequate to avoid the negative social, environmental, and economic consequences of climate change.[2]

Beyond the NCA, many important initiatives related to climate change have continued to take place, yet most seem weak or even counterproductive in light of the severe consequences of ineffective and delayed corrective action.[3] In spite of some seemingly positive developments, and even as more

---

2. "National Climate Assessment."

3. Here is a sample of the variety of initiatives: Yale Project on Climate Change Communication, June 3, 2014, *Climate Notes,* "Public Understanding vs. Scientific Consensus," http://environment.yale.edu/climate-communication/article/public-understanding-v -scientific-consensus; Cook and colleagues (2013), who examined nearly 12,000 peer-reviewed papers in the climate-science literature and found a 97 percent consensus among the papers that stated a position on the reality of human-caused global warming; see the report at Pontifical Academy of Sciences, www.casinapioiv.va/content/accademia/en/ events/2014/sustainable.html; Elizabeth Douglass, "America's Oil Consumption Is Rising, Not Falling, Outpacing China's," *Inside Climate News,* July 14, 2014, http://insideclimate-news.org/news/20140714/americas-oil-consumption-rising-not-falling-outpacing-chinas; Daniel R. DiLeo, "Should U.S. Bishops Weigh In on the Carbon Emissions Policy?" *In All Things,* June 2, 2014, 10:52am, http://americamagazine.org/content/all-things/should-us -bishops-weigh-carbon-emissions-policy. See also Dan DiLeo, "Catholics against Climate Change: Faithful Advocates for the EPA's Clean Power Plan," *Millennial Journal,* June 16, 2014, http://millennialjournal.com/2014/06/16/catholics-against-climate-change-faithful -advocates-for-the-epas-clean-power-plan; Justin Gillis, "Bipartisan Report Tallies High Toll on Economy from Global Warming," *The New York Times,* June 24, 2014, www.nytimes .com/2014/06/24/science/report-tallies-toll-on-economy-from-global-warming.html; "World Council of Churches Pulls Fossil Fuel Investments," *Guardian,* July 11, 2014, http:// insideclimatenews.org/breaking-news/20140711/world-council-churches-pulls-fossil-fuel -investments. See also Doug Demeo, "Getting out of Oil: Catholic Universities Can Make a

people accept and experience the real impacts of climate change, haunting and sobering questions bear down on us: Are we acting soon enough and strong enough to prevent climate collapse? Even under the best conditions, are we simply doing "too little, too late"? Where can we find genuine reason for hope in this picture? These questions challenge the faith, spirit, and psyche of the people of God.

A vast interdisciplinary literature has long linked the causes of human-forced global climate change and other environmental devastation to negative Western influences, including some appropriations of Christianity.[4] Often the loss of life's meaning, alienation, and a spiritual malaise are specifically named as the root causes.[5] Furthermore, science has shown with great certainty that the consequent impudent raping of the earth, poisoning of its atmosphere, and breaking down of its major ecological cycles have forced unprecedented life-threatening global warming, bringing us to the brink of a shutdown of earth's vital climatic functions.[6]

Some hope lies in the fact that things were not always this way, and thus need not remain so. Indeed, Christianity and other religious traditions offer alternative healthy modes of living. With great urgency, we need to recover those life-giving resources, again lay hold of moral meaning, and become emboldened to act immediately to halt and reverse anthropogenic

---

Difference through Divestment," *America* 210, no. 14 (April 21, 2014), http://america magazine.org/issue/getting-out-oil.

4. A sampling of this literature includes Christiana Peppard, *Just Water* (Maryknoll, NY: Orbis Books, 2013); Robin Attfield, "Social History, Religion, and Technology: An Interdisciplinary Investigation into Lynn White's 'Roots,'" *Environmental Ethics* 31, no. 1 (Spring 2009): 31-50; Michael S. Northcott, *A Moral Climate: The Ethics of Global Warming* (Maryknoll, NY: Orbis Books, 2007), 45-80; Leonardo Boff, *Cry of the Earth, Cry of the Poor,* Ecology and Justice Series, trans. Phillip Berryman (Maryknoll, NY: Orbis Books, 1997), 63-85; David Toolan, *At Home in the Cosmos* (Maryknoll, NY: Orbis Books, 2001), 41-74.

5. See "An Open Letter to the Religious Community" and "Statement by Religious Leaders at the Summit on Environment," in *Ecology and Religion: Scientists Speak,* ed. John E. Carroll and Keith Warner (Quincy, IL: Franciscan Press, 1998), ii-xv. Also Peter H. Raven, "The Sustainability of the Earth: Our Common Responsibility" (paper presented at "Without Nature: A New Condition for Theology," University of Chicago Divinity School, October 26-28, 2006), 4-5. See Eric Doyle, *St. Francis and the Song of Brotherhood and Sisterhood* (New York: Seabury Publishers, 1981), 72.

6. See Intergovernmental Panel on Climate Change, Fifth Assessment Report (AR5), for the three-part report: "Summary for Policymakers: Climate Change 2013: The Physical Science Basis"; "Summary for Policymakers: Climate Change 2014: Impacts, Adaptation, and Vulnerability"; "Summary for Policymakers: Climate Change 2014: Mitigation of Climate Change," www.ipcc.ch.

global warming. One Christian resource, ripe for retrieval of a renewed and ecological ethical vision, is the *imitatio Christi,* or agapistic (love oriented) virtue ethics, of Bonaventure of Bagnoregio (1217-74).[7]

Bonaventure's Franciscan Christology provides the theological anchor for a hope-filled and morally compelling vision that can address the very root of the moral and spiritual malaise attached to anthropogenic global warming.[8] Jesus is the divine clue to the structure and meaning not only of humanity, but of the entire universe. Integral to Bonaventure's *imitatio Christi* is the intimate and necessary integration of Christology and incarnational spirituality. This characteristic of the Franciscan moral vision places it in a unique position to respond to the moral and spiritual malaise that undergirds climate change today.[9]

In Bonaventure's Franciscan Christology the incarnation is integral to the possibility of creation itself; one is integral to the other. Christ is the inner ground of creation and its inner goal. Franciscan theologians thus hold that "the whole world is structured Christologically." Though solidly set in the Christian tradition, Bonaventure presents a cosmic vision with universal implications that invites dialogue, a quality so necessary when dealing with forced global warming.[10]

While Bonaventure's Christology is central to his entire theological project, its more practical, tangible effect is seen in his *imitatio Christi* and ethics. The incarnate Christ is the formal norm; we are compelled to imitate according to the key virtues perfectly exemplified in his incarnation, life, death, resurrection, and ascension — and modeled by St. Francis of Assisi (1182-1226).

In this chapter, I claim that Bonaventure's *imitatio Christi* constitutes

7. The *imitatio Christi,* or imitation of Christ, is nothing less than an embrace of Christ's poverty, humility, and charity. See Zachary Hayes, *The Hidden Center: Spirituality and Speculative Christology in St. Bonaventure,* Franciscan Pathways (St. Bonaventure, NY: Franciscan Institute, 1992), 27. See *Sent.* IV, d. 3, p. 2, a. 3, q. 1, ad 3 (4.84). For a listing of the Latin and English titles of Bonaventure's works, see J. M. Hammond, s.v. "St. Bonaventure," *New Catholic Encyclopedia,* Supplement 2012-13: Ethics and Philosophy, 2013 (vol. 2, 2nd ed.; Detroit: Gale, 2003), 479-83.

8. See my "Bonaventure's Franciscan Christology: A Resource for Eco-Conversion toward Halting Human-Forced Global Warming," in *Confronting the Climate Crisis: Catholic Theological Perspectives,* ed. Jame Schaefer (Milwaukee: Marquette University Press, 2011), 101-24.

9. See Zachary Hayes, "Christ, Word of God and Exemplar of Humanity," *Cord* 46 (1996): 16-17; also Ilia Delio, *Christ in Evolution* (Maryknoll, NY: Orbis Books, 2008), especially chs. 3 and 7.

10. Hayes, "Christ, Word of God and Exemplar of Humanity," 6, 16.

an agapistic virtue ethics and that it is a resource for ecological conversion[11] and empowering Christian action to halt global warming. The chapter has three parts. The first situates Bonaventure's thought within the Franciscan theological tradition. The second outlines the key theological tenets that undergird Bonaventure's hope-filled vision. For Bonaventure, the triune God is fully relational and the one who, out of overflowing love, created a thoroughly related, relational, and connected world. The incarnation is God's complete self-revelation, which opens the fullness of life to humans and the entire universe. In such an interrelated world, humans are created co-creators with the divine and are called to take on the mediating role as guardians of creation. Bonaventure's Christology unifies his understanding of God, the human person, Christian discipleship, and ethics expressed in practical terms in the *imitatio Christi*. The third and final part focuses on four key virtues of the *imitatio Christi* and how they inform and support Christians in their efforts to halt anthropogenic global warming.

Bonaventure's *imitatio Christi* within the Franciscan Theological Tradition

How we think about God, the material universe, and humankind bears religious and moral significance. The *legendae* of St. Francis of Assisi reveal the effect of the saint's life on others.[12] Unquestionably, Francis's ministry, teaching, and profound religious experiences placed serious ethical demands on him, and these shaped the Franciscan intellectual and spiritual life. Indeed, his experience of the "poor Christ" was the driver behind his spiritual and ethical understanding of radical poverty.[13]

Francis of Assisi was acknowledged as a "vernacular theologian."[14] Francis's theological authority originated *ex beneficio,* not *ex officio.*[15] Three major

11. Pope John Paul II, general audience address, January 17, 2001, http://w2.vatican.va/content/john-paul-ii/en/audiences/2001/documents/hf_jp-ii_aud_20010117.html.

12. Joseph Ratzinger, *The Theology of History in St. Bonaventure,* trans. Zachary Hayes (Chicago: Franciscan Herald Press, 1971).

13. David Burr, *Olivi and Poverty: The Origins of the Usus Pauper Controversy* (Philadelphia: University of Pennsylvania Press, 1958), 1-37.

14. Bernard McGinn, *Meister Eckhart and the Beguine Mystics* (New York: Continuum, 1983), 6-7, and his *The Flowering of Mysticism: Men and Women in the New Mysticism, 1200-1350* (New York: Crossroad, 1998), 21.

15. See Congregation for the Doctrine of the Faith, "Instruction on the Ecclesial Vocation

themes in Francis's vernacular theology irrevocably link Franciscan spirituality, theology, and ethics: the humanity of Christ, the mystery of God as
generous love, and the sense of creation as family (John 14:6-9).[16]

Significantly, Francis of Assisi, the patron of ecologists, also asserted
the life-sustaining virtue of mutual obedience among all the creatures.[17] The
obedient one "is subject and submissive to all persons in the world, and
not only to human beings, but even to all beasts and wild animals so that
they may do whatever they want with that person, in as much as it has been
given to them from above by the Lord."[18] Furthermore, Francis denounced
abusive relationships that humans create with others.[19] Humans use other
creatures to meet daily survival needs, yet they are ungrateful to them, failing
to recognize the Creator of such gifts and blessings. Bonaventure develops
these linkages between the triune God, creation, Christ, the incarnation,
creatures, and humans, solidifying an inseparable connection between the
Franciscan theology, spirituality, and ethics.[20] Bonaventure's interpretation
of Francis shaped his own vision and articulation of highly integrated works
of theology, spirituality, and ethics.

St. Bonaventure's Theology, Spirituality, and Ethics:
A Hope-Filled Vision

Some Key Sources

A university professor, Bonaventure became the founder of the Franciscan
theological tradition,[21] as well as the clearest interpretive voice of St. Francis

---

of the Theologian," *Origins* 20, no. 8 (July 5, 1990): 119. Also United States Conference of Catholic Bishops, "Doctrinal Responsibilities: Approaches to Promoting Cooperation and Resolving
Misunderstandings Between Bishops and Theologians," *Origins* 19, no. 7 (June 29, 1989): 101.

16. See St. Francis, "Admonition I.1-4," in *Francis and Clare*, ed. Regis Armstrong and
Ignatius Brady (Mahwah, NJ: Paulist Press, 1982), 25-26.

17. See John Paul II, apostolic letter, *Inter Sanctos, Franciscus Assisiensis Caelestis Pa-
tronus Oecologiae Cultorum Eligitur,* http://w2.vatican.va/content/john-paul-ii/la/apost
_letters/1979/documents/hf_jp-ii_apl_19791129_inter-sanctos.html.

18. Francis of Assisi, "Salutation to the Virtues, 14-18," in *Francis and Clare*, 151-52.

19. See the "Mirror of Perfection," in Marion A. Habig, *Omnibus of Sources* (Chicago:
Franciscan Herald Press, 1972), 1236.

20. Hayes, "Christ, Word of God and Exemplar of Humanity," 6.

21. See Kenan B. Osborne, ed., *The History of Franciscan Theology* (St. Bonaventure,
NY: Franciscan Institute, 1994), vii-ix. See Zachary Hayes, "The Life and the Christolog-

of Assisi's Christocentric connected spiritual and ethical vision.[22] Augustine, Pseudo-Dionysius, and Richard of St. Victor informed Bonaventure's thought.[23] Bonaventure stressed God as the supreme Good; the great love, respect, and responsibility of the world for God's creation; and a Christocentric spirituality formulated in metaphysical terms and as integral to the Christian cosmological vision. Bonaventure's evangelical theological synthesis gives Francis's vision intellectual structure and method.[24] The result was an integration of a rigorous theology and a powerful spirituality that gives Bonaventure's work great promise for our time.[25] The three themes of St. Francis's run deep in Bonaventure's theology and are visible in the *imitatio Christi.*

Bonaventure's Method

St. Augustine's concern with integrating many levels of human and religious meaning into a unified vision of reality strongly influenced Bonaventure's work. Thorough self-knowledge leads ultimately to a more profound knowledge of God. Such knowledge is accrued only through contemplation of the cosmos and the divine.[26] The motivation for such activity progresses from

---

ical Thought of St. Bonaventure," in *Franciscan Christology: Selected Texts, Translations, and Introductory Essays,* ed. Damian McElrath, Franciscan Sources 1 (St. Bonaventure, NY: Franciscan Institute, 1980), 62-64.

22. See Timothy Johnson, "Lost in Sacred Space: Textual Hermeneutics, Liturgical Worship, and Celano's *Legenda ad usum chori,*" *Franciscan Studies* 59, no. 1 (2001): 112. See E. R. Daniel, *The Franciscan Concept of Mission in the High Middle Ages* (New York: Franciscan Institute, 1975), 48.

23. See J. Guy Bougerol, *Introduction to the Works of Bonaventure,* vol. 1, trans. José de Vinck (Paterson, NJ: St. Anthony Guild Press, 1964), especially 23-49.

24. Ilia Delio, "The Franciscan Intellectual Tradition: Contemporary Concerns," in *The Franciscan Intellectual Tradition,* ed. Elise Saggau, CFIT/ESC-OFM Series no. 1, Washington Theological Union Symposium Papers, 2001 (St. Bonaventure, NY: Franciscan Institute, 2002), 8. See Ilia Delio, *Crucified Love: Bonaventure's Mysticism of the Crucified Christ* (Quincy, IL: Franciscan Press, 1998). Also Hayes, "The Life and the Christological Thought of St. Bonaventure," 62-63.

25. See *Aeterni Patris,* encyclical of Pope Leo XIII on the restoration of Christian philosophy (1879), §14, www.vatican.va/holy_father/leo_xiii/encyclicals/documents/hf_l-xiii _enc_04081879_aeterni-patris_en.html. See Gerald A. McCool, *From Unity to Pluralism: The Internal Evolution of Thomism* (New York: Fordham University Press, 1989), 163, 171-72, 190, 196-97.

26. St. Augustine, *Confessions,* trans. Mark Vessy and Albert C. Outler (New York:

an initial desire for something beyond oneself to, ultimately, responding to God's offer of love. This contemplative process opens one to knowledge of the deeper mysteries of humanity, creation, and God, and moves one to act with ever more complete conformity to God.[27] Bonaventure's theology utilized a holistic wisdom *(sapientia)* approach that integrated the various ways of knowing, including the intellect *(scientia)*. All forms of knowing must serve the singular goal of life, not known to philosophy alone — namely, Jesus Christ.

Two Works and the imitatio Christi

Bonaventure's integrated approach is seen in his masterful *Itinerarium mentis in Deum* (The Journey of the Mind into God).[28] The spiritual life and the intellectual life mutually inform one another, with the ideal of the imitation of Christ always in the foreground and shaping the moral life. Seekers begin their journey, conforming themselves primarily according to the paradigmatic values of Christ. They move from contemplating external realities (the natural world), God the Creator (nature mysticism), to the interior world of human consciousness (sensations, the natural faculties; mysticism of the soul), to a state where the natural faculties are transformed by God's grace (metaphysical mysticism), and finally, to full union with God, both in this life (mystical experience) and in death (the beatific vision). Through the six stages, the person develops and matures in knowledge of God (theology), relations with God (spirituality), and the imitation of Christ (ethics).

Bonaventure's *De reductione artium ad theologiam* (On the Reduction of the Arts to Theology) is influential in our understanding of the *imitatio Christi* and the moral life.[29] Here Bonaventure asserts that all forms of knowledge — the liberal and the mechanical arts — can all be traced back to their origin in the highest form of wisdom, namely, divine revelation. If

Barnes & Noble, 1992), bk. 13, sec. 18, p. 326: "In your great wisdom you, who are our God, speak to us of these things in your Book, the firmament made by you."

27. Zachary Hayes, "Franciscan Tradition as a Wisdom Tradition," *Spirit and Life* 7 (1997): 32.

28. *Itinerarium mentis in Deum,* in *Works of St. Bonaventure,* vol. 2, rev. and exp. ed., trans. Zachary Hayes (St. Bonaventure, NY: Franciscan Institute, 2002), 9-32.

29. *St. Bonaventure's On the Reduction of the Arts to Theology,* trans. Zachary Hayes (St. Bonaventure, NY: Franciscan Institute, 1996). See especially Zachary Hayes, "Introduction," 1-3.

we consider how human reason works, by deduction and by induction, we can see that this is the case, presuming that we accept God as the Creator of all. This is of great significance for understanding the moral and religious significance of global warming, and for a well-reasoned dialogue today between economics, politics, earth sciences, and theology, so necessary when utilizing inductive methodologies in environmental ethics. Bonaventure sees human cognition as one way in which the human spiritual journey is involved in creation's return to God. Hayes explains:

> To lead the arts back to theology means, for Bonaventure, to show the organic connection between all the arts and the central concern of scripture and theology. None of the arts, including philosophy, ought to be allowed to stand as an independent and self-sufficient discipline. All ought to be brought into relation to the highest form of wisdom available to human beings in this life: namely, theology. Only then will all forms of human knowledge serve effectively in realizing the true end of human existence.[30]

Every form of knowledge bears moral meaning and holds potential for shaping the Christian spiritual journey to God.

Bonaventure's Wisdom Theology and Imperial Ecology

All knowledge, especially theology, is for the sake of deepening love in the human person and the world. Theological wisdom is wisdom of the will, including both intellectual and cognitive knowing, as well as affective ways of knowing. Theology is *(habitus affectivus)* knowledge that is situated between what is purely speculative and what is purely practical or ethical, "embracing both and partaking in both."[31] Indeed, all knowledge is integrated into a process of human transformation and thus enhances one's desire for the good and for the ultimate Good, God. Theology is thus practical in the sense that it contributes to the ethical, moral, and spiritual transformation of humanity. Any authentic transformation will be visible in actions — in lifestyle and living the moral life.

If Bonaventure is right about this integration of knowledge and process of human transformation, then from the very start it matters how we name

30. Hayes, "Introduction," in *St. Bonaventure's On the Reduction of the Arts to Theology,* 2-3.
31. See Bonaventure, *Sent.* I, prooem. q. 3.

God. In the shadows of climate collapse we need to ask, Can whatever or whomever we claim as god supply adequate meaning for the ultimate questions of life: Who am I? Why am I? What is my purpose for living? Can this god inspire a sufficient motivation in us to respond to the urgent ecological, social, political, and economic realities of global warming, climate change? What is the relationship between god and moral and political will to support the immediate necessary actions to enable the continuation of human life on planet Earth beyond this generation?

Clearly, the "imperial ecology" promoted by the Enlightenment Deists resulted in gradual theoretical and actual alienation from and dismemberment of the earth. They ignored the radically related triune Creator God, of whom Bonaventure speaks, and were blinded to the reality that all creation is interrelated to its core.[32] The god of Francis Bacon (1561-1626) and René Descartes (1596-1650), Isaac Newton (1642-1727), and ultimately Pierre Simon LePlace (1749-1827) — likely not imagined with ill-will — nonetheless opened the door to wanton misuse and abuse of creation. In the seventeenth century the Western worldview shifted from a sacramental perception (Augustine) to scientific materialism; from sacramental sensitivity to mathematical objectivity; from reliance on Plato and Aristotle to belief in the laws of Newton; and from seeing the planetary systems as dynamic and relational "Sister, Mother Earth" to seeing them as mere cogs in a vast indestructible machine that could be torn apart, rearranged, and torn apart again at the command of human masters of the universe. As Alfred North Whitehead so aptly put it, "Nature became meaningless matter in motion" with no moral standing, and thus none could make any moral claims about its well-being.[33]

A diminishment in the value of the human person accompanied this mechanistic worldview. Atomized individualism replaced biblical notions of human nature. Social contracts, theoretically modeled on seventeenth-century Newtonian physics, require and assume autonomous individuals, not interdependent or socially connected communities.[34] Religion, including Catholicism, often reinforced individualism by separating salvation and creation, making creation a mere context for human activity, but no longer related to it. Moral obligation was reduced, and justice became merely the obligation to fulfill contracts. Commerce and culture shifted from efforts

---

32. Dawn M. Nothwehr, *Ecological Footprints: An Essential Franciscan Guide for Faith and Sustainable Living* (Collegeville, MN: Liturgical Press, 2012), 64-66.

33. See Toolan, *At Home in the Cosmos,* especially pt. 2, "The Development of Scientific Materialism," 42.

34. Toolan, *At Home in the Cosmos,* cites Mary Madgley, 61.

to cooperate with nature, to strident efforts to tame, conquer, destroy, and reconstruct it.

Have We Become like Gods?

In an ironic twist to the Genesis story, in a sense, humans have become like gods! We *have* gained "control" over the earth! We *do* know the fundamental workings of the biosphere; we *are* to blame for many catastrophic events! It is *this* fundamental intuition — "We are responsible" — that, conscious or not, threatens to paralyze us in the face of global warming. We fear the end of the natural world, and we are shocked by our responsibility for the loss! Like our forebears in Eden, our guilt threatens our relationship with God. While there is a "healthy guilt," we must not remain there.

In Genesis 3, when confronting the sin of our tragically enlightened first parents, God's first words to Adam and Eve are relational: "Where are you?" God's question originates in life-giving love; it is an effort to restore the divine/human relationship, to reverse what has gone wrong. Unfortunately, Adam responds with a blame game! The man blames the woman (v. 12), and the woman blames the snake (v. 13). I believe these responses indicate how our ancestors failed to know the heart of God! Today as we stand at the intersection of global climate collapse and the reversal of its known causes, I think Bonaventure's *imitatio Christi* supports a clear way forward. Will we have the wisdom to openly and fully engage God's offer of love in our day?

Bonaventure's Trinitarian Theology

Bonaventure's theological starting point was the Trinity, and he ended up with a highly relational Christocentric system.[35] His *imitatio Christi* is best understood in the context of his Trinitarian theology. He followed the questioning of the Cappadocians trying to understand the relationship of the Christ of the Gospels and the God of creation.[36] Thus, Bonaventure (unlike

---

35. See Ilia Delio, *Simply Bonaventure: An Introduction to His Life, Thought, and Writings* (Hyde Park, NY: New City Press, 2001).

36. Delio, *Christ in Evolution*, 55. Also Catherine Mowry La Cunga, *God for Us: The Trinity and the Christian Life* (New York: HarperCollins, 1991), 53-81.

Augustine's focus on the unity of God's substance) focused on the divine persons of the Trinity. Implicit in the notion of persons is the experience of relationship; to be a person is to be social, a person-in-relationship. Bonaventure described this relationship of Trinitarian persons as *circumincessio* (to move around one another in a communion of love).[37] The Trinity is self-diffusive goodness (Pseudo-Dionysius) and ultimate love (Richard of St. Victor). The three persons are not only related to one another, but they mutually inhere in one another.[38]

Bonaventure's Doctrine of Creation

The Trinity is the starting point for Bonaventure's examination of creation and the *exitus/reditus* of creatures in relation to God, the Creator. The triune God creates the entire cosmos. Using modified Platonic models, Bonaventure explained that God freely created everything as ordered, oriented, and directed toward its goal, in a manner such that all of creation is fully interrelated and interdependent.[39] The community of creation is the product of the overflowing self-diffusive and self-expressive love of the community of the Trinity. Based on hylomorphism (everything is open to change) and the Platonic doctrine of seminal principles (everything has potential), creation is dynamic and open to transformation.[40] Simply put, Bonaventure held that it was God's plan that all creation would desire to be perfected (become its most perfect self).

Creation is God's means of expressing divine goodness, indeed God's very self, in the incarnation in Jesus Christ. All creation comes from God and returns to God. The Father's goodness is expressed in the Word, who proceeds from the Father as the perfect expression of the image of God. In Bonaventure's view, the Word is the inner self-expression of God, and all of creation is the external expression of the inner Word. Christ, the Word is the Art of the Father, and the creation is the expression of the Artist. Of

---

37. Delio, *Simply Bonaventure,* 41nn4-5. Also LaCugna, *God for Us,* 272.

38. Delio, *Simply Bonaventure,* 40-41.

39. See Zachary Hayes, "The Cosmos, a Symbol of the Divine," in *Franciscan Theology of the Environment: An Introductory Reader,* ed. Dawn M. Nothwehr (Quincy, IL: Franciscan Press, 2002), 249-67.

40. Delio, *Simply Bonaventure,* 56-57. See Zachary Hayes, "Bonaventure: Mystery of the Triune God," in *The History of Franciscan Theology,* ed. Kenan B. Osborne (St. Bonaventure, NY: Franciscan Institute, 1994), 72-79.

all in creation, human beings are those most capable of participating in and manifesting God's glory.[41]

Christian Anthropology: Humans in Creation[42]

Humans are "the ones in creation who freely choose God, and in choosing God, become like God — perfect in love."[43] Humans, the *imago Dei*, are both spirit and matter, and they can unite everything with God. Humans thus stand in the middle of creation as the creatures who can lead it to perfection (or destruction). For Bonaventure, that humans are in the center, indicates a position of mediation, not anthropocentric priority or greater value in relation to others. Humans and other creatures of creation serve one another in relationship. Humans advocate for the other creatures, giving them voice before God and the world.[44] The other creatures inspire, thrill, and arouse human awareness of the magnificence and generosity of God, moving them to contemplation. The Uncreated Lover communicates love in an unlimited variety of ways (through all beings in creation), and in Christ incarnate the entire cosmos is united and transformed.[45]

Contemplative, Ethical Human Beings

Bonaventure's speculative Christology serves to ground spirituality and agapistic virtue ethics. This integration defines humans as both spiritual and ethical beings at the center of creation. In *The Soul's Journey into God,* Bonaventure extends Francis's insight of the kinship of creation. Bonaventure saw union with God reflected not only in the external world, but also within the human person "in the inner act of sensation, in aesthetic experi-

---

41. Delio, *Simply Bonaventure,* 65. See *Sent.* II, d. 1, p. 2, a. 2., q. 1. concl. (2.44b).

42. See Dawn M. Nothwehr, *The Franciscan View of the Human Person: Some Central Elements,* Franciscan Heritage Series 3 (St. Bonaventure, NY: Franciscan Institute, 2005), 31-44.

43. Delio, *Simply Bonaventure,* 59. See Zachary Hayes, "Incarnation and Creation in St. Bonaventure," in *Studies Honoring Ignatius Brady, Friar Minor,* ed. Romano Stephen Almagno and Conrad L. Harkins (St. Bonaventure, NY: Franciscan Institute, 1976), 318.

44. See Nothwehr, *The Franciscan View of the Human Person,* 38-39; Ewert Cousins, *Christ of the Twenty-First Century* (Rockfort, MA: Element, 1992), 152-55.

45. Bougerol, *Introduction to the Works of Bonaventure,* 40.

ence, in the activities of memory, understanding, and will, and in the contemplation of Being and self-diffusive goodness, or God."[46] Bonaventure used a series of analogies to explain:

> The entire world is a shadow, a road, a vestige, and it is also a book written without (Ex 2:8; [Rev] 5:1). For in every creature there is a shining forth of the divine exemplar, but mixed with the darkness. Hence creatures are a kind of darkness mixed with light. Also they are a road leading to the exemplar. Just as you see a ray of light entering through a window is colored in different ways according to the colors of the various parts, so the divine ray shines forth in each and every creature in different ways and in different properties; it is said in Wisdom: In her ways she shows herself (Wis 6:17). Also creatures are a vestige of the wisdom of God. Hence creatures are a kind of representation and statue of the wisdom of God. And in view of all of this, they are a kind of book written without.[47]

Creation was executed by God like an artist who conceives an idea in his or her imagination and then expresses it externally. Beginning with time, God created everything from nothing, setting the cosmos on a journey that moves forth from God and moves toward a return to God, revealing God-self along the way. The role of the material and natural world is to arouse the human consciousness to praise and love God, and in turn, humanity is to serve nature by giving it a voice that would not otherwise be heard in the cosmos.[48] Bonaventure thus demonstrates how there is an intimate relationship between God and each creature of the cosmos, and with each of them with one another through Christ. If humans ignore this relationship, they fail to comprehend their position in the cosmos! As Bonaventure puts it:

> Therefore whoever is not illuminated by such great splendors in created things is blind. Anyone who is not awakened by such great outcries is deaf. Anyone who is not led from such great effects to give praise to God is mute. Anyone who does not turn to the First Principle as a result of such signs is a fool. Therefore open your eyes, alert your spiritual ears,

46. Cousins, *Christ of the Twenty-First Century*, 151. See Ewert Cousins, *St. Bonaventure: The Soul's Journey into God — The Tree of Life — The Life of St. Francis* (Mahwah, NJ: Paulist Press, 1978).

47. Bonaventure, *Hexaem.* 12.14, quoted in Cousins, *Christ of the Twenty-First Century*, 152.

48. Bonaventure, *Brevil.* 2.4 (5.221), cited by Hayes, "Bonaventure: Mystery of the Triune God," 67-68.

unlock your lips and apply your heart, so that in all the creatures you may see, hear, praise, love and adore, magnify and honor God, lest the entire world rise up against you.[49]

Humans created in the *imago Dei* with the faculties of memory, intellect, and will are drawn by the goodness in creation to comprehend and value it as sacred in the panentheistic sense as a revelation of the Creator.[50] In so doing, humans find their role as the mediators between God and creation and as guardians of the multiple manifestations of God's self-revelation in Christ.[51]

Bonaventure's *imitatio Christi* as an Agapistic Virtue Ethics and Forced Global Warming

Bonaventure's Virtue Ethics

Bonaventure's understanding of "imitation" has roots in Plato's notion of *mimesis,* which had three levels of meaning: ontological, aesthetic, and ethical. At the ethical level, the divine order defined the moral order. For humans, the rational beings and copies of the eternal Ideas, the Ideas also hold the rules for the moral life. To become moral, humans require engagement with enlightened teacher-liberators who awaken them to the vestiges of the divine within themselves. The teacher-disciple is a communion of life and love, which begets Beauty and ultimately entices the disciple back to the divine Ideas.[52]

Bonaventure also utilized Augustine's adaptation of a Neoplatonic sche-

---

49. Bonaventure, *Itinerarium mentis in Deum* 1.15, in *Works of St. Bonaventure,* 61.

50. Note carefully the distinction between pantheism and orthodox Christian panentheism. See John T. Ford, CSC, ed., *St. Mary's Press Glossary of Theological Terms,* Essential Catholic Theology Series (Winona, MN: St. Mary's Press, 2006), s.v. "pantheism": "This word (from the Greek *pan-,* meaning 'all,' and *theos,* meaning 'god') refers to the belief that identifies God with the universe; that is, the whole universe is God." By contrast, see *New Catholic Encyclopedia,* 2nd ed., vol. 10 (Detroit: Gale, 2003), s.v. "panentheism," by E. R. Naughton and S. Sia: "Panentheism (Gr. παν, all; εν, in; θεος, God), in its simplest form, is the view that the world is in God, but God is not the world. In metaphysics, it utilizes a real distinction between the essence of God and God's existence, or considers God as having accidents really distinct from God's nature."

51. Cousins, *Christ of the Twenty-First Century,* 152-55.

52. Ambroise Van Si Nguyen, "The Theology of the Imitation of Christ according to St. Bonaventure," trans. Edward Hagman, *Greyfriars Review* 11 Supplement (1997): 13-15.

ma.[53] The archetype of all likenesses is the Word, the perfect likeness of God. The entire cosmos originated through the Word at the moment of creation (John 1:1-14). People are created in the image of the triune God, endowed with memory (Father), intelligence (Son), and will (Spirit). Humans are thus naturally capable of knowing themselves and of desiring the supreme Good. There is human freedom to act on their desire in response to God's offer of grace and to cooperate with it toward their final fulfillment in God. Bonaventure follows Augustine closely but elaborates how each being participates in the divine Being to varying degrees: similitude, vestige, or image. Through those intimate relationships with the divine, of whom the Word is the only perfect expression, all creation is sustained and perfected. Simply, for Bonaventure, "[The Word] is the form we imitate."[54]

Bonaventure holds that Christ is the ethical center, the exemplar of all virtues, and the source of grace. Christ is simultaneously in God and in the world. Following and imitating Christ is a spiritual and ethical journey of moral perfection and union with God. Christ possesses the *ethica generalis:* "'To act as Christ acted, to live as he lived, to suffer as he suffered, and to die as he died,' this is the general science of human behavior" (*Serm. in Nativ. Domini,* Serm. 2 [9.107b]).[55]

Bonaventure taught that "a moral act is a free and conscious commitment by which we determine ourselves in the presence of the one who calls out to us. The presence of Christ, seen as a model of the virtues, arouses a response in each of us."[56] Christians are challenged to engage in a personal encounter with the living Christ as the primary influence in daily living. For this engagement, human acceptance of God's grace and love is essential. In a remarkably modern move, Bonaventure explained, "Our affections are moved more strongly by examples than by mere argumentation, by promised rewards than by reasoning, by devotion more than by dogma" (*Brevil.,* prol. 1 [5.202a]).[57] Just as sunflowers attracted by sunlight turn toward the sun, so the soul turns to God, drawn into relationship with Christ (John 12:45).

---

53. Nguyen, "The Theology of the Imitation of Christ," 16.
54. Nguyen, "The Theology of the Imitation of Christ," 18, cites *Sent.* I, d. 27, p. 2, a. un., q. 2, ad 5 (1.486b).
55. Nguyen, "The Theology of the Imitation of Christ," citing *Sent.* 1.147.
56. Nguyen, "The Theology of the Imitation of Christ," citing *Sent.* 1.148.
57. See Timothy E. O'Connell, *The Making of Disciples* (New York: Crossroad Publishing, 1998), especially chs. 6-8.

Imitatio Christi *and Virtue Ethics*

The *imitatio Christi* has both an internal and an external dimension. Humans are embodied and spiritual earth-creatures who seek union with God while on a journey through time and space in this world, a place that is utterly bursting forth with the signs and wonders of God. Because Jesus Christ shows us most fully who God is and what God is like, Jesus is also the concrete, embodied source for our understanding of the moral life. According to Bonaventure, we can learn how to live morally by studying the whole life of Jesus as it is explained in the Gospels and interpreted by St. Francis.[58] Significantly, the Gospels speak of Jesus as the Word incarnate, who though divine, became our human brother, Jesus of Nazareth, a Jew who also knew God as the loving Creator.

But Jesus is far more than a mere ethical model. Following Jesus takes us beyond merely mimicking Jesus' actions, to spiritual transformation. Our interior disposition changes. Grounded in a loving relationship with God in Christ, we become more loving. The whole point of Jesus' life was to help us to be genuinely free from sin and free for becoming fully the persons we are meant to be.

In Bonaventure's ethics, there is a constant interplay between our *being* and *doing* the good (ethical, external) and the process of our *becoming* good (spiritual, internal). In these two ways God's grace assists in the moral life, and we are able to grow in goodness and wholeness and become more like God.[59] As Bonaventure sees it, the spiritual life directs the moral life of the Christian. Central to this transformation are the virtues of humility, poverty, obedience, and love.

Humility

Humility is the virtue most central to the God-human relationship. The English word "humility" is derived from the Latin word for "earth," *humus.* We human earth-creatures are not to grovel before God but, rather, to revel in God's love. Such love inspired God, in the incarnation, to humbly join in our concrete embodied reality, coming into intimate relationship with humanity.[60]

---

58. Hayes, *The Hidden Center,* 27. See *Sent.* IV, d. 3, p. 2, a. 3, q. 1, ad 3 (4.84).
59. Hayes, *The Hidden Center,* 42, literally translated "rendered deiform."
60. Bonaventure, *Sermon on the Nativity* (9.106): "love that so moved God in the In-

This is the childlike humility (Matt 18:4) Jesus proclaims as the characteristic of those "greatest in the kingdom of heaven." Yet, the depth of moral maturity is exemplified in Jesus' Eucharistic washing of the disciples' feet (John 13:1-15). Jesus, knowing full well who he was, consciously chose to serve those not his equal, and he then commissioned them to do likewise.

Ilia Delio explains: "As the Image of God therefore, Christ not only reveals God to us but he reveals who we are in relation to God, that is, the truth of our humanity. This becomes important to Bonaventure because he sees the poverty and humility of Christ not only expressive of God as love but expressive of the human person who, being created by God, is by nature poor and humble. The truth of oneself in God, therefore, is found in relationship to Jesus Christ." Bonaventure held that humility is the root and guardian of all other virtues.[61] Imitating Christ's humility, one keeps personal self-identity in integral balance — gifts with needs, strengths with limits. People need to see themselves intimately loved by God, yet creatures amid others beloved of God in the cosmos.[62]

I suggest that imitating Christ's humility today calls us to claim our identity as creatures of the earth, with distinct capabilities. We must use our scientific and technological prowess to care for one another and the planet in sustainable ways.[63] For example, before building huge structures that vastly change the terrain, destroy countless habitats, driving numerous species to extinction, permanently destroying ecosystems, we need to reflect on one of the most fundamental principles of modern science. Wetlands expert R. Eugene Turner clarifies:

> Embracing doubt, a signature of strength of science, is an essential core component of an Ignorance Based World View (IBWV) that assumes the areas of [scientific] certainty are small and relative. The contrasting Knowledge Based World View (KBWV) assumes small and mostly insignificant [scientific] knowledge gaps exist. When the KBWV is combined with a sense of urgency to "do something," [e.g., about flooding] then the intellectual landscape is flattened, the introduction of new ideas is

---

carnation to humbly bend down and lift the lowliness of our nature into unity with his own person."

61. Delio, *Simply Bonaventure*, 72-73, 117, which cites *M. Trin.*, q. 1 (5.121); *Lignum vitae* 5 (8.72).

62. Leonard J. Bowman, "The Cosmic Exemplarism of Bonaventure," *Journal of Religion* 55, no. 2 (April 1975): 187.

63. Bowman, "The Cosmic Exemplarism of Bonaventure," 187.

impeded, monitoring and adaptive management is marginalized, risky behaviors continue, and social learning is restricted.[64]

Much of the human contribution to global warming is rooted in a KBWV approach to technology and energy use. Such a response reflects a kind of scientific egotism, or hubris, that has been ecologically disastrous.

Poverty

Bonaventure held that material poverty must go hand in hand with humility in Christ. Jesus was born in a manger, thrived in relationships with the marginalized, and died like a common criminal on the cross. Many of us materially wealthy people know only a false poverty (material), the illusion of never having enough "stuff" and always ultimately craving something more (spiritual poverty). Human poverty is rooted in our existence as creatures. We did not bring ourselves into existence.[65] True poverty is the recognition of the need for God in every aspect of life. False poverty is to live in the illusion of never having enough. Today, we must choose to live with what is sufficient for a life of dignity, not opulence! Key to the virtue of poverty is accepting God's gifts with open hands and heart, ready to give away whatever we have as a gift to another in need (Matt 10:8).

Today, we know that one of the main drivers of global climate change is pumping ever more CO_2 into the atmosphere. The demand for more and more energy to create more and more "stuff" — things that many buy, use for a short time, and then toss out and that are not necessities of life — continues to exacerbate an already serious threat to the global climate. Imitating Christ in a society driven by consumerism and a world threatened with climate collapse calls us to a life of simplicity, not opulence. This commitment requires change of heart and change of behavior, fewer gadgets and more gracious engaging with creatures — humankind and otherkind — and our Creator.[66]

64. R. Eugene Turner, "Doubt and the Values of an Ignorance-Based World View for Restoration: Coastal Louisiana Wetlands," *Estuaries and Coasts* 32 (2009): 1054.

65. Delio, *Simply Bonaventure*, cites *Hex.* 4.8 (5.350); 10.17 (5.379); *Sent.* II, d. 1, p. 1, a. 3, q. 2, ad. resp. (2.34-35).

66. See Kyle T. Kremer, "Eco-Asceticism: Preparing for the Future with Discipline Today," *America*, November 25, 2007, 21-24. Also Jack Nelson-Pallmeyer, "By Their Spending You Shall Know Them," in *Christian Simplicity: A Gospel Value* (Louisville, KY: Passionist

Obedience

The word "obedience" comes from the Latin *oboedire,* meaning "to pay attention" or "to hear." Jesus Christ modeled this virtue by listening to his Father's will (Heb 10:7, 9; John 5:30; 14:31) and by caring for the needs of people and nonhuman others.[67] This attentiveness empowered him to embrace the cross and to bring us the postresurrection hope of a new creation. Christians are connected to Christ through bonds that are personal and moral, to the Obedient Lover and his command to love (John 15:4, 10). Obedience is motivated by the love of Christ, who acts in humans as the inspired Word and transforms them. Obedience thus opens people to life's meaning, the motives for action, and the basis for all values.

For Bonaventure it was the dual call to attend to and love God and our neighbors that made this virtue so eminent.[68] Today, we must heed the groaning of the suffering earth, listen to the cries of people already burdened by poverty who are now disproportionately suffering the effects of climate change, become ecologically literate, engage in prayerful discernment, and then act to halt environmental destruction.

Love

God's love overflows to humankind and all of creation. It is most perfectly demonstrated in the incarnation and in all of the acts of the incarnate Christ.[69] Having first received God's love, humans then share it among themselves and with all of creation (John 13:34-35). But humans love imperfectly, so justice and the discipline of law are necessary. Justice is able to restore beauty to the world by making upright what was deformed by sin. Christ is the ultimate norm and negotiator of justice (love).[70] Today we must re-

---

Earth & Spirit Center, 2011), 46-47. Also see The Story of Stuff Project, http://storyofstuff .org/about.

67. Hayes, *The Hidden Center,* 37. Bonaventure's commentary on Luke stresses Jesus' obedience to people.

68. *Ex Reg* 4.1, cited in Krijn Pansters, *Franciscan Virtue: Spiritual Growth and the Virtues in Franciscan Literature and Instruction in the Thirteenth Century* (Leiden: Brill, 2012), 75.

69. Hayes, *The Hidden Center,* 38-39. In Bonaventure's speculative theology and spirituality, love drives the Christ-mystery.

70. Hayes, *The Hidden Center,* 202-3. See *Hex. 1,* 31-33 (5.334). Aristotle, *Ethics* II, ch. 6. See also *Hex.* 1.34-36 (5.335).

late with the nonhuman world with justice and love as God relates to us. If we truly love God and neighbor, we will seek the common good. Today this effort means joining together as local communities and states to create public policies that protect the sustainability of the environment and, most certainly, to halt global warming. As John Paul II wrote, "The task of the state is to provide for the defense and preservation of common goods such as natural and human environments, which cannot be safeguarded simply by market forces."[71]

Christ: Paradigm and Norm

Bonaventure rightly taught that Christian morality requires us to make Christ's fundamental attitudes and values our own. Those standards need to truly define our relationship to all reality.[72]

Jesus was a Jew, with a worldview in which God was actively present always and everywhere. His life, ministry, and teaching were radically relational and were intimately connected with the earth. Beginning with his inaugural sermon (Luke 4:16-22), he shows us the vital bond between care for the earth and care for the poor. That bond was based on the Jewish theological understanding that the land is God's. In Leviticus 25 the Sabbatical Year and Jubilee Years mandate debt forgiveness and return to one's own land (economics), restoration of the land and rest for animals (ecology), and liberation of all enslaved (ecumenicity).

71. *Solicitudo rei socialis,* no. 40, cited in Kenneth R. Himes, *Christianity and the Political Order: Conflict, Cooptation, and Cooperation* (Maryknoll, NY: Orbis Books, 2013), 206. Also USCCB, *Renewing the Earth,* part 5A, www.usccb.org/issues-and-action/human-life-and-dignity/environment/renewing-the-earth.cfm. See USCCB, *Global Climate Change: A Plea for Dialogue, Prudence, and the Common Good,* especially "The Public Policy Debate and Future Directions," www.usccb.org/issues-and-action/human-life-and-dignity/environment/global-climate-change-a-plea-for-dialogue-prudence-and-the-common-good.cfm.

72. Hayes, *The Hidden Center,* 39: "To perceive the life of Christ as a paradigm is to accept its fundamental values as normative for human life. The fundamental attitude and values of Christ must be so personalized in one's life that they truly define one's relationship to reality." The spiritual life in Christ is a journey deeper into the foundational realities of the world. Understanding those realities also shapes Christian ethics.

Conclusion: *Imitatio Christi,* Virtue Ethics, and Human-Forced Global Warming

Bonaventure believed in Christ's presence throughout the cosmos from the moment of creation. Bonaventure thus held a positive and radically relational view of God, creation, redemption, and ethical praxis (see John 1:3, 14; Heb 1:2; Col 1:15-20; Eph 1:3-14; Rev 1:8; 21:6).[73] All creation is loved by God for its own sake. Humans have the capacity to read the signs of the divine in creation and then take up their proper relationship to God, creation, and fellow humans.

Bonaventure rooted this belief in the Gospel of John, specifically 1:14: "The Word became flesh [*sarx*] and dwelt among us, full of grace and truth." The Johannine writer used the Greek word *sarx* to show the relationship of the incarnation to the material world. Created things are perishable, fragile, and finite — conditions that also characterize human flesh.[74] The incarnation unites humans with the whole cosmos, and Jesus Christ incarnate embodies and exemplifies the norm and standard for all ethical relations. By following the example and teachings of Jesus, humans can participate with Christ as created co-creators and co-redeemers of the cosmos. Through Christ Jesus, our relationship with God brings us into relationship with the world. That relationship requires humility, poverty of spirit, austerity of life, and genuine charity (John 13:34-35).[75]

Considering Bonaventure's grasp of the cosmos and his open attitude toward science,[76] I think that, if he were present here today, he would hold that his love-centered virtue ethics requires that we *act* to halt global warming.[77] Jesus' engagements with the marginalized, sick, and poor model what is currently (and what will be) required concerning caring for the needs of

73. See Boff, *Cry of the Earth, Cry of the Poor,* 174-86, also Ilia Delio, *A Franciscan View of Creation: Learning to Live in a Sacramental World,* The Franciscan Heritage Series 2 (St. Bonaventure, NY: Franciscan Institute, 2003), 31. See also Hayes, "Christology — Cosmology," *Spirit and Life* 7 (1997): 41-58.

74. See discussion of "deep incarnation" in Denis Edwards, *Ecology at the Heart of Faith* (Maryknoll, NY: Orbis Books, 2006), 58-60; also Duncan Reid, "Enfleshing the Human," in *Earth Revealing — Earth Healing: Ecology and Christian Theology,* ed. Denis Edwards (Collegeville, MN: Liturgical Press, 2000), 69-83. See Neils Henrick Gregersen, "The Cross of Christ in an Evolutionary World," *Dialog* 40 (2001): 205.

75. Hayes, *The Hidden Center,* 39. See *Dom. IV in Quad. I* (9.232).

76. Hayes, "The Cosmos, a Symbol of the Divine," 249-67. Also see *St. Bonaventure's On the Reduction of the Arts to Theology.*

77. See Intergovernmental Panel on Climate Change.

the poor, who are — and who will be — victims of the perils of desertification and flooding, famine and disease that are predicted to immediately result from unchecked human-caused global warming.[78]

Let us pray for the grace of faith in God's abiding love and the moral courage to take seriously our role as the guardians of God's creation, in the words of St. Francis of Assisi:

Almighty, eternal, just and merciful God, give us miserable ones the grace to do for you alone what we know you want us to do, and to desire always what pleases you. Inwardly cleansed, internally enlightened, and inflamed by the fire of the Holy Spirit, may we be able to follow in the footprints of your beloved Son, our Lord Jesus Christ. And, by your grace alone, may we make our way to you. Most High, who live and rule in perfect Trinity and simple Unity, and are glorified God all powerful, forever and ever.[79]

---

78. See Gerald Baum, Monika Hellwig, and W. Malcolm Byrnes, "Global Climate and Catholic Responsibility: Facts and Responses," *Journal of Catholic Social Thought* 4 (Summer 2007): 313-401; also Elizabeth A. Johnson, "An Earthy Christology: 'For God So Loved the Cosmos,'" *America*, April 13, 2009, 27-30.

79. Francis of Assisi, "Letter to the Entire Order," 50-52, quoted in Nguyen, "The Theology of the Imitation of Christ," 34.

CHAPTER 7

Restoring Land Stewardship through Household Prudence

John A. Cuddeback

Pope Francis's frank challenge in *Evangelii gaudium* to the structures of the global economy has generated much controversy. It is noteworthy that economic issues dominate his reflections on challenges the Church faces today in evangelization. While his treatment does not constitute an in-depth analysis of specific economic structures, it focuses our attention on a fundamental issue, one that is at once theological and philosophical, moral and political: what gives order to economic activity, or what gives order to the production and distribution of wealth.

This pope and his predecessors have been clear in rejecting an economy in which the production and distribution of wealth is fundamentally determined by market forces, ungoverned by a prudence that directs us toward the common good of society.[1] Among the numerous negative consequences

1. See, for instance, Pope Francis: "This imbalance [between rich and poor] is the result of ideologies which defend the absolute autonomy of the marketplace and financial speculation. Consequently, they reject the right of states, charged with vigilance for the common good, to exercise any form of control. A new tyranny is thus born, invisible and often virtual, which unilaterally and relentlessly imposes its own laws and rules" (*Gaudium evangelii,* §56). Likewise, see Pope Emeritus Benedict XVI: "*Economic life* undoubtedly requires *contracts,* in order to regulate relations of exchange between goods of equivalent value. But it also needs *just laws* and *forms of redistribution* governed by politics, and what is more, it needs works redolent of the *spirit of gift.* The economy in the global era seems to privilege the former logic, that of contractual exchange, but directly or indirectly it also demonstrates its need for the other two: political logic, and the logic of the unconditional gift" (*Caritas in veritate,* §37). There is also Pope St. John Paul II: "In the struggle against such a system, what is being proposed as an alternative is not the socialist system, which

of such an economic system, one is the degradation of land and environment. Pope Francis singles this out for attention: "The thirst for power and possessions knows no limits. In this system, which tends to devour everything which stands in the way of increased profits, whatever is fragile, like the environment, is defenseless before the interests of a deified market, which become the only rule."[2]

Civil authority has an irreplaceable role in the stewardship of land and environment. The difficulty of determining just how governmental authority can and should exercise what Thomas Aquinas would call regnative prudence regarding the economy — which would, for instance, foster the appropriate freedom of economic activity — does not make it any less crucial for the common good. Francis and his predecessors are clear on the duty of civil authority to assure that economic structures serve the common good, and one major aspect of this duty is that land be properly used and protected.

Yet in this chapter I would like to turn to another locus of the exercise of prudence over the realm of economics: the household. I want to connect the right practice of prudence at the household level to the right practice of land stewardship.

The household, like civil society, is a natural society that by its very nature is ordered, among other things, to the fulfillment of the material needs of the body. Authority in the household, then, is likewise entrusted with a critical role in the production and use of wealth. Household or domestic prudence, the virtue that pertains to authority in the household, has the task

---

in fact turns out to be State capitalism, but rather *a society of free work, of enterprise and of participation.* Such a society is not directed against the market, but demands that the market be appropriately controlled by the forces of society and by the State, so as to guarantee that the basic needs of the whole of society are satisfied" (*Centesimus annus,* §35). Going back further, we read from Pope Paul VI: "However, certain concepts have somehow arisen out of these new conditions and insinuated themselves into the fabric of human society. These concepts present profit as the chief spur to economic progress, free competition as the guiding norm of economics, and private ownership of the means of production as an absolute right, having no limits nor concomitant social obligations. This unbridled liberalism paves the way for a particular type of tyranny, rightly condemned by Our predecessor Pius XI, for it results in the 'international imperialism of money'" (*Populorum progressio,* §26). Finally, Pope John XXIII first taught: "Thus Pius XI's teaching in this encyclical can be summed up under two heads. First he taught what the supreme criterion in economic matters ought not to be. It must not be the special interests of individuals or groups, nor unregulated competition, economic despotism, national prestige or imperialism, nor any other aim of this sort" (*Mater et magistra,* §38).

2. *Gaudium evangelii,* §56.

of guiding the economic side of household life in view of the higher good of the virtuous flourishing of the household and broader community.

My thesis is that the practice of household prudence is an essential means for achieving the right practice of land stewardship. The thought of Aristotle and Aquinas will provide the principles for my treatment.

Two Kinds of Household Managers

I begin with Aristotle's distinction between two fundamentally diverse practices of *oeconomia,* or household management. For Aristotle, and Thomas Aquinas following him, *oeconomia* names the science or art practiced by household managers. As in all practical sciences or arts, the end is the key.

Aristotle writes: "Thus it is clear that household management attends more to men than to the acquisition of inanimate things, and to human excellence more than to the excellence of property which we call wealth."[3] The end of the household manager, then, the good that gives order to all that he does, is the good life — meaning the complete virtuous life — of the household community.[4] The virtue that especially enables the household manager to exercise this art well, to direct the household community to this end, is domestic prudence.[5] Domestic prudence, as all the species of prudence, is an intellectual virtue that has a strong moral component: it requires the moral virtues, and in a special way requires right intention of the end, in this case the good of the household. In other words, the good and prudent household manager is one who properly wills the common good of the household community and, putting that good above his private good, proceeds to order the life of the household toward its true flourishing.

Of particular significance for Aristotle is the right understanding of the place of the pursuit of wealth in household management. In what seems a

---

3. Aristotle, *Politics* 1.13, 1259b18-20, in *The Complete Works of Aristotle,* vol. 2, ed. Jonathan Barnes (Princeton: Princeton University Press, 1984). All Aristotle citations will be from this volume.

4. Aquinas insists on this point — that the end is not riches — in his *Commentary on Aristotle's Nicomachean Ethics* I.1, sec. 15, and in *Summa theologiae* (hereafter *STh*) II-II, q. 50, art. 3, ad 1, where he says, "Riches are related to *oeconomica* not as its last end, but as its instrument. On the other hand the ultimate end of *oeconomica* is the whole good life of the household. In Ethics I.1 the Philosopher speaks of riches as the end of *oeconomica* in accordance with the opinion of the many."

5. Aristotle, *Nicomachean Ethics* VI, 1141b29, 1142a9.

much overlooked text — in both Aristotle and in Aquinas's commentary — Aristotle points to a fundamental mistake to which household managers are prone, namely, that they conflate the end of household management and money-making. One reason for this confusion is that household management does in fact seek money, especially for the exchange of necessary things, though it seeks it as an instrument for its end. Here the key distinction is between the limited pursuit of money as a means to fulfill the needs of the household, versus a pursuit of money that is intrinsically unlimited and pertains to the merchant.[6] But the more fundamental and significant reason for the conflation pertains to moral character. In a very striking line Aristotle gives his explanation of *why* some household managers seek to increase their money without limit: "The origin of this disposition in men is that they are intent upon living only, and not upon living well; and, as their desires are unlimited, they also desire that the means of gratifying them should be without limit."[7]

This text deserves a much more thorough treatment, but here we will simply note that central to proper governance of the household, which governance is of course necessary for the household to achieve its end, is the rightly ordered desires of household managers. Right order here can be characterized in terms of willing the virtuous life first, and as a consequence, willing material goods only as necessary for complete and proper human flourishing. Here Aristotle and Aquinas specifically raise the specter of a pursuit of wealth that is not directly limited by its immediate ordination to a higher, fully human, end.

We have, then, already seen the basic outline of a second kind of household manager. It is one who, to paraphrase Socrates in the *Apology,* acts as though lower things are higher, and higher things are lower. More specifi-

6. See, for instance, Thomas Aquinas, *Commentary on Aristotle's Politics,* trans. Richard Regan (Indianapolis: Hackett, 2007), I, ch. 8, §3, p. 56: "Then he resolves the foregoing difficulty, saying that the reason for the aforementioned difference seems to be the close relationship of the two kinds of moneymaking. That is to say, there is a close relationship between the moneymaking that serves household management, which seeks money for the exchange of necessary things, and commerce, which seeks money for its own sake." See also I, ch. 8, §6, p. 58: "He also spoke about necessary moneymaking, namely, the moneymaking that is different from the foregoing kind. For necessary moneymaking acquires money up to a limit because of another end, namely, to provide for the necessities of life. And household management, properly speaking, concerns things in accord with nature, e.g., things pertaining to food, and this kind of moneymaking is limited, unlike the first kind of moneymaking."

7. Aristotle, *Politics* I.9, 1257b41-1258a2.

cally, this household manager does not take the virtuous flourishing of the household community as the defining end, the first principle and source of order for running the household. The main instance of such a disorder in Aristotle's treatment is the household manager who acts as though his task is to acquire money without limit. Such a one is incapable of the virtue of domestic prudence.

It seems that here we touch on a very significant moral matter. In the persons of household managers we have the opportunity to see in a unique way the fundamental lines of the human moral drama: do we will first things first, do we will the common good above our private good, do we will the bodily for the sake of the spiritual, and then do we actually order our lives through prudence according to these right appetites? Furthermore, it is clear that Aristotle and Aquinas see this moral drama as the core issue in *oeconomia,* and thus the distinction of two kinds of household managers is at the root of the distinction between well-ordered and disordered economic structures.[8]

Land Stewardship

In turning to the matter of land stewardship, I focus on two things: (1) a historical assertion about the connection of the market economy and the misuse of land, and (2) the philosophical connection of a market economy and the misuse of land, rooted in the points made in the first section of this chapter.

A historical assertion, especially one made by a philosopher, is perhaps particularly vulnerable to attack. We need to be careful to distinguish claims about actual historical connections from claims about philosophical connections. Yet since moral philosophy ultimately is about what happens in the particular, it behooves us to be especially aware of how various practical theories have played out in the theater of the past couple of centuries.

My historical assertion is this: the practice of what is fundamentally a

8. I contend that the modern market society, by its nature, fosters the second, or disordered, kind of household management, inasmuch as it fosters making monetary profit the first principle of the production of wealth. On this point, see Christopher A. Franks, *He Became Poor: The Poverty of Christ and Aquinas's Economic Teachings* (Grand Rapids: Eerdmans, 2009), for instance, "Our economic practices condition us to consider ourselves entitled to whatever we can get in the struggle of the marketplace," 3; see also, "Market society evokes the sense that welfare depends first of all on securing exchange value for oneself. This sense is at the root of the assumption common in modern economics that all economic activity begins in self-interest," 50.

market economy has fostered the reduction of land, as well as human labor, to a commodity. My use of the term "market economy" I take from Karl Polanyi in *The Great Transformation:* "A market economy is an economic system controlled, regulated and directed by markets alone; order in the production and distribution of goods is entrusted to this self-regulating mechanism. An economy of this kind derives from the expectation that human beings behave in such a way as to achieve maximum money gains." Commodities, according to Polanyi, "are here empirically defined as objects produced for sale on the market; markets, again, are empirically defined as actual contacts between buyers and sellers."[9]

A critical shift in the economic system and practices of the Western world, a change that especially came to fruition in the industrial revolution of the nineteenth century, is that labor and land become fundamentally subject to market forces. As Polanyi puts it, "order in the production and distribution of goods" is determined by market prices.[10]

Particularly interesting in Polanyi's historical account is the assertion that both labor and land had never before been systematically reduced to objects of commerce.[11] His account of the consequences is stark. Concerning the reorganization of labor, he writes, "No market economy was conceivable that did not include a market for labor; but to establish such a market, especially in England's rural civilization, implied no less than the wholesale destruction of the traditional fabric of society."[12]

The fate of the land is intimately tied to that of labor, as of course the two had always been so closely associated. What Polanyi calls the "commercialization of the soil" was fundamentally at the same time a separation of man from the soil. The market economy demanded that land be freed from its precapitalistic ties so that it could play its necessary role in the self-regulating market.[13] It seems to me that we can in principle connect many

9. Karl Polanyi, *The Great Transformation: The Political and Economic Origins of Our Time* (Boston: Beacon Press, 2001), 71, 75.

10. Polanyi, *Great Transformation,* 71.

11. "Mercantilism, with all its tendencies toward commercialization, never attacked the safeguards which protected these two basic elements of production — labor and land — from becoming the objects of commerce" (Polanyi, *Great Transformation,* 73).

12. Polanyi, *Great Transformation,* 81.

13. "The aim was the elimination of all claims on the part of the neighborhood or kinship organizations, especially those of virile aristocratic stock, as well as of the Church — claims, which exempted land from commerce or mortgage" (C. Brinkmann, *Das soziale System des Kapitalismus,* quoted in Polanyi, *Great Transformation,* 188-89).

of our current problems with land and environment with the fact that the disposition and use of land became fundamentally a matter determined by market principles.

The philosophical assertion of the connection of market economy and use of the land, to which I now turn, is bolstered by, but not dependent upon, this historical assertion. In giving his account, Polanyi expresses what I take to be a key insight about the true place of land in human life:

> The economic function is but one of many vital functions of land. It invests man's life with stability; it is the site of his habitation; it is a condition of his physical safety; it is the landscape and the seasons. We might as well imagine his being born without hands and feet as carrying on his life without the land. And yet to separate land from man and organize society in such a way as to satisfy the requirements of a real-estate market was a vital part of the utopian concept of a market economy.[14]

At root the point seems to be this: the place of land in human life, as is certainly also the case with labor, is far too noble and complex a reality to be given order by the demands of a market economy. In view of our earlier considerations, we can also put it this way: the disposition of land and labor in human life should be subject to the ordering of the prudent deliberations of human persons who have an understanding of the complex richness of land and labor.

Returning to Aristotle's understanding of the science and art of *oeconomia,* we see that it is precisely the managers of households, as well as in some cases those entrusted with the care of the civil society, that are called to exercise such prudence. It is these who by their office are entrusted with and well-situated for a holistic approach to the land, ordering its use in view of higher ends. It is they, not the forces of the market, who can and must understand land and labor for what it is and thus dispose of it accordingly.

I am aware of the argument that runs as follows: it is precisely the complexity of the disposition of land and labor that puts it beyond the scope of any human comprehension and planning. The self-regulating market, this argument asserts, is the fortunate, or even God-given, solution to this problem. It seems to me that this argument fails to appreciate the central role of prudence in human life. To relegate the disposition and use of land to market forces constitutes an abdication of prudence. By way of comparison, the

---

14. Polanyi, *Great Transformation,* 187.

rearing of children is a profoundly complex affair. Yet while market forces can be a real factor in prudent deliberation regarding the bearing and raising of children, they must not be taken as a primary source of this order. Similarly, while market forces are real factors in the prudent disposition of land and labor, they should not be first principles of that disposition.

Household Prudence and the Land

The relation of the household manager to the land stands as a special instance of, and opportunity for, the exercise of the virtue of prudence. To appreciate how land stewardship should be an exercise of household prudence, we can look to Thomas Aquinas's understanding of prudence, which locates it within a theology of creation.[15]

Prudence always receives its first principles from a given moral order, from principles of the natural law.[16] Central to prudence, then, is a perception of what is given — a natural order with set ends, and a hierarchy of goods in the order to the end. There is much freedom and creativity in the exercise of this queen of virtues, yet its exercise always remains a conforming to a received order — indeed an order received as a gift, and so an order mine, but not primordially mine.

Prudence exercised vis-à-vis the land, which we can also call stewardship, should have these characteristics in a special way. Land is surely for human use, and the prudent stewardship of it is ordered to the human good. But it is for human use precisely in and through, not despite, its wonderfully complex inner teleology. Here the prudent man is faced with a realm that is truly for him, but not for him as his tool or instrument. The natural world is not man's artifact, but God's artifact, and as such Aquinas calls the natural world God's instrument.[17]

As the natural world is God's instrument, used by him for his ends, we do well to consider more specifically how the natural world serves God's ends. It of course serves God by providing for the bodily needs of man.

---

15. For instance, Aquinas speaks of man's being "provident" for himself and others, precisely as a fruit of the way in which he is subject to eternal law (*STh* I-II, q. 91, art. 2). And in *Disputed Questions on Truth*, trans., Robert William Mulligan, SJ (Chicago: Henry Regnery, 1952), q.5, art. 7, Aquinas says: "Divine providence extends to men in two ways: first, in so far as men are provided for; second, in so far as they themselves become provident."

16. See *STh* I-II, q. 47, art. 6c, ad 3.

17. *STh* I-II, q. 1, art. 2; I, q. 22, art. 2, ad 4; I, q. 103, art. 1, ad 3.

But there is more. The natural world serves God by providing men with an opportunity for stewardship.

In a remarkable article in his consideration of divine providence in the *Disputed Questions,* Aquinas asks: "Are all material creatures governed by God's providence through angels?" He proceeds to give a fundamental principle: God communicates his goodness to creatures not only by making them be good in themselves, but also by enabling them, like him, to be the cause of goodness in others. One form this takes is God's causing rational creatures to be the cause of goodness in lower material creatures.[18]

The providence of angels and men are, then, both ways of participating in God's providence over themselves. It is noteworthy that, in Aquinas's eyes, God does not consider it below the angels for them to exercise governance over material things, a governance that directs those natural things to their own God-given ends. Here we see angels being Godlike by causing goodness in lower things, precisely through the providential, we could also say prudential, governance of them.

Man's providence, says Aquinas, is restricted in comparison to the angels, being limited to the realm of "human affairs and practical matters of human life."[19] But if we consider the reply to the fourth objection, in which Aquinas further specifies how angels govern material creation, it seems that Aquinas still places a stewardship of the natural world within human providence. The objector asks: Since material things have their own nature from God, what is there for an angel to do in governing it? Aquinas replies:

> Even though the establishment of nature by which material things receive a tendency to an end comes directly from God, their motion and action can take place through the instrumentality of angels, just as natures in seeds possess their undeveloped nature from God alone but, by the providence of a farmer, are helped to develop into act. Consequently, just as a farmer supervises the growth of the crops in his fields, so do angels direct the entire activity of material creation.[20]

18. Aquinas, *Disputed Questions on Truth* I, q. 5, art. 8.

19. "But even in rational creatures an order can be found. Rational souls hold the lowest place among these, and their light is shadowy in comparison with that of the angels. Consequently, as Dionysius says, their knowledge is more restricted, and their providence is likewise restricted to a few things, namely, to human affairs and practical matters of human life. But the providence of angels is universal and extends to all material creation" (Aquinas, *Disputed Questions on Truth,* vol. 1, q. 5, art. 8).

20. *Disputed Questions on Truth* I, q. 5, art. 8, reply to 4, trans. Robert William Mulli-

What an image — angels are like farmers. And *agricola gubernat pullulationem agri* — literally, "the farmer governs (exercising a providence) the sprouting of the field." It is important to bear in mind the context: Aquinas has said that God shares his goodness by making some creatures capable of causing goodness in lower ones. In other words, to illustrate how angels in their governance cause goodness in material creatures, Aquinas points to how the farmer does precisely that in his field. There is a real aspect here, in angels *and* in men, of directing the natural world to its own good, according to the order and ends that God has established.

I suggest, then, that this disposition of the farmer should be shared, in varying degrees, by all human persons. What again precisely is this disposition? The good farmer intends, in his governance of the natural environment, to harvest the fruit of his labor. But at the same time, he intends that the fruit that serves human needs comes about *through* his working with, and conforming his actions to, the given natural order. The farmer knows that, properly speaking, he himself is not making or even producing something. His labor bears a fruit, the principal agent of which is the living thing he cultivates, or God as the cause of the nature of the productive living thing.[21]

We can begin to ponder here the danger of reducing the cultivation of the earth to the production of a certain amount of wealth — especially as measured simply in monetary terms — and of subjecting its fundamental disposition to the determination of market forces. Of the first importance here is the conviction that human governance, stewardship, dominion of the earth is, as Polanyi suggested, a powerfully complex reality, one shot

---

gan, SJ (Chicago: Henry Regnery, 1952): "Ad quartum dicendum, quod quamvis institutio naturae, per quam res corporales inclinantur in finem, sit immediate a Deo; tamen eorum motus et actio potest esse mediantibus Angelis; sicut etiam rationes seminales sunt in natura inferiori a Deo tantum, sed per providentiam agricolae adiuvantur, ut in actum exeant; unde, sicut agricola gubernat pullulationem agri, ita per Angelos omnis operatio creaturae corporalis administratur."

21. We might consider 1 Cor 3:6-9: "I planted, Apollos watered, but God gave the growth. So neither he who plants nor he who waters is anything, but only God who gives the growth. He who plants and he who waters are equal, and each shall receive his wages according to his labor. For we are God's fellow workers; you are God's field, God's building." We might also consider Xenophon: "Do you think it is any less necessary [than in war] to ask the gods for mercy where agricultural affairs are concerned? Sensible farmers, I can assure you, worship and pray to the gods about their fruits, grain, cattle, horses, sheep — yes, and all their property" (*The Estate Manager* V, in *The Conversations of Socrates* [London: Penguin, 1990], 308).

through with multiple levels of providential teleology. By God's providential design, humble stewardship of the natural world — an image of which is the farmer in his field — bears at least a threefold fruit: one inside the steward himself, one in the material fruits of the land, and one in the well-cared-for land itself, a blessing to others now and in the future. Something that we see again and again throughout agrarian folk wisdom is the conviction that doing what is best for the land, the plants, and the animals ultimately redounds to the good of all. The point here is not that lower natural things are ruled "for their own sake." Indeed, Aquinas is explicit that, in the proper sense, only rational creatures are ruled by God "for their own sake."[22]

Rather, the point is that, when we look first to the given order of nature and, in accord with that order, put first things first, such as putting the common good before the private, then — in ways beyond our comprehension — the common good is achieved.

I suggest that, when the complexity of teleology is beyond our full comprehension, it is not the time to put self-interest first or to abandon the disposition of things to market forces. Now is the time to put first things first and to exercise our prudence according to the light of the natural order.

Returning to Aristotle's moral analysis of the danger for household managers, we recall that, for Aristotle, the fundamental moral reason for the demise of the practice of *oeconomia* is that men "are intent upon living only, and not upon living well; and, as their desires are unlimited, they also desire that the means of gratifying them should be without limit."[23] In his commentary Aquinas lists three abuses that follow upon this disposition — abuses that are hauntingly redolent of contemporary society. The first is that men "strive to acquire money without limit because they do not have the right endeavor for the good life." The second is that "unnatural and unnecessary moneymaking is included in household management." The third is that men "abuse their faculties, i.e., their virtues, arts, or position." Of particular interest is how Aquinas notes Aristotle's two examples of arts that come to be abused precisely by being ordered toward money: "So also, military skill is for the sake of victory, and medical skill for the sake of health, but neither skill is for the sake of money. But some use military and medical skills to acquire money and so make both into instruments to make money, subordinating such skills to money as the end to which all other things need to be

---

22. See *Summa contra gentiles* III, ch. 112: "That Rational Creatures Are Governed for Their Own Sakes, While Others Are Governed in Subordination to Them."
23. Aristotle, *Politics* I.9, 1257b41-1258a2.

directed." Aquinas ends with a scriptural reference: "And so Eccl 10:19 says: 'All things yield to money.'"[24]

Agriculture perhaps was not used as an example, since prior to the modern age and especially the industrial revolution, agriculture was not as likely to be an art misused in this way. Polanyi says of a famous nineteenth-century English manufacturer: "[Richard] Cobden set the landlords of England aghast with his discovery that farming was a 'business' and that those who were broke must clear out."[25] Less than a hundred years later the southern agrarian Andrew Lytle found it necessary to scold: "A farm is not a place to grow wealthy; it is a place to grow corn."[26]

A renewal of land stewardship today will require a rejection of the logic of the market as a first principle of land use. The proper approach to the natural world is especially instantiated in the household manager of good character, who at once both respects the natural order and orders land use in view of the true flourishing of household and community. One certainly need not be a farmer to have such a disposition — and indeed all too many farmers might not, but the good farmer in his field provides an archetype for renewing land stewardship in our households.

Conclusion

I conclude with words from Plato's contemporary, Xenophon: "For you'll gain more produce by sowing and planting what the land readily grows and nurtures than by sowing and planting what *you* want."[27] This simple yet profound piece of agrarian wisdom captures much. There clearly have always been, and always will be, those whose approach to the land is fundamentally one of "I do what do I want." But it has not always been the case that dominant economic and social structures both presuppose and cultivate such an approach.

Some might even wonder whether Xenophon was wrong. Haven't we in fact gained more produce by sowing and planting exactly what we want? This is not the place to argue about how to evaluate our current situation.[28]

24. Aquinas, *Commentary on Aristotle's Politics*, I, ch. 8, §§4-6, pp. 57-58.
25. Polanyi, *Great Transformation*, 192.
26. Andrew Lytle, "The Hind Tit," in *I'll Take My Stand: The South and the Agrarian Tradition* (Baton Rouge: Louisiana State University Press, 1977), 205.
27. Xenophon, *The Estate Manager* XVI, p. 341; italics are original.
28. The difficulty and disagreement about how to judge the current situation is clear

But what comes to mind is Wendell Berry's concern that we have lost the ability to subtract. In other words, seeing the sheer quantities and efficiency of our industrial production, we can become blinded to the wide array of costs, material and spiritual, that we, and the land, have endured.

Contemporary economic structures and practices do not encourage a sense of responsibility for stewarding the natural world. A robust and principled practice of household management, *oeconomia,* does. At the end of the day, perhaps the most practical question that each of us can ask ourselves is: What will the *nomos* of our *oikos* be? What order will prevail in our own household? Will we sow and plant what we want, or will we sow and plant in prudence, guided by a vision of what the land readily grows and nurtures? For the good of us all.

---

in ISI's *A Student's Guide to Economics,* by Paul Heyne (Wilmington, DE: Intercollegiate Studies Institute Books, 2000), 26: "Those who are tempted to suppose that the loss of community is too high a price to pay for the advantages of a market-coordinated economy should reflect carefully on the full range of benefits that 'capitalism' has brought with it" (31). Earlier he writes: "What can those who contrast *material* with *human* welfare possibly have in mind? . . . People who talk this way literally do not know what they are talking about" (26). While I am very concerned to avoid the pitfall of overspiritualizing the human good, it seems to me that *properly* distinguishing *material* and *human* welfare is in fact central not only to a proper assessment of our economic situation, but also to understanding human life itself.

CHAPTER 8

Flourishing and Suffering in Social Creatures

Faith Pawl

My present task is to ask what on its face seems like a very simple question: What matters most for the good animal life? More specifically, I will ask about the good life for social, nonhuman animals. Though I take this question to be philosophically interesting in its own right, two immediate applications for such inquiry come to mind. First and foremost, it is important to reflect on animal flourishing for the sake of the proper care of creation. If proper stewardship requires that we concern ourselves with the flourishing of nonhuman animals, we ought to do our best to understand what animal flourishing consists in. This is especially true if stewardship involves valuing and cultivating the natural goodness of the creatures entrusted to our care.

Philosophical reflection on the nature of animal flourishing is also important for the sake of addressing one of the more strident objections to traditional theism that has been surfacing in the philosophy of religion in the past decades. Consider an atheistic challenge sometimes called the problem of animal suffering: is it rational for the theist to maintain belief in an omnipotent, omniscient, omnibenevolent God in light of all the suffering we witness in the animal kingdom? The stories that theists traditionally tell concerning God's permission of human suffering seem inapplicable to cases of animal suffering, or so the charge goes. If theists wish to respond to the atheistic challenge, more needs to be said about what sorts of goods animals can actually enjoy before we can ask whether their suffering can be defeated, outweighed, or redeemed. If we do not know what a good animal life is like, how can we say anything about the place of suffering therein?

It is not my aim here to offer a theodicy for the suffering of social animals, or to spell out the ethical implications for my conception of the good life for social animals, though I will make a few suggestions in conclusion about how either endeavor might go. Rather, my goal is to address questions upstream from those applications, more fundamental questions about the nature of the animal good.

We rational animals are the prime examples of social creatures, and since antiquity our reflection on the good life has taken it for granted that human flourishing depends on social connection. In the Christian tradition, we believe that the central good for human beings is to be in relationship — with God and with others. I will argue here that, for very many nonhuman animals, social connection is one of, and perhaps chief among, the ingredients that make for a good life. That is, for many creatures in addition to just humans, relationships are at the core of well-being, even if animal relationships are radically different from human ones. I will also argue for a more speculative claim, that relationships have value for animals that extend beyond the biological, adaptive value that those relationships confer.

To make the case, I will first offer some clarification on the notion of a social creature. I will do so by focusing on empirical research on one species of social creature, the savannah baboon, in order to illustrate what I mean when I say that social creatures are able to share their world with other beings. Then I will say something about flourishing in general and the role of social connection for baboon flourishing. I will conclude with some suggestions about the implications of what I say about animal social flourishing, both for the two motivating applications above, and for our general view of the place of animals in the created order.

Social Creatures

As I am using the term, a social creature is a being that, in virtue of possessing some degree of cognitive sophistication in the domain of social interaction, is able to share its world with other beings, especially its conspecifics. What kind of sharing do I have in mind? Social creatures depend upon one another, are responsive to the cognitive and emotional states of one another, and in many cases have some level of conscious awareness of those states. Most important, social creatures have strong natural desires to be with those animals to which they are closely bonded. This loose definition makes space for a very broad range of levels of sociality.[1]

In order to unpack this definition of a social creature and to make plain what I mean when I say social creatures share their world with one another, I will focus on a particular species of animal, the savanna baboon. Savanna baboons are old-world monkeys who dwell primarily in sub-Saharan Africa. They are highly social creatures, and their social intelligence has been extensively researched because of the structure of their social groups.

As is the case for very many species of large-brained, group-living animals, baboons develop close, long-term bonds with their conspecifics. These sometime include mating pairs, but more often do not. Biologists studying this social pattern in a number of species, not just primates, are primarily concerned with the way that long-term social bonds and the altruistic behavior associated with such relationships enhance fitness.[2] Research indicates that, just as is the case for humans, having close, stable social bonds makes for healthier individuals. Baboons and other animals that are successful at forming such bonds have longer lives and fewer stress-related illnesses, and their offspring have a better chance at survival.[3]

Researchers call these stable, closely bonded relationships among baboons "friendships."[4] Using longitudinal data from two subspecies of ba-

1. I will not try to specify exact boundaries for which species count as social and which do not. First, I think those boundaries might in fact be vague. Second, I am not a scientist, and thus I am not qualified to say which species of animals qualify as sufficiently social and which do not. Furthermore, though there have been tremendous strides in research on animal social intelligence in the past decades, there is still very much scientists themselves do not know about how animals relate to one another, and so there will be very many cases where we simply do not know enough yet to draw conclusions relevant to my concerns about social flourishing.

2. Robert M. Seyfarth and Dorothy L. Cheney, "The Evolutionary Origins of Friendship," *Annual Review of Psychology* 63, no. 1 (2012): 153-77.

3. Joan B. Silk, Jeanne Altmann, and Susan C. Alberts, "Social Relationships among Adult Female Baboons *(Papio cynocephalus)* I: Variation in the Strength of Social Bonds," *Behavioral Ecology and Sociobiology* 61, no. 2 (December 1, 2006): 183-95; Barbara B. Smuts, *Sex and Friendship in Baboons*, 2nd ed. (Piscataway, NJ: Aldine Transaction, 2007); Jorg J. M. Massen, Elisabeth H. M. Sterck, and Henk de Vos, "Close Social Associations in Animals and Humans: Functions and Mechanisms of Friendship," *Behaviour* 147, no. 11 (September 1, 2010): 1379-1412; Seyfarth and Cheney, "The Evolutionary Origins of Friendship"; Robert M. Seyfarth, Joan B. Silk, and Dorothy L. Cheney, "Variation in Personality and Fitness in Wild Female Baboons," *Proceedings of the National Academy of Sciences* 109, no. 42 (October 16, 2012): 16,980-85.

4. I will follow the convention of calling these bonding pairs friendships. Should the

boons in Kenya and Botswana, Joan Silk et al. found that female baboons' bonds remain fairly stable across time and are not spread out indiscriminately among many partners. Silk explains, "Females gain benefits from establishing and maintaining highly individuated relationships with a relatively small number of partners, rather than interacting less selectively with a wider range of social partners."[5] So while we might expect that positive social contact in general is good for animals, it is interesting to note that, for baboons, what matters is being attached to *particular* individuals.

Close, relaxed physical contact is one hallmark of baboon friendship, and grooming is the glue that holds it all together. Grooming is very important for baboon hygiene, and baboons who are groomed more frequently tend to be healthier.[6] However, according to Dorothy Cheney and Robert Seyfarth,

> Grooming involves far more than just the removal of ecto-parasites. When two animals groom, their behavior not only provides immediate satisfaction but also strengthens the bond between them. This not only causes them to groom each other again but also reinforces their tendency to spend time together, tolerate each other at feeding times, huddle together on cold days, and support each other in aggressive alliances. . . . All of these interactions forge a relationship that is more than the sum of its parts.[7]

This relationship is subserved by the biological mechanisms of bonding and attachment. Grooming feels good. When animals groom one another, they secrete the hormone oxytocin, which not only reduces stress hormones but bonds animals together.[8] This is roughly the same sort of chemistry at work when mammal mothers (including humans) nurse their young.

---

reader worry that the label runs the risk of inappropriate anthropomorphism, the label may be taken as a technical term, as it is used in the empirical literature.

5. Joan B. Silk et al., "Stability of Partner Choice among Female Baboons," *Animal Behaviour* 83, no. 6 (June 2012): 1512.

6. Mercy Y. Akinyi et al., "Role of Grooming in Reducing Tick Load in Wild Baboons (*Papio cynocephalus*)," *Animal Behaviour* 85, no. 3 (March 2013): 559-68.

7. Dorothy L. Cheney and Robert M. Seyfarth, *Baboon Metaphysics: The Evolution of a Social Mind* (Chicago: University of Chicago Press, 2008), 63.

8. Cheney and Seyfarth, *Baboon Metaphysics*, 88. For a related discussion on rhesus macaques, see Steve W. C. Chang et al., "Inhaled Oxytocin Amplifies both Vicarious Reinforcement and Self Reinforcement in Rhesus Macaques (*Macaca mulatta*)," *Proceedings of the National Academy of Sciences* 109, no. 3 (January 17, 2012): 959-64.

Having close relationships really matters to baboons, even if they do not understand the ways in which such relationships are good for them. Among baboons, friendships occur most frequently between maternal kin. Studies on baboon friendship indicate that, even if baboons have *no* maternal kin, they still manage to seek out at least one "enduring friendship." In fact, when a female baboon loses a friend, she has a strong inclination to find others with whom she can bond. Seyfarth and Cheney write,

> Data from several species suggest that, when individuals are under stress or their long-term bonds are challenged, they respond in ways that seem designed either to restore and strengthen existing relationships or to form new ones. Such behavior also has the effect of reducing [stress hormone] levels. . . . If a female's mother dies, her bonds with sisters grow stronger. . . . Evidence that animals strive to restore and maintain social bonds when challenged finds parallels in studies in humans, where the loss of a close companion is a potent stressor, and individuals show an increased tendency to associate with others when under stress.[9]

It is tempting, parroting Aristotle, to say that no baboon would choose a life without "friends," even with all other goods besides.[10]

Studies tell us that having long-term social bonds with a select number of partners is good for baboons, both because it promotes long-term health and because it increases the chances that baboons will help each other in the future. It would be a mistake to think, though, that baboons cultivate these relationships because they have calculated the benefits they stand to reap from their friends. As several researchers point out, to attribute such forward thinking to primates gives them too much cognitive credit.[11]

9. Seyfarth and Cheney, "The Evolutionary Origins of Friendship," 161, 169. The authors cite Silk, Altmann, and Alberts, "Social Relationships among Adult Female Baboons *(Papio cynocephalus)*"; and Kenneth S. Kendler, John Myers, and Carol A. Prescott, "Sex Differences in the Relationship between Social Support and Risk for Major Depression: A Longitudinal Study of Opposite-Sex Twin Pairs," *American Journal of Psychiatry* 162, no. 2 (February 1, 2005): 250-56.

10. See *Nicomachean Ethics* XIII, ch. 3. Aristotle had something very different in mind when he spoke about friendship, though there is a very weak sense in which the baboon friendships I've described resemble what Aristotle termed "friendships of pleasure" — the kind of friendship shared most often between young people.

11. Frans B. M. de Waal, "Putting the Altruism Back into Altruism: The Evolution of Empathy," *Annual Review of Psychology* 59, no. 1 (2008): 279-300; Gabriele Schino and Filippo Aureli, "Reciprocal Altruism in Primates: Partner Choice, Cognition, and Emo-

As far as monkeys' immediate motivations go, Gabrielle Schino and Fillipo Aureli explain that, even if monkeys had the capacity to forecast the ways in which their current behaviors might pay off well into the future (and it appears they do not), monkeys demonstrate strong temporal discounting, or "the tendency to devalue future rewards."[12] In other words, they are not interested in delayed gratification. Thus, it is hard to see that monkeys could or would be motivated to maintain friendships because of the promise of future reward, since they do not tend to prioritize long-term gratification over present gains.

More likely, there are emotional rewards built into the frequent interactions that occur between friends, and those immediate rewards are part of the mechanisms that motivate so-called altruistic behaviors. "The simplest way for evolution to build these mechanisms would have been to recruit the social bonding that (presumably) originally evolved in the context of mother-infant attachment. The recent application of the concept of 'friendship' to nonhuman primates is coherent with this interpretation."[13] As Schino and Aureli go on to argue, the memory of past interactions coupled with positive emotional associations can sufficiently explain the proximate cause of altruistic behaviors in primates, without making any hefty assumptions about cognitively demanding tasks like long-term scorekeeping of past interactions or predictions about future rewards. This suggestion is helpful, because it highlights that having close relationships does not necessarily require much cognitive sophistication.

I do not mean to suggest, though, that baboons are not cognitively sophisticated creatures, especially when it comes to social cognition. Baboon troops range in size from about 20 to 150 animals. Each savanna baboon troop has several adult males and females, as well as many young baboons, and all the members of the troop fall somewhere in dominance hierarchies. The dominance structure is dizzyingly complex, and what researchers have discovered is that baboons are remarkably adept at keeping track of where everyone belongs in the dominance hierarchy, as well as keeping track of other facts such as who is mating with whom and who is friends with whom.[14] They even seem to keep track of which baboons are friendly and

---

tions," in *Advances in the Study of Behavior*, vol. 39, ed. Timothy J. Roper and H. Jane Brockmann (London: Academic Press, 2009), 45-69.

12. Schino and Aureli, "Reciprocal Altruism in Primates," 55.

13. Schino and Aureli, "Reciprocal Altruism in Primates," 58. See also de Waal, "Putting the Altruism Back into Altruism," 218.

14. Cheney and Seyfarth, *Baboon Metaphysics*.

which are not.[15] Furthermore, baboons' vocalizations are individually distinct, and they are able to identify one another by those distinct vocalizations. They can tell when they are the intended audience of another baboon's vocalization, even when they cannot see the other baboon.[16] These are all remarkable feats given the size of a baboon troop.

Baboons have evolved to have highly specialized cognitive capacities for processing complex and dynamic social information.[17] Since evolution has shaped baboons with brains so highly specialized for social tasks, their experience of the world is thoroughly colored by their sociality. What, though, might the subjective character of baboons' social relationships be like? Any answers to such questions are highly speculative, since we cannot know what it is like to be a baboon, any more than we can know what it is like to be a bat. However, recent research on empathy and so-called altruistic behaviors in primates offers some insight into the affective dimensions of primates' interactions with one another.

Frans de Waal and his colleagues are interested in the phenomenon they call empathy, understood very broadly as the capacity to share in other creatures' emotional states. As de Waal describes it, empathy comes in layers, and he likens the layers of empathy to those of a Russian doll. At the most basic layer, the subject and the other share emotional responses through something called "emotional contagion." To illustrate emotional contagion, de Waal points to the whole flock of birds that immediately startles and takes flight in response to one bird's emotion of fear. Similarly, when one newborn in a nursery full of human babies starts to cry, they all cry. "At the core of these processes is adoption — in whole or in part — of another's emotional state, i.e. emotional contagion."[18] Emotional contagion is automatic, a sort of unreflective mimicry of the emotion of the other. The emotional distress of the other arouses distress in the subject, and often the subject's desire to alleviate its own distress prompts it to do something on the behalf of the other. On this model, the pro-social behavior of monkeys like baboons is made possible by an integral emotional link between animals.

Emotional contagion, de Waal and his team theorize, is subserved by

15. Seyfarth, Silk, and Cheney, "Variation in Personality and Fitness in Wild Female Baboons."

16. Anne L. Engh et al., "Who, Me? Can Baboons Infer the Target of Vocalizations?" *Animal Behaviour* 71, no. 2 (February 2006): 381-87.

17. Cheney and Seyfarth, *Baboon Metaphysics,* 274.

18. De Waal, "Putting the Altruism Back into Altruism," 283.

neural mechanisms that allow animals to experience one another's emotions by a sort of state-matching process. When some animal subject perceives the distress or joy of another animal (the object), the object's representation of its emotional state automatically elicits a matching state in the subject.[19]

Neurological research on the now-famous "mirror neurons" suggests that at least some kind of system that matches brain states between observer and observed is in play in various forms of empathy. Mirror neurons, discovered more than twenty years ago, were first detected in macaques.[20] Mirror neurons fire in the brains of both monkeys and humans when subjects observe another individual performing an action, and when the subject performs that same action herself. The subject's brain mirrors the object's.

Mirror neurons are thus hypothesized to play a role in action understanding. Pier Francesco Ferrari and Leonardo Fogassi explain that the mirror neuron system "represents a neural model that, through a matching mechanism, enables the emergence of important cognitive functions such as the understanding of the other's behavior. This mechanism is automatic and pre-reflexive, that is, does not imply any inferential mechanism or verbal processing."[21] The system is implicated in not just action understanding, though, but emotional understanding as well.[22]

Social cognition is no doubt distributed through other brain systems beyond the mirror neuron system, but mirror neuron research is helpful because it demonstrates the embodied nature of social cognition. Vittorio Gallese et al. put it nicely when they say, "Social cognition is not only thinking about the contents of someone else's mind. Our brains, and those of other primates, appear to have developed a basic functional mechanism, a mirror mechanism, which gives us an *experiential insight into other minds.*"[23]

19. Stephanie D. Preston and Frans B. M. de Waal, "Empathy: Its Ultimate and Proximate Bases," *Behavioral and Brain Sciences* 25, no. 1 (2002): 1-20.

20. Pier Francesco Ferrari and Leonardo Fogassi, "The Mirror Neuron System in Monkeys and Its Implications for Social Cognitive Functions," in *The Primate Mind: Built to Connect with Other Minds,* ed. Frans B. M. de Waal and Pier Francesco Ferrari (Cambridge, MA: Harvard University Press, 2012), 14.

21. Ferrari and Fogassi, "The Mirror Neuron System in Monkeys," 29.

22. Jaime A. Pineda et al., "Hierarchically Organized Mirroring Processes in Social Cognition: The Functional Neuroanatomy of Empathy," in *Mirror Neuron Systems,* ed. Jaime A. Pineda (Totowa, NJ: Humana Press, 2009), 135-60.

23. Vittorio Gallese, Christian Keysers, and Giacomo Rizzolatti, "A Unifying View of the Basis of Social Cognition," *Trends in Cognitive Sciences* 8, no. 9 (September 2004): 401 (emphasis mine). The authors use the term "mind" here in a very broad sense.

When animals experience emotional connections with one another, they do not need to go through an inferential process whereby they reason about what is going on inside one another. They experience the other's emotions themselves, directly.

If de Waal's model is apt, primates like baboons share their lives with each other via integral emotional connections. This emotional sharing is but one remarkable aspect of their social capacities. To summarize, baboons see one another as distinct individuals. They are keenly aware of one another's social roles and relationships. Baboons are highly motivated to form close, stable bonds with one another, and those bonds are maintained by helping and grooming behaviors that are probably motivated by emotional rewards. Like very many mammals, baboons are subject to emotional contagion, the emotional core of empathy. All this makes possible some basic level of inter-subjectivity. It is no stretch to say that to understand the nature of the baboon is to understand that baboons are connected to one another.

Flourishing and Social Connection

Now we should ask, What does it mean to say that a social creature like a baboon has a life that is good? What is baboon flourishing? To answer these questions, we need some grasp on what flourishing is in the first place. Rather than spell out my own theory of flourishing, I will borrow one contemporary account from the philosopher Richard Kraut. What I wish to say about baboon flourishing might work just as well with a different conception of flourishing, though, so long as the alternate account of flourishing is tightly connected with nature-fulfillment.

Kraut approaches the fundamental question of what is good by insisting that it makes no sense to construct an ethical theory around a purely abstract notion of the good. We must always ask what is good *for* some being or other. For the most part, our ethical inquiry is concerned with what is good *for* humans, though it is of course sensible to inquire what is good *for* other beings as well. It is good for living things to flourish, he argues, and while we can come up with a general account of what flourishing is, what will constitute one being's flourishing will vary greatly from what will constitute the flourishing of a being of another kind. "When we think about the good of animals, our thoughts vary according to the kind of animal we have in mind. We must ask what is good for a member of this species or that, and the answer to that question will not necessarily be uniform across species.

Unimpeded flying is good — that is, good for a bird."[24] In fine Aristotelian form, Kraut takes it that to know what is good for an animal, we must think about what is distinctive about that kind of animal.

Kraut bases his own conception of flourishing and account of what is good for living things on the commonsense notion that flourishing is tightly connected with health. He says,

> What is good or bad for a living thing always has to do with its closeness to or distance from living the kind of life available to a flourishing member of its species. Animals that have perceptual systems do well if the organs and mental processes that are part of those systems operate well, and those animals fare well, as sensory beings, to the extent that they have certain kinds of experiences and not others.[25]

Thus, to flourish, one's physical and psychological health must support, rather than impede, having the kind of life a member of a species is capable of having, complete with certain kinds of positive experiences that go along with that life. According to Kraut, a subject comes to flourish under favorable conditions "by developing properly and fully, that is, by growing, maturing, making full use of the potentialities, capacities that (under favorable conditions) they naturally have at an early stage of their existence."[26] He calls this view of flourishing "developmentalism."

In the quick sketch I have presented of Kraut's view, flourishing is primarily a functional notion. A subject is flourishing if he or she is functioning properly, in a way that allows fulfillment of the various potentialities this subject has in virtue of being a member of the species to which he or she belongs. But why is it good for a subject to be able to fulfill his or her potentialities? One insufficient answer, in my view, is that the goodness of fulfilling one's potentialities can be explained solely in terms of the goodness of achieving such excellence. It is true that an individual that flourishes is an exemplary member of his or her species, and the achievement of excellence can indeed be a very great good for that individual.

However, the goodness of being an exemplary member of the species "cow," for instance, has very little to do with the blue ribbon that cow wins at the state fair, and everything to do with the kind of life that a blue-ribbon

24. Richard Kraut, *What Is Good and Why: The Ethics of Well-Being* (Cambridge, MA: Harvard University Press, 2009), 89.
25. Kraut, *What Is Good and Why*, 152.
26. Kraut, *What Is Good and Why*, 131.

cow can lead.[27] A better answer to the question about the goodness of realizing one's potentialities — the answer Kraut himself would give — is that the relevant potentialities of a subject are what make possible certain kinds of experiences for him or her, and as a matter of common sense, we take those experiences to be constitutive of the good life for the species capable of enjoying those experiences.

Now think about what is good for baboons. Following Kraut, we can understand what is good for baboons by considering what it looks like for baboons to grow, mature, and make "full use of the potentialities, capacities that (under favorable conditions) they naturally have at an early stage of their existence."[28] In addition to sharing with all living things certain physical capacities for growth and reproduction, baboons also have rich sensory, cognitive, affective, and social powers, so we can conclude that baboon flourishing will involve the exercise of all those powers, complete with the kind of positive experiences made possible by those powers.

As I have been at pains to show, though, baboons' social powers are of crucial importance for them — sociality permeates every aspect of baboon life. Baboons' social experiences are indeed among the catalog of great goods baboons can desire and enjoy, but I think there is a sense in which the social experiences that baboons enjoy are at the top of the list. Social connection is very good for baboons because it makes possible relationship.

Why think that relationship — having "friends" — is a great good for baboons? One straightforward answer is that having "friends" is adaptive — it makes possible greater longevity and reproductive success. I wish to speculate here, though, that the goodness of baboon friendship extends beyond the adaptive value of such relationships.

Permit me to begin with an analogy that is, on its face, somewhat simplistic. Humans enjoy increased longevity and reproductive success when we have strong social connections. We do not think, however, that our human relationships are valuable simply because they promote our fitness. Furthermore, though we value the pleasure we experience when we are with our friends, we do not think friendship adds value to our lives just because of that pleasure. Rather, we humans value one another as individuals, and we value the relationships we have with one another because it is good to share

27. Sadly, the qualities that are assessed when we judge animals in such contexts are often qualities that do not contribute to an animal's having a good life but, rather, qualities well suited merely to our human interests and at the expense of animal flourishing.

28. Kraut, *What Is Good and Why*, 131.

life's experiences with others. You might even say it is part of our nature as social creatures to want to share our lives.

Why think the case is different for baboons? Certainly, there are tremendous differences in the ways that humans relate to one another and baboons relate to one another. We should ask, though, Do baboons value one another as individuals? That depends on what we mean. When someone mentions valuing another human as an individual, it might mean something like this person values the other as an end in himself or herself, or recognizes and appreciates the intrinsic dignity of the other, or something else sufficiently Kantian. It makes no sense to attribute such valuing to baboons, since baboons cannot take up these kinds of reflective, evaluative attitudes about what matters to them. Indeed, if by "valuing" we mean taking up such an evaluative stance, baboons probably do not value anything at all.

There is another important sense, however, where when we say that we value humans as individuals, we simply mean that we like *them*. We want to spend time with *them*. We want *them* to be happy. There is a particularity about our preference for being with that individual. It is Timothy and not some stranger whose company I prefer. In this way, baboons clearly have preferences for one another as individuals, since they recognize one another as individuals, and they desire to spend their time with particular baboons. A baboon's friends matter to him or her.

Do baboons care about the relationships they have with one another because it is good to share life's experiences with others? Again, it is hard to know how to fill out the analogy. Humans are probably unique in the way we wish to explicitly share with one another what we are thinking or feeling.[29] Within the animal domain, there is a uniquely human impulse to communicate our inner lives with one another, and our linguistic abilities allow this desire to reach fruition. We are capable of sophisticated kinds of emotional sharing, and it is fair to say that there is a depth to human relationships that is hard to imagine outside our species. It does not follow, however, that animals' relationships are shallow, whatever that means, or that animals do not enjoy whatever aspects of their experiences they *do* share. Again, baboons' relationships matter to them. Baboons (for the most part, anyway) do not want to be alone. They seek out friends. They long for physical contact. These pursuits give them pleasure, and they give them something to care about.

Is it part of a baboon's nature as a social creature to want to share its life

---

29. Cheney and Seyfarth, *Baboon Metaphysics*, 198.

with others? The answer to this question seems to me to be a resounding Yes. Social connectedness is at the very core of what it means to be a baboon. The good baboon life, then, is one where a baboon has what it needs to flourish, and its central desires are not ultimately frustrated. Strong social bonds are necessary for baboon flourishing and are at the core of their motivational structure.

Mutatis mutandis, what I have said here about baboon flourishing will apply to the flourishing of other species to the extent that those species have social capacities similar to those of baboons. So long as other species of animals have strong natural desires for social connection, the flourishing of members of those species as well will depend on such connection. Since phenomena like friendship and emotional contagion seem to be fairly widespread among mammalian and avian species, there is reason to think that what I have said here about baboons can be generalized to very many species of animals.

Applications

As I warned at the outset, I will not go very far toward drawing out the practical implications of how I am conceiving of animal social flourishing. That is the difficult work of applied ethics, work I will save for another day. Here I have only two suggestions. If we ought to treat things in a way that respects the sorts of natures that they have, then we must pay attention to the social dimension of the lives of social creatures. Concerning animals on our farms, in our homes and workplaces, and in captivity in zoos (justifiably or not), we should take care to allow those animals to develop and maintain the close bonds that hold such value for them, so far as we reasonably can. Should the conditions of domestication or captivity prevent animals from having the sorts of social attachments they naturally desire, we have good reason to provide surrogates. This suggestion seems modest enough, but I suspect that many of our practices, especially in large-scale farming operations, would need to be radically revised were we to take the social good of animals more seriously. Concerning animals in the wild, we have yet another motivation to minimize habitat loss, since scarcity of land, food, and water can place considerable stress on the health of animal social groups.

What, then, is the upshot of this conception of the good of social animals for the atheistic challenge posed by the problem of animal suffering? In my work, I have focused on the social good of animals as a sort of corrective to a trend in the still nascent philosophical literature on the problem of animal suffering. Until very recently, the discussion has tended to focus exclusively on animal pain to the exclusion of other evils that animals can suffer. Likewise within this same dialectic, discussions of the animal good have been focused mostly on pleasure and goods associated with biological fitness, like longevity and reproductive success.[30] The good animal life is one with the adaptive stamp of evolutionary approval. I think that picture of the good animal life is too shallow.

One of the most common responses to the problem of human suffering is to look for goods that we can gain (or evils that can be prevented) only because of the existence of suffering. Those goods (or the prevention of those evils) are hypothesized to provide morally justifying reasons for God's permission of suffering. In my view, pessimism about the existence of any morally justifying goods for the defeat of *animal* suffering — or at least, any goods that have to do with the actual animals who suffer — stems from the sense that we have already figured out what an animal's greatest good consists in, namely, biological flourishing and the absence of pain, and the observed facts about animal suffering show that those goods are just hopelessly frustrated.

However, if what I say about social flourishing in creatures is apt, we should take a more capacious view of animal sentience and appreciate a rich array of goods that many animals can enjoy in addition to the goods of pleasure, longevity, and reproductive success. If relationships are a key ingredient of the good animal life for social creatures, this opens up logical space for a broader range of responses to the problem of animal suffering.

By focusing too narrowly on the discontinuities between animals and humans — particularly when it comes to rationality and freedom — we have too hastily dismissed the possibility that God's permission of animal suffering might depend on reasons analogous to the reasons for God's permission of human suffering. Here I have in mind the reasons proposed in various responses to the problem of evil like certain versions of soul-making theodicies, or Marilyn Adams's or Eleonore Stump's relational defenses for human suffering.[31]

My point is not that we can tell the very same stories for animal suffering

---

30. There are some notable exceptions, especially in Trent Dougherty's recent work.

31. Marilyn McCord Adams, *Horrendous Evils and the Goodness of God* (Ithaca, NY: Cornell University Press, 2000); Eleonore Stump, *Wandering in Darkness: Narrative and the Problem of Suffering* (New York: Oxford University Press, 2010).

that we can tell for human suffering. To assert as much would be to overlook the tremendous differences between the lives of humans and the lives of animals, especially when it comes to the enjoyment of the great goods of rationality, free will, and the ability to make meaning of one's life. However, the goods that matter *most* for the kinds of defenses just mentioned are goods of relationship — with God and with other creatures, and these stories might help shed some light on why God allows animals to suffer too.

Concluding Reflections on the Place of Social Creatures in the Created Order

I want to finish here with another reason the theist has for taking a more capacious view of animal sentience, particularly in the social domain, and this reason is independent of questions of applied ethics or theodicy. As we learn more and more about the social intelligence of various animals, it becomes clear that we humans are not the only creatures who have the kind of perspective on the world that allows for rich intersubjective connection, which is something that should inspire awe and wonder at the beautiful complexity of God's creation. Just as consciousness itself is a curious, marvelous feature of the world that God has made, the ability to share conscious experiences with others adds a further layer of complex beauty to the world.

How amazing is it that primates are able to have some grasp, however fleeting, into the mental states of their conspecifics? How lovely for us that the domesticated animals in our care are sensitive and responsive to our feelings and intentions! How wonderful that mammals and birds are empathically connected to one another, that animal families are born out of the natural mechanisms of bonding and attachment! These great goods are the stuff of the peaceable kingdom. Indeed, it should be no surprise that a Creator God who values community and family has liberally sown the seeds of such connection, in varying degrees, throughout the created order. We need not attribute full-blown rationality or thought to creatures in order to see that their lives are made better by these goods. My hope, then, is that reflection on the social good of animals can affect something like a gestalt shift in the way we conceive of their lives, because I believe such a shift will transform the way we care for animals, and might even help us gain insight into the mystery of their suffering.

CHAPTER 9

Unfinished Creative Business:
Maximus the Confessor, Evolutionary Theodicy,
and Human Stewardship in Creation

Paul M. Blowers

In 1896 John Augustine Zahm, a distinguished physicist at the University of Notre Dame, made the bold claim that "it was [Augustine] the great bishop of Hippo who first laid down the principles of theistic Evolution as they are held to-day."[1] By the early twentieth century, some studies appeared exploring Augustine's *De Genesi ad litteram,* especially his doctrine of *rationes seminales,* the principles implanted by God in the world that sustain all created things in relation to their Creator's providential purposes, in the light of evolutionary theory.[2] By 1994 William Mallard had even ventured a positive comparison between Augustine's *rationes seminales* and the DNA of animate creatures as unveiled in modern genetics.[3]

But while Augustine has been drawn into the conversations between theology and evolutionary science for better than a century, Maximus the Confessor, the eminent Byzantine monastic theologian of the early seventh century often considered to have provided an authoritative synthesis of Greek patristic thought, has been a relative latecomer to them. Those conversations have meanwhile intensified and their stakes exponentially risen

---

1. John Augustine Zahm, *Evolution and Dogma* (Chicago: D. H. McBride, 1896), 71.

2. E.g., Henry Woods, *Augustine and Evolution: A Study in the Saint's* De Genesi ad litteram *and* De trinitate (New York: Universal Knowledge Foundation, 1924); Michael John McKeough, *The Meaning of the* Rationes Seminales *in Augustine* (Washington, DC: Catholic University of America Press, 1926).

3. William Mallard, *Language and Love: Introducing Augustine's Religious Thought through the* Confessions *Story* (University Park: Penn State University Press, 1994), 90, referencing *De Genesi ad litteram* 10.20.35 (CSEL 28/1:323).

because of the continued barrage of biological data not only reinforcing evolution itself but also unveiling the cruelties and vagaries operative in the processes of natural selection. Evolutionary theodicy, which itself has evolved significantly over the past twenty-five years,[4] has attempted to stay apace of this barrage. One of the few studies to draw Maximus into the conversation is Christopher Southgate's excellent monograph *The Groaning of Creation: God, Evolution, and the Problem of Evil* (2008). Southgate, a trained scientist as well as theologian, has become an important conversation partner for me in trying to reflect how the Christocentric cosmology of Maximus might inform, challenge, or enrich contemporary Christian theodicies that presuppose evolution. Southgate is thoroughly candid in setting out some principal pieces of the dilemma that evolution poses for Christian theodicies, notably the theodicies that aspire to address the suffering and strife of nonhuman as well as human creation, such as are warranted by Paul's musings on the "vanity" and "groaning" of creation in Roman 8. To frame my essay, then, I first broach four broad considerations from Southgate that indicate the enormity of the challenge for Christian evolutionary theodicy, before turning to Maximus's protology and teleology of creation as a resource for addressing some of the philosophical difficulties thus posed.

1. Biological evolution presents overwhelming evidence that the biosphere thrives on *developmental* processes of adaptation in which "happenstance, contingency, incredible waste, death, pain, and horror" (David Hull) are not only par for the course but intrinsically necessary to the continued flourishing and development of the system *as a whole*. The trajectory of the development of species is littered with the "tragedy" of lost individuals, victims of the ruthlessness of what Richard Dawkins has called the "selfish gene,"[5] the relentless but necessary egoism built into the evolutionary chain. Thus, as Dostoyevsky voiced in the persona of Ivan Karamazov, "package deal" theodicies morally justifying whole ecosystems are little comfort to the innocent suffering of individuals, whether human or nonhuman.[6]

2. Theories of a "cosmic fall" from a semi-transcendent or material paradise, while theologically compelling, not to mention deeply grounded

---

4. For an excellent review of some of the major approaches to theodicy, in particular to evolutionary theodicy, see Nicola Hoggard Creegan, *Animal Suffering and the Problem of Evil* (New York: Oxford University Press, 2013), 56-70.

5. Richard Dawkins, *The Selfish Gene*, 2nd ed. (New York: Oxford University Press, 1989).

6. See Southgate, *The Groaning of Creation: God, Evolution, and the Problem of Evil* (Louisville, KY: Westminster John Knox Press, 2008), 7-15. Southgate quotes from David Hull, "God of the Galapagos," *Nature* 352 (1992): 68-86.

PAUL M. BLOWERS

in Christian tradition, lack any substantiation whatsoever from biological evidence.[7] So far as evolutionary biology is concerned, the character and dynamics of natural selection have been and always will be the same. Natural selection is a cosmic constant.

3. The influential theodicy of the great second-century Christian thinker Irenaeus of Lyons, according to which natural and even moral evils serve instrumentally to educate human free will and to enable the thriving and maturing of the human creature, has the advantage of supporting real development in creation, but it also has the perennial liability of being strongly anthropocentric, and it does not resolve the uncomprehended suffering of countless subhuman creatures, or what C. S. Lewis famously targeted as the moral problem of "animal pain."[8]

4. *Kenosis*-centered theodicies that emphasize the Creator's deep identification, through the incarnation and passion of Christ, in the "groaning" of creation and the eschatological birth-pangs of the new creation (Rom 8:19-22) have significant merit but, in the view of Southgate and others, must avoid making the cross ontologically "necessary" — built into the system, as it were — rather than preserving its properly salvific efficacy as a historically contingent event in the history of a Creator who assumes full responsibility for the contingencies of his creation.[9]

It would be both anachronistic and pointless, of course, to try to extract from Maximus (or any other patristic theologian, for that matter) anything like a straightforward response to these accumulated and itemized modern concerns. My goal, then, will be rather modest. I will limit myself here to bringing some key aspects of Maximus's doctrine of creation to bear on a Christian theodicy that, like Southgate's own, presupposes evolutionary biology while also rejecting untenable options such as concordism (a forced or rationalized harmonization between science and revelation) and process theology. My suggestion is that, although Maximus may not greatly meet the apologetical needs of an evolutionary theodicy, certain of his theological instincts and intuitions, especially regarding the Creator's kenotic involvement in the micro- and macrostructures of creation, may help provide historical-theological grounding for those things that Southgate, among others, recommends as properly basic for a theologically coherent evolutionary theodicy and environmental ethics.

7. Southgate, *The Groaning of Creation*, 28-35.
8. Southgate, *The Groaning of Creation*, 11, 16, 165-66n96. On the problem of anthropocentrism, see 41, 83, 92-94, 105, 130-32.
9. Southgate, *The Groaning of Creation*, 49-50, 53, 57-59, 66.

Southgate specifically includes the following as indispensable conditions and convictions:[10]

- Creation is intrinsically good and gives rise to a multiplicity and diversity of goods (benefits not restricted solely to human creatures).
- Pain, suffering, death, and extinction are intrinsic to the evolving creation, but such a creation was the only one that God could create in order to give rise to this multiplicity and diversity of goods. (Otherwise put, there is a certain kind of "necessity" imposed even on the Creator.)
- The Creator actively shares in the suffering of *all* sentient creatures.
- The cross of Jesus Christ is the epitome of divine compassion and embodies the Creator's ultimate taking responsibility for the pain of creation, while the resurrection inaugurates the Creator's ultimate transformation of all creation.
- Because the loving Creator would never consider any creature a mere evolutionary expedient, there will be, in the eschatological transformation of creation, justice for all those creatures that did not flourish in this life.
- Christian commitment to the biblical Creator's special concern for human creatures does not undermine the principle that the Creator values *all* creatures emerging within evolution; it only heightens the crucial and positive vocation of humans to cooperate in the Creator's healing of the evolutionary process.

Let us turn, then, to consider how elements of Maximus's theology of creation may be seen to contribute in certain ways to the work of sustaining and advancing these principles of an evolutionary theodicy.

Maximus's Doctrine of the *Logoi* of Creatures: Universality and Particularity

Maximus's celebrated theory of the *logoi* of created beings, paralleling in some respects Augustine's *rationes seminales,* serves various functions in the Confessor's thought, but among the most important is its grounding

---

10. Southgate gives a synopsis of the main points of his evolutionary theodicy in *The Groaning of Creation*, 16, before arguing for their coherence in the body of his monograph. I abbreviate them here.

of universality *and particularity*, and of unity *and diversity*, in the created order. At one level, the *logoi* constitute the divinely premeditated and exemplary plan of created beings. They are ontological "codes" that establish the salutary interconnections and interactions between creatures spiritual and material, grand and minute, macrocosmic and microcosmic, and that situate those beings in networks conducive to their peculiar development and thriving, and to their participation in the uncreated Logos.[11] Because they define a creature's nature (φύσις), the *logoi* are also *teleological* codes. We might say they are the theological and metaphysical counterpart of DNA, since they encompass a creature's "historical" beginning, middle, and end; and yet they even project creatures beyond themselves "ecstatically" toward their eschatological transformation and deification, the sublime condition that Maximus sometimes calls "eternal well-being" (τὸ ἀεὶ εὖ εἶναι).[12]

Many will see Maximus's theory of *logoi* as reflecting the Middle Platonic and Neoplatonic notion of the divine ideas or archetypes "located" in the Logos, or divine Mind. The difference is that, by Maximus's account, the Creator-Logos, who cannot be conceptually separated from the Logos *incarnate* in Jesus Christ, personally and actively holds together the taxonomy of being. He both contains and sustains the *logoi* of every essence, genus, species, and individual within a species,[13] and by extension the same could be said even of the microstructures — including the genetics — of all organic beings. The *logoi* of individuals are contained by the *logoi* of species, the *logoi* of species by the *logoi* of genera, and all these are enfolded within the Creator-Logos. More precisely, says Maximus, the Logos as divine Wisdom contains the *logoi* of universals, while as divine Prudence he contains the

---

11. See especially *Amb.* 7 (PG 91:1077C-1080A, 1080C), 10 (1133A-1137C), 15 (1216A-B), in *On Difficulties in the Church Fathers: The Ambigua*, ed. and trans. Nicholas Constas (Cambridge, MA: Harvard University Press, 2014); *Qu. Thal.* 2 (CCSG 7:51). On Maximus's developed doctrine of the *logoi*, see especially Irénée-Henri Dalmais, "La théorie des 'logoi' des créatures chez saint Maxime le Confesseur," *Revue des sciences philosophiques et théologiques* 36 (1952): 244-49; Torstein Tollefsen, *The Christocentric Cosmology of St. Maximus the Confessor* (Oxford: Oxford University Press, 2008), 64-137; Alain Riou, *Le monde et l'Église selon Maxime le Confesseur* (Paris: Beachesne, 1973), 88-91; Jean-Claude Larchet, *La divinisation de l'homme selon Maxime le Confesseur* (Paris: Cerf, 1996), 112-23, 125-31, 141-51; and Andrew Louth, "St. Maximos' Doctrine of the *logoi* of Creation," in *Studia Patristica* 48, ed. Jane Baun et al. (Leuven: Peeters, 2010), 77-84.

12. *Amb.* 42 (PG 91:1345A-C), 7 (PG 91:1073C, 1084B-C), 42 (1325B-C); also *Qu. Thal.* 2 (CCSG 7:51), 60 (CCSG 22:80).

13. For extensive analysis, see Tollefsen, *The Christocentric Cosmology of St. Maximus the Confessor*, 93-110.

logoi of particulars[14] — a sure signal that there is "no waste," no creature left behind, in Maximus's cosmic vision.

At the same time, Maximus is a stark realist about the contingencies — the hazards and vagaries — encumbering the concrete life of created beings. He strictly distinguishes an individual creature's *logos*, its ontological predisposition to fulfill its divinely intended end, and its *tropos* or "mode of existence" (τρόπος ὑπάρξεως), whereby it exercises its own freedom, its own proclivities and aversions, in a world where creatures "both bear up and are borne along,"[15] where the dialectic of activity and passivity both bolsters and buffets them. Creatures' natural *logoi* are stable within the Creator's providence, but in their *tropoi*, or proper trajectories, they constantly fluctuate and undergo change. In fact,

> they are in motion according to the principle of flux and counterflux, and so they increase and decrease in quantity, and undergo alteration in terms of their qualities, and, to speak strictly, by their mutual succession, inasmuch as those that come earlier perpetually make way for those that come later. And, simply, to sum it all up, all beings are absolutely stable and motionless according to the principle by which they were given subsistence and by which they exist, but by virtue of the principle of what is contemplated around them, they are all in motion and unstable, and it is on this level that God's stewardship (οἰκονομία) of the universe wisely unfolds and is played out to the end.[16]

Maximus, to be sure, is a far cry here from identifying what Southgate and others call the tragic vicissitudes of natural selection, the relentlessness of change and variation in the processes of evolution. For Maximus, stability rather than flux belongs to nature itself; mutability as such must lie within the register of creaturely movement and actualization. And yet created "nature," as intrinsically "graced" by the Creator, is itself open-ended and permeable to the dynamic activity of the Creator, who continually renders his creation malleable and adaptable.

Because the *logoi* are the loci, or staging-points, of the work of the Creator-Logos in his creatures and constitute his immanent "intentions"

14. *Amb.* 41 (PG 91:1312B-1313A), 17 (PG 91:1225B-C), 41 (PG 91:1313A-B).

15. *Amb.* 8 (PG 91:1105B), 42 (1348D-1349A), 71 (1412B-C, 1416A-B); *Qu. Thal.* 64 (CCSG 22:191); *Ep.* 10 (PG 91:449B-C). On this dialectic of activity and passivity, see also *Amb.* 7 (PG 91:1073B-1077B).

16. *Amb.* 15 (PG 91:1217A-B), in *The Ambigua*, 367 (slightly altered).

PAUL M. BLOWERS

(θελήματα) for them,[17] his continued dynamic involvement in their flourishing, the *logoi* themselves retain a certain malleability or suppleness. Southgate, in his brief treatment of Maximus, suggests that the Confessor conceives the *logoi* "not as static aesthetic ideals but dynamically in terms of peaks in fitness landscapes, peaks that shift over time as God draws the biosphere onward."[18] In other words, the *logoi* embody the Logos's freedom to bring about new variations and possibilities in the development of any given species. From creatures' standpoint, the *logoi* are inalterable, but since the Creator-Logos "incarnates" himself in the *logoi*, as Maximus describes it, he can also innovate on the existential modes (τρόποι) through which individual created natures, in accordance with their *logoi*, realize their full potential.[19] Though Maximus sees such innovation most dramatically in miraculous phenomena, where the Logos empowers a given creature to act beyond its normal bounds,[20] more subtle alterations or reorientations could be imagined in the microsphere of genetic development that would, in principle, be comprehended under a creature's natural *logos*. Furthermore, Maximus speaks of the "law of nature," not as an implacable system built into the fabric of the cosmos, but as intrinsically and perennially interconnected with the "scriptural law" (i.e., Scripture's salvific narrative and embedded existential instruction) and the "spiritual law" of divine grace that effectively fulfills the other two laws.[21] These three laws interpret each other, as it were, and together reveal the triune Creator's creative and redemptive freedom and providence at every level of the created order.

17. *Amb.* 7 (PG 91:1085A); *Qu. Thal.* 13 (CCSG 7:95).
18. Southgate, *The Groaning of Creation,* 61. On the notion of "fitness landscapes," see 159-60n40.
19. See especially *Amb.* 42 (PG 91:1341D-1345C).
20. *Amb.* 42 (PG 91:1344A-D).
21. On the reciprocity of "natural" and "scriptural" laws, see especially *Amb.* 10 (PG 91:1128D-1133A). On the function of the three laws as conjointly supporting the realization of authentic love of fellow creatures, see *Qu. Thal.* 64 (CCSG 22:233-37). For analysis of their significance in Maximus's thought, see Hans Urs von Balthasar, *Cosmic Liturgy: The Universe according to Maximus the Confessor,* trans. Brian Daley (San Francisco: Ignatius Press, 2003), 291-314; Paul Blowers, *Exegesis and Spiritual Pedagogy in Maximus the Confessor: An Investigation of the* Quaestiones ad Thalassium (Notre Dame, IN: University of Notre Dame Press, 1991), 117-22; and Assaad Kattan, *Verleiblichung und Synergie: Die Grundzüge der Bibelhermeneutik bei Maximus Confessor* (Leiden: Brill, 2003), 126-47.

All Creatures Great *and Small?*

Among the key challenges to an evolutionary theodicy in Southgate's appraisal is the "tragedy" of both whole species and weak individuals within species being cast off, lost forever, within the seemingly ruthless processes of natural selection. Of course, Maximus does not directly address these cruelties, any more than he addresses animal pain as such. He shares the strong anthropocentrism prevalent in patristic cosmology, reserving his concerns for physical suffering to the human corporeal condition. And yet Maximus's overall cosmology dignifies particularity in relation to universality of being, and not only with respect to humans but also to the nonrational creation. In Maximian ontology, the individual of any species, rational *or nonrational,* is still a *hypostasis,* a kind of "person,"[22] insofar as it is "an essence with particular properties."[23] This dignity cannot belong exclusively to rational, relational, communicative beings like angels or humans but must extend even to individual dogs or mice, as Melchisedec Törönen has recently emphasized in his work on Maximus's metaphysical logic.[24] Certain Eastern Orthodox "personalist" theologians like John Zizioulas have taken issue with Törönen, insisting that, whatever the technicalities of his metaphysical language, Maximus's preoccupation is the hypostatic status, or "personhood," of human beings, who are uniquely created in the image of God.[25] Zizioulas's criticism, however, comes at the cost of unnecessarily narrowing the scope of Maximus's theological cosmology and of shutting the door on its implications for nonhuman creation.

Törönen finds these implications abounding. From his reading of Maximus, he presses the issue of the "hypostatic" dignity even of nonrational creatures who are capable of "relating" and "communicating" in their own unique ways:

> Is not the way in which different plants, trees, and other creatures form an ecosystem a kind of relationship? Is not the interdependence of the

22. Cf. *Ep.* 15 (PG 91:549C); *Opusc. theol.* 10 (PG 91:557D).
23. *Ep.* 15 (PG 91:557D).
24. See Melchisedec Törönen, *Union and Distinction in the Thought of St. Maximus the Confessor* (Oxford: Oxford University Press, 2007), 55-59; cf. Tollefsen, *The Christocentric Cosmology of St. Maximus the Confessor,* 126-27.
25. See Zizioulas's "Person and Nature in the Theology of St. Maximus the Confessor," in *Knowing the Purpose of Creation through the Resurrection: Proceedings of the Symposium on St. Maximus the Confessor, Belgrade, October 18-21, 2012,* ed. Maxim Vasiljević (Alhambra, CA: Sebastian Press, 2013), 88.

species in nature, and the way in which they seek for light, nutrition, or protection, a kind of relationship or relatedness? Of course, these types of relations are bound to certain natural processes. Their relations, as Maximus would put it, are governed by their *logos* of essence and the "law of nature." But a certain relatedness is undeniable.[26]

Southgate goes much further. Appealing to Hans Urs von Balthasar (a notoriously huge devotee of Maximus), he embraces the idea that an intra-Trinitarian *kenosis,* specifically the Father's generation and "abandonment" of the Son, grounds the Creator's act of creating the world and making possible other selves for whose sake his only begotten Son will suffer. Southgate further draws on Gerard Manley Hopkins's poetic image of "selving" non-human creatures, proposing that the Trinitarian *kenosis* already operative in creation includes making room for *new* biological "selves," ontologically funded by the Son (Logos) and nurtured by the Holy Spirit, but also demanding human creatures ethically to make room for them and to cooperate in nurturing them.[27] Southgate acknowledges that there is much ambiguity in this idea, since we would be speaking of the "selving" of creatures without reason or free will, creatures whose instincts are toward self-interest and rivalry, creatures who with rare exceptions show no capacity for a self-giving that mirrors the Creator's own *kenosis.* Can such creatures truly be "selves"? Southgate says yes, as do certain other postmodern theologians. Sarah Coakley insists that even the most basic instinctual abilities of lower creatures to "sacrifice" and to cooperate with others for the thriving of the biosphere make possible real altruism at the level of higher creatures,[28] though this proposal does not totally answer the problem of sacrificial "victims" of predation and the built-in cruelties of natural selection.[29] At this point, Maximus provides little real help for an evolutionary theodicy as such, other than resoundingly affirming that all individual creatures still have a vocation in the universe by virtue of their very difference and mutual "otherness" as created beings.[30]

26. Törönen, *Union and Distinction,* 57.

27. Southgate, *The Groaning of Creation,* 57-60, 63-64.

28. Sarah Coakley, *Sacrifice Regained: Reconsidering the Rationality of Religious Belief* (Cambridge: Cambridge University Press, 2012).

29. Creegan, *Animal Pain and the Problem of Evil,* 65.

30. See Törönen, *Union and Distinction,* 58-59; also Balthasar, *Cosmic Liturgy,* 87, noting that, for Maximus, createdness is not an imperfection per se because "even being different from God is a way of imitating him."

The Protological Dilemma: Is Creation *Fallen* or Only *Fragile?*

An enormous challenge for the theological construction of an evolutionary theodicy is to give account of how or why creation took *this* particular shape, or outward "form" (σχῆμα), as Paul calls it in 1 Corinthians 7:31. If there was an original paradisaical state of humanity and of the rest of creation, how could the cosmos have lapsed into physical and moral chaos unless it was already flawed? — a question that vexed a number of patristic theologians. Was the thrusting of creation into a trajectory of rivalry, suffering, and death really the domino effect of an original trespass by angels or human protoplasts? Evolutionary science insists, on the contrary, that the natural world *began* and endures with predation, violence, parasitism, suffering, extinction, and all the features of natural selection.[31]

For his part Maximus, much like Irenaeus, does not dwell at great length on the "prelapsarian" creation, focusing instead on the empirical fact that creation, virtually from the beginning, was compromised by its fledgling status, as well as by human disobedience. Already, everything created *ex nihilo* was, by its very materiality, ontologically vulnerable and liable to relapsing into chaos and in need of divine sustenance.[32] Indeed, Maximus shares with Athanasius the view that, without the addition of grace, creation remains in a state of ontological poverty and is susceptible to lapsing into nonexistence.[33] In addition, Maximus determines that Adam fell virtually the moment he was created (ἅμα τῷ γίνεσθαι), by squandering his faculties of spiritual fulfillment on material pleasures.[34] The Creator, he suggests, either saw this coming and had already fused human souls with passible and mortal bodies, or else he did so at the instant Adam compromised his nature. Such was God's subjection of creation to the corruption or vanity described in Romans 8:20,[35] a subjection that integrated *all* of corporeal creation. Maximus affirms that human sin has made the world "like a place of death and destruction,"[36] and yet suffering and death are punitive as well as rehabilitative only for rational

---

31. See Southgate, *The Groaning of Creation,* 28ff.

32. *Amb.* 8 (PG 91:1101D-1105B).

33. See Athanasius, *Contra gentes* 3-5, 41, 46; *De incarnatione* 4-6, ed. Robert Thomson (Oxford: Oxford University Press, 1971), 8-14, 112-14, 130, 142-48.

34. *Qu. Thal.* 61 (CCSG 22:85).

35. *Amb.* 8 (PG 91:1104B).

36. *Qu. Thal.* 65 (CCSG 22:255).

creatures.[37] Nonrational creatures do not share Adamic sin but are victimized by it, as sin exposes again the ontological vulnerability of all creation. But much like Irenaeus, Maximus asserts that the subjection of all creation to futility is still also, as Paul says, a subjection *in hope,* meaning that the intentions of the Creator-Logos are frustrated but hardly nullified. Maximus's whole cosmology thrives on the ambiguity, the "contradiction" and "tragedy" of historical existence, as Balthasar called it in his theo-dramatic reading of the Confessor.[38] The postlapsarian history of creation is not a "plan B," since the Wisdom of the Creator, engrained in the *logoi* of all creatures, comprehends every contingency. Maximus is, moreover, a biblical "realist" who understands the economy of creation and redemption to be seamless. Creation is already in some sense a "redemption" from chaos, since the chaos or disorder endemic to materiality and corporeality actually turns out to be the raw material, the "fruitful potentiality,"[39] of stability, beauty, and ever new creation, as the Creator-Logos works, with the aid of his human agents, to resolve the anomalies and inequalities in the corporeal realm.[40]

Maximus, once more like Irenaeus, reads the beginning of creation through the lens of its end. Teleology trumps protology in explicating the divine economy. The history of creation is providentially pointed, not simply toward recovering a lost prelapsarian paradise, as if the beginning point of creation is to be reduplicated, but instead toward attaining an *unprecedented* transformation and deification, the "new heavens and new earth" (Isa 66:22; Rev 21:1).[41] Though Maximus is not a chiliast (millenarian) like Irenaeus, he unquestionably projects the deification of *all* creatures, first because all creatures' *logoi* project them toward "eternal well-being,"[42] and second because Christ's realization of a new eschatological humanity abounds into the transfiguration of the full network of creation, which altogether is like a majestic, perfectly integrated human being.[43]

37. On death as punitive, see, e.g., *Amb.* 7 (PG 91:1076A-B, 1093A), 8 (1104A), 10 (1156C-D, 1157A).

38. Balthasar, *Cosmic Liturgy,* 188-93.

39. This phrase is John Polkinghorne's, quoted by Southgate, *The Groaning of Creation,* 141n72.

40. *Amb.* (PG 91:1104B-1105B).

41. See Irenaeus, *Adv. haer.* 5.36.1-2 (SC 153:452-60).

42. Cf. *Amb.* 7 (PG 91:1073A-C); *Capita theologica et oeconomica* 1.56 (PG 90:1104C).

43. Cf. *Amb.* 41 (PG 91:1308C-1312B); *Mystagogia* 7 (CCSG 69:33-36). On the incarnation as the original "mystery" of creation, see *Qu. Thal.* 60 (CCSG 22:73-81). On the deification of *all* creatures as a theme in Maximus, see Larchet, *La divinisation de l'homme selon saint Maxime le Confesseur,* 105-12.

The Cross within the Plan of Creation

Christopher Southgate — and he is certainly not alone — insists that a viable evolutionary theodicy demands a heavy emphasis on divine *kenosis* and deep identification with the suffering of creatures at every twist and turn in the evolutionary chain, especially those creatures that are either forced into extinction or else never genuinely thrive. Here again, it cannot be denied that the principal concern of patristic writers like Maximus or Irenaeus is Christ's identification with the suffering and fallenness of *rational* creatures. And yet for both these patristic writers, the "recapitulation of *all* things" (cf. Eph 1:10), the "mystery hidden from the ages" (Col 1:26), is not complete unless the Creator-Logos suffers and dies for all creatures.[44] In Irenaeus, as John Behr has consistently emphasized, the cross is already immanent in the plan of creation because the very act of creation is motivated foremost by the Creator's desire to disclose, in Jesus Christ, the depths of his grace and his love for the creation.[45] Incarnation and cross are intrinsic to "plan A" because the Creator has already comprehended all future contingencies in the drama of the divine economy and seeks to enable the creation to freely play out its role in the true "play within the play," which is the revelation of Jesus Christ.[46]

For Maximus, there is perhaps no clearer statement of the immanence of the cross in the plan of creation, and of the Logos's suffering on behalf of all created beings, than in a statement from his *Chapters on Theology and Economy:* "The mystery of the incarnation of the Logos holds the power of all the hidden *logoi* and figures of Scripture as well as the knowledge of visible and intelligible creatures. Whoever knows the mystery of the cross and the tomb knows the *logoi* of these creatures. And whoever has been initiated in

44. In Maximus, cf. *Amb.* 7 (PG 91:1096D-1097B), 41 (PG 91:1308D-1309A); *Qu. Thal.* 60 (CCSG 7:73-81).

45. Irenaeus, *Adv. haer.* 4.20.2 (SC 100:628-30). It was to the Crucified, the "Lamb who was slain," says Irenaeus, that the Father opened the "book" containing the secrets of "heaven and earth." Cf. *Adv. haer.* 3.22.3 (SC 211:438), where he states that "insofar as [the Creator] preexisted as the one who saves, it was necessary that what would be saved should also come into existence, in order that the Savior should not exist in vain." See also John Behr, *The Mystery of Christ: Life in Death* (Crestwood, NY: St. Vladimir's Seminary Press, 2006), especially 73-114; cf. also Daniel Wanke, *Das Kreuz Christi bei Irenäus von Lyon* (Berlin: Walter de Gruyter, 2000), especially 143-339.

46. For this theme in Irenaeus, Athanasius, the Cappadocians, and Maximus, see my *Drama of the Divine Economy: Creator and Creation in Early Christian Theology and Piety* (Oxford: Oxford University Press, 2012), 263-68.

the ineffable power of the resurrection knows the purpose [*logos*] for which God originally made all things."[47]

In a number of texts, Maximus makes clear that the whole incarnational work of Christ is a *paschal* ministry, a *kenosis* into the possibility, pain, and mortality of creation across all of its levels.[48] At this point we can begin to discern how Maximus might lend credence to a *kenosis*-centered evolutionary theodicy. The cross, Christ's putting creaturely death to death, is the climax of his "incarnation" and paschal ministry within the *logoi* of all creatures, which began at the very moment of creation and which will continue to its final consummation. Southgate expresses misgivings about a theology of the cross that would make the death of Christ ontologically necessary to the thriving of creation rather than God's free response to the historically contingent crisis of evil. But again, like Irenaeus, Maximus is reading creation *teleologically,* from the standpoint of its eschatological consummation,[49] and he sees the creation as a work in progress, an economy in which, as he suggests by way of an exegesis of John 5:17, the Father is "working still" through the cosmic ministry of his Son, the Creator-Logos.[50]

As for the redemption and transformation of the many nonrational and subhuman "selves" in creation, Southgate has posited that there must be, in words he borrows from Jay McDaniel, a "heaven for pelicans," referencing the phenomenon of the white pelican, which, having birthed two chicks, allows one to be pushed aside and ignored in order to assure the survival of the other chick, the focus of the mother's nurture. If the justice and integrity of God's stewardship of creation is to be maintained, says Southgate, the lost or expendable victims of every species must also enjoy a share in the eschatological consummation and perfection.[51] For Maximus, the incarnation, death, resurrection, and ascension of Jesus Christ have, in principle at least, opened a way for that very possibility, even if the firstfruits of the coming eschatological transformation are creatures of reason and free will.

---

47. Maximus, *Capita theologica et oeconomica* 1.66 (PG 90:1108A-B).

48. Cf. *Qu. Thal* 21 (CCSG 7:127-33), 42 (CCSG 7:285-89). See also my "The Passion of Jesus Christ in Maximus the Confessor: A Reconsideration," in *Studia Patristica* 37, ed. M. F. Wiles and E. J. Yarnold (Leuven: Peeters, 2001), 361-77.

49. See, e.g., *Qu. Thal.* 22 (CCSG 7:137-43).

50. *Qu. Thal.* 2 (CCSG 7:51).

51. Southgate, *The Groaning of Creation,* 46, 78-91.

The Human Vocation in the Healing of Creation

An obviously lingering issue for evolutionary theodicy is how precisely to make sense of biblical, let alone patristic, anthropocentrism. Paul's own reflection on the vanity and hope of the world in Romans 8:19-23 still centers on the "revealing of the sons of glory" (v. 19), the "glorious liberty of the children of God" (v. 21), the "adoption as sons" and "redemption of [human] bodies" (v. 23). The strategy of Southgate and others is to distinguish a salutary anthropocentrism from an unhealthy "anthropomonism," and to refocus on the human vocation of aiding the Creator in the healing of creation. Southgate — perhaps in the name of a *sensus plenior* of the Romans 8 passage — ventures to reread creation's "vanity" or "futility" as the evolutionary process itself, redirected in hopeful expectation of an eschatological transformation of all things through the incarnation, death, and resurrection of Jesus Christ. In the light of God's action in Christ, Southgate proposes, human creatures are called actively and positively to "groan" with fellow (especially nonrational) creatures in two principal forms. That "groaning" must first operate through *contemplation* of the deep solidarity of all particular creatures and discernment of the suffering of Christ as immanent within the whole creation, summoning humanity to have the "mind of Christ," a spirit exemplifying Christ's suffering servanthood. Second, groaning with creation must mean the actual *practice* of that servanthood, an "ethical *kenosis*" as Southgate describes it, demonstrated in a more disciplined asceticism that curbs human acquisitiveness and that works toward an ever deeper (and nonsentimental) *love* of the created "other."[52]

Maximus was no ancient environmentalist, but his theological cosmology and anthropology in their own way go far to undergird Southgate's concerns for human stewardship and servanthood in creation. As in many of the Greek (and monastic) fathers, the twin disciplines of *contemplation* (θεωρία) and ascetic *praxis* (πρᾶξις) go hand in hand in defining the moral and spiritual life of Christians. Maximus has a highly developed doctrine of the contemplation of created nature, specifically of the *logoi* of creatures, and of deepening stages of that contemplation.[53] But the *logoi* are not just metaphysical

---

52. Southgate, *The Groaning of Creation*, 94-95, 97-103, and see his larger discussion, 92-115.

53. See especially *Amb.* 10 (PG 91:1133A-1137C). Maximus's view of natural contemplation is balanced by a recognition of the fact that human knowledge cannot comprehend the most infinitesimal creatures (*Amb.* 17, PG 91:1224D), let alone the uncreated nature of the infinite God.

principles providing evidence of the Creator's ordering of the universe. For Maximus, as I noted earlier, they are God's very intentions for the world. Through them the Logos has "pre-evangelized" the creation, invested it with the gospel of his own kenotic action in creating, redeeming, and transforming the world. I would reiterate Maximus's statement (quoted above) that only through the perspective of the cross and resurrection of Christ does the believer have any hope of understanding the *logoi* of created beings. The "contemplation of nature," as he calls it, is less about reaching a transcendent vision beyond corporeality than preparing oneself through knowledge and virtue for the eschatological transformation of creation.[54] This contemplative knowledge is a "sanctified intuition" that patiently discerns the Christocentric mystery at the core of the overlapping networks of creation.

As for the practical dimension of human stewardship in creation, Maximus's signature contribution is his emphasis on the mediating work of humanity analogous to Christ's own work as cosmic mediator and reconciler. Because human nature is the "workshop" (ἐργαστήριον) of all creation, a perfect microcosm of and connecting "link" (σύνδεσμος) within the universe,[55] human beings are uniquely ontologically positioned to cooperate with Christ in the healing and perfecting of creation, a work still in progress. Maximus describes it as a joint mediation of five polarities in the universe:

1. As Christ, by his virgin birth, has healed the divide between male and female, human beings participate by working to overcome the passions of desire and ire that alienate the sexes.
2. As Christ, through his resurrection from the dead, has mended the divide between "paradise" and "inhabited earth," that is, between the irenic state of creation and the deviance of human civilization, humanity aids the healing by imitating Christ's holiness and virtues.
3. As Christ, by his bodily ascension into heaven, has reconciled "heaven and earth," humanity ascends with Christ by taking on a likeness to the angels.

54. For a thorough analysis, see Joshua Lollar's excellent study *To See into the Life of Things: The Contemplation of Nature in Maximus the Confessor and His Predecessors* (Turnhout: Brepols, 2013), 171-330; also Michael Harrington, "Creation and Natural Contemplation in Maximus the Confessor's *Ambiguum* 10:19," in *Divine Creation in Ancient, Medieval, and Early Modern Thought*, ed. Michael Treschow et al. (Leiden: Brill, 2007), 191-212.

55. *Amb.* 41 (PG 91:1305A-C); *Mystagogia* 7 (CCSG 69:33-36). See also the groundbreaking work of Lars Thunberg, *Microcosm and Mediator: The Theological Anthropology of Maximus the Confessor*, 2nd ed. (Chicago: Open Court, 1995), especially 95-330.

4. As Christ, by his bodily ascension through and beyond the higher intelligible orders, has healed the relation between "sensible" and "intelligible" creation, humanity shares the mediation by being true to its
microcosmic spiritual and material nature.

5. And as Christ has at last united Creator and creation by presenting his
perfected humanity enthroned at the right hand of the Father, humanity's participation is its ultimate perfection of the love of God that leads
to deification.[56]

Since Maximus states that sin was precisely an abuse of the dominion
that the Creator granted to humanity, the clear inference is that a strong
mortification and asceticism are necessary for humans to find their true role
in the world. Difficult as it might be for contemporary environmentalists to
grasp, Maximus the monk presupposed that humanity's internal command
of the acquisitive and defensive passions was part of the healing of the irrational penchant of the whole creation. Acknowledging the intrinsic chaotic
element in material creation and recognizing that there is much anomaly
and inequality among human beings, Maximus appropriates a phrase from
Paul's encouragement to the Corinthians in the collection for the poor in
Jerusalem: Christians must be about filling others' deficiencies with their
own abundances (see 2 Cor 8:14).[57] But what he has in mind here, as in his
constant admonitions about equal love for all human beings,[58] is larger than
proactive mercy or an equalizing ethics. Christians, by the grace of the Creator, are resisting chaos and helping to usher in a new creation that benefits
all creatures. From a soteriological perspective, the mystery of deification
that Maximus conceives as humanity's true telos, or goal, is not a final tran-
scending of corporeality but a cosmic transfiguration in which all things are
made new, in which God becomes "all things in all" (1 Cor 15:28).[59]

Even if Maximus cannot at last fully assuage our twenty-first-century

56. For the derivative human role in the cosmic mediations, see *Amb.* 41 (PG
91:1305A-1308C); for Christ's supreme work as Mediator, 41 (1308C-1312B). Maximus explicitly recalls here the Irenaean doctrine of the "recapitulation" (ἀνακεφαλαίωσις) of all
things in Christ, inspired by Eph 1:10 and Col 1:16.

57. *Amb.* 41 (PG 91:1308C), 8 (PG 91:1105A-B). I have essayed this theme at length in
"Bodily Inequality, Material Chaos, and the Ethics of Equalization in Maximus the Confessor," in *Studia Patristica* 42, ed. Frances Young et al. (Leuven: Peeters, 2006), 51-56.

58. *Capita de caritate* 1.17 (PG 90:964D), 1.24-25 (965A-B), 1.61 (973A), 1.71 (976B-C),
2.10 (985D-988A); *Ep.* 2 (PG 91:392D-408B).

59. See *Amb.* 7 (PG 91:1076A-B, 1076C, 1092C).

doubts about a future state of creation in which the competition and rivalry of natural selection are overcome, and in which a perfect symbiosis of all creatures endures, his vision of the crucified Creator-Logos gradually seizing a new world from the jaws of chaos and vanity still speaks for itself as an ancient witness to the Christian faith and hope in the ever provident, resourceful, and all-wise Creator. Balthasar and, more recently, the scientist and theologian Celia Deane-Drummond under his influence are correct, I believe, to read Maximus through a "theo-dramatic" lens, for his cosmological vision, deeply indebted to biblical images of the divine economy, projects real elements of tragedy, of suspense, of the complex plot in which the "characters" who inhabit creation move and play in unpredictable ways, and in which the resolution of the drama of creation in Jesus Christ is delayed and defiant of human imagination.[60] This sense of theo-drama, I believe, will be essential to the continuing construction of an evolutionary theodicy — at least one that looks for support from the cosmic vision of St. Maximus the Confessor.

---

60. See Balthasar, *Cosmic Liturgy*, 263-71; Balthasar, *Theo-Drama: Theological Dramatic Theory*, vol. 1: *Prolegomena;* vol. 2: *The Dramatis Personae: Man in God;* vol. 3: *The Dramatis Personae: The Person in Christ;* vol. 4: *The Action,* trans. Graham Harrison (San Francisco: Ignatius Press, 1988-94; German ed., 1973-80]), 1:249; 2:201-2, 215-16, 222, 328; 3:257-58; 4:252-54, 259, 364, 380-83. Cf. Celia Deane-Drummond, *Creation through Wisdom: Theology and the New Biology* (Edinburgh: T&T Clark, 2000), 76-78; Deane-Drummond, *Christ and Evolution: Wonder and Wisdom* (Minneapolis: Fortress Press, 2009), 149-51.

CHAPTER 10

Knowing Our Place: Poverty and Providence

Christopher A. Franks

In his recent apostolic exhortation, *Evangelii gaudium,* Pope Francis made the following remark about the economies so prevalent in our time that resist being secondary to social and moral concerns: "In this system, which tends to devour everything which stands in the way of increased profits, whatever is fragile, like the environment, is defenseless before the interests of a deified market, which become the only rule."[1] Writers attentive to this fragility and to the power of Christian convictions to form gentler living have sought to renew our appreciation of the doctrine of creation for an ecological age. One frequent strategy is to appeal to the last few chapters of the book of Job and to emphasize Job's confrontation with a menagerie of creatures that could hardly help but instill in Job a new "ecological" awareness. That awareness is thought to play a crucial role in displacing Job from his former anthropocentric views, and we must, we are told, learn a similar ecologically astute sense of our creatureliness.

This strategy has great promise to deepen the grip of the doctrine of creation on our lives, helping us to "know our place" in two senses. First, it can teach us a contemplative attention to the nonhuman members of our communities. Often, we do not know our place because we do not know the neighborhoods and landscapes we inhabit and their members. This is partly because, on account of our automated and climate-controlled lives, we have less contact with those landscapes than we once did. It is also partly because

---

1. Pope Francis, *Evangelii gaudium,* cited in the editorial in *The Christian Century,* December 25, 2013.

we are increasingly trained to view things primarily under the aspect of their market value or their capacity for financial return on investment, or more broadly, in terms of their susceptibility to human calculation and manipulation. The ecological reading of Job can mold a more-than-economic concern for our nonhuman neighbors for their own sake.

Second, these readings can prompt us to retrace our interdependence with those neighbors, upending our tendency toward individualism. We often do not know our place in the sense that we see ourselves as sovereign over, rather than enmeshed within, the networks of interdependence that surround us. As our society increasingly makes our access to the means of sustenance depend on our participation in exchanges that assume we are law-abiding strangers rather than friends, it trains us to understand ourselves as proprietors and competitors in an agonistic world. This pressure distorts our sense of what it is to be human, as we habitually act as though our flourishing were to be found in lives of independence and self-sufficiency. We therefore fail to know our place as social and organic creatures whose flourishing can come only through building up the networks of interdependence with other people and other nonhuman creatures that make our lives possible.

Thus, we instead aim ourselves at building up fences of security and wealth around ourselves that we think will establish our happiness and insulate us from danger, while in fact we continue to exacerbate the dangerousness of our world. Our insulated so-called happiness, after all, always excludes and neglects some people and places (usually the most fragile), numbing us to their pain and struggle, and blinding us to the ways in which our good is inseparable from theirs. As Rowan Williams has suggested, although we cannot escape our sociality, we can deny it by seeking a freedom "to cut our ties, to unravel the knots binding us in one world, to break the humiliating cords of interdependence," which is ultimately a way of aiming at suicide, whether sudden or gradual, individual or collective.[2]

In this chapter I begin by considering these lessons in the writings of four authors, but for the sake of going on to examine a further lesson we can draw from the reading of Job, a lesson often underappreciated among these authors. It is a lesson at least as significant as ecological awareness for forming gentler lives. Indeed, I would argue that this lesson is more important. I will go further: without this lesson, the lessons of ecological awareness could easily backfire and yield more brutalizing of what is fragile. This lesson is about the trustworthiness of the order in which we find ourselves

2. Rowan Williams, *The Truce of God* (Grand Rapids: Eerdmans, 2005 [1983]), 43.

circumscribed. In addition to the two ways of knowing our place that the ecological readings of Job can help us press toward, there is a third way we often fail to know our place, namely, as creatures in the unfolding story of God's providential ordering. But it is exactly a lack of trust in the dispenser of all good gifts that keeps us wary of our own vulnerability and determined to keep up our defenses. These defenses seem necessary to secure our future in a world where the existence of so many other people and creatures with their own agendas often seems a threat to our own welfare. The commentary on Job by Thomas Aquinas focuses just here, on trusting God's providence when we cannot see how God can weave even threatening events into a plan for our good. Without such trust, our environmental problems themselves are likely to frighten us into even more self-protection, with its negative consequences for all that is excluded and fragile.

In contrast to such self-protection, this trust is embodied in a lowering of our defenses that makes sense only in light of the faithfulness of God. Such a lowering of defenses is part of a trajectory drawing toward Godlikeness, a trajectory whose contours are best glimpsed in terms of the defenseless poverty of Christ. To elucidate this trust, therefore, I will offer some meditations on voluntary poverty and its importance for living into the fullness of our creatureliness. After all, our creatureliness is most fully realized in the calling to give ourselves away for the sake of communion.

Creatureliness in the Book of Job

First, I turn to the book of Job, and specifically to how it has been used by four recent interpreters to elucidate the conditions of creatureliness. These authors all challenge our proprietary and competitive habits by deepening our appreciation of what is involved in coming to grips with being small moments in a much larger pattern, living lives that are intertwined with a world of wild diversity that is in many ways out of our control.

Ecologically and theologically minded interpreters turn to the book of Job primarily because it contains, in the speeches of God in chapters 38–41, the most extended treatment of creation in the entire Bible. And whereas a number of passages in the Bible might be thought to reinforce the separation or at least distinctness of humanity from the rest of the material creation, or might appear to deal with creation in abstract generalities that do not draw the reader's attention to the stunning diversity of particular creatures, these chapters of Job linger exquisitely over a wide range of arenas and their wild

·inhabitants, emphatically refusing to refer all these things to humanity or to subordinate them to human concerns.

Twenty years ago, the United Methodist environmentalist Bill McKibben used Job's transformation to call for a transformation in our own lives. McKibben used God's speeches in Job to offer an understanding of our createdness quite at odds with our society's anthropocentric goals of perpetual economic growth and ever-rising standards of living. McKibben wanted to apply these lessons to our day because our environment is talking back to us, he says, teaching us something that echoes artists, sages, and saints through the ages, who held that "nonattachment and simplicity and the flight from materialism are necessary for the good life."[3] God's speeches take Job on a tour of a world far from people, and through this tour God reorients Job to see himself and all humanity as merely a part of the whole order of creation, a part that is not disproportionately more important than all the rest. This new vision calls, McKibben says, for humility and joy — humility that puts God or nature or some combination back at the center, rather than at the periphery of a human-focused culture, and joy that delights, as God seems to in these speeches, not just over domesticated beauty, but over the sometimes revolting, sometimes silly, sometimes monstrous, yet always ebullient and wild and glorious creation. This vision can transform our aesthetic judgment, he says, so as to thirst for and delight in the natural wildness we are so quickly destroying.

In his wonderful meditation on theology and ecology, Norman Wirzba, too, finds in God's speeches to Job the transforming offer of a wider vision of creation. That vision dovetails in important ways, Wirzba notes, with lessons taught by contemporary ecological science. In particular, God's speeches highlight three features of this complex creation. First, there are destructive forces that are not entirely eliminated by God and in which God even sees a positive sign of dignity and strength. Second, all the diverse elements of creation matter to God precisely in their own integrity and not merely in relation to human beings. And third, God extends significant freedom to these diverse elements to exercise their power, so that there is "an openness and unpredictability about creation." The upshot of Job's tour of creation is that he is no longer so sure we can assume that "life will be to our advantage and benefit." Job has come to see that the ideas of justice he had previously tried to apply to God were naive and shortsighted. Wirzba also suggests

3. Bill McKibben, *The Comforting Whirlwind: God, Job, and the Scale of Creation* (Grand Rapids: Eerdmans, 1994), 28.

that the epilogue of the story reveals how Job's new vision of justice altered his engagement with the world. Specifically, the detail that Job's daughters were given a share in the inheritance along with his sons signals that "Job is now ready to welcome the world of the other on its own terms rather than in terms of the conventional understanding. . . . Job emerges from his long plight ready to embrace the creation with the selfless care and joy that marks God's own involvement in the world."[4]

In William Brown's powerful treatment of biblical accounts of creation, through which he strolls with the biblical text in one hand and the findings of modern science in the other, he too discovers in God's speeches to Job the delivery of a wider vision that, by acquainting Job with creation's extremities, transforms Job's perception. But Brown emphasizes not so much that God's speeches displace Job's anthropocentrism, but that they induce in Job a disorienting vertigo by bringing him to precipices where no human belongs. Furthermore, Brown stresses that God's speeches confront Job with his own disturbing kinship with the wild, frightening, and ultimately God-dependent world beyond the realms of human settlement and control. Brown goes further than McKibben and Wirzba to emphasize the unruly elements in creation. But he resists associating the forces of chaos symbolized by Leviathan with evil. Rather, Brown emphasizes how creation's chaotic and violent aspects play important positive roles, contributing to the provisions for living creatures and epitomizing, in the forms of Behemoth and Leviathan, the wild freedom and fearless vitality in creation that God has no intention of subjugating. Like Wirzba, Brown stresses also God's affirmation of each creature's unhindered expression of its own identity and God's refusal to micromanage its affairs. The upshot, Brown suggests, is for Job to begin to share in God's *biophilia,* in God's delight in the otherness, wildness, and diversity of creation. Through exploring the wondrous and fearsome taxonomy of creatures, which we are able to do now much more thoroughly than Job, humans ought to find comfort as our fear and loathing of the wild gives way to a sense of community with it. It is not that we should stop trying to create humane habitats at a distance from threatening wildness, but that we should retain our awe and wonder at such wildness, in the knowledge that "our flourishing depends on theirs." Furthermore, by recognizing our kinship with the wild, we begin to overcome our alienation from the "otherness," the "wildness" within ourselves. And so, reveling in

4. Norman Wirzba, *The Paradise of God: Renewing Religion in an Ecological Age* (New York: Oxford University Press, 2003), 45, 41, 47.

such wild dignity, we can affirm all life, in order "to step lightly on God's beloved, vibrant Earth."[5]

Finally, in his ecologically oriented reading of the Bible, Richard Bauckham also agrees that God's speeches in Job fundamentally displace Job, and humans in general, from the central place in the story of creation. They thus offer a salutary corrective to readings of the Bible that support the hubristic project of dominative and exploitative rule over nature. Bauckham is distinctive for focusing on what this taxonomy of creatures teaches Job about God, and not just about creatures: God's speeches evoke cosmic humility before the wisdom and power of God, particularly as seen in the otherness of the cosmos. In this way, Bauckham is closest of these four to the focus we will see in Aquinas. Bauckham suggests we can learn the same humility, even though, given the breadth of human impact today, we now have responsibilities to such creatures that Job never had.[6] Bauckham's interpretation is also distinguished for his attention to the distinction between the creatures mentioned in God's first speech and Behemoth and Leviathan, who are the focus of God's second speech. McKibben discusses these two creatures only to draw the lesson that only God can create any way God pleases, although through genetic engineering we are encroaching on that prerogative.[7] Wirzba mentions only Behemoth, and then only to highlight the comparison God makes between Behemoth and Job, which he suggests displays God's equal concern for all creatures.[8] Bauckham, though, discusses them even more than Brown does. Unlike Brown, Bauckham sees them not as positive forces but as the "anti-God powers in creation."[9] The emphasis is on the unbowed and fearless arrogance and power of these creatures, and on the futility and even the horror for Job to think of trying to control them. Yet, it is also affirmed that God is their maker and master, who alone can cope with them. There are two upshots. First, although we humans cannot subdue creation's destructive forces, we can help to unleash them, and then we join their arrogant rebellion, forsaking our proper humility. Second, we understand better Job's decision to relent in his case against God, as he appreciates the true scope of the forces of chaos with

5. William P. Brown, *The Seven Pillars of Creation: The Bible, Science, and the Ecology of Wonder* (New York: Oxford University Press, 2010), 128, 137, 140.

6. Richard Bauckham, *The Bible and Ecology: Rediscovering the Community of Creation* (Waco, TX: Baylor University Press, 2010), 52.

7. McKibben, *The Comforting Whirlwind*, 78.

8. Wirzba, *The Paradise of God*, 46.

9. Bauckham, *The Bible and Ecology*, 61.

which God contends, and he experiences relief that he, as a mere mortal, is not in charge of such things.

For my purposes, I do not need to settle the debate among these writers about whether the destructive forces in the world represented by Leviathan are to be understood positively or negatively. In either case, God is patient with such forces. Perhaps this is because they are a delight to God and are crucial to the vitality and life-fostering abilities of creation. Perhaps it is only because God sees how to bring good out of them, although they are fundamentally opposed to God. Perhaps it is a little bit of both. In any case, these interpreters help us to grasp what would be involved in learning a joy and humility and even sympathy that can acknowledge that we are encompassed in a larger order that conditions and limits us.

One way of turning away from the proprietary self, then, is to be displaced, as Job was, so that we may avoid the temptation to engage the stories of other creatures only insofar as they can be made to serve the interests of the story we want our lives to tell. Instead, we must prepare to bear with the stories of many, in light of the distinct contribution each may make to the story of creation. One could summarize what Job learns according to these four as a sort of contemplation that trains the attention on the being of another. Such contemplation is the wellspring of compassion, and such compassion has the power to foster delight in each thing's being what it was made to be for its own sake, and it forms in us a desire to play our role in making room, in enabling each creature to be what God made it to be. To see what such turning away from the proprietary self would mean, consider some of its implications for our use and consumption.

Of course, we must use and consume some other created things, but our use and consumption will be transformed if shaped by this contemplation. I suspect that something like such contemplation of the depth and wonder of created things is what the long tradition of Christian critics of modern political economy had in mind when they insisted that capitalism's promoters are misnamed when they are called "materialists." G. K. Chesterton, for example, characterized the stockbroker as a most ethereal fellow, transposing everything into figures, which so enchant him that he scarcely pays attention to the prosaic delights of actual material objects.[10] To see the creatures of the world first for what they are before God, even in those cases when what they are before God ultimately subordinates them to our use, is to enjoy them in all their fullness; in contrast, to refer them

---

10. G. K. Chesterton, *The Outline of Sanity* (London: Dodd, Mead, 1927), 184-93.

only to our own interests is to treat them abstractly and to miss much of their wonder.

When we learn such contemplation, the things we use can begin to become luminous to us as reflections of God's glory. Such attention, then, can awaken one to the cost of one's use and consumption. The more one is able to delight in each thing's being what it is for its own sake, the more one feels the sacrifice involved in one's using and consuming, and the more one's gratitude for one's sustenance becomes true gratitude by being tinged with mourning for the loss involved. To know this sort of gratitude is to learn a complex delight, not only in using and consuming, but in serving the good of the things one uses and their contexts. Here is the supreme motivation to seek to reuse and to sustain in use, eschewing the notion of "throwing away."

Consider in this connection how the terms "saving" and "wasting" have swapped places in our everyday consideration of economic processes. "Saving" once applied to the created things we must use and the by-products of our using them. People saved the products of labor by canning, preserving, economizing, reusing and repairing, and by limiting consumption. They saved the by-products of such use through composting, salvaging, and so forth. "Wasting," in contrast, applied to our own bodily energy, when the lazy or profligate failed to pull their weight and contribute to the ongoing vitality and fertility of productive processes and to the exchange of services that builds up a community. Today, the term "waste" is more often applied to the created things we must use and their by-products. The products we use become "waste" because they quickly become trash as we, uncontemplative as we are, find ever new rationales for replacing them with something new, and the by-products of our use are also waste because we can find little use for them and try to stash them in no one's backyard. "Saving," however, is what we do with our own bodily energy, since we no longer need to use it, surrounded as we are by "labor-saving devices." My point is not to disparage technological innovations but to suggest that our decisions about what sort of innovations to invest in are shaped by whether or not we are drawn out of ourselves to sense our connection to the things we use and consume. As Rowan Williams has suggested, we need "a model for our use of the material world that is not simply dominating, but allows us to be and feel part of things, not detached and superior to the objects we use (let alone the persons we deal with)."[11]

Fostering this sort of contemplation might be helped if Christians con-

11. Williams, *The Truce of God*, 102.

sidered the words of James in the book of Acts, where he advised Gentile Christians to "abstain from what has been sacrificed to idols and from blood and from what is strangled" (Acts 15:29). This advice does not require Christians to keep kosher, but it does call on them to recognize that the way their meat is slaughtered has something to do with the quality of their worship. Our worship, after all, should be marked by our gratitude for the lives of those beasts, by our reverence for the gift of life God has given them, and by our acknowledgment of the permission God has given us to take it away (under certain circumstances).

McKibben in particular gives a number of other practical suggestions of how this humble and joyful contemplation might affect our use and consumption. For example, he suggests focusing our transit more on bicycles than on cars, and replacing a materialist Christmas celebration with alternative, joy-filled gifts focused on the spiritual meaning of the season. On a larger scale, we should recognize, he says, that God was telling us something about God's intentions for our economic activity through the Torah's safeguards against overconsolidating ownership and overworking the land, and through its commands about leaving untouched open space in the midst of humanly managed land.

Job, Creaturely Poverty, and Trust in God

Our four ecologically minded interpreters of Job go a long way toward helping us to move out of the stance of the proprietary self and to share Job's displacement, so that we too can be "put in our place" and learn humility and wonder at the incredible diversity of life. All four agree in seeing something like a contemplative attitude toward that diversity as one of the major lessons that modern readers can take away from Job.

But it is important to make clear something that is not always clear in these authors. What makes such contemplation possible is not simply an encounter with biological difference, but encountering these incredible species in light of their relation to God. Brown suggests that the vertigo Job would experience from being verbally drawn alongside everything from a lion to an ostrich to a warhorse to the very underbelly of Leviathan is similar to the disorienting awe Brown himself felt when he witnessed a video presentation called "Powers of 10," in which the screen zooms out from a city by powers of 10 until the whole galaxy is in view, and then zooms in on a human body by powers of 10 to the other extreme. The implication is that the author's visual experience itself, and Job's verbal experience likewise, would be sufficient to evoke the awe and wonder to transform Job in the appropriate ways. Mc-Kibben, for his part, gives the impression that encountering wild nature can hardly help but evoke intimations of the romantic sublime. In both cases, I suspect the authors' views are shaped by their Christian conviction that such creaturely life is a gift from the Creator, a Creator who is good and who calls "good" all that is made. But these theological convictions are left in the background, as though contemplative compassion is the natural reaction to any encounter with difference. On the contrary, I submit that accepting our role as part of a whole without hostility is very difficult without trust that the whole is governed with our good in mind.

It is especially important to bring out this suppressed premise because all of these authors besides McKibben acknowledge the terror some of the creaturely powers could inspire. Bauckham does make clear that it is the encounter with God that transforms Job, but Wirzba and Brown gloss over this point. In fact, Wirzba gives the impression that Job is inspired to welcome the other with selfless care and joy simply by learning of the dignity of destructive beasts that overturn his human-centered ideas of justice. And Brown suggests that, when we see the freedom and vitality of the chaotic forces, as well as our own kinship with them, we will begin to affirm all life.

Now, ecological knowledge by itself could perhaps in some cases do the job of displacing one from the center of things in such a way that one learns to be joyfully patient of one's membership in a larger order, even apart from trust in God. But it is still important to bring out the suppressed premise of theological conviction about creation because it highlights the difference between simply being a member of a larger order and being a creature. The notion of creation, that life is a gift, brought out of nothing by an absolutely gratuitous love, is not a given. As Jon Levenson argues in *Creation and the Persistence of Evil*, canonically, the very notion of creation, of "the emergence of a stable community in a benevolent and life-sustaining order," rather than being a given, is but a corollary of God's faithfulness, so that creation itself is a covenantal notion, tied to God's promises to be *for* God's people.[12] Simple ecological knowledge of biological diversity, outside the notions of covenant and creation, might evoke one's admiration or one's horror. But when one sees the world from within those notions, the proper response is gratitude for God's gifts and trust in God's continuing faithful-

12. Jon D. Levenson, *Creation and the Persistence of Evil: The Jewish Drama of Divine Omnipotence* (San Francisco: Harper & Row, 1988), 12-14.

ness. Without this gratitude and trust, it is harder to see how Job's experience could usher in contemplative attention and delight, or even a willingness to go on without despair. Despite the forces that challenge God's creative ordering, the revelation of God's wisdom and power and benevolence offers an anchor for Job's (and the reader's) ability to go on, even when sometimes the darkest of our experience makes it especially difficult to see precisely how providence is at work for our good.

When our membership in a larger order is set within this providential context, we are also displaced even more radically. It is then that we truly learn humility, for we learn to acknowledge that, apart from God's sustaining action, we are literally nothing. As we draw near to God and sense the disproportion between humans and God, we learn true poverty of spirit, and we learn to despise "all superficial exaltation of spirit feeding on honors or wealth."[13] This is the true displacement that leads Job to repent in dust and ashes. We learn also to entrust ourselves more and more to the faithfulness of God, both when God's ordering of our steps seems more apparent, and when it seems more obscure. And for Christians these lessons are inseparable from seeing God's faithfulness through Jesus Christ, who is the very wisdom by which we were created, and who calls us out of our proprietary and self-protective habits to a surprising extent, for the sake of bearing witness to the unexpected degree of communion with God to which we are called. The crucial point I want to stress here is that the Christian way of being pulled out of our defensive competitiveness involves a great deal of trust in God's faithfulness.

If our four authors leave this crucial premise a bit hidden, some thinkers have left it out entirely. Thomas Berry, for example, has proposed that the unfolding of the multitude of stories that make up our world be understood rather pantheistically as a "new story of cosmic emergence."[14] David Burrell and Elena Malits point out that, among the theological difficulties raised by such an approach, it downplays the drama of redemption through Christ to such a degree that it obscures what is new in the new creation. According to Burrell and Malits, what is new is "a transformation of human potential for friendship with God. And when friendship with the creator of all is pos-

13. William J. Hill, OP, *Hope: Summa theologiae IIa IIae, 17-22*, Blackfriars edition, vol. 33, ed. Thomas Gilby et al. (New York: McGraw-Hill, 1966), 173.
14. See Thomas Berry, "The New Story," *Teilhard Studies* 1 (1978): 1-13; Brian Swimme and Thomas Berry, *The Universe Story: From the Primordial Flaring Forth to the Ecozoic Era — a Celebration of the Unfolding of the Cosmos* (San Francisco: Harper, 1994).

sible, an entirely new relation of human beings with the rest of creation is possible as well."[15]

Next, I want to explore this trust in God's providence in the midst of uncertainty by looking at Thomas Aquinas's commentary on Job. Aquinas cannot quite match the contemplative wonder at specific creatures of our four authors, and modern scholars would dispute some of the texts on which he depends, but his commentary has the virtue of being quite clear on exactly this point of God's trustworthy providence. We see here, then, something crucial to what it means to be patient in our creatureliness.

Whereas both Aquinas and our modern interpreters find Job transformed, for all the modern ones except for Bauckham, that transformation is rooted in Job's being overwhelmed by his new ecological knowledge. For Aquinas, though, that transformation is a matter of Job's new knowledge of God. God's speeches are filled with knowledge about creatures, but their main aim is not to give Job an ecology lesson, as important as that is. The entire catalog of features of creation is aimed at unsettling and reorienting Job's understanding not of creation, but of God. Thus, Job is changed because, as Aquinas restates Job's words, "I know You more fully than before."[16] And what does he know about God more fully? Two things. First, he knows more fully that only God has the wisdom and power even to know what it means to bring order and justice to this manifold universe. This recognition of the disproportion between a human being and God is, according to Aquinas, the primary aim of God's first speech: "In the preceding words the Lord, by mentioning the marvels which appear in His effects, demonstrated His wisdom and power so that from this demonstration it may be manifest that no man can contend with God either in wisdom or in power."[17] Second, Job knows more fully not only that God is the only one in the position of mastering the world, but also that God is trustworthy to exercise that mastery for our good. God is even master of Leviathan and all the forces of rebellion he represents.[18] If Leviathan works destruction,

15. David Burrell, CSC, and Elena Malits, CSC, *Original Peace: Restoring God's Creation* (Mahwah, NJ: Paulist Press, 1997), 21.

16. Aquinas, *The Literal Exposition on Job: A Scriptural Commentary concerning Providence,* trans. Anthony Damico, American Academy of Religion: Classics in Religious Studies (Atlanta: Scholars Press, 1989), 470.

17. Aquinas, *The Literal Exposition on Job,* 443.

18. Modern interpreters debate whether Job 41:10-12 indicates God's mastery of Leviathan or God's refusal to master him. Aquinas's reading reflects not only the text he had but also the influence of his Christian reading of providence. See the readings of these verses

that is his agency departing from God's perfect intention, because "for God, only one work is properly suited to His goodness, namely, to benefit and to show mercy."[19] But Leviathan's destructive acts do not escape the ordering of God's providence. When God gives Leviathan room to act, Leviathan can do only as much as God permits — even, one presumes, when Leviathan is us human beings, with our ability to unleash chaos! As Burrell and Malits note, "Much of what might be called 'natural evil' now bears the stamp of human rapacity."[20] And God can be trusted to allow only what can be somehow ordered to the good, since God is the one who has gifted all things with life and freedom, and who particularly desires the salvation of human beings.[21]

For Aquinas, although we trust that God orders all things toward the good, we cannot always see how. As William Placher has observed, Aquinas "did not say that, looking over the world, we can determine how each of the world's evils contributes to some greater good. . . . We can only trust that, if we could see all the things that God has created as God sees them, then, in a way we cannot imagine, we would consent that they should be. We would see them, moreover . . . as in some relation to God we cannot now imagine."[22] Aquinas does offer a few examples of trying to see God's providential purpose. He proposes that an earthquake may be used by God to frighten sinners into desisting from their sins. And he affirms that the whole story of Job serves God's purpose of making Job's saintly virtue conspicuous so that others may be drawn to the truth.[23] But the debate around which the book of Job revolves is concerned with refuting the false view that God's favor or the absence of it could easily be read off the history of a person's prosperity or lack of it. That view stems from the mistaken assumption that this life is the final horizon in which our end must be achieved. According to Aquinas, Job realizes the error of that view, for he knows of the hope of resurrection.[24] This life, in contrast, is more like a military campaign, in which we must be prepared for an arduous path of adversities. The wise

in Bauckham, *The Bible and Ecology*, 58, whose reading is not far from that of Aquinas, and Brown, *The Seven Pillars of Creation*, 122, whose reading is quite different.

19. Aquinas, *The Literal Exposition on Job*, 452.
20. Burrell and Malits, *Original Peace*, 17.
21. Aquinas, *The Literal Exposition on Job*, 459.
22. William C. Placher, *The Domestication of Transcendence: How Modern Thinking about God Went Wrong* (Louisville, KY: Westminster John Knox Press, 1996), 116.
23. Aquinas, *The Literal Exposition on Job*, 422, 81.
24. Aquinas, *The Literal Exposition on Job*, 88, 269.

person, then, will place hope not in temporal goods, but in the eternal. For this reason, it is less true that prosperity passes by wise men than that they pass it by.[25]

Being placed in the story of God's providential work thus deepens our trusting receptivity and strengthens us for acts of mercy that are unhindered by excessive fear of insecurity. This solid anchor of trust enables us to put our own property at the service of the universal destination of all goods. We can be confident that nature's processes of nourishment and productivity have produced enough for all, and that our participation in the divine economy of mutual benefit now may help it get where it is needed. Compare this view of providence with that of Thomas Malthus, who asserted that God intentionally makes goods scarce to reward the hard working and punish the lazy, and to reduce the excess population if some may starve. That is the self-justifying and cruelly uncharitable ideology of the proprietary self, which rebels against our creatureliness and its necessary patience.

When we yield to the true story of God's providence, however, we are trained for patience with the time-bound nature of our creatureliness. As beings whose createdness unfolds in time, we face the poverty of those who live before the end; that is, in this life we only "have" and "know" a part of the story. Furthermore, even the part of the story we "have" is not adequately "known" by us immediately. For if it requires time for us to develop prudence over our own affairs, how much more does it require time for us to learn to see the wisdom of God's providence over all things! Indeed, we almost never see it very clearly. But we do see Jesus. While we do not know how the multitude of stories in creation will be woven together into their ultimate destiny, what we know is the glimpse we have seen in Christ and the saints of the divine economy of mercy, penitence, and reconciliation that anticipates that destiny. What we know is that we participate in this economy ourselves and witness to it when we hear the summons of Christ's defenseless love that makes sense only in light of an unshakable trust in the faithfulness of the Father. What anchors that trust is that the Master of the story has revealed that mastery to us, not in such a way that we can always see what sense everything makes in light of the end, but in such a way that we can go on as creatures destined for love, even when we are not sure how it can come out right. In light of this trust, the miseries that have sometimes been our lot, and that we have often caused, do not have to fuel an endless determination to remake the world in order to erase those memories, since

25. Aquinas, *The Literal Exposition on Job*, 145, 178.

that history, with all its miseries and missteps, is not beyond God's mastery to gather up in Christ in the story of creation's redemption.

Christian Poverty, Creatureliness, and the Life of Christ

In this section, I reflect a bit on the poverty of Christ, insofar as it gives us a vivid picture to illustrate some of the qualities of the self-offering love toward which the story of God's providence summons us. This love, I suggest, although it is beyond the gifts of our nature, helps us see the depths of the meaning of our creatureliness.

I confess that I am not qualified to address poverty, since I am neither involuntarily nor voluntarily poor. But I am emboldened to address this topic partly because I can call upon the words of others, some of whom know the vow of poverty firsthand. I was comforted to read the words of the late Dominican theologian Herbert McCabe that poverty, like riches, is best understood not as a status some have achieved but as an ideal or a direction in which we might aim. His distinction between these two aims is a helpful place to start thinking about poverty. He writes, "Riches represent the ideal of taking the world for your own use; poverty represents the ideal of complete freedom from possessions." McCabe elaborates on this distinction by contrasting *possession,* which always involves taking, and *being,* which can only be received and bestowed, never taken. He continues, "To aim at riches is to aim at taking possession of things, even, perhaps, taking possession of people. To aim at poverty is to aim at the giving of life, and this comes from gratitude for receiving life ourselves."[26] McCabe's point is perhaps a bit obscure. But God, he notes, never takes but only gives, and never possesses but only is. In this sense, McCabe says, God is poor, and in this sense poverty is to be aimed at. McCabe is not denying that our being, unlike God's, must be sustained by some degree of taking, but he is cautioning us that, if we aim our lives at taking rather than at self-diffusive being, we will be sorrowful like the rich young man in the Gospel story, because we will become less like God and we will corrode the friendship with God and with others that is our true maturity and joy.

Admittedly, these characterizations of riches and poverty are found in a sermon, and McCabe has simplified matters to suit his homiletical purposes.

26. Herbert McCabe, OP, *God, Christ, and Us,* ed. Brian Davies, OP (London: Continuum, 2003), 54.

McCabe's characterization of poverty might just be another way of talking about gratuitous love — it never takes, but only gives. But he does point us toward something of what we mean by the term "poverty." What McCabe does not go into in much detail here is what difference it makes for poverty to be lived out in a human life. When the divine characteristics of poverty, the lack of a possessive attitude and the concern with self-expenditure for the sake of others, become incarnate, poverty must involve some additional features. After all, while God's being is inexhaustible, we human beings can bestow good things to others only to the extent that we have received good things ourselves. And that means that our self-expenditure always runs a risk that God's never does, that the fund from which we bestow will run thin, especially if we are determined to aim at utter nonpossessiveness. So it is important to recognize the oddity of calling God poor (except in reference to the Son, who has become a human being). For when we speak of poverty, we typically mean not only a lack of possession and a willingness to give, but also the vulnerability that, for human beings, comes with it. Since we are temporal beings who need regular sustenance, and since our social orders mediate our access to sustenance through the institution of property, to divest ourselves of possessions always exposes us to insecurity and a sharpening of our dependence, and usually to weakness as well — if not physically, then at least with respect to our command of material resources. And since the ability to command resources correlates with social status, poverty generally implies humility, too.

These features of what poverty means for human beings — vulnerability, insecurity, dependence, weakness, humility — are left aside in McCabe's sermon, but they are the reason that the thought of poverty more often drives us to protect ourselves from it than to pursue it. Because we recoil from such a state, pursuing riches instead of poverty can seem not only more satisfying, but more humane. Even if McCabe is right that we should avoid the pursuit of riches, maybe his implication that we must be moving in one direction or the other is misleading. Can't we aim simply at a moderation somewhere between poverty and riches? Isn't that the counsel of Proverbs 30:8, "Give me neither beggary nor riches"?

The sage of Proverbs is right that neither deprivation nor wealth is to be desired in itself, but Christ invites the moderate sage, and us as well, to an unexpected beatitude, pursuing a sort of love constituted by an ever deeper self-offering vulnerability. This love moves toward doing without some of the hedges against deprivation we reasonably cling to (but which in practice often become rationalizations for exclusion). Through that love, the features of poverty we fear — insecurity, dependence, weakness, humility — become features of the path to beatitude. In one sense, their appearance there is surprising. As Thomas Hibbs comments, the embrace of poverty could make no sense as part of the perfection of an Aristotelian nature in an Aristotelian cosmos, but once that nature becomes a wayfarer, part of a story open to God's dramatic intervention, embracing poverty can become part of the road to our final end.[27] In another sense, though, once we have seen Christ's poverty, we can grasp some of the ways in which it points to the fulfillment, not only of our being in the image of God, but of our very creatureliness.

Consider two conditions of our creatureliness, both of which we can use riches to obscure from our view: temporality and being parts of a larger whole. Our temporality means that our createdness unfolds moment by moment. But it is easy for us, when we look to the future, to grow weary of the thought that our toil today will have to be repeated tomorrow, and so we may look to riches for an escape. It is easy for us, when we look to the future, to grow anxious about what might threaten tomorrow's sustenance, and so we look to riches for security. The fact that we are parts of a larger whole means that our createdness is never merely our possession but is always received through the intersection and interpenetration of our own lives with the lives of many other creatures who each have their own agendas. But it is easy for us to prefer our own agenda to such an extent that we seek to bend other creatures to the service of our own interests, or at least to dismiss the interests of others as irrelevant to our own, and so we look to riches to give us power over others and to build fences that insulate us and bolster our sense of independence. Rowan Williams offers a formulation of our createdness I have found very helpful that ties together the temporality and the membership in a larger whole: "Contemplation for men and women is looking and listening and being moulded by what is other. It is recognizing that you are created — limited, living in time — and allowing yourself to go on being created in and by the world of things and persons in time, all of them mediating the obscure universal initiative of an uncreated action, so wholly regardless of 'self' that it lets the whole universe be."[28]

To learn to inhabit our creatureliness, then, involves a disposition of receptivity toward each new moment and toward the stories of many other creatures whose stories intertwine with our own and help to constitute them.

27. Thomas S. Hibbs, *Dialectic and Narrative in Aquinas: An Interpretation of the "Summa contra gentiles"* (Notre Dame, IN: University of Notre Dame Press, 1995), 174.
28. Williams, *The Truce of God*, 40.

Receptivity entails vulnerability, of course. And it is no good ignoring our responsibility to exercise some foresight against the risk. Of course, we are responsible to seek reasonable security and to develop our knowledge, our skill, and our art. But the wrong sort of security or the wrong use of our skill can become a sort of rebellion against our creatureliness. We must judge, in the particular circumstances of our time and place, what sort of security and what sorts of arts are "appropriate." The question, then, is what sort of people we must be to make these judgments well.

Apart from Christ, we might have made these judgments differently. Aristotle, for example, recognizes that only a small amount of riches is required for a good life, but he affirms that we need enough wealth so that our bodily needs do not distract us from the development of our capacities, and furthermore we ought to have a modest stock from which we can draw in order to exercise our generosity. Since virtue rather than wealth is the key to stability of character and a good life, one should not seek too much security through wealth, but for Aristotle, dependence, weakness, and humility diminish the goodness of life. To fail to maintain a modicum of nobility and apparent self-sufficiency would undermine our flourishing.[29]

What becomes evident in the life of Christ, however, is that humanity is called toward a universal love that aims to encompass all things, and that the universality and trustworthiness of this aim invites us to a defenselessness that refuses many of the means of security and barriers we might otherwise have thought appropriate. In this way, we learn just how far we can go in "allowing ourselves to go on being created." Christ allows himself to go on being created in the interpenetration of his own story with the stories of a multitude of others — not that he exercises no action shaping that interpenetration; he is supremely active, bringing new possibilities of life, love, reconciliation, and truth. But his action is also patient to attend to how many stories are coming together in any given circumstance, in order to discern in the confluence of stories the opportunity to bear witness to the kingdom, which is the miraculous, divine "weaving together" into one destiny all the stories of creation. Christ's "allowing himself to go on being created" is also a matter of his patience with creation's fertility (which includes human labor) to provide what it will, and thus he regularly renews his material dependence

29. Alasdair MacIntyre suspects, as do I, that Aristotle's disdain for receptivity reflects "an illusion of self-sufficiency, an illusion . . . that is all too characteristic of the rich and powerful in many times and places" (Alasdair MacIntyre, *Dependent Rational Animals: Why Human Beings Need the Virtues* [Chicago: Open Court Press, 1999], 127).

and trust. These two stances, his patient and compassionate attention to the multitude of stories, and his patient material simplicity, are inseparable. The compassion helps to motivate the simplicity, and the simplicity helps reduce the barriers of insulation and exclusion that might hinder his availability to bear with so many stories.

Christ's "allowing himself to go on being created" has a further dimension that clarifies the depth of his receptivity and the meaning of his poverty. Christ's bold enactment of new possibilities in light of an allegiance to the Father that challenges society's settled strategies for self-protection makes him a sign of contradiction. For this reason, as he seeks to engage with love the confluence of stories, some of the elements within society he seeks to engage, such as Caiaphas, end up rejecting him and becoming a danger to him. Yet, he allows himself to go on in defenseless openness to the world he loves, even as it kills him, refusing to betray the love he must have even for his enemies. And his courageous defenselessness here is but the continuation of his whole pattern of living, empowered by the same unshakable trust in the Father through the Spirit to weave all things into the story of a creation drawn to communion.

In this way, Christ enacted in human form the contours of the divine poverty of which McCabe speaks, adding to divine nonpossessiveness and self-expenditure an active refusal of the insulation, the security, and the protection offered by riches. So Christ's person offers a way of being that is not opposed to all prudential hedging against risk, but that judges such hedging by whether it would betray the love Christ has for others, which calls all people into a trajectory toward defenselessness and insecurity — in short, toward a self-abandon that invites and anticipates the communion that is our destiny in Christ.

Poverty, Repentance, and the Small Gesture

As Herbert McCabe has said, to aim at poverty is to aim at giving life. I hope it is now more evident why that is so. To aim at poverty is to aim at giving life because it aims to be patient of God's giving of life to all. To receive the life God gives, moment by moment, not resentful that it must be shared with other creatures whose presence we did not choose, trustful that somehow one day we will be able to survey the whole and call it "gift," is to make room for others in light of the "roominess" of God. To aim at poverty calls us to an ever greater virtuosity in this kind of patience, as we look for ways to live into the extremity of insecurity, self-abandonment, and courageously defenseless love we have witnessed in Christ. What holds us back is partly our selfishness and love of riches, of course. But I suspect that, if we are honest, we are also held back by doubt that we are up to the arduousness of it, by doubt that such ferocious trust in the Father can really be ours.

But Christ meets us at the Table to keep inviting us to renew our repentance, to come once again and lay down our defenses in trust. It is such trust that empowers us to repudiate the distrust (of our neighbors, of the natural world, and of God) that is instilled in us by a society organized around addressing a so-called scarcity. But "scarcity" usually just means how we describe creation's fertility when our desires cannot find rest in what has been given or acknowledge the trustworthiness of the Giver. When we do repudiate that distrust, we may become what E. F. Schumacher called "home-comers." He alluded to the parable of the prodigal son to suggest the difference between two types of people. On the one hand are those who continue to be driven by this distrust into what Schumacher called a "forward stampede," an acquisitive, controlling Leviathan of a society that wastes and wrecks its inheritance. On the other hand are those who have come home to the joy of the Father, who no longer aim at riches or self-aggrandizement or godlike mastery of the world.[30]

This is not a counsel of passivity. In fact, in some ways it is our continued captivity to the self-protective habits of a marketized society that is passive. It is when we are stripped of such bondage to the service of our own egos that we gain real freedom to act and to love. Furthermore, this is not a counsel of rashness. Any degree of voluntary poverty makes sense only to the extent it is ordered to participate in a mutuality of benefit in which one's need will be supplied by others, while one also offers one's own gifts. But to aim at poverty is to be free of the compulsion of felt needs. Instead, one interrogates one's needs for the sake of others.[31] That is, instead of taking felt needs as givens, the one who aims at poverty asks of any supposed need whether it can be forgone in the interest of freeing up, for the benefit of others, the resources we might have used and the attention we might have paid to them. Or one interrogates an alleged need in the interest of refusing to insulate oneself from the experiences and needs of others. The questions

30. E. F. Schumacher, *Small Is Beautiful: Economics as if People Mattered* (New York: Harper & Row, 1973), 138-51.
31. For this way of formulating the matter, I am indebted to Rowan Williams, *The Truce of God*, 95.

this poverty asks cannot be asked all at once, any more than one can have all one's alleged needs before one's attention at once. But to aim at poverty is to commit continually to renew one's efforts at need-interrogation for the sake of love.

Consider a recent example. It is well known that Pope Francis has chosen not to live in the papal apartments in the Apostolic Palace but to live in a more modest suite in the Domus Sanctae Marthae guesthouse. The gesture is in some ways symbolic and does not necessarily free up a home for someone else, but it does reflect the pope's concern to avoid the isolation and self-deception that can accompany the embrace of status and luxury. To embrace them without interrogation can be a temptation to convince ourselves that we are not really changed by them or attached to them. Then we ignore how riches form a self-protective barrier, and we reassure ourselves that we nonetheless understand the world we claim to love, even as we grow less and less sensitive to the reality of what is fragile in it.

This is only a small gesture toward the defenseless openness of Christ to the world he loves, but it is a sign that God is not without God's saints, who, knowing their place on the way to God, continue to gesture their trust in the Father. By their witness, their lives become transparent to the workings of God's providence, which uses their example, like Job's, to bring others toward the friendship with God that is the human participation in the ultimate destiny of all creation.

CHAPTER 11

Nature and the Common Good: Aristotle and Maritain on the Environment

Jonathan J. Sanford

Why should we be concerned to promote a proper care of the environment? The deepest reason, and the one that ultimately matters, is that God ordered human beings to keep and till the earth,[1] and so the earth is ordained to human stewardship, and human beings are ordered by their Creator to share in the work of bringing to completion the rest of creation.[2] Adam's fall does not vitiate the original command, though it does make it that much harder to fulfill: the fundamental and divinely given responsibility for each human is to steward well the created order.[3] Though this biblical answer encapsulates every legitimate answer to the question, it does not explain each of them.

---

1. "The Lord God took the man and put him in the garden of Eden to till it and keep it" (Gen 2:15; all quotations from *The Holy Bible*, Revised Standard Version, Catholic Edition [San Francisco: Ignatius Press, 1966]).

2. "And God blessed them, and God said to them, 'Be fruitful and multiply, and fill the earth and subdue it; and have dominion over the fish of the sea and over the birds of the air and over every living thing that moves upon the earth.' And God said, 'Behold, I have given you every plant yielding seed which is upon the face of all the earth, and every tree with seed in its fruit; you shall have them for food. And to every beast of the earth, and to every bird of the air, and to everything that creeps on the earth, everything that has the breath of life, I have given every green plant for food.' And it was so" (Gen 1:28-30).

3. "[God said to Adam,] 'Cursed is the ground because of you; in toil you shall eat of it all the days of your life; thorns and thistles it shall bring forth to you; and you shall eat the plants of the field. In the sweat of your face you shall eat bread till you return to the ground, for out of it you were taken; you are dust, and to dust you shall return.' . . . — therefore the Lord God sent him forth from the garden of Eden, to till the ground from which he was taken" (Gen 3:17-19, 23).

Because we are complex creatures, social by virtue of our rationality, there are multiple spheres of concerns that need to be addressed to answer why we should promote proper care of the environment. In this chapter, I am primarily concerned with the human, which is to say the properly social, spheres of concern.[4]

Here too the book of Genesis offers some guidance, but its message is not so easy to interpret. Recall that it was Cain, not Abel, who was the farmer, and that it was Abel, not Cain, whose burnt offering found regard from the Lord God (Gen 4:2-7). Though warned by God that temptation was crouching at his door, Cain failed to resist it, was overcome with jealousy at God's favor for Abel, and murdered his brother. Doubly cursed now in his efforts to bring forth the fruit of the earth, first through his father's sin and then through his own,[5] Cain is sent forth from his homeland. He goes east of Eden and builds the first city, named after his son, Enoch (Gen 4:17).

What conclusions concerning caring for the earth are we to draw from this account? Is it not strange that he who denies he is his brother's keeper founds the first polis? What is the relation between farming and the city? Are cities the fruit of murder and disobedience? Are cities contrary to the original plan of God for man? We will return to these questions. Here, let's note that, at the very least, there is clearly a tension between Cain the farmer and Cain the city-founder, and the murder of Abel marks the division between those two Cains. Elements of this tension have found their way into some features of the debates concerned with environmental ethics, with the more industrial-minded city-dwellers on the one side, and the bucolic farmers and naturalists on the other. I think a conception of the common good that includes both sides of this division, and one that takes its orientation from both Aristotle and Jacques Maritain, can go some way toward ameliorating the tension.

---

4. I heartily embrace the long-standing Christian view that nonrational creatures are ordered to God's glory and that we need to preserve them for this reason. Nothing I will say about the polis and the common good is meant to compete with or contravene this principle, though I will not be focusing on it.

5. The first curse being the curse of Adam, to which is added: "And now you are cursed from the ground, which has opened its mouth to receive your brother's blood from your hand. When you till the ground, it shall no longer yield to you its strength; you shall be a fugitive and a wanderer on the earth" (Gen 4:11-12).

Narrowing the Motivational Concern

The question with which I began — Why should we be concerned to promote a proper care for the environment? — is ultimately one about motivation. Should we be motivated to pursue the good of the environment?
What does that even mean? Assuming we should promote the well-being
of the natural world in some fashion, what ought to be our reasons? Questions about motivations are ultimately questions about reasons. My initial
question also, it stands pointing out, is ambiguous. As a philosopher, I am
perhaps oversensitive to the debates that words like "should" and "we" inspire. With some effort I place those aside, at least for the moment, but I
would like to take up the term "environmentalism" because this term is often
used as shorthand for "promoting a proper care for the environment." What
is environmentalism? Does this term name a cohesive movement, one with
a coherent ideology? It often is regarded as a wellspring of obligation: does
that make it a moral theory, or something else?

Few movements come in more shapes and sizes than environmentalism. Some of those permutations, particularly those of the New Age, earth-
mother-worshiping pagan variety, encourage some Christians to become
morally opposed to promoting any strong version of environmentalism. Of
course, Christians come in all shapes and sizes too, with some Christians embracing elements of environmentalism and others wary even of the admirer-
of-nature-and-careful-to-recycle versions of environmentalism. The source
of that wariness is not doubt as to whether we have an obligation to tend and
care for the earth, for the Bible and the Magisterium are both clear on this
point. Rather, the concern springs from a mostly visceral reaction against the
extreme variety of environmentalism that carries with it features not merely
ideological but fanatical and sometimes violent as well. It also prompts a fair
question: Is the environmentalism that wishes there were far fewer humans
to walk upon and so pollute the earth perhaps even pining for large-scale
demise to see that wish fulfilled, in a continuum with the environmentalism
that insinuates moral failure on the part of those driving larger-than-strictly-
necessary vehicles? Are either of those environmentalist positions the sort
that inspires a family to buy some land, move out of town, and start growing
their own food? For some environmentalists, love of nature leads more or
less directly to hatred of anything, or anyone, who harms it. For other environmentalists, there is not the companion misanthropy to complement one's
philo-naturalism, but, rather, an acceptance of the principle that the enemy
of your enemy is your friend. "Sure," the modest environmentalist says to

himself, "I don't agree with all that bosh about humanity being a scourge on the earth and in need of radical thinning, but I have to admit that my extreme friends have a point and, after all, it's not like they are acting on those extreme views but are advancing the sort of policies I care about." So, you see, there is something to be said for what I call the *continuum view,* which collects all forms of environmentalism under a single umbrella.

At the heart of the continuum view is the conviction that there is a battle being waged over the environment with typical citizens of First World economies on the one side, whose consumerism has become so ingrained into the fabric of their characters that they no longer care if the rest of the world is decimated, just so long as they get their stuff, and atypical citizens of First World economies who are lovers of the wild wastelands and who make every effort to tread lightly in their nevertheless carbon-strewn paths through life.[6] To be sure, I am painting with a broad brush, but consider the many ways in which this conflict plays itself out in our popular discourse: hydraulic-fracturing advocates on the one hand, Josh Fox's *Gasland* on the other. Opponents of the EPA's oversight of manufacturers on the one hand, Al Gore's *An Inconvenient Truth* on the other. Both sides in these debates build upon the conviction that there is an ineluctable conflict between civilization and the environment. This conviction works hand-in-glove with the continuum view of environmentalism for the same reasons that one's list of allies always swells in times of global conflict; fundamental differences are overlooked for the sake of winning proximate goals.

I think Christians, and Catholics especially, should reject the continuum view. Though there can be short-term gains in achieving some measure of protecting the environment by joining forces in legislative efforts with those who do not share our regard for the dignity of persons,[7] we run a greater risk by seeming to align our reasons for stewardship with those advancing a "hands-off of nature" sort of environmentalism. Rousseau's *Second Dis-*

6. Sometimes that mentality leads to a new sort of "mercy killing," such as in the case of the UK woman who recently flew(!) to Switzerland to have assistance in killing herself (legally) for the sake of reducing her carbon footprint.

7. The long-term goals have been articulated by Pope Emeritus Benedict XVI in *Caritas in veritate,* where he has made clear that the healing of our whole world, not only of human persons but including the world of nature, is of a piece with the healing of our own personal natures (see especially §51). See also Stratford Caldecott, "At Home in the Cosmos: The Revealing of the Sons of God," *Nova et Vetera* 10 (2012): 105-20: "The healing of the world around us depends on a re-ordering and a healing of the inner world of the imagination, intelligence, and will" (108).

course, at least with respect to the yarn he spins concerning man's original nature and idealization of the rest of nature that attends it, is the inspiration for the bulk of environmentalisms we see today.[8] That is to say, there is an underlying presumption that man cannot but be a despoiler of the earth, that cultivation by its very nature is tantamount to violence. In the Christian view, although indeed there is the tension mentioned already between Cain the farmer and Cain the city-builder, the *original* dispensation of man is to keep and till the earth, and in the original prelapsarian condition, that cultivation of the earth maintained it in its perfected state. Lapsed man is still ordained to cultivate the earth, and his task is, among other things, to return it to its perfected state.

It is also important to bring Rousseau to mind in light of the tension between the two Cains raised before, since, from Rousseau's perspective, all political order is fundamentally artificial. His view of uncultivated nature, on the one hand, and of man who originally is not ordained to cultivation, on the other, can do no more than cement the conflict between the city and the environment. Rousseau misses, even renders himself incapable of appreciating, because of his distorted positions on human nature and the nature of beings in the world, precisely what Aristotle and Maritain so aptly reveal regarding the common good, namely, that it is by means of an adequate understanding and appreciation for the true ends of community that any human action is best guided. Any proper care of the environment needs, then, to be articulated from within political philosophy.[9]

Aristotle is convinced that, not only are cities made for human beings, but human beings are made for cities. That is to say, we flourish as the sort of beings that we are only within a well-established political order. So much of environmentalism, in contrast, seems to take its cue, however remotely, from

8. Descartes performs the critical groundwork in the modern period for the denaturing of nature, so to speak, in his *Discourse on Method,* books 5-6, and in *Meditations on First Philosophy,* books 2 and 6. Christopher Thompson reminds us that, just as secular contemporary philosophy makes no room for form and finality and thus has left contemporary environmental ethics with relatively few resources for addressing our significant problems, so too has there been an inadequate response on the part of the Church. See Christopher Thompson, "Perennial Wisdom: Notes toward a Green Thomism," *Nova et Vetera* 10 (2012): 79.

9. John Rist's reflections on the paucity of modern, and the richness of ancient, philosophical resources for confronting environmental challenges, despite large-scale environmental concerns not being a matter of philosophical concern for them, are apropos here. See his "Why Greek Philosophers Might Have Been Concerned about the Environment," in *The Greeks and the Environment,* ed. Laura Westra and Thomas M. Robinson (Lanham, MD: Rowman & Littlefield, 1997), 19-32.

a Rousseau-esque suspicion that man is made for the woods, mountains, and streams, and that the artifice of political community has distorted our genuinely free and solitary natures. What I would like to propose, among other things, is that with Aristotle you get your woods, mountains, and streams *because* of your churches, schools, and parliaments. What I explore in the rest of this chapter is whether Aristotle's view of the city and man really can provide suitable motivation for genuine concern for the environment, and, still further, whether this Aristotelian foundation for environmentalism can be subsumed into a Christian environmentalism; it is Maritain who will help us answer that latter question.

From the Common Good to the Environment

I have stressed Aristotle's political philosophy as the point of departure for a responsible environmental ethic,[10] because a fulsome environmental ethic receives its legitimacy through its incorporation within the common good as held out as the ideal of political life.[11] Three related observations are in order. First, it is worth reminding ourselves that, from an Aristotelian perspective, ethics is but a part of the architectonic science of politics.[12] Second, there is no such thing as a stand-alone environmental ethic. Any concern for the environment needs to be part of the sphere of concerns proper to human beings. Third, there can be, despite appearances to the contrary, no insuperable conflicts between an ethic of the environment and the ethic of other matters

---

10. It should be noted that Aristotle, and the Greeks in general, have been described in some recent environmental ethics literature as being in some way responsible for the ecological crises of our ideas. Westra and Robinson outline some of those criticisms and work to rebut them in their introduction to *The Greeks and the Environment*, 3-10. Westra has done a great deal of work in the course of her career to make the case that Aristotle provides the essential ingredients for a sound ecology on a global scale. See her *An Environmental Proposal for Ethics: The Principle of Integrity* (Lanham, MD: Rowman & Littlefield, 1994) and *Living in Integrity: Toward a Global Ethic to Restore a Fragmented Earth* (Lanham, MD: Rowman & Littlefield, 1998), and the many efforts of the Global Ecological Integrity Group (see www.globalecointegrity.net).

11. In other ways, one could draw elements of an environmental ethics from Aristotle, though none as potentially comprehensive. See, for instance, Richard Shearman's study, which connects man's desire for contemplation as perfective of the self with the preservation of species, in "Self-Love and the Virtue of Species Preservation in Aristotle," in *The Greeks and the Environment*, 121-32.

12. *Nicomachean Ethics* (hereafter *NE*) I.2, 1094a26-1094b12.

pertaining to human life. The notion of the common good does the work of harmonizing every sphere of human concern, assuming, that is, that we have a more or less correct and sufficiently rich conception of the common good at our disposal. Do we?

Before attempting to answer this last question, and in order to correct a possible misunderstanding predicated on the way in which I seem to be privileging the political sphere, it is worth stressing that nothing I have just said undermines the deep regard we should have for the distinct dignity and value proper to the beings that compose what we often loosely refer to as "the environment." Indeed, Aristotle is the first thinker, outside of the Jewish tradition, to articulate a deep appreciation for the goodness of the natural order, and his natural philosophy is predicated on a conception of nature that infuses every being with finality and beauty. Aristotle never articulates the transcendental properties of being in the manner in which they come to be described later in the tradition, but in critiquing Plato for, among other things, dividing particular beings from their essences,[13] Aristotle does couple good with being and recognizes that good is said in as many ways as being is.[14] He recognizes, moreover, that the goodness of the natural order is ultimately grounded on its imitation of and orchestration toward the first and divine being, when he writes:

We must consider also in which of two ways the nature of the universe contains the good or the highest good, whether as something separate and

13. *Metaphysics* (hereafter *Meta.*) I.9, 991b1-3.
14. *NE* I.6, 1096a19-35: "But things are called good both in the category of substance and in that of quality and in that of relation, and that which is *per se*, i.e. substance, is prior in nature to the relative (for the latter is like an offshoot and accident of what is); so that there could not be a common Idea set over all these goods. Further, since things are said to be good in as many ways as they are said to be (for things are called good both in the category of substance, as God and reason, and in quality, e.g. the virtues, and in quantity, e.g. that which is moderate, and in relation, e.g. the useful, and in time, e.g. the right opportunity, and in place, e.g. the right locality and the like), clearly the good cannot be something universally present in all cases and single; for then it would not have been predicated in all the categories but in one only. Further, since of the things answering to one Idea there is one science, there would have been one science of all the goods; but as it is there are many sciences even of the things that fall under one category, e.g. of opportunity (for opportunity in war is studied by strategy and in disease by medicine), and the moderate in food is studied by medicine and in exercise by the science of gymnastics. And one might ask the question, what in the world they *mean* by 'a thing itself,' if in man himself and in a particular man the account of man is one and the same" (all quotations of Aristotle's texts are taken from the *The Complete Works of Aristotle*, 2 vols., ed. Jonathan Barnes (Princeton: Princeton University Press, 1984).

by itself, or as the order of the parts. Probably in both ways, as an army does. For the good is found both in the order and in the leader, and more in the latter; for he does not depend on the order but it depends on him. And all things are ordered together somehow, but not all alike, — both fishes and fowls and plants; and the world is not such that one thing has nothing to do with another, but they are connected. For all are ordered together to one end.[15]

In this quotation we find expressed the ultimate reason for the beauty and goodness apparent in the natural order, namely, its being ordered toward the perfect and first being. However, one hardly needs to have completed a course in first philosophy to be moved to appreciate the wondrous beauty of the natural world; in fact, the avoidance of certain methods of philosophizing may be required to maintain one's admiration for nature's beauty.

Aristotle, ever the champion of natural beauty, chides those who seek to turn away from an appreciation of the world that surrounds them and to fly into the upper reaches of the cosmic order. This world, the one through which we walk and of whose elements our bodies are composed, is replete with objects for our study:

We therefore must not recoil with childish aversion from the examination of the humbler animals. Every realm of nature is marvelous: and as Heraclitus, when the strangers who came to visit him found him warming himself at the furnace in the kitchen and hesitated to go in, is reported to have bidden them not to be afraid to enter, as even in that kitchen divinities were present, so we should venture on the study of every kind of animal without distaste; for each and all will reveal to us something natural and something beautiful. Absence of haphazard and conduciveness of everything to an end are to be found in nature's works in the highest degree, and the end for which those works are put together and produced is a form of the beautiful.[16]

So, indeed, from Aristotle we first learn the vocabulary by means of which we can adequately express the unity of each being, its orientation toward its end, and its participation in beauty itself. Not only are each of these beings what they are because of their telic participation in the first and divine being, but a study of such beings brings a deepening of our own participation

15. *Meta.* XII.10, 1075a11-19.
16. *Parts of Animals* I.5, 645a15-25.

in the divine being's life, since, "In every case the mind which is actively thinking is the objects which it thinks,"[17] and, "the actuality of thought is life, and God is that actuality."[18] To study nature is to share in God's activity, the very same activity that gives life to all natural things. All of this gives us reasons for recognizing the goodness, the value, the beauty of those beings composing our environment, but it does not yet give us an ethic.[19]

It is the naturally bequeathed quest for the fulfillment distinctive of our nature on the one hand, and the power to deliberate on the other, which provides two of the pillars for a basic Aristotelian and commonsense ethics.[20] Added to this is a third pillar, the education that each person receives at the hands of parents, teachers, and other important persons. This education provides the formation in what counts as noble or ignoble, courageous or cowardly, and so forth, and so which provides the necessary culturally informed ingredients out of which, among other naturally occurring ingredients, particular virtues, and indeed our characters as a whole, are baked.[21]

The virtue whose possession most ostensibly connects an individual's pursuit of the good life with the flourishing of the whole community is justice, and especially justice in the general sense. Aristotle writes of it that "this form of justice, then, is complete excellence — not absolutely, but in relation to others. . . . And it is complete excellence in its fullest sense, because it is the actual exercise of complete excellence. It is complete because he who possesses it can exercise his excellence towards others too and not merely by himself; for many men can exercise excellence in their own affairs, but

17. *De anima* III.7, 431b16-17.

18. *Meta.* XII.7, 1072b26-27.

19. The distinction between elements of an ethics, and an ethics, is a point not always fully appreciated by those who (rightly) turn to Aristotle for a rich appreciation of the natural world. For instance, Susanne E. Foster, in "Aristotle and the Environment," *Environmental Ethics* 24 (2002): 409-28, makes an excellent case for why we should have a significant regard for nonhuman beings, speaking of them as deserving moral concern (427). It is not clear, however, what "moral concern" means within the context of an Aristotelian approach to ethics, since it is an expression that owes its contemporary meaning to the Kantian tradition. She claims that, although Aristotle never discussed environmental ethics, one can be developed from his biological and ethical works (411). I think a case can be made that Aristotle has an environmental ethics, but only if granted a less familiar use of "environmental."

20. "Commonsense ethic" in the manner in which G. E. M. Anscombe's position on virtue theory is characterized by Christopher Miles Coope in his "Modern Virtue Ethics," in *Values and Virtues: Aristotelianism in Contemporary Ethics*, ed. Timothy Chappell (Oxford: Clarendon Press, 2006), 20-52.

21. *NE* I.4, 1095b3-8.

not in their relations to excellence."[22] If one has this social virtue of justice, then one has, at least to some degree of firm formation,[23] each of the other virtues.[24] That is what makes justice a complete excellence. But more significantly from the perspective of our genuinely social or political natures, it is justice that advances the common good by putting our virtues at the service of others.

Before filling in with a little more detail what that common good entails for Aristotle, and to cut short the typical Hobbesian-inspired objection that Aristotle's view of the common good assumes far too much about the better lights of the human being, it is worth reminding ourselves that Aristotle's view of the human condition is by no means naive. Though virtue's value is not reducible to it, it is in part measured by its scarcity.[25] Only those who have been raised well — which is to say, raised with a thorough education in what counts as virtuous and what counts as vicious — stand a chance at living virtuously. Given that so much of our moral success depends upon what our elders have yielded to us, or have failed to do so, it can be surprising that Aristotle insists that human beings are responsible for their bad actions, and still further, that we can voluntarily put ourselves into the position of being incapable of reformation — which, though chilling, seems to me just the right conclusion to arrive at if we take seriously our own need for divine aid.[26]

A moral theory that holds that very few people can live up to its standards, and that everyone is responsible for failing to do so, is not one that

22. *NE* V.1, 1129b26-27, 30-35.

23. Aristotle describes virtues by their paradigms, which does not need to be seen to imply that one needs virtue in the fully developed state to have a virtue at all. I think that his arguments in *NE* VI.13 allow for a "more" or "less" approach to virtue, with some minimum threshold needing to be met for a good-habit-still-being-solidified to qualify as a virtue.

24. *Politics* (hereafter *Pol.*) III.13, 1283a38-39: "For justice has been acknowledged by us to be a social excellence, and it implies all others."

25. *NE* II.9, 1109a24-29: "Hence also it is no easy task to be good. For in everything it is no easy task to find the middle, e.g. to find the middle of a circle is not for every one but for him who knows; so, too, any one can get angry — that is easy — or give or spend money; but to do this to the right person, to the right extent, at the right time, with the right aim, and in the right way, *that* is not for every one, nor is it easy; that is why goodness is both rare and laudable and noble."

26. *NE* III.5, 1114b16-1115a3, 1114a17-22: "In that case it was *then* open to him not to be ill, but not now, when he has thrown away his chance, just as when you have let a stone go it is too late to recover it; but yet it was in your power to throw it, since the moving principle was in you. So, too, to the unjust and to the self-indulgent man it was open at the beginning not to become men of this kind, and so they are such voluntarily, but now that they have become so it is not possible for them not to be so."

warms the heart of the egalitarian. The scarcity of virtue and the common tendency to vice are why, Aristotle suggests, we need not only encouragements to virtue but punishments for vicious actions. We cannot forbid every vice, but we can arrange our polis in such a manner that those who would wreak havoc on it are corrected in their actions if not their characters, or otherwise banished.[27] This is, in other words, why we need the law, and the city thrives that is ruled by genuine laws, "for most people obey necessity rather than argument, and punishments rather than what is noble."[28] The constitution that (1) embraces the role of law as the governing principle and (2) sees magistrates as servants of the law, is the only one that has the chance of moving the whole community — even those for whom arguments are of no avail — toward its most fitting end.[29]

Regardless of the extent of deadweight those who refuse to embrace the path of virtue bring to the ship of state, their lives and the lives of the virtuous must somehow be woven into an organized community if any of the members of that community are to thrive. Although indeed there are cities that fail to promote the common good as it should be promoted, and so particular families are forced in those communities to take over some of the duties that fall naturally to the state,[30] the sort of beings that we are — which is to say, political, or in other words, rational, animals — can flourish only within a community. The city's development is posterior to the most basic natural community, the family, with respect to generation; but with respect to perfection, the city is ultimately prior because the thriving city is the end of man. In Aristotle's words:

> Further, the state is by nature clearly prior to the family and to the individual, since the whole is of necessity prior to the part. . . . The proof that the state is a creation of nature and prior to the individual is that the individual, when isolated, is not self-sufficing; and therefore he is like a

27. *NE* X.9, 1179b4-19. I follow Peter Simpson, *A Philosophical Commentary on Aristotle's* Politics (Chapel Hill: University of North Carolina Press, 1998), in regarding *NE* X.9 as the introduction to the *Politics*.

28. *NE* X.9, 1179b4-5.

29. *Pol.* III.16, 1287a19-22, 28-32: "And the rule of the law, it is argued, is preferable to that of any individual. On the same principle, even if it be better for certain individuals to govern, they should be made only guardians and ministers of the law. . . . Therefore he who bids the law rule may be deemed to bid God and Reason alone rule, but he who bids man rule adds an element of the best; for desire is a wild beast, and passion perverts the minds of rulers, even when they are the best of men. The law is reason unaffected by desire."

30. *NE* X.9, 1180a25-32.

part in relation to the whole. But he who is unable to live in society, or who has no need because he is sufficient for himself, must be either a beast or a god: he is no part of a state. A social instinct is implanted in all men by nature, and yet he who first found the state was the greatest of benefactors. For man, when perfected, is the best of animals, but, when separated from law and justice, he is the worst of all; since armed injustice is the most dangerous, and he is equipped at birth with arms, meant to be used by intelligence and excellence, which he may use for the worst ends. That is why, if he has not excellence, he is the most unholy and the most savage of animals, and the most full of lust and gluttony. But justice is the bond of men in states; for the administration of justice, which is the determination of what is just, is the principle of order in political society.[31]

The state is not the institutional deception that an ancient group of masters built to contain their slaves, nor is it the artificial compact for mutual protection of a collection of individuals too weak to live as nature made them. Human beings are made for the city, and the city for human beings.

The common good is, then, ultimately the expression of the shared life of excellence within the city. Its highest expression is a shared life of genuine friendship.[32] The city, though it is established to address mutual needs, is not "a mere society, having a common place, established for the prevention of mutual crime and for the sake of exchange." Of course, those necessities must be taken care of by any city worthy of the name, but this initial level of the common good is far from encompassing. To appreciate the difference implied between meeting needs and thriving, consider how it is often remarked in our times that citizens feel closest to each other in times of crisis, whether a war or a natural disaster. For Aristotle, however, the true measure of a community's embrace of the common good is the quality of its peacetime life: "If it is disgraceful in men not to be able to use the goods of life, it is peculiarly disgraceful not to be able to use them in time of leisure — to show excellent qualities in action and war, and when they have peace and leisure to be no better than slaves."[33]

What are the excellent qualities, the virtues, that Aristotle references in this passage? First, to be able to establish a time of peace, the virtues of courage and endurance are especially required. Second, with peace and relative prosperity secured, the examined life of philosophy can be embraced, knowl-

31. *Pol.* I.2, 1253a8-20, 25-39.
32. *Pol.* III.9, 1280a37-39.
33. *Pol.* III.9, 1280b29-31; VII.15, 1334a36-39.

edge can be advanced, and the education of all can be pursued. Whether in times of crisis or in times of peace, Aristotle points to the virtues of justice and temperance as being of particular importance. We see, then, that the common good is ultimately a life lived in common, marked by friendship of both the family relation and political varieties, with the cardinal virtues of temperance, courage, and justice in force at all times, and prudence ordering the whole toward a shared life of reflection and study.[34] I have already remarked on how Aristotle is attuned to the reality that few citizens may in fact embody these virtues, and even fewer fully embrace the greatest good of philosophical activity. Those few need the whole, however, not simply to support a robust economy that makes possible the leisure required for philosophical pursuits, but as political friends with whom justice is fully shared. So too do the nonvirtuous, most of whom stand a good chance of at least usually being self-controlled, benefit when there is a critical mass of leading citizens actually embracing the best life. The whole city, from bottom to top, is well-ordered when the conditions are in place in which man can fully flourish as the political animal he is.

This conception of the common good is necessary, I think, to articulate a responsible environmentalism that can motivate us, at least the striving-to-be-virtuous among us, in the same way in which the activities of virtue motivate us. That is to say, caring for the environment is like caring for our other needs, and the flourishing of the environment is both necessary to the flourishing of the whole community and a necessary outcome of those same virtues of temperance, courage, justice, and prudence.

Particular care for the environment, as John Cuddeback notes in his *Nova et Vetera* article on the subject,[35] falls for Aristotle within the art of economics, that is to say, household management,[36] and relies heavily on a distinction between two sorts of wealth-getting, one natural and the other unnatural. The natural one concerns farming, animal husbandry, and the other skills that are part and parcel of cultivating plants and animals in a manner that puts them to good use without exhausting the soil, decimating

---

34. *Pol.* VII.15, 1334a11-1334b27.

35. John A. Cuddeback, "Renewing Husbandry: Wendell Berry, Aristotle, and Thomas Aquinas on 'Economics,'" *Nova et Vetera* 10 (2010): 121-34, especially 127-28.

36. In his reflection on Aristotle's elements and notion of place as the seeds for environmentalism, David Macauley draws out some connections between the notions of place and home in Aristotle's works; see "The Place of the Elements and the Elements of Place: Aristotelian Contributions to Environmental Thought," *Ethics, Place, and Enviornment* 9 (2006): 187-206, especially 199.

herds, or polluting our common airways and waterways. It is natural because there are fixed boundaries to the acquisition of this sort of wealth:

> Of the art of acquisition then there is one kind which by nature is a part of the management of a household, in so far as the art of household management must either find ready to hand or itself provide, such things necessary to life, and useful for the community of the family or state, as can be stored. They are the elements of true riches; for the amount of property which is needed for a good life is not unlimited. . . . But there is a boundary fixed, just as there is in the other arts.[37]

There is no point in storing more than you can use, whether for one's own community directly or for the sake of selling so as to acquire other things conducive to the good life. There is no point, moreover, in causing harm to the earth one tills or the water one drinks or the air one breathes, since doing so undermines the harmony with one's immediate environment needed for continued healthy living for oneself and one's kith and kin — and indeed, one's future generations. No point, that is, as long as one is seeking to utilize the fruits of the earth to meet one's natural needs.[38]

This sort of household management is natural in another sense too, insofar as it is an expression of nature's provision for human flourishing. Aristotle provides an intriguing argument to the effect that property, "in the sense of bare livelihood," belongs to all. He means not only all human beings, but every living thing, noting for example, how nature provides milk for mammals to be sustained on. Similarly, the apple seeds are encased in fruity flesh to enrich the early life of the seedling. The same purposive nature that provides for seedlings provides for nonhuman animals, and humans as well, as Aristotle notes: "In like manner we may infer that, after the birth of animals, plants exist for their sake, and that the other animals exist for the sake of man, the tame for use and food, the wild, if not all, at least the greater part of them, for food, and for the provision of clothing and various instruments. Now if nature makes nothing incomplete, and nothing in vain, the inference must be that she has made all animals for the sake of man."[39] If all the animals are

---

37. *Pol.* I.8, 1256b26-39.

38. John A. Cuddeback's discussion of moneymaking in "Renewing Husbandry: Wendell Berry, Aristotle, and Thomas Aquinas on 'Economics'" is helpful on these points; see especially 129-33.

39. *Pol.* I.8, 1256b9-15, 15-22. Anthony Preuss argues, wrongly I think, that a "straight-line" can be drawn from this passage of Aristotle to Herbert Spencer's notion of the survival

for the sake of man's good use, and plants for the sake of animals, plants too are ultimately for the sake of man's good use. And in fact Aristotle explicitly says as much when he writes, "For as political science does not make men, but takes them from nature and uses them, so too nature provides with earth or sea or the like as a source of food."[40]

By means of these two senses of "natural," this latter one by means of which all plants and animals are provided to man for his good use, and the former, by means of which man's household management — and so proper stewardship of plants and animals — is governed by the natural limits of his needs and telic orientation toward virtuous living, we find a fundamental convergence between Aristotelian political philosophy and the book of Genesis. This should not surprise us, since God's commands communicated directly to Adam, particularly those having to do with naming the animals and keeping and tilling the earth, are written into nature as well. Nevertheless, it is remarkable that Aristotle has read so well the naturally encased words of the Creator.

To round out the distinction just mentioned, and to bring this discussion of Aristotle to a practical point and a conclusion, I should mention the other sort of wealth-getting — the unnatural variety. This variety trades on money. There is no money in nature, and so it fails the one test of being natural, nor is there any limit to the acquisition of money because, by its very nature, there is no use to be had by it directly, and so it fails the second test of being natural. This sort of wealth-getting, Aristotle notes, consists in exchange:

[It] is justly censored; for it is unnatural, a mode by which men gain from one another. The most hated sort, and with the greatest reason, is usury, which makes a gain out of money itself, and not from the natural object of it. For money was intended to be used in exchange, but not increase at interest. And this term interest, which means the birth of money from money, is applied to the breeding of money because the offspring resembles the parent. That is why of all modes of getting wealth this is the most unnatural.[41]

Perhaps Aristotle did not fully understand or appreciate the way in which interest keeps pace with markets, and perhaps there are ways to uti-

---

of the species, in "Some Ancient Ecological Myths and Metaphors," in *The Greeks and the Environment*, 11-18.

40. *Pol.* I.10, 1258a22-24.
41. *Pol.* I.10, 1258b1-7.

lize some Aristotelian arguments to defend free markets, as Michael Novak has argued,[42] but one must nevertheless recognize that Aristotle has a significant point, one that resonates with the biblical injunction against usury as well (Exod 22:25-27; Deut 23:19-20; Lev 25:36-37). There is something fundamentally unlimited about the desire for money, and when this desire replaces our natural desires and becomes fixated on more and more, this pleonexic disposition becomes the very essence of greed and so the opposite of justice. Unnatural desire for gain does indeed imperil the common good of cities. So too does it do great harm to the environment in ways too obvious to need to be mentioned here.

We have seen, then, that human beings can flourish only in cities, and that an essential part of flourishing in a city is the proper care and cultivation of the lands surrounding cities. This notion of the common good is what makes possible the harmony between the city and the environment. We have also seen that no city is free of incontinent and even bad men, for although the city exists for the sake of the exercise of virtue within the bonds of friendship, those who are truly virtuous are rare indeed. Laws are needed, then, and not just inducements, for the sake of commodious living, and the result of those laws can serve as a great encouragement to self-control, if not virtuous living. Those laws ought to be exercised in such a fashion as to prevent harm to the common good, which includes, as we have seen, harm to the environment. These laws, if well made, will result, not in the equalization of property, but rather in a meritorious division of it, as Aristotle remarks:

> And the avarice of mankind is insatiable; at one time two obols was pay enough; but now, when this sum has become customary, men always want more and more without end; for it is of the nature of desire to be unlimited, and most men live only for the gratification of it. The beginning of reform is not so much to equalize property as to train the nobler sort of nature not to desire more, and to prevent the lower from getting more; that is to say, they must be kept down, but not ill-treated.[43]

This last quotation opens up a proverbial can of worms — talk of keeping down those undeserving will necessarily do that, and for good reasons. I want to make sure that we do not throw overboard the general principle at work in this last quotation in a hasty reaction against Aristotle's claim, for

---

42. Michael Novak, *The Spirit of Democratic Capitalism* (New York: Simon & Schuster, 1982).
43. *Pol.* II.7, 1267b1-9.

it is a principle from which many practical applications can and should be derived.

What is this principle? It is simply this: when a certain activity imperils the common good, it should be prevented or, at the very least, kept from increasing its scope of harm. This principle is the heart of any legislation that looks to protect from harm natural resources such as water, air, and soil quality for the sake of common use, as well as to promote activities that are an expression of the sort of household management that Aristotle recognizes to be natural. I also think it can be used to support legislation in favor of preserving parts of the environment from human cultivation, on the basis that such territories preserve species whose loss would deprive us of the joy and wonder of appreciating them, and that, in short, tracks of uncultivated natural beauty are an important ingredient in our common good.[44] Our support or motivation for such legislation, after of course much scrutiny to ensure that it does indeed do the sorts of things it is supposed to, should be of the same sort as our support or motivation for living well — which is to say, virtuously and philosophically. We have arrived, then, at a very general but nevertheless practical principle for a serious environmentalism that is fundamentally political in nature.

Maritain's Radicalization of the Aristotelian Model

The foundation for a proper concern for the environment motivated by the promotion of the common good has been laid well by Aristotle. Does anything remain to be done on the theoretical level? Does Maritain really have something to add to this? Without a doubt, he does, though the need for such an addition is easily overlooked when Christian Aristotelians forget that Aristotle is no Christian. The Christian perspective makes a tremendous difference on every issue that touches upon the nature of God, the relation between nature and God, our reliance upon God's providence in every facet of our lives, and the ultimate destiny of human beings. Though Christian Aristotelians regularly take note of these differences, they too often stop short of seeing the difference these differences make with respect to political and

---

44. Of course, there are additional reasons for maintaining nature preserves, including respect for the living organisms themselves and the manner in which, through their very existence, they glorify the Creator. The political reasons I am emphasizing are not meant to trump those reasons.

moral philosophy. Tracing out some of those differences is where, at least for the purposes of this reflection, I find Maritain to be of particular importance. Here I have room only to indicate three areas in which the approach of Maritain proves to be a necessary supplement to what I have already sketched with respect to Aristotle's conception of the common good and the environment.

First, and perhaps one of Maritain's most controversial claims, the genuine common good of any political body can be reached only within a community that embraces Christianity. In its essentials, the vision of the common good as articulated by Maritain is that endorsed by Aristotle; and yet, though Aristotle properly saw that the common life of virtue, including the virtues of the mind woven together via friendship, which is our proper end as social animals, that end is unrealizable for any political community in which Christianity does not have a significant influence on political life. Here, in Maritain's words from *Man and the State,* is the claim:

> I should like to add that such a task [of securing the common good] requires historic achievements on so large a scale and is confronted with such obstacles in human nature that it cannot conceivably succeed — once the good tidings of the Gospel have been announced — without the impact of Christianity on the political life of mankind and the penetration of the Gospel inspiration in the substance of the Body Politic. As a result we are entitled to state that the end of the Body Politic is by nature something substantially good and ethical, implying, at least among peoples in whom Christianity has taken root, an actual — though always imperfect — materialization of the Gospel principles in terrestrial existence and social behavior.[45]

One of the ironies of Maritain's claim is that it would be regarded by many contemporary political theorists as blatantly undemocratic and discriminatory, and yet throughout *Man and the State* Maritain proves himself to be a great champion of democratic regimes and the highest ideals of democracy with respect to establishing the rational order of the moral life. What Maritain finds in Christianity, however, among other things, is a profound respect for the human person, and that respect is foundational to any full pursuit of the common good. Moreover, Maritain's position is not

---

45. Jacques Maritain, *Man and the State* (Washington, DC: Catholic University of America Press, 1998 [1951]), 55. See also 61: "Democracy can only live on Gospel inspiration. It is by virtue of the Gospel inspiration that democracy can overcome its direst trials and temptations."

that such a state needs to be a Christian state or that the citizens need all be Christian. Rather, it is in fact because of the Christian character of genuine democracy that those of different creeds and a variety of ethnicities can all embrace one and the same common good.[46]

Following closely on the first point, then, the radical insistence on the dignity of the human person is the second significant point to be drawn from Maritain. In many respects, this feature of Maritain's political philosophy can hardly be called Maritain's at all, for it is, or should be, the proud heritage of any Christian to have the means at his or her disposal to recognize the dignity of every single human being, a dignity grounded in our being *imagines Dei*. To be sure, Aristotle, like Plato, recognized there to be a divine spark in the human soul, but Aristotle had no notion of God the maker of Adam and Eve. Neither did he hesitate to exclude from full engagement in the life proper of the political community any number of people, including women, children, and slaves. In fact, the only people who fully participate in the polis of Aristotle are free, adult, Athenian men. Not so for Maritain. In fact, so great is the dignity of each human person that Maritain does not hesitate to acknowledge the good of persons to extend even beyond the common good:

> Now the Christian knows that there is a supernatural order, and that the ultimate end — the absolute ultimate end — of the human person is God causing His own personal life and eternal bliss to be participated in by man. The direct ordination of the human person to God transcends every created common good — both the common good of the political society and the intrinsic common good of the universe. Here is the rock of the dignity of the human person as well as of the unshakeable requirements of the Christian message.[47]

The source of the human person's dignity is God himself, and so by its very nature the good of that ordination toward God must trump any other good, since God is the very ground of all good. This does not, Maritain insists, relegate the political common good to a mere means, for it is a proper end in itself, but the primacy of the spiritual good in fact provides a wellspring for all other goods,[48] including of course the good of caring for and cultivating the natural world.

The primacy of the spiritual also brings to the fore the third significant

---

46. Maritain, *Man and the State*, 109, 113, 156.
47. Maritain, *Man and the State*, 149.
48. Maritain, *Man and the State*, 149-50.

contribution that Maritain makes to enhancing an Aristotelian account of the common good, and so wrapping a proper concern for the environment into a comprehensive ethic, namely, Maritain's thoroughgoing efforts to order the various sciences properly. In these efforts he is building on the foundations of Aristotle and Aquinas, but he goes beyond them both. One of the advantages that Maritain has on them is chronological; Maritain's historical position allows him to track the destructive effects caused by elevating mechanistic and technological sciences above the practical and speculative. For instance, in his critiques of mechanistic science in *The Degrees of Knowledge* and elsewhere (by "mechanistic science" he means empirio-metric analysis), it is not its legitimacy per se that he calls into question but, rather, its masquerading as a philosophy of nature.[49] No idea has been more destructive to the world of nature than the mechanistic idea of things as merely extended, flexible, mutable, and so fully comprehensible by means of empirical-mathematical analysis. Even those who come to the defense of the environment do so too often armed with a denatured view of nature, and so a view of nature that does not begin with a proper regard for a realism, in other words, about the beings that surround us. Maritain's insistence that knowledge is not just one sort of thing but that there are degrees of knowledge, and that different sorts of things require different sorts of knowing, is absolutely essential to the work that needs to be done to see the world of nature for what it is, and on that realism to build an environmental ethic that is but one feature of the political philosophy that embraces a robust common good.

On the same theme of establishing the proper order of sciences, one of the remarkable things about Maritain's career, at least given the current state of the question of the relationship between philosophical and theological science, is the way in which Maritain unapologetically embraced suprarational knowledge. I say remarkable because not only was Maritain celebrated in the world of Catholic academia, but, one could argue, he was even more celebrated within the secular academic world, having held positions at Columbia University, the University of Chicago, and Princeton University. In his *Degrees of Knowledge,* in fact, Maritain argues that there is a wisdom above

49. "We can see that the central error of modern philosophy in the domain of the knowledge of nature has been to give the vaule of an ontological explanation to the type of mechanist attraction immanent in physic-mathematical knowledge, and to take the latter for a philosophy of nature. It is not a philosophy of nature. It is an emperiological analysis of nature, mathematical in form and control (an 'empirio-metric analysis')" (Jacques Maritain, *Distinguish to Unite; or, The Degrees of Knowledge,* trans. Gerald B. Phelan [New York: Charles Scribner's Sons, 1959], 184).

even theological science, which is mystical wisdom, which he tells us is an "experimental knowledge of the deep things of God, or a suffering of divine things." Metaphysical wisdom is an expression of our knowledge of God as first cause, theological wisdom yields knowledge of God as revealed to us, and mystical wisdom is the experience of God.[50] In Maritain's following St. John of the Cross in this robust defense of mystical knowledge, one might think that Maritain inspires flight from the world, and so in turn apathy with respect to the world of nature. Just the opposite is the case, however. In recognizing both theology and mystical wisdom to surpass in certainty and depth the wisdom that can be drawn from reason's unaided explorations of the world, Maritain provides the groundwork for a genuinely *philosophical* appreciation for the role of God as the Creator, as Lawgiver, as Providential Caretaker of the souls of men, and as the Wondrous Artist of nature, whose power and love are manifest in the goodness of every being. By means of this wisdom the humble human citizen of earthly cities can see that his or her pursuance of the common good is ultimately motivated by God's having given it to us to pursue, and that each of our roles in that pursuit is infinitely ennobled by being but a part in a divinely orchestrated dance.

Environmental Ethics from within a Christian Aristotelian Framework

What do these contributions of Maritain to an enriched Aristotelian account of the common good have to do with the environment? Recall that the case has been made that, by means of a robust understanding of the common good, one finds common ground between environmental concerns and the concerns of human happiness. They are mutually supportive, so much so that what is good for the environment is what is good for human beings. With the enhanced understanding of the common good that Maritain's unapologetically Christian and democratic political philosophy brings, including an enhanced respect for human persons, an appreciation for humanity's source and destiny in God, an appreciation for the brotherhood of all persons, and the creative energies to apply Thomistic principles to contemporary problems, the imperative to cultivate well — that is to say, so as to preserve and perfect — the environment is strengthened well beyond what Aristotle's view of the common good enables.

50. Maritain, *The Degrees of Knowledge,* 247, 253.

To return, then, finally to Genesis and the curse of Cain. We should not understand Cain the city-builder as Cain the antifarmer. Cain's sin of murdering his brother the shepherd did indeed cause a rupture in the civil order of the first family. That rupture, however, was not made permanent by Cain's building of the city of Enoch. For, indeed, human beings are made to live in community, and though teeming with sin, the city is nevertheless a proper community for man grown beyond the clan structure of his early days. The realm of such a city's concern, however, includes the environment. It is the genuinely common good that stretches a city's concern well beyond its gates to include all its environs. The environs, in turn, are part and parcel of the city, and whatever walls separate one field from another are nevertheless open to the shared good of the city. The route, then, ultimately, to the reparation of the separation between man the farmer and man the city-dweller is the healing of the human family. Even if the work they perform is separate, the good they share is one and the same.

CHAPTER 12

Knowing the Good of Nature:
St. Augustine and George Grant

Paige E. Hochschild

Wendell Berry articulates a human place within the natural order as one of cultivated presence:

> We are [kept in touch with natural cycles] not by technology or politics or any other strictly human device, but by our necessary biological relation to the world. It is only in the processes of the natural world, and in the analogous and related processes of human culture, that the new may grow usefully old, and the old made new. . . . The only life we may hope to live is *here*. It seems likely that if we are to reach the earthly paradise at all, we will reach it only when we have ceased to strive and hurry so as to get there. There is no "there." We can only wait here, where we are, in the world, obedient to its processes, patient in its taking away, faithful to its returns.[1]

Berry's "necessary biological relation to the world" is a nonnegotiable foundation for ethical reflection about the environment. While it has priority over "technology or politics or any other strictly human device," Berry does not understand the human relationship to nature with simplistic romanticism. The "analogous and related processes of human culture" mediate this relationship with great complexity. The character of human life and its "useful growth" assumes a rich dependence of human culture — the structures of human knowing and acting — upon a primal biological sense of being at home

1. Wendell Berry, "Discipline and Hope," in *A Continuous Harmony: Essays Cultural and Agricultural* (San Diego, CA: Harvest Books, 1970), 150-51 (italics added).

in the world. Berry's writings develop the argument that the world cannot be understood as an abstraction: the particularity of a place makes a cultural claim upon human imagination and memory. The possibility of knowing nature and articulating its good is arguably a central matter for the renewal of culture that should be a prime concern for ethicists of the environment.

There are significant obstacles to such a cultural and intellectual renewal. *Caritas in veritate* is a foundational text for Catholic environmental ethics; few interpreters, however, reflect seriously upon the pessimistic tone of the encyclical.[2] The absence of a fruitful social reason and a "public morality" is said to cripple theoretical environmental ethics. Pope Emeritus Benedict XVI argues that we are intellectually complicit with the functionalizing of rationality that results from subjectivizing valuation. This is an understandable but unfortunate retreat from the improbable criterion of certitude set up by modern epistemologies.[3] In *Christianity and the Clash of Cultures,* he identifies the subordination of reason to praxis as a prime cause of weakened "moral energy," awkwardly combined with an overconfidence in technological power.[4] This combination can result in an ethics that is a mere moralism, in which "the key words are justice, peace, and the conservation of creation, and these are words that recall essential moral values, of which we genuinely stand in need. But this moralism remains vague and almost inevitably remains confined to the sphere of party politics, where it is primarily a claim addressed to others, rather than a personal duty in our own daily life." The problem of valuation is presented as the central dilemma. We are incapable of responding substantively, Ratzinger charges, to the essential question: "What does *justice* mean?"

2. June 29, 2009. Accessed at www.vatican.va/holy_father/benedict_xvi/encyclicals/documents/hf_ben-xvi_enc_20090629_caritas-in-veritate_en.html.

3. Benedict describes this situation as the divergence between immanent reason and a reason open to its own finitude (*Caritas in veritate,* §74), and as the ejection of metaphysics from the "human sciences," which damages the possibility of dialogue between science and theology (§31). This limitation "makes it harder to see the integral good of man in its various dimensions. The 'broadening [of] our concept of reason and its application' is indispensable if we are to succeed in adequately weighing all the elements involved in the question of development and in the solution of socio-economic problems." See also *Spe salvi,* §17 (November 30, 2007): "The restoration of the lost paradise can only come from the newly discovered link between science and *praxis.*" An important source for Ratzinger on the critique of modern practical reason is H.-G. Gadamer; cf. "What Is Practice? The Conditions of Social Reason," in *Reason in the Age of Science,* trans. Frederick G. Lawrence (Cambridge, MA: MIT Press, 1981), 69-87.

4. Joseph Ratzinger, *Christianity and the Crisis of Cultures* (San Francisco: Ignatius Press, 2006), 27-28, 30.

This essay argues for the metaphysical reenriching of the concept of nature for environmental ethics. Such a metaphysical enrichment invites a contemplative openness to things as they are, addressing — in an admittedly academic way — Berry's exhortation to "wait here, where we are." It also addresses nature as the precultural basis for the "analogous and related human processes" of culture. Nevertheless, the complexity with which culture mediates dependence precludes the idea that nature is an open book, generating meaning for ethics with easy self-evidence. The limited intelligibility of nature provides potentially normative content for the orderly negotiation between the levels of cultural-intellectual "process," and therefore the possibility of responding to the question of the nature of justice. This essay will more specifically propose a metaphysical defense of nature for *theological* environmental ethics. First, it identifies unhelpful anxieties about intrinsic value and the naturalistic fallacy. Second, it engages parts of Augustine's *De Genesi ad litteram,* in which natural philosophy reveals the robust concept of nature needed for the exegesis of the theological concept of creation. Even in later writings, Augustine deliberately preserves the co-terminous functions of theological and philosophical reflection, insofar as a correct understanding of nature remains useful for understanding rightly the activity of the Trinity in creation. Third and finally, George Grant will enter the conversation as a contemporary writer who locates the question of nature philosophically within a larger problem of *justice.* Grant defines justice as the whole order of nature by which the value of particular natures are measured; justice is also what is owed to things by virtue of their nature, proper function, or relationship to the moral agent. The balance between these two aspects of justice reflects a similar and very classical position in Augustine. The impossibility of reducing the *ratio* of the whole to the useful good of the particular suggests a christological pedagogy for theologians of the environment. Grant, like Wendell Berry, looks cautiously to the modern academy as the place where the recovery of the integrity of nature is most pressingly needed for a renewed conversation between the disciplines about social justice and the natural world.

Valuing the "Processes of the Natural World": Concerns in Contemporary Ethics

In contemporary environmental ethics, nature is generally approached as "other"; whether it is matter for human activity or the sphere of human activity, the natural environment describes something enclosed and entered into by the human subject from without. The *good* of nature is handled as a matter of objective valuation: it is first an epistemological problem, and subsequently an ethical problem of deliberating between various models of man-in-relation-to-nature. J. Baird Callicott writes: "The intrinsic-value-in-nature question has been, and remains, the central and most persistent cluster of problems in theoretical environmental philosophy."[5] Ethicists ask whether things in nature have value intrinsically and of themselves, or whether their value is derived indirectly, for example, through an instrumental relation — of human use, or of use by nonhuman animals.[6] This dichotomy generates a further line of questioning, that of subjective versus objective valuation: to say that nature is valuable intrinsically is itself ambiguous, and this ambiguity seems to strike a decisive blow at objective valuation. Concerns about anthropocentrism need to be taken seriously; however, the fact that thinking animals alone appear to make valuative judgments for the

---

5. J. Baird Callicott, *Beyond the Land Ethic: More Essays in Environmental Philosophy* (Albany: State University of New York Press, 1999), 15.

6. The pragmatic approach of valuing nature "indirectly" puts intrinsic value (also described as ecological value) in tension with anthropocentrism; see Ben A. Minteer, "Intrinsic Value for Pragmatists," *Environmental Ethics* 22 (Spring 2001): 57-75; Bryan G. Norton, "Why I am a Nonanthropocentrist: Callicott and the Failure of Monistic Inherentism," *Environmental Ethics* 17 (1995): 341-58. On intrinsic value, see J. Baird Callicott, "On the Intrinsic Value of Nonhuman Species," in *The Preservation of the Species,* ed. Bryan G. Norton (Princeton: Princeton University Press, 1986), 138-72; see also Holmes Rolston III, *Environmental Ethics: Duties to and Values in Nature* (Philadelphia: Temple University Press, 1988), particularly the sections on "value ownership," "human dominion over animals," "duties to species," and ch. 6, on the "concept of natural value." Note that Rolston describes argumentation in favor of "why nature counts" morally as "nonanthropocentrism" in the introduction to *Environmental Ethics: An Anthology,* ed. Andrew Light and Holmes Rolston III (Oxford: Wiley-Blackwell, 2002), 2. Ethicists have observed that anthropocentrism need not take the extreme form of giving exclusive or arbitrary power to humans over and against other animals; e.g., Tim Hayward, "Anthropocentrism: A Misunderstood Problem," *Environmental Values* 6 (1997): 49-63. The further question about value (not addressed in this chapter) concerns the distinctions between animal and plant life, and living and nonliving things, given that modern ethical theory often assumes an Enlightenment privileging of consciousness and active over passive suffering; these important distinctions can be honored by approaching valuation as a matter of whole ecosystems, e.g., in "land ethics." "Deep ecology" is arguably a more individualist and experiential form of the "land ethic," with the qualification that it can entail a romantic objectification of nature that ethicists argue is too hopelessly and luxuriously "Western"; cf. Ramachandra Guha, "Radical American Environmentalism and Wilderness Preservation: A Third World Critique," *Environmental Ethics* 11, no. 1 (1989): 71-83.

sake of ethical reflection about action makes the responsibility of rigorous valuation more pressing.[7] Intrinsic value, regardless of the presence of some valuator, seems to offer a clear advantage for ethicists.[8] At the very least, it avoids the tendency after John Locke to narrow "value" to a merely economic standard of utility.[9]

Given the concerns generated by the idea of objective valuation, environmental ethicists look at nature through a lens colored by anxiety about the naturalistic fallacy. Environmental writing takes on the moralizing tone identified by Ratzinger, precisely when it assiduously avoids accounts of why particular practices are right or wrong, given the binding obligations that might exist in relation to natural structures. From a theological perspective, some writers propose *theological method* as a way to bypass a value-embedded nature and enter into ethics from the authority of revelation or the safer hermeneutic of a particular religious tradition. As one example, Jame Schaefer writes, "The is-ought problem of appropriating behavior norms from empirical facts is avoided, because the beginning point is always religious faith in God as the creator-initiator and continuous sustainer of the [cosmos]."[10] Schaefer argues — not without merit — that ancient and modern worldviews are so radically divergent that there is no possible scientific correspondence between them. As a result, theology and science (or natural philosophy) have nothing to say to one another. Rather than rendering theological ethics impotent, this *frees* theological texts to provide "conceptual behavior trajectories" that are more palatable to a modern, scientific worldview. These trajectories might take the form of skills training in

---

7. Aristotle, *De anima* 434a; a realistic philosophical anthropology will be crucial for negotiating the place of humans-in-nature. By classical accounts, all living beings engage in valuation, based in the natural appetites and ordered by the instinct to preserve life. The foundation of ethics for Aristotle in these appetites provides common moral ground between human and nonhuman animals.

8. Rolston, in *Environmental Ethics*, ed. Light and Rolston, 143-53; John O'Neill, "The Varieties of Intrinsic Value," *Monist* 75 (1992): 119-37.

9. For example, in the *Second Treatise on Government* (5.28-33; and 5.37: ". . . in the beginning, before the desire of having more than man needed had altered the intrinsic value of things . . . which depends only on their usefulness to the life of man"). Environmental ethicists must nevertheless engage economists on models for quantifying environmental value; R. Turner et al., "Valuing Nature: Lessons Learned and Future Research Directions," CSERGE Working Paper EDM (Center for Social and Economic Research on the Global Environment, University of East Anglia, UK, 2002), 02-05.

10. Jame Schaefer, *Theological Foundations for Environmental Ethics: Reconstructing Patristic and Medieval Concepts* (Washington, DC: Georgetown University Press, 2009), 6.

"sacramental sensibility." There is nothing wrong with this idea; a vague type of sacramentality is present in recent Catholic theology, often as a reaction against an excessive nature-grace polarity.[11] But the lack of clear content, particularly any clear theological content, limits the ability of this language to have a universal pedagogical reach even within faith communities where particular sacraments are central to practice. More important, while the intent to converse with a modern worldview is surely correct, this conversation should not be an occasion for giving over discourse about nature to the mechanistic-reductionist language presupposed by the many forms of the so-called naturalistic fallacy.[12] The dangers of anthropocentrism become more pressing when nature is a dead thing.

The characteristically Anglo-American disjunction of value from science (the locus of "facts") seems to make intrinsic value in nature *metaphysically* incoherent. Callicott writes, "The bankruptcy of the naturalistic approach to a fitting axiology for environmental ethics is . . . quite general."[13] The central issue for both the philosophical and theological tradition is the strong

11. Cf. Bernard Cooke, *Sacraments and Sacramentality,* rev. ed. (Mystic, CT: Twenty-Third Publications, 1994). For a more felicitous popular presentation of sacramentality, see Michael J. Himes, "'Finding God in All Things': A Sacramental Worldview and Its Effects," in *As Leaven in the World,* ed. Thomas M. Landy (Franklin, WI: Sheed & Ward, 2001), 91-102.

12. Especially given that Hume, presumably the originator of the "naturalistic fallacy," was mainly concerned with appeals to divine command or religious authority, which might found strong moral-political claims. This remains the prevailing concern; for example, James Boyle writes that "naturalistic arguments use the multiple meanings of the word 'nature' to solder a dubious claim about . . . [a] Divine Plan to a negative value judgment, and then to make the whole look like a mere statement of fact" (*Times Literary Supplement,* July 24, 1998, in a review of Phil Macnaghten and John Urry's *Contested Natures* [New York: Sage, 1998]). Philosophical skepticism alone reveals the damning "anthropomorphism" of argument that "attributes knowledge and insight to a world of brute facts and organic processes." By this account, Schaefer cannot avoid the "is-ought problem" by turning to theology, any more than the environmental ethicist might avoid it by turning away from anthropocentrism; cf. Hayward's critique in "Anthropocentrism" (1997).

13. J. Baird Callicott, "Intrinsic Value, Quantum Theory, and Environmental Ethics," *Environmental Ethics* 7, no. 3 (1985): 124. The only way that value can be identified as a property of a thing is if it is *primitive* and *nonnatural.* Natural properties can be identified empirically; nonnatural properties by definition cannot be known or inferred except by "some mystical intuitive faculty." Callicott proposes an "axiological subjectivism" that allows instrumental valuing to be a basis for intrinsic valuing: for example, "I value this other person (as a resource to me); in this, I value them in their own right." Assuming the universality of such valuation, some "consensus of feeling" should serve as a "functional equivalent" to objective value.

rejection of the concept of the good, despite its admitted usefulness for ethics.[14] Like Moore before him, Callicott considers good to be a nonnatural property, possibly a transcendental. But Moore makes an unjustifiable move from language (observing that "good" is *said of* different things in many ways) to ontology (concluding that "good" is therefore not *in* natural things in any way).[15]

Missing from this modern worldview is any commonsense account of how goodness is evaluated. The relatively abstract behaviorist accounts of early psychology assume a disjunction between the subject and the world, one that is not easily overcome by phenomenology's attention to objects, or existentialism's hope in the transcendental ego.[16] In classical psychology, "good" denotes an appetitive response to some thing in the world, and it is thus immediately valuative — even if not fully ethical. The language of valuation assumes a relationship of fittingness between the perceiver and the world. At a basic level, if valuation is a properly human activity, it assumes that there are things external to the valuator, and they are intelligible enough to reveal ontological valence and entertain aesthetic distinction. The particularization of principles necessary for ethics clearly depends upon the difference between kinds of things. Environmental ethics is concerned with morally appropriate being-in-the-world and the just use of nature. It must therefore attend to the value revealed by natural distinctions, ideally

14. G. E. Moore, *Principia Ethica,* 2nd ed. (Cambridge: Cambridge University Press, 1993 [1903]), 15-18; Peter Phillips Simpson, *Vices, Virtues, and Consequences* (Washington, DC: Catholic University of America Press, 2001), 24-30. For one genealogy of "good," see Alasdair MacIntyre, *A Short History of Ethics* (New York: Macmillan, 1966), especially 5-83. For an intellectual-historical account, see G. E. M. Anscombe, "Modern Moral Philosophy," *Philosophy* 33 (1958): 1-19; Philippa Foot, *Theories of Ethics* (Oxford: Oxford University Press, 1967); cf. John Rawls, *A Theory of Justice* (Cambridge, MA: Harvard University Press, 1971). Alasdair MacIntyre's account in ch. 5 of *After Virtue,* 2nd ed. (Notre Dame, IN: University of Notre Dame Press, 1984), oversimplifies to an extent, because of the context-determined and "fragmented traditions" theses; cf. Simpson, *Vices, Virtures, and Consequences,* 28. In contrast, MacIntyre makes a crucial move when he acknowledges that any coherent moral philosophy, and thus any account of the good, will have to be grounded in an understanding of human nature; cf. *First Principles, Final Ends, and Contemporary Philosophical Issues* (Milwaukee, WI: Marquette University Press, 1990), 15, 29-31.

15. Moore, *Principia,* 38-40. According to Simpson (*Vices,* 119), Moore's assertion about the requirements of logic becomes an unwarranted assertion about the nature of nature.

16. Whereby valuative responses are seen as psychological states created *ex nihilo:* according to Sartre, the consciousness is unified not through actualization, but through *technique* as "poetic production," in *The Transcendence of the Ego,* trans. F. Williams and R. Kirkpatrick (New York: Farrar, Straus & Giroux, 1991), 76-77.

accompanied by a rich psychology of human nature, as well as realism in approaching moral formation.[17]

To Schaefer and Callicott, one might observe that the rationalist subjectivism of the Anglo-American tradition threatens environmental ethicists with an epistemology far *more* hospitable to domination models of man-in-nature.[18] Theologians cannot bypass the problems of modern worldviews by disregarding the history of philosophy of science, particularly the shift away from nature as a basis for induction.[19] Holmes Rolston III offers an alternative approach, a "biocentrism" whereby natural kinds are valued on the basis of differentiating living from nonliving things.[20] Life, according to Rolston, is a primary characteristic, including within itself degrees of complexity marked by natural behaviors (or operations) determined by genotype — from nutrition and self-preservation, to locomotion and complex linguistic and social structures. Genotype alone is not determinative; phenotype describes the unfolding of the formality of the genotype *in response* to the natural environment.[21] The good of a species is thus determined simultaneously by intrinsic nature and environment-dependent actualization — or, by the interrelation of formal cause and final cause.

Rolston finds a biological basis for intrinsic value in what is effectively the systemic sociality of nature. Ecosystemic dependence is true of nature as a whole, including living beings, whether they are moral subjects or not. The genetic set is normative in that it directs living things to self-preservation. Rolston describes it as the "know-how" of each particular species; classical

17. Richer than that assumed by the human sciences; Pierre Manent argues that modern philosophy evidences a central tension in the indecision between the perceiving subject as unknowable or nonexistent. Human essence "or nature is simultaneously cast out and recalled, and it can then be no more than pure fact deprived of meaning, an opaque and mute frame, a vague cause." The absence of human nature from ethical reflection constitutes at once "a duality and a duplicity"; *The City of Man,* trans. M. A. LePain (Princeton: Princeton University Press, 1998), 154.

18. Mike Hawkins, *Social Darwinism in European and American Thought, 1860-1945: Nature as Model and Nature as Threat* (Cambridge: Cambridge University Press, 1997), 21-38; Francois Jacob, *The Logic of Living Systems,* trans. B. E. Spillman (London: Allen Lane, 1974).

19. William Wallace, *The Modeling of Nature: Philosophy of Science and Philosophy of Nature in Synthesis* (Washington, DC: Catholic University of America Press, 1996), 200.

20. Holmes Rolston III, *A New Environmental Ethics* (New York: Routledge, 2012), 110. Rolston uses the term "biocentrism" to contrast his approach to one more strongly anthropomorphic, which makes human subjectivity the dominant criterion of species value.

21. Rolston, "Environmental Ethics," in *Ecology, Economics, Ethics: The Broken Circle* (New Haven: Yale University Press, 1991), 73-96.

faculty teleology describes this genetic set in terms of species-appropriate capacities and operations, for example, the capacity for locomotion in regard to some perceived good. The intrinsic good of individual living things or persons is common across a species. Individual intrinsic good is therefore dependent upon, but not necessarily reducible to, the species good. The species good (or the common good of the species) is in turn dependent upon and therefore subordinate to the ecosystemic good of the whole. Rolston paints a nested, threefold picture of analogous senses of natural good; he then invokes the language of obligation as appropriate to natural-scientific description of this kind. He argues that our language of valuation is directly dependent upon ecological description, because "one's beliefs about nature, which are based upon but exceed science, have everything to do with our beliefs about duty. The way the world *is* informs the way it ought to be. . . . What is ethically puzzling and exciting is that an *ought* is not so much derived from an *is* as discovered simultaneously with it."[22]

"The Way the World Is": Augustine, Bad Science, and Revelation

Origen is one example of early appropriation of natural philosophy into Christian pedagogy. He proposes "physics" as a discipline mediating ethics and theology, because physics considers the way the world is; or "the nature of each individual thing, according to which nothing in life happens contrary to nature."[23] These three disciplines, rightly ordered together, prepare one to be a good student of the biblical text. Augustine's relationship to natural philosophy is more ambiguous than the one suggested by Origen's threefold schema.[24] He sees natural philosophy as necessarily part of the liberal arts; however, his youthful experience with the bad science used to justify Manichaean cosmology and practices makes him cautious.

---

22. Rolston "Environmental Ethics," 95.

23. *Commentary on the Song of Songs,* trans. R. P. Lawson, Ancient Christian Writers Series, from W. A. Baehrens, ed., *Die Griechischen Christlichen Schriftsteller der ersten drei Jahrhunderte* 33 (1925). Origen's distinction echoes the fourfold distinction in Clement's *Stromata* (1.28) of the "Mosaic philosophy" into historic, legislative, sacrificial, and theological *(enoptic);* the first two are gathered under ethics, and the "sacrificial" is said to pertain to physical sciences.

24. On the place of "natural knowledge" in relationship to the liberal arts, see Siver Dagemark, "Natural Science: Its Limitation and Relation to the Liberal Arts in Augustine," *Augustinianum* 49, no. 2 (2009): 439-502.

A metaphysics of God and the natural world corrects Augustine's basic intellectual errors, serving as a propaedeutic to reading Scripture correctly.[25] Augustine describes himself as subject to a kind of mental entrapment in the physical: "I was still in externals!" (*Conf.* 7.7.11). This cry is misunderstood as one of introspective spiritualism; however, Augustine clearly states that his mind came to no finality in the natural world, no "rest" of understanding, only because he could not imagine divine causality in any other mode than the material (7.1.2). At the high point of Augustine's intellectual frustration, when he was nevertheless daily drinking in the "norm of doctrine" (7.5.7), he is finally made free from the pseudoscience of astrology. He attributes his liberation to the influence of a trustworthy teacher, who shows how improbable it is that physical entities could determine the fortunes of persons in basically identical circumstances; this argument is made based simply on logic and the observation of the lives of these persons. Divine providence is nothing like this, Augustine says, moving things with a coercive natural necessity; God is intimately present in nature as "he who is," abiding in all things without change (7.10.16). The first truth of the natural world is that it is not God. The nonphysicality of the divine and the nondivinity of the physical reveal to Augustine at last that the good of both is vested in their distinct determining characteristics. He confesses to God with new clarity and relief: "You made all things good, and there are absolutely no substances which you did not make. . . . Individually they are good, and all things taken together are very good" (7.12.18).

Scripture is written so that the understanding of faith can be "exercised and nourished."[26] Augustine is aware that Scripture is not meant for the study of the natural world; nevertheless, a certain rigor and natural philosophical attentiveness is present in Augustine's writings, especially his "literal commentary" on Genesis. Much like the simple, metaphysical clarity eagerly sought after in the *Confessions,* this attentiveness serves as a deliberate contrast to the irrationalism of Manichaean cosmology.

Modern biblical scholars argue that scriptural texts do not contain a single, coherent view of nature. Environmental writers tend to focus on a limited range of passages, typically Genesis 1–3 and selections from the wisdom literature.[27] While extrabiblical literature provides more comparative

---

25. This bad science clearly involves confusion for Augustine of moral and metaphysical orders of good and evil. On false views of nature as an obstacle to correct views about God, see *Conf.* 5.3.5; 5.10.20; 7.6.8.

26. *Io. Ev. Tr.* 18.1.

27. These scholars' questions therefore tend to reflect "ethnocentric" concerns foreign

resources, the theological-philosophical cosmology of the Christian intellectual tradition has clear hermeneutic potential to bring the biblical text into conversation with a contemporary scientific worldview.

Like Rolston, Augustine argues for both intrinsic and systemic good in nature in his interpretation of Genesis. He employs philosophical wisdom in the service of biblical interpretation, much as he would the tools of liberal learning.[28] The role of philosophical wisdom is clearly subservient to the *regula fidei,* which orders interpretation to the end of building up faith and charity in the Church.[29] Augustine's early attempts at a commentary on Genesis are more open to the tendency to allegory familiar from the Hexaemera of Ambrose and Basil. The "literal commentary" on Genesis has a more transparent pedagogy, taking the time to consider points of consistency between the book of Scripture and the "book of nature."[30] Augustine takes a non-Plotinian delight in the distinctions and complexity of the created order, insofar as they serve to clarify the meaning and intent of the biblical text.

Augustine is consistent about the basis for natural goodness: it is vested in the way the world is, and therefore in the intelligibility of being.[31] Everything is good insofar as it is a nature *(species).*[32] From his *Confessions,* we have

---

to the Bible; cf. Jeanne Kay, "Concepts of Nature in the Hebrew Bible," in *Franciscan Theology of the Environment,* ed. Dawn M. Nothwehr, OSF (Quincy, IL: Franciscan Press, 2002), 25. Kay's own conclusions are surprisingly close to those of Rolston: nature participates in the story of sin, covenant, and redemption for the Hebrew people. On the whole, nonhuman living things are rightly subject to human use and cultivation; they also stand over and above human history, as a power beyond human instrumentality and a tool for divine punishment and blessing. Kay argues for a general biblical view of nature as one of complex interdependence, with strong intrinsic goodness confirmed by the clear limits of human knowing (as in Job 42) and the prohibition against misunderstanding nature as divine (as in Exod 20:4).

28. Cf. *Doctr. Chr.* 2.16.42; on philosophy, 2.37.55.

29. *Doctr. Chr.* 1.26.39 and 2.9.14; *Conf.* 12.25.35. These two principles are given practical form in books 2 and 3 of *Doctr. Chr.,* with clear priority to the literal meaning of the text; cf. K. Pollman's entry "Hermeneutical Presuppositions," in *Augustine through the Ages: An Encyclopedia,* ed. A. Fitzgerald and John C. Cavadini (Grand Rapids: Eerdmans, 1999), 426-29.

30. *C. Faust.* 32.20; *En. Ps.* 45.7; *s.* 68.6.

31. *De natura boni* 1: "in quantum natura est, bonum est."

32. *Nat. bon.* 18; usually translated as "form" or "appearance." From a philosophical perspective, "nature" has many meanings; the primary sense, however, is of something that is complete as given, and the secondary sense is of the whole aggregate of natures existing or coming into being. The primary specification within the aggregate, common to Rolston and classical natural philosophy, is that of *life,* which marks a certain spontaneous activity that is in accord with the nature of a thing; cf. A. Whitehead, *Process and Reality* (Charlottesville, VA: Social Science Bookstore Reprint, 1941), 16-20; and James A. Weisheipl, *Nature and*

seen that the primary truth of natural things is that they are not God — that is, that they are finite.[33] Even impermanent being describes a completeness of nature that is a veritable perfection. By contrast, God is maximal being *(summum bonum),* not as one thing compared to many things, but by being perfect in the attributes of being, such as magnitude of power (infinite). The perfection of God is evident above all in his mode of being incomparably greater than that of creaturely beings.

Nature is also good in the completeness and functional unity of the whole. This is variously called the law of nature, its *ordo* or *gradus.*[34] The most important element of this functional unity, beyond the good of being itself, is the difference within it. The hierarchies of the natural order reveal interdependence in the subordination of both species and individuals to the good of the whole. That some things are *greater* than others is simply obvious to Augustine, as a matter of observation: "I considered the totality. Superior things are self-evidently better than inferior. Yet with a sounder judgment I held that all things taken together are better than superior things by themselves."[35] The intrinsic goodness convertible with the being of things is described as a *bona generalia;* the intrinsic and functional goodness of lowly things is particularly misunderstood by the Manichees.[36] Nothing in creation evades the "order imposed upon it" by God, and the principle of hierarchy (or difference) is therefore essential to the greater goodness of the whole.[37] This is an ontological claim, not only an aesthetic one; the "scale

---

Motion in the Middle Ages (Washington, DC: Catholic University of America Press, 1985), 1-24. Sarah Byers rightly sees Augustine as closer to Aristotle than Plotinus in his approach to natural things; as a minor note, Byers misreads the internal "efficient cause" of the being of a person (at *Civ. Dei* 12.26) as the animating principle, rather than God as Creator; cf. "Augustine and the Philosophers," in *A Companion to Augustine,* ed. Mark Vessey (Malden, MA: Blackwell Publishing, 2012), 178.

33. *Conf.* 7.15.20, trans. Chadwick (Oxford: Oxford University Press, 1991).

34. *Conf.* 2.4.9; *En. Ps.* 118.25.4; also the numbering of creation *(numerus);* cf. *Gen. litt.* 4.3.7. Thomas calls this the good of *diversitas; Summa contra gentiles* II, ch. 45.2: "Oportuit . . . esse multiplicitatem et varietatem in rebus creatis, ad hoc quod inveniretur in eis Dei similitudo perfecta secundum modum suum."

35. *Conf.* 7.13.19. More complex beings are differentiated by more complex operations ordered to the preservation and flourishing of life at both the individual and species levels. As in Rolston's biocentrism, the key criterion for Augustine is that of life, which he defines as a kind of vital and enforming principle; cf. *V. rel.* 11.22; Byers, "Augustine," 177.

36. *Civ. Dei* 8.6.

37. Augustine goes so far as to insist that simple things should not be valued according to their magnitude, for "they have none, except by the wisdom of their Creator. . . . Beauty is not constituted by size, but by the balance and proportion of the parts. God is a great

of value" *(sunt aliis alia bona meliora)* reveals an inequality that makes the very existence of things to be possible *(ad hoc inaequalia, ut essent omnia).*[38]

For Augustine, the intrinsic and systemic good of natural things is understood through complementary metaphysical and biblical analyses. The strong message of the goodness of creation in Genesis 1 requires classical metaphysical language in order to be more than literary flourish or part of a narrative unity. The argumentative unity of salvation history requires a rich ontology of the good of nature. While this sense of goodness is a mere starting place for moral valuation, it is a nonnegotiable one for Augustine. To love a thing rightly is to love it justly, that is, as its nature demands. Augustine differentiates the orders of utility, pleasure, and judgment; these all have their proper function in the moral life, for example, in the way utility directs persons to value a lesser thing over a greater one at the appropriate time.[39] Nevertheless, utility and pleasure direct the will to goods in a way that must be subordinated to the order of judgment as the prudential correspondence of a rational norm to the natural place of things in the whole. Prudence requires ethical disinterestedness, as well as epistemic humility, before the staggering scope of systemic good presented in Genesis. Moreover, the centrality of human persons in Genesis 1 is clearly secondary to the order in which things are created: the *importance* of the human species cannot be separated from its *dependence* upon the rest of creation.

Two Examples: A Natural Philosophical Posture Clarifies the Biblical Text

In the second book of *Gen. litt.,* Augustine distances himself from interpreters who argue about whether the moon was created in its full or waxing stage, on the fourteenth day or the first day of its natural cycle.[40] The

---

worker in great things; but that is not to say that he is less so in little things" (*Civ. Dei* 11.22, trans. R. W. Dyson [Cambridge: Cambridge University Press, 1998]; see also 11.16 and *Gen. litt.* 3.14.22).

38. *Civ. Dei* 11.22.

39. *Civ. Dei* 11.16: "Who would not rather have bread in his house than mice, or gold than fleas?"

40. *Gen. litt.* 2.15.30. Augustine's letter from 400 to Januarius (*Ep.* 55) criticized the musings of the Manichees on this subject; he considers two possibilities: first, that the moon has its own proper kind and source of luminosity (a position more common in Greek astronomy), and second, that the moon receives its light from the sun.

only point of significance, he says, is that it was created; if so, it was created *perfectam*. If God is the author and maker of all *naturae*, these natures are made as containing in themselves potentially *(continebat occultum)* all that is necessary to account for species-appropriate behavior. Changes in the lunar cycle can be explained by physical mass *(mole corporis)* or simply as a matter of appearance due to accidents of circumstance and position. Augustine offers a simple and scientifically cautious hypothesis: the natural difference between things, he says, is not always explained by differentiation of species. Essential and accidental characteristics cannot be confused one with another.

Augustine illustrates this point with an image of a living thing: a tree in the winter sheds its leaves and no longer produces seed, and yet this condition is not an imperfection. God creates living things with the potency to come to full development, and their dependence upon the whole of nature for the necessary conditions for growth argues strongly for the developmental integrity of nature. Augustine is not saying that a celestial body is alive in the same way as a tree. The image of the tree in seasonal rather than nutritional-developmental stages serves to show that accidental factors of circumstance — season, as compared with the moon phase — do not touch upon the perfection of a thing as a complete nature.

The varying luminosity of the moon and other celestial bodies receives a similar commonsense treatment. Paul's differentiation of the glory *(claritas)* of the sun from that of the moon at 1 Corinthians 15:41 suggests two hypotheses: the difference is a matter of circumstance such as our distance from the source of luminosity, or Paul is simply illustrating the difference *and* similarity that exist between natural and resurrected bodies.[41] Augustine observes that different stars seem to be similar in kind with respect to luminosity. If differences of appearance cannot be explained by relative distance from the earth, then an alternative explanation should be sought after. There is no good reason to attribute differences of appearance or behavior to other "more mysterious causes."[42] It would be misleading to read the biblical text as making a scientific claim when commonsense observation suggests otherwise. In this instance, the intelligibility of nature clarifies the meaning and literary form of a doctrinally significant passage.

---

41. *Gen. litt.* 2.16.33.

42. Augustine gives more attention to astrology and questions of providence, demonology, and fate in *Gen. litt.* 2; cf. Jean Pépin, "Influences paiennes sur l'angélologie et la démonologie de Saint Augustin," in *Entretiens sur l'homme et le diable* (Paris: Mouton, 1965), 51-56.

A second text illustrates Augustine's willingness to put natural philosophical induction at the service of exegesis. The balance of predation in
nature often appears to be savage, and many patristic commentators associate the harshness of interdependence with the regime of sin. Augustine,
by contrast, argues that if creation is good, the intelligibility of the laws of
nature must be referred to the divine law.[43] What *appears* to be savage and
even unjust may not be, because the efficiency of the order of predation
is evidence of the good of the systemic whole. All things act according to
their nature, "from elephants to worms"; where the good of order is not
discerned, the failure must be attributed to limited scientific observation.

An explanatory appeal to moral evil is a particularly pernicious eva-
sion. Natural bodily suffering, Augustine says, is an unavoidable result of
the passivity of being embodied and alive.[44] This is no less true after the
introduction of moral evil into creation, which is not *substantially* changed
by sin. Basil interprets the troublesome *spinas et tribulos* of Genesis 3:18 as
placed deliberately in the cultivated fields of humans for the correction of
sin. Augustine takes a different approach, arguing that "thorns and thistles"
must play some role in the systemic functioning of nature, even if this role
is not obvious.[45] Ambrose interprets them as existing primarily for spiritual
pedagogy; he contrasts them to the beauty of the rose, and this comparison
generates a rich allegorical interpretation.[46] Augustine admits that obstacles
to cultivation might teach perseverance, given the greater labor that would
be required for successful agriculture. Moral pedagogy could play out in
different ways, however, depending on the relationship between farmer and
field, and above all the particulars of situation and spiritual disposition. The
thorns and thistles do not become evil because they are experienced as an
obstacle; any potential moral dimension must be secondary to a clear natural
end such as nutrition.[47]

43. On the law of nature as the manifestation of divine law, on the one hand, and, on
the other, correspondence to the immutable moral law ("written in the heart") and the
changeable human law, see *Civ. Dei* 19.12 and 11.27 (on its intelligibility); *C. Faust.* 22.27;
Sol. 81.2; *An quant.* 36.80.

44. *Gen. litt.* 9.17.32; *Doctr. Chr.* 1.26.27.

45. Karla Pollman, "Human Sin and Natural Environment: Augustine's Two Positions
on Genesis 3:18," *Augustinian Studies* 41, no. 1 (2010): 69-85.

46. *Hexaemeron* 3.11.47-48.

47. *Gen. litt.* 3.19.28. Cf. *Mor.* 2.14-17; Pollman, "Human Sin," 83-84. Pollman observes
the strong cultural-religious contrast between Augustine and many of his opponents: "In ancient theories of cultural development, the pessimistic theory claims nature to have changed
as a punishment for human insubordination, i.e., the change in nature was both objective

If thorns and thistles are not present in nature prior to the expulsion of Adam and Eve from paradise, then some explanation must be found: Augustine suggests spontaneous generation, possibly from vegetable or animal putrefaction, given that both are necessary for plant life.[48] Species can emerge at the time when material and environmental conditions for survival are exactly right. For even small animal life forms, however, Augustine argues that some kind *(quasi)* of inseminated natural power must be fully present.[49] For both possible scenarios, Augustine posits the presence of "numbering reasons" *(numerosae rationes)* as the *incorporeal texture* of things inscribed in them *corporeally.*[50] Augustine here articulates the developmental priority of form to matter, precisely to account for the autonomy and integrity of natural kinds.[51]

With these two examples from *Gen. litt.,* Augustine shows that he has overcome any remaining tension between natural philosophical inquiry and revelation.[52] The rightful autonomy of nature is contextualized early in the literal commentary within a Trinitarian theology of creation. The *ratio* of nature manifest in time and human history is identified with the creative *ratio*

---

and external. This line of thinking easily opens the door for mechanical explanations for any kind of misfortune as being specifically divine punishment. . . . The optimistic theory sees nature as being permanently hostile to humans and as having been so from the very beginning. Thanks to its ability to advance through the acquisition of more and more skills, however, human beings are increasingly able to tame hostile environments. . . . In contrast, Augustine develops a third way, in which nature, as created by God, is always good, but in which human nature has changed for the worse . . . when viewed subjectively, the natural environment seems to have turned into something bad and harmful, but, *de facto,* it has only become a permanent reminder of our own changed nature."

48. Cf. *Gen. litt.* 3.14.22, where plant life is described as the *subplementum habitationis* for animal life.

49. *Gen. litt.* 3.14.23: "praeseminata et quodammodo liciata."

50. *Gen. litt.* 4.33.52: "corporeis . . . intextae." Augustine's illustration does not do justice to the possible interpretations of the Latin. He compares this to the way in which an egg yolk contains all the material needed to form a chick. Without some organizing principle that cannot simply be the sum of the material elements, there is no reason why this matter should develop into a formed chick.

51. Marcia Colish, *The Stoic Tradition from Antiquity to the Middle Ages,* vol. 2 (Leiden: Brill, 1985), 203-6; see also the relevant *Notes complémentaires* in the *Bibliothèque Augustiniennes* edition (vol. 7.48) of *Gen. litt.,* ed. Agaesse and Solignac, especially 667-68.

52. Kim Paffenroth argues compellingly that *Conf.* 9 marks the official resolution of this tension, through the objective but therapeutic and liturgical use of Scripture; cf. "Book Nine: The Emotional Heart of the Confessions," in *A Reader's Companion to Augustine's Confessions,* ed. Kim Paffenroth and Robert P. Kennedy (Louisville, KY: Westminster John Knox Press, 2003), 137-54.

of divine wisdom — this is creation considered "at once" *(simul)*, the production of all being coterminous with time itself.[53] The *ratio* of nature and the *ratio* of the creative activity of God are in turn related analogously with the divine wisdom itself, *in principio* — a perspective completely inaccessible to human understanding. The relationship between these three senses of *ratio* — guaranteed by the biblical account of creation and the Trinitarian account of providence[54] — allows for the coexistence of faithful reverence of the mystery of divine causality, along with wonder at the ever-unfolding intelligibility of the natural environment. The internal pedagogy of revelation encourages this approach; in *Civ. Dei* 10, Augustine says that the law given through the angels is the decisive correction of the human tendency to idolatry. The law testifies to the order of things *evident to the understanding;* the miracles accomplished with the ark of the covenant in hand only confirm this order.[55] Finally, the sacrifices of the priesthood established under the law reveal and even partially restore the orderliness of creation. If the natural order reveals the goodness and power of God, the tendency to forgetting that accompanies cultural processes is decisively corrected through the liturgical knowledge of creation as an offering, returned to God at the hands of his stewards.[56]

George Grant: A Call for the Restoration of a Rich Concept of Nature

Pope Emeritus Benedict XVI charges environmentalism with thin moralism, as cited above, desiccated by an abstract sense of justice and "party politics."

---

53. *Gen. litt.* 5.3.6; on this approach to time, see *Ver. rel.* 7.13. The identity of historical time with creation in the word is negotiated in *Conf.* 11; its complex reunification through the Church, modeled on the Sabbath-peace of the *caelum caelorum,* is treated in *Conf.* 12-13.

54. Cf. *Ver. rel.* 13, where each person of the Trinity is associated with a particular blessing: form comes from the Word; beauty, from the Holy Spirit. At *Gen. litt.* 2.23.44, Augustine attributes a tree's growth, fertility, and abundance of fruit to the perfecting work of the Holy Spirit.

55. *Civ. Dei* 10.15; 10.19.

56. Thomas Aquinas, *STh* II-II, q. 81, art. 6, argues that religion is the chief moral virtue, since religion directs appropriate reverence to God as God. In art. 5, Thomas says that religion requires rendering to all things in creation what is due to them as well, since it is a virtue that falls under justice; this is accomplished by referring all things to God as end, and in q. 85, sacrifice is said to be the chief way God is honored perfectly through the sensible order. This offers an image of the human person in creation as not only steward and cultivator, but as priest.

While a restored, metaphysically rich conception of nature is not likely to constitute a quick fix, the literary and intellectual struggles of Augustine over the natural philosophical coherence between revelation and nature exemplify a multidisciplinary attitude worthy of imitation, even by theological ethicists. A primary locus for the renewal of cultural processes and human remembering should therefore be the university. George Grant, like Wendell Berry after him, writes as a contemporary critic within and (later) without the university, calling for intellectual renewal in the service of cultural and moral-political well-being. Where Berry advocates a remembered dependence upon nature through literary thanksgiving and reflective habits of living, Grant critically articulates a broader problem of justice as the insuperable metaphysical and political obstacle to such a remembered dependence.

The university is not an obvious place to begin. Grant, as a student of Heidegger, frames his critique in terms of technique (technological thinking) as the "ontology" of our age and of our basic ethical posture.[57] Contemporary academic language reveals a shift toward a privileging of the pragmatic, in the "antidogmatic tone of the word *practice*, [in the] suspicion against the merely theoretic, rote knowledge of something of which one has no experience whatsoever." Theory has become "a notion instrumental to the investigation of truth. . . . It suggests nothing of what *theoria* was to the eye disciplined enough to discern the visibly structured order of the heavens and the order of the world and of human society." The isolating logic of the dominantly experimental model of science has become the very essence of science. The net effect is a loss of "flexibility" in our relationship to the natural world, through the anthropomorphic transformation of nature itself. The evidence of this lost flexibility is seen in the way we become silent before nature, even as we submit ourselves to technology we cannot possibly understand or master; we trustingly inhabit a regime of experts, privileging their technical skill over anything like practical wisdom. Disciplinary over-specialization thus limits the possibility of unity between the different forms of human knowing with human living.[58]

57. The logic of will-as-freedom, Grant argues, is the hallmark of contemporary democracy, and it is a difficult logic to overcome; cf. his *Technology and Justice* (Notre Dame, IN: University of Notre Dame Press, 1986), 17.

58. Hans-Georg Gadamer, "What Is Practice? The Conditions of Social Reason," in *Reason in the Age of Science* (Cambridge, MA: MIT Press, 1983), 69, 72. This is a line of critique developed by Wendell Berry, particularly in his early writings on agricultural policy in the United States (e.g., *The Unsettling of America* [New York: Random House, 1982]). On the subject of human well-being, Berry writes in "The Body and the Earth" (103): "It is absurd

Grant resigned from his post teaching philosophy at York University after witnessing the transition from undergraduate collegiate-style education to a committed research model.[59] The justification offered was practical application and technical preparation. While acknowledging that these are not unworthy ends, Grant warned that their justification was framed in the language of an experimental mode of relation of persons to nature. It was a model of man-in-nature, he observed, committed to human progress for the sake of mastery and transcendence of self through personal-technical improvement. A receptive-contemplative model of man-in-nature, embodied in an older philosophy of education as human formation, was rejected as an antiquarian, impractical luxury.[60] Grant lamented that philosophy was being reduced to analytic competence; philosophy, he said, is not "in essence a technique. Its purpose is to relate and see in unity all techniques, so that the physicist, for instance, can relate his activity to the fact of moral freedom, the economist see the productive capacity of his nation in relation to the love of God."[61] For Grant, the rejection of a historical, literary, or *wisdom* dimension in education signaled an overall loss of purpose for both the humanities and the sciences.

---

to approach health piecemeal with a departmentalized band of specialists. A medical doctor uninterested in nutrition, in agriculture, in the wholesomeness of mind and spirit. . . . Our fragmentation of this subject cannot be our cure, because it is our disease. The body cannot be whole alone. Persons cannot be whole alone." On the university and the humanities: "The scientific ideals of objectivity and specialization have now crept into the humanities and made themselves at home. This has happened, I think, because the humanities have come to be infected with a suspicion of their uselessness or worthlessness in the face of the provability or workability or profitability of the applied sciences. . . . A poem is a relic as soon as it is composed; it can be taught, but it cannot teach. . . . In the humanities as in the sciences the world is increasingly disallowed as a context." Without "the world" as a context, Berry observes, the university is given over to accomplishments of mere intellectual bureaucracy, "promotion, technological innovation, publication and grant-getting." The sciences and humanities will "have to come together again in the presence of the practical problems of individual places . . . [where people] see, know, think, feel, and act coherently and well without the modern instinct of deference to the 'outside expert'" ("An Argument for Diversity," in *What Are People For?* [New York: Farrar, Straus & Giroux, 1990], 116-17).

59. See the following essays in *The George Grant Reader,* ed. William Christian and Sheila Grant (Toronto: University of Toronto Press, 1998): "The Paradox of Democratic Education" (1955); "Letter of Resignation" (1960); "The University Curriculum (The Multiversity)" (1975); and "The Battle between Teaching and Research" (1980).

60. George Grant, *English-Speaking Justice* (Notre Dame, IN: University of Notre Dame Press, 1974), 120.

61. Grant, "Philosophy," in *The George Grant Reader,* 159.

Grant's argument that the modern research university is uniquely unfit for addressing questions of substantive justice is compelling. In Grant's opinion, it is properly the task of philosophy to restore disciplinary conversations adequate to the rich layers of "cultural process" that mediate human dependence upon nature. Most pressing is the eliding of nature, both intellectually and institutionally:

> What doctrine of nature will be adequate to express [the idea] that nature is a sphere for our timeless enjoyment and yet also a sphere that we must organize, that it has meaning apart from our ends and yet is also a part of redemptive history? . . . A philosophic reconstruction of the concept of nature is necessary, but of consummate difficulty, because it must take into itself what modern scientists have discovered. . . . [This reconstruction must] overcome the distinction between nature as the simply dominated and nature as the simply contemplated.[62]

Contemplated nature over and against dominated nature describes an object for study and for wisdom.[63] Wisdom is intrinsically valuable knowing, with no eye to practical outcomes; its genuine practical value is real but secondary. Education for wisdom presupposes the immeasurable value of things as they are, and this presupposition should result in a basic posture of epistemic humility. Contemporary educational models would describe the habits of the psychology of learning — the virtues of inquiry, personal disinterestedness, critical discernment, judgment, even delight and wonder — as "values" and therefore not properly goals of learning. Nature, in contrast, is a "fact," a thing potentially known and actually studied by more than one discipline. It is the pedagogical victory of the so-called naturalistic fallacy that students are taught very early that facts and values are not only distinct, but have nothing to do one with another. The isolation of valuation from the experience of the world almost guarantees that environmental ethics will appear to many as political moralism, as Ratzinger argued. This isolation makes it difficult to imagine an environment as a particular place in which one is dependently at home — inclined to know it well, use it well, and make the time to love it well.[64]

A strong epistemological and cultural critique of modernity is an im-

62. George Grant, *Philosophy in the Mass Age* (Toronto: University of Toronto Press, 1995), 102-3.
63. Grant, "Philosophy," 172.
64. Cf. Wendell Berry, "Nature as Measure," in *What are People For?* 207.

portant element of a rich and effective environmental ethics. For the philosopher and the theologian, a restored metaphysical foundation for speaking about nature is even more necessary. The temptation to bypass metaphysics, even for sympathetic rhetorical reasons, appears as nothing less than a fideism that refuses the responsibility of ethicists to speak in a language that can be universally understood. Grant rejects this option; overly simplified faith, he says, is too close in form to nihilism. Moreover, faith cannot be a basis for law, since modern democratic citizens need a morality "that can be thought."[65] The cross of the crucified Christ reveals the good of creation with shocking clarity. The Matthean beatitude "happy are those who are hungry and thirsty for justice" reaches beyond Jesus' contemporary Jewish audience to describe the poverty and radical dependence upon God that is the very definition of the *creature.* To live as though constantly aware of the perfection of God, says Grant, would require the kind of mindfulness that comes only with the normal deprivations of creaturely dependence — what Wendell Berry calls "disciplines."[66] The words of Jesus here are not for practical application, to some or to many; they are simply a "true proposition," and whether it is justice for which one hungers or something else, the truth of the words grasps at the listener and, until hunger is awakened, does not let go.

Grant laments the incoherence of the modern rejection of the good of nature, or of what is. He speaks of the good as a matter of "justice" in order to communicate the immediately ethical character of human knowing: to know the nature of a thing is to owe what is due to that thing by virtue of what it is. Grant is primarily concerned to defend the intelligibility of things in particular, but he recognizes that a metaphysical cosmology is necessary for doing so. Like Augustine and Rolston, Grant distinguishes the good of order from the intrinsic good of each kind of thing. The order of good, or of justice, is the measure or rule of nature, by which we judge particular goods in the world.[67] Modern justice, particularly in the form of contractual liberalism, is immediately flawed because of its origin in "human freedom . . . [both] individual and social."[68] If freedom is conceived of as wholly indeterminate,

65. Grant, *Philosophy in the Mass Age,* 96.

66. Grant, "Justice and Technology," in *The George Grant Reader,* 435-36.

67. Given that a total knowledge of the rule of nature is impossible, Grant is not proposing a rationalist natural law theory. Since partial knowledge is possible, and even demanded by the human thirst for scientific truth, a more modest Thomistic-Augustinian form of natural law is possible.

68. Grant, *English-Speaking Justice,* 77. In *Philosophy in the Mass Age,* 37, Grant calls this the "humanist view," in which we "make the world" and reduce the complexity of human

justice at best appears as self-determination; socially, it appears as negotiated self-interest and, if necessary, force. Grant insists, however, that practical induction from the experience of actually making judgments suggests that self-interest can be *calculated* only by recourse to the order of justice that stands over and against freedom. While the order of justice may seem to limit the scope of freedom, in truth it makes it individually and socially coherent.

Justice is thus primarily the valuative framework of the whole, or "the overriding order which we do not measure and define, but in terms of which we are measured and defined."[69] The intrinsic good of species or individuals, vested in their nature, is willfully lost from sight before the logic of freedom as self-assertion, enframed and enabled by technique. Grant argues brilliantly in *English-Speaking Justice* against modern genealogies of justice, particularly that of Rawls; he charges his readers with accepting the abstractions of modern ethics and politics — self-determination and fictional "states of nature" — while hoping to retain some intellectual remnant of human nature and justice from the philosophical and theological tradition. The result of this intellectual incoherence is an unhappy state of profound cultural tension. Grant criticizes Rawls for using Kant to overcome the limitations of merely utilitarian justice, while neglecting the primary place of the "good will" in Kant's ethics, as a first principle of practical reason. "Good will" functions as a normative principle for Kant, but while he attempts to establish it in the firm soil of human *nature* — by grounding it in human reason — Rawls refuses any such attempt. "Facts of reason" constitute an unjustifiable rationalist optimism. Rawls nevertheless borrows Kant's optimism, while arguing that justice "cannot be justified as coming forth from the universal morality given us in reason itself."[70] Rawls needs rationality but reduces it to mere "analytic instrumentality."

It is not surprising that philosophical language invoked by Rawls, such as "person" or "rights," is oddly lacking in content. When a Harvard professor, Grant wryly observes, talks about freedom as the pursuit of maximal self-interest, freedom ends up looking like a typical elite professor's imagining of the ideal "union of individualism and egalitarianism" — which of course limits "egalitarianism" for others to little more than basic consumption and welfare.[71] By Grant's account, the naturalistic fallacy is an epistemological

willing to voluntariness; in this picture, value is simple to determine (yes or no), but virtually impossible to negotiate at the political level.

69. Grant, *English-Speaking Justice*, 20, 86-87.
70. Grant, *English-Speaking Justice*, 29.
71. Grant, *English-Speaking Justice*, 40.

deceit that serves a new need to clear the ground for an ethics suitable for a truly modern worldview. The rejection of human nature and any account of the psychology of evaluation, based on an assumed fitness between man and world, relegates reflection upon the good to the social sciences, with self-justifying criteria of health and normalcy. For this reason, Grant and Berry both reject the university as a place of culturally and socially embedded moral reflection. And yet the responsibility of renewal falls most of all upon the university, particularly Catholic universities, who must answer to a long tradition calling for cross-disciplinary conversation, particularly between theology and philosophy, and philosophy and natural science.[72]

George Grant paints a gloomy picture. It cannot be a matter of mere historical interest that Augustine's mature approach to Scripture exemplifies the fruitfulness of a critical but integrated approach to literary-theological analysis, done within the hermeneutic of a premodern metaphysical cosmology in conjunction with practical and scientific mindfulness about the natural world.[73] This is one mode of historical cultural recovery; it is also an example for the theological ethicist, in showing that *nature* need not be bypassed for the sake of *the environment*. The Enlightenment justification for the devaluing of nature, in order to establish a new foundation for ethics and epistemology, gives rise to a new conception of justice. This new conception, according to Grant, is inextricably bound up with a view of man-in-nature marked by technological domination and a thin political moralism. Nature appears to persons as "the other," into which they enter as though from "some safe standpoint outside it"; they owe it nothing. Berry proposes habits

72. Pius XI, *Divini illius magistri* (1929), §§21, 28, 55-56; Pius XII, *Humani generis* (1950), §43; *Gravissimum educationis* (1965), §10; Congregation for Catholic Education, *The Religious Dimension of Education in a Catholic School* (1988), §§53-54, 60, 72; Sacred Congregation for Catholic Education, *The Catholic School* (1997), §46; John Paul II, *Ex corde Ecclesiae* (1990), §§7, 10, 18, 46; cf. §46: "An area that particularly interests a Catholic University is the *dialogue between Christian thought and the modern sciences*. This task requires persons particularly well versed in the individual disciplines and who are at the same time adequately prepared theologically, and who are capable of confronting epistemological questions at the level of the relationship between faith and reason. Such dialogue concerns the natural sciences as much as the human sciences which posit new and complex philosophical and ethical problems."

73. For the best historical study of this approach to Scripture in the Greek tradition, see Paul M. Blowers, "Entering 'This Sublime and Blessed Amphitheater': Contemplation of Nature and Interpretation of the Bible in the Patristic Period," in *Nature and Scripture in the Abrahamic Religions: Up to 1700*, vol. 1, ed. Jitse M. van der Meer and Scott Mandelbrote (Leiden: Brill, 2008), 147-76.

of deprivation to correct this falsehood, to remind persons of the hunger and thirst of ordinary creatureliness; Grant, despairing of the university, points to the suffering of the cross as revelatory of the good.[74] Augustine proposes to theologians the consoling wisdom of revelation in conversation with other disciplines attentive to the good of creation. From this kind of conversation, a doctrine of nature might emerge, adequate to the needs of contemporary cultural and environmental renewal.

74. Berry, "Nature as Measure," 207. Grant, "Justice and Technology," 240: "Justice is demanding . . . it is an unchanging measure of all our times and places, and our love of it defines us. In affirming that justice is what we are fitted for, one is asserting that a knowledge of justice is intimated to us in the ordinary occurrences of space and time, and that through those occurrences one is reaching towards some knowledge of good which is not subject to change, and which rules us in a way that is more pressing than the rule of any particular goods. In the *Phaedrus,* Plato writes of the beauty of the world, and Socrates states that beauty is what leads to justice. Beauty is always seducing while justice often appears unattractive. If in this world we could see justice as it is in itself, it would engulf us in loveliness."

CHAPTER 13

Rethinking Gluttony and Its Remedies

Chris Killheffer

Before we *re*think gluttony, we first need to ask why we'd want to think about gluttony at all. It used to be something you couldn't help thinking about, back when the Church took gluttony very seriously as one of the seven deadly sins, when you heard about it from the pulpit and in popular literature, when it was just part of the background of everyday life. But that was a long time ago — we pretty much never hear about gluttony anymore, not in our everyday speech and not in the discourse of the Church. The word appears exactly once in the Catechism, and there it's not even defined as a term but shows up only as a historical footnote.[1] That seems to be about all that's left of gluttony — and that's good news, isn't it? To not have to worry anymore about a deadly sin hanging over us whenever we eat? It's bad enough living with all the food guilt we already have — feeling we have to count calories all the time, that we have to always balance how much we eat with how much we're exercising, that we somehow have to meet our culture's impossible standards of thinness. Who would want to add religious anxiety onto all of that? Who wants to think that, not only am I counting my calories, but God is counting them too? Who wants to feel that, after eating some cake, you've got to go to the gym *and* to confession?

Not me — I certainly don't have any desire to make our food guilt any worse. For this very reason I think it would be worth our while to try to re-think gluttony. Because I believe that gluttony still haunts us; we may have dropped the word out of our speech, but it still lingers with us as a moral

---

1. *Catechism of the Catholic Church* (Mahwah, NJ: Paulist Press, 1994), §1863.

concern, or at least as a source of moral anxiety. Gluttony has survived into our time by morphing into a modern form, sneaking by way of the Protestant ethic and capitalism into our worries about calories and waistlines.[2] It lurks behind words like "overweight" and "obesity," words we hear very often and that are meant to sound more neutral than the word "gluttony" but that actually carry a strong association of moral failure, of poor discipline, of a kind of character flaw we believe we can somehow see in each other's body shape. To the modern mind, gluttony is about getting fat: to overeat is to become heavy, and to be heavy is to be unacceptable to a society obsessed with lean, youthful bodies. That's how gluttony is still with us today, this old idea that is somehow behind our diet fads and eating disorders, behind all the bullying and shaming of large-bodied people that happens in our culture.

If that is what gluttony had always been about, then we could be glad that the Church abandoned it as a moral concept. We could simply say "Good riddance!" and hope that the idea eventually falls out of our social thinking as it has fallen out of our theology. But when we look back at the history of the idea of gluttony, we find that in the early and medieval church it was something very different from what we experience today, so different that we may wonder whether it might be a good thing to try to revive it, to bring it back into our moral thinking.

Cassian: Gluttony in the Monastic Setting

Susan Hill, a scholar of religion at the University of Northern Iowa, has done fascinating research into the different meanings of gluttony over time, and her work is important for us because our modern sense of gluttony is so entrenched that we can find it hard to step outside and imagine how it might have been experienced in the past.[3] Consider this example she points to: among patristic and medieval theologians it was fairly common to refer to

2. On the modern evolution of gluttony, see Marie Griffith, *Born Again Bodies: Flesh and Spirit in American Christianity* (Berkeley: University of California Press, 2004); Francine Prose, *Gluttony* (New York: Oxford University Press, 2003); and William James Hoverd, "Deadly Sin: Gluttony, Obesity, and Health Policy," in *Medicine, Religion, and the Body,* ed. Elizabeth Burns Coleman and Kevin White (Leiden: Brill, 2010), 205-30.

3. Susan E. Hill, "'The Ooze of Gluttony': Attitudes toward Food, Eating, and Excess in the Middle Ages," in *The Seven Deadly Sins: From Communities to Individuals,* ed. R. Newhauser (Leiden: Brill, 2007), 57-70, and *Eating to Excess: The Meaning of Gluttony and the Fat Body in the Ancient World* (Santa Barbara, CA: Praeger, 2011).

gluttony as the first sin, the one committed by Adam and Eve when they ate the forbidden fruit.[4] One piece of fruit, and somehow it constituted gluttony and was serious enough to have been involved with our initial alienation from God. Why? Clearly not because it had anything to do with calories or body size; I think it's safe to assume that what Adam and Eve did didn't make them fat. What it did involve was eating in a way that broke a limit set by God — eating, we might say, that was heedless or disdainful of a divinely established reality.

The limit set for Adam and Eve was very clear: don't eat from that tree! And because the limit is clear, the nature of the abuse is also clear: they ate from the tree that God told them not to eat from. But how did this idea translate into daily life? To the early and medieval Christian mind, what were the divine limits set on eating?

Many thinkers during this period gave consideration to the problem of gluttony, but the two who made the most influential contributions to the Christian understanding of the sin were John Cassian, writing in the early fifth century, and Gregory the Great, writing in the late sixth century. Cassian devoted attention to gluttony in his two principal works, the *Institutes* (ca. 420) and the *Conferences* (ca. 425), both part of his efforts to establish norms for monastic life. Gregory, as pope, gave consideration to gluttony in his *Morals on the Book of Job* (ca. 590), in which he built on Cassian's ideas in a way that made them relevant more widely in the Church, of concern not only to those living in religious communities but to all Christians. Between the two of them, they laid the foundation for the Christian sense of gluttony, which would last more than a thousand years, right up to the modern period.[5]

Cassian spent many years with the Egyptian desert fathers, and he was strongly influenced by what we might call their semi-gnostic understanding of gluttony, characterized by a suspicion of the body and its desires, which they sometimes viewed as encumbrances weighing down the soul. That negative stance toward the body is present in Cassian, who frames much of his discussion of gluttony in terms of heroic asceticism. At times he almost seems to wish we didn't have to eat at all, and the next best thing is to eat

4. Hill, "Ooze," 59-61.
5. Morton Bloomfield, *The Seven Deadly Sins: An Introduction to the History of a Religious Concept, with Special Reference to Medieval English Literature* (East Lansing: Michigan State University Press, 1952), 42-104; and Carole Straw, "Gregory, Cassian, and the Cardinal Vices," in *In the Garden of Evil: The Vices and Culture in the Middle Ages,* ed. R. Newhauser (Toronto: Pontifical Institute of Medieval Studies, 2005), 35-58.

just enough to keep the body going, while making sure that the portions are so small and the flavor so bland that no pleasure is involved. That pleasure-denying aspect is certainly part of the Church's tradition when it comes to food; we see it even in someone as appealing as St. Francis, who early in his career mixed ashes with his food to make it taste bad.[6] And this ascetic strain may be the most persistent aspect of the tradition; it may very well be what lies behind modern worries about our body size making us look like we're undisciplined and ruled by the pleasure of food. But the ascetic suspicion of pleasure isn't all there is in Cassian, or in the tradition he helped to shape. In the course of his meditations on gluttony, he classifies three distinct ways the sin is expressed, an attempt to define specific practices that constitute breaking the divine limits on eating.[7] And when he gets to this specific level, we find concerns informing his understanding of the sin that are very different from the semi-gnostic urge to be rid of bodily desire.

The first way of gluttony he defines as taking any food outside of "the lawful station and usual time for eating, apart from table." That is, eating outside of regular community mealtimes — what we would call "snacking." Why is that considered to be a problem? Not, as we today might worry, because it loads up the calories, and not, as the gnostics might worry, because it's enjoyable. Cassian's concern with eating outside of communal meals is that it causes discord among the brethren: "Whatever is eaten that does not fall under regular practice and common usage is polluted by the disease of vanity and ostentation."[8] Consuming food alone and on one's own terms leads to "hatred for the monastery";[9] it makes eating an individual act, one that is against the structure and discipline of the group. Cassian is pointing here to the reality that eating is an act that necessarily affects the community we belong to. He's pointing to what looks like a limit: we must not eat in a way that fails to acknowledge that our eating has an effect on those around us.

Cassian's second way of gluttony is "that which rejoices only in filling the belly to repletion with any food whatsoever." So what we'd call overeating,

6. Prose, *Gluttony*, 28. On attempts by the saintly to remove all pleasure from food, see David Gentilcore, "Body and Soul; or, Living Physically in the Kitchen," in *A Cultural History of Food in the Early Modern Age*, ed. Beat Kumin (London: Berg, 2012), 143-64.

7. John Cassian, *The Institutes*, trans. Boniface Ramsay (New York: Newman Press, 2000), 131.

8. Cassian, *Institutes*, 129, 132.

9. Cassian, *The Conferences*, trans. Boniface Ramsay (Mahwah, NJ: Paulist Press, 1997), 190.

but we should note that the concern here has nothing to do with gaining body weight but rather with a desire to maintain spiritual and ethical rigor. For Cassian, eating until we're full "dulls the heart's keenness." It "suffocates" and "weighs down" the mind, robbing it "of every possibility of integrity and purity."[10] At issue here is how the quantity of food we consume can hinder our ability to be reasonable, to be fully conscious of God and our ethical responsibilities, to be available for good works. We see here another limit: as we must be conscious of how our eating influences the community, so must we be aware of the effect of what and how much we eat on our own spiritual lives.

The third way of gluttony is "that which is delighted with more refined and delicate foods." The problem with seeking out these kinds of foods is not the ascetic worry that they might taste too good or the modern worry that they're too fattening; rather, Cassian is concerned here with the expense and labor involved with such food choices. "Food must be selected," he says, that is "easy to prepare, cheap to purchase and appropriate for the way of life of the brothers and their needs."[11] There's a recognition here that food involves a burden, that human beings, outside of the Garden, acquire food only through an arduous and costly interaction with the creation. To demand refined and delicate types of food is to increase that burden, to make the processes necessary to sustain our lives more costly to ourselves and the community. Here is a third limit: responsible eating seeks instead to minimize the costs involved with food, to make the burden of food production as light as possible.

In these definitions of gluttony, Cassian offers a view of responsible eating that, despite his frequent use of ascetic language, has little to do with the ideal of eliminating desire, and certainly has nothing to do with the modern ideal of maintaining a trim figure. Instead, we find an emphasis on eating as an act with profound spiritual and communal significance, an act that necessarily involves effects that reach far beyond the conditions of our own individual bodies. As Hill argues, Cassian's view of gluttony has to do with our consciousness of these realities, with "one's recognition of the proper place of food in one's life and in the community as a whole."[12]

10. Cassian, *Institutes,* 131, 120.
11. Cassian, *Institutes,* 132, 131.
12. Hill, "Ooze," 63.

Gregory: Gluttony's Expanding Meanings

When Gregory takes up gluttony, he draws heavily on Cassian, but with an emphasis that moves the concern of gluttony even more clearly outside the ascetic ideals of the monastery. He follows Cassian's classification scheme but makes a couple alterations: for Gregory, it's five ways of gluttony instead of three — he puts eating foods that are too difficult to prepare and eating foods that are too expensive into separate categories, and he adds the category of eating with "unbounded desire."

Gregory's exploration of the problem of desire is where his treatment of gluttony departs from the semi-gnostic stance more definitively than Cassian's. The semi-gnostic approach to the desire for bodily pleasure is not to "bound" it as Gregory suggests, but rather to try to deny it completely: the ascetic strategy is to try to take no pleasure in food — to eat enough to satisfy the body's need but not to satisfy its desire for pleasure. Gregory uses some of that kind of language himself, but he also challenges and complicates it. The problem with trying to deny ourselves all pleasure in eating is that, first of all, it's impossible in practical terms, since we find that even just satisfying the body's need produces pleasure. There's simply no clear way to separate pleasure and need, because "pleasure so veils itself under necessity that a perfect man can scarcely discern it." More important, Gregory challenges this approach because we can't completely deny our desire for pleasure without doing a kind of spiritual damage to ourselves. Why? Because of how integral eating is to what we are as human beings. Gregory refers to eating as a "kind of debt" we owe to the outward man, the bodily aspect of ourselves, which "requires even by nature the daily fruits of human labor to be spent upon it." Eating is not something we do grudgingly or with condescension to our bodily existence; it's something we *owe* to that aspect of ourselves, a kind of exchange between the inward and outward man. The very nature of our outward man is to be embedded in the material creation; it exists only in the framework of that arduous and costly interaction with the created order. The inward man must respect and attend to that reality. To do otherwise, to ignore or despise that bodily reality, is to attack the sustenance of our virtue: "For our vices become proud upon the same food on which our virtues are nourished and live." We must bound bodily desire, but we must not try to root it out or too stringently discipline it; to do so he likens to attacking an enemy with a violence that causes us to "kill also a citizen whom we love."[13]

---

13. Gregory the Great, *Morals on the Book of Job* (Oxford: John Henry Parker, 1850), 405, 407, 404, 408.

This more affirmative view of eating that Gregory developed not only removes the issue of gluttony from the context of monastic discipline, but also makes it clearer why it's a matter of such importance: at stake in our eating is the health of the relationship of our inward and outward man, and the outward man's relationship to the community and world outside of it.

In this way, Gregory took Cassian's conception of gluttony, with its emphasis on eating as an act that affects the community and our relationship with God, and expanded it far beyond the monastic setting. He made the moral problem of gluttony relevant for all Christians, and in the wake of his writing the idea spread throughout the Christian West, with the sin's different classifications acquiring new meanings as they entered a lay context. Eating outside of communal mealtimes became understood as eating before Mass or certain times of prayer, but also as eating and drinking late into the night, which was seen as a defiance of the natural order. This idea was vividly expressed in medieval sermons; in one from the fifteenth-century collection *Jacob's Well,* the glutton is told, "You ignore the time that God has ordained, for you make day of night, and night of day."[14] In another, gluttons are described as "turning the time against kind [nature]. . . . Men should spend the day in good works and the night in rest of the body, as need asks."[15]

The type of gluttony involved with eating to the point of fullness was expanded in the medieval period to include drinking, which even more clearly hinders a person's spiritual and ethical capacities. Eating and drinking too much figure prominently in many sermons and literary contexts, with emphasis not only on how participation in communal religious practice is undermined, but also on the immensely destructive social consequences of drunken behavior.[16] Gluttons, one sermon notes, "get so intoxicated that they fall to ribaldries, obscenities and idle talk, and sometimes to brawls, by reason of which they fight amongst themselves, sometimes mutilating and

14. Hill, "Ooze," 65-68.
15. British Library Harleian Manuscripts 45, 139b, as quoted in G. R. Owst, *Literature and Pulpit in Medieval England: A Neglected Chapter in the History of English Letters and of the English People* (New York: Barnes & Noble, 1961), 444. This and all following translations of sermons from Owst are mine unless otherwise noted.
16. On medieval views of drunkenness, including the popular idea of the tavern as an anti-Church, see Hill, "Ooze," 66-67; Owst, *Literature and Pulpit,* 425-41; and Mireille Vincent-Cassy, "Between Sin and Pleasure: Drunkenness in France at the End of the Middle Ages," trans. Erika Pavelka, in *In the Garden of Evil: The Vices and Culture in the Middle Ages,* ed. R. Newhauser (Toronto: Pontifical Institute of Medieval Studies, 2005), 393-430.

killing each other."[17] The sin is sometimes associated with more pervasive social ills; one sermon warns that "of drunkenness comes war, pestilence and hunger. For where drunkenness and gluttony reign, there befall many diverse perils."[18]

The type of gluttony involving the demand for costly foods became particularly important in the medieval world, acquiring wider social-justice concerns as it spread beyond the monastery. A common symbolic representation of gluttony during this period was the bear, a symbol considered appropriate not only because of the animal's reputation for appetite, but also because of its habit of taking honey from bees — that is, of demanding a highly refined food that requires much labor on the part of others to produce.[19] As the demand for more luxurious foods increased throughout the Middle Ages, this luxury-craving aspect of gluttony became an area of great concern for medieval preachers, who saw it as a fall from the simplicity of the past: "For at the beginning of the world, man's food was bread and water, but now gluttony is satisfied only with the fruit of every kind of tree, with every kind of root, herb, fowl and fish from the sea. Now men must have [all sorts of expensive wines] and various confections, all of which requires great busyness to prepare and much work for the cooks."[20] Grasping after such costly food is associated in the medieval mind with injustice and neglect of the poor. Another sermon calls gluttons those who "reckon not what they spend so that their mouths might be fed deliciously," and asks, "Where is the compassion of such men that they should have upon the poor?"[21]

Reclaiming Gluttony Today

Such concerns informed Christian ideas about gluttony for a thousand years, right up to the modern period, when the sin turned into calorie anxiety and

---

17. British Library Harleian Manuscripts 4894, 28, as quoted in Owst, *Literature and Pulpit*, 435. This quotation appears in Owst in translated form, but the translator is not specified.

18. British Library Harleian Manuscripts 2398, 33, as quoted in Owst, *Literature and Pulpit*, 432.

19. E.g., British Library Bodleian Manuscripts 95, 35b, as quoted in Owst, *Literature and Pulpit*, 445.

20. British Library Harleian Manuscripts 2398, 31b, as quoted in Owst, *Literature and Pulpit*, 442.

21. British Library Harleian Manuscripts 2276, 36, as quoted in Owst, *Literature and Pulpit*, 445.

body-shaming. This tradition poses a question for us: what would it be like if, instead of worrying about our love handles, we reclaimed the old idea of gluttony? What if we raised the questions about eating today that Cassian and Gregory asked 1,500 years ago? What are the limits set by God on eating in a globalized, pluralistic world? What is eating that's too costly, or that involves too much preparation? What is eating just to feel full, without regard for what kind of food or how it affects us? What is eating that has no concern for how we're affecting the community?

One way we might try to engage with those questions is to ask them with a narrow focus — that is, to think of them only in reference to our immediate community. For instance, being a husband and father, I might ask: How do my food choices affect the community of my family? I might ask whether the foods I choose to eat are too expensive for our family budget, or whether I'm demanding food that requires my wife to work too hard to prepare. I might ask whether I sometimes eat so much that it leads me to neglect being patient with the kids or attentive to my wife's needs.

I think those are good questions to ask, and exactly what many everyday Christians do ask when they think about the ethics of food. But why do we tend to ask *only* those questions? Why don't we ask about the effects of my eating that go outside my family? About how others outside my family might bear some of the burden of my eating? Why do we tend to keep our sphere of concern so narrow? We've seen that, as the idea of gluttony moved from the monastery to the wider world, its sphere of concern expanded to include not just the interests of each person's immediate family or monastery, but also the interests of society as a whole, and particularly the interests of the poor. Why in our time has the sphere of concern gotten smaller, even as human society has become more globally interdependent, and as we've gained more awareness of how much our human communities are connected to everything else?

The wider concerns of gluttony don't occur to us because, for most people, food doesn't seem in any real way linked to a world outside our families. Food in a medieval village had a context that was *known,* but our food doesn't. Our food doesn't seem to have any context at all — it doesn't come from a place or community that's in any way apparent or thinkable. It's just stuff that we see in the supermarket, at the restaurant, in the vending machine. Our food feels that way because of the kind of food system we have, one that is very different from what our ancestors experienced. Our food comes from a system that's industrial and global, which means a system that has very few people involved with producing food, that transports food over great distances, and that tends to rely on complex processing to change food into products that have very little resemblance to their original form. With a system like that, it's not surprising that we don't know much about our food, or that we don't give much thought to the old social concerns about gluttony. In one sense that was the aim of creating the industrial food system: the whole idea was to make food so hugely available to everyone that the questions associated with the old idea of gluttony would become irrelevant. To make food available not just in huge quantities, but also of tremendous variety, all sorts of food once thought exotic or luxurious — to make it available at very low cost to everyone who wants it. And seen from one perspective, the system has been wonderfully successful. Meat, which throughout history was mostly considered an occasional luxury, is now available to billions of us three meals a day. Coffee, sugar, chocolate, bananas, and a whole host of other foods once enjoyed by only a tiny percentage of humanity are now consumed as staples all over the planet. The variety of foods present in an average supermarket would have astounded even our most fabulously wealthy ancestors. What sense does it make to fret over the costs of our food when there's such an overabundance that we throw out half of what we produce every year?

The standard explanation for how the industrial food system was able to achieve such success is that it created more efficient ways to produce food — that is, that it *eliminated* many of the costs of production, usually through changes in technology. Following that explanation, we can see how the system has obviated many concerns about gluttony: eating a little meat or some cake seemed extravagant to John Cassian, since he wrote at a time when an immense amount of labor was needed to produce those things and process them into their final form, but should it still seem extravagant to us, who know that nearly all of that labor is now done by machines?

The logic of this narrative about industrial food makes a lot of sense and actually seems like really good news — we can eat what we want and don't have to worry about our food choices burdening anybody. But that logic holds up only if we don't ask too much about how the magic of efficiency actually works. And it doesn't take much scrutiny to start noticing problems; any basic economics textbook will point out that the burdens of production often aren't actually eliminated by advances in efficiency; instead, they continue to exist as what economists call *external costs*. External in the sense that the burdens of production are often borne somewhere outside of the concern and responsibility of the particular economic operation in question. The medieval preachers would ask, Where? Where do the costs of production go when we replace a food system based on human and animal labor with one based on chemicals and machines?

Let's take that example of eating some meat — let's say we're eating a ham sandwich. It doesn't seem very costly to us because it's widely available for a price just about anyone can afford. And that's because ham production is more efficient than it used to be; with confined feeding operations we no longer need much land, and with mechanized husbandry and butchering it no longer involves as much human labor. So the costs aren't in land and labor anymore. Where did they get pushed to? What are the costs of a confined feeding operation for the pig, who never goes outside, who lives his whole life in a crowded pen, who never digs his snout into the dirt? What are the costs for the people who work in a place like that? And for the people who kill the pigs? What are the conditions of an "efficient" slaughter operation — how many pigs do those people have to kill every day? I know that if I had to kill thirty pigs a day, there would be a huge psychological burden for me. Instead, that burden goes to the person who killed the pig in my sandwich.

Meat might seem like an extreme example — what about the other foods we eat? The other day I bought a small bottle of apple juice for my kids, and on the label it said that it contained juice from apples grown in seven different countries (China, Turkey, New Zealand — all over the world), and yet it cost me only a couple of bucks. Apparently they've made production very efficient with artificial fertilizers and pesticides, and they make transportation efficient with fossil fuels. For the company producing the juice, the costs of making it and getting it to me have gone way down, and then they pass those savings on to me the consumer. Great! But where did those costs really go? To make artificial fertilizer, we have to extract natural gas and turn it into ammonium nitrate — what are the costs of that process for the people involved with it, and for the towns where it happens? What's the cost of making organophosphates and other pesticides and spraying them in huge quantities? What is the cost for the workers who are exposed to those chemicals? Or the cost of emitting tons and tons of carbon in order to maintain the efficiencies of a global operation? And what about the plastic bottle the juice is in — that's a more efficient way of storing and transporting it, right? But what is it like for the people who work in the places where the petrochemicals for that bottle are extracted and refined?

We can ask these kinds of questions about everything we eat, even about the foods that might seem pretty responsible. I sometimes buy a kind of organic cracker that I like a lot, and I think — well, they're organic, so the way they're produced can't be too bad. But in reality I don't really know much more about the crackers than I do about any industrial food. There are a whole bunch of ingredients on the box, some of which I've never heard of. I do know that the crackers contain palm oil, which is in nearly every processed goodie we eat these days; it's what they're using instead of hydrogenated trans fats, because palm oil doesn't cause the health problems trans fats do. So that's good — they've made my food healthier, more natural. That's eating that's at least somewhat more ethical, right? But what are the costs of growing palm oil "efficiently"? What are the costs of bulldozing rain forest to make way for palm plantations? What are the costs for the people who used to subsist off what they could harvest in those forests? For the Sumatran tigers and orangutans who simply can't live at all without the habitat the forest provides? What are the costs of converting a complex ecosystem into an agricultural extraction enterprise?

Those are the kinds of questions that the old concept of gluttony poses to us about the food we eat, about the packaging around the food we eat, really about everything we consume, food or otherwise. We'll find that in almost every case it's very hard to get answers, and that's a big part of the problem in itself. To consume responsibly is to be conscious of the effect my consumption has on others, to try to minimize the burdens of how my food is produced, but I don't know those effects or those burdens. As they've been made external, they've also been hidden; it's as if the realities of where our food comes from have been screened off behind a wall we can't see past, like the wall put up around a construction site. That wall has been erected very deliberately by the business interests of industrial food but also by us, who have willingly given up the right and responsibility to know something about what we eat. They don't tell us much about where our food really comes from, and we don't ask.

But if we're going to take the old concerns of gluttony seriously, then we have to ask. And while we may not get full answers, if we ask, we will get enough. There's already lots of information out there; if we look, we can already see over the wall enough to know that the costs and burdens of our food haven't really been eliminated, they've only been shifted. And not only shifted, but also magnified: as the industrial food system has externalized costs, it has made them much bigger, much more severe than they've ever been before. Producing food in the medieval world did not involve lagoons of manure poisoning watersheds. It didn't involve massive dead zones in the oceans, or cancer-causing pesticides, or cooking the climate with carbon. The industrial food system has taken the old burdens and has transformed them into catastrophes. And if we're often not very aware of those terrible burdens, it's because they're not pushed onto us, because our role in the system is to consume comfortably. No, the burdens are pushed onto the powerless — onto migrant workers or pigs or tigers. As the medievals knew, the cost of luxurious eating always falls on the poor; today we realize that among the poor are not only human beings and communities, but also the many nonhuman beings and communities that we are inextricably tied to.

Although the costs aren't pushed onto us, they are still linked to us, since we are the beneficiaries of the system that has externalized them. We don't bear many of the burdens of our own food; we spend much less money buying food and much less time preparing it than has been typical for most human beings. Those burdens have been shifted away from us, and those externalized burdens have become how our outer man is interacting with the creation. We don't really have any justification for keeping our sphere of concern confined to our families. We can choose not to worry about where the costs of our food went only because they're not costs that we ourselves have to pay. We can choose not to concern ourselves because we're some of the lucky ones; maybe we don't live in the town with the petrochemical plant. Maybe we don't have to kill pigs all day for a living. Maybe we don't have to cart in bottled water because our wells have been contaminated by runoff or fracking waste. Maybe we're not cows trapped in veal pens, or tigers whose forest is disappearing. Let the costs of my consumption go to all of them, to the migrant workers and the pigs and the kids with poisoned wells, let them go to everybody not as lucky as me and my own kids. That's what we're staking a claim to when we try to keep a narrow sphere of concern. Not a kind of eating that somehow magically doesn't affect the world around us — that kind of eating doesn't exist. What we're choosing instead is a kind of eating that says to the rest of the world — its creatures, its communities, its capacities for health and beauty — let all of you bear my burdens.

And that is where there is a terrible cost of gluttony for us, the gluttons. We would never consciously and deliberately want our burdens pushed out to the rest of the world. We don't want the migrant workers to get sick or the pigs to suffer or the tigers to go extinct — we don't want any of that. But because of the system we're entangled with, that is the real nature of our relationship to pigs and tigers; our inner man is all full of blessings on them, while our outer man is engaged with their ruin. The industrial food system has not made concerns over gluttony irrelevant; rather, it has institutionalized gluttony, producing a kind of consumption that is unconscious of its effects on others and that maximizes burdens as an inevitable and continual fact of our lives. It's a system that has bound us to gluttony, making it nearly impossible to eat in a way that is not totally at odds with our spiritual selves.

This is why the tradition was right to treat gluttony so seriously. Adam committing gluttony by eating the apple — that's not just a trope, not just a bit of overwrought medieval rhetoric. Everything in the creation is interconnected; it's a web of life ordered by God. And every time we consume something, we're intervening into that web, into that order, with consequences for the health of all the members and for the health of the whole. To consume with no consciousness of that reality, to consume with no care for how we're intervening into that goodness — that is an interaction that leaves *me* diminished. That is eating in a way that leaves my inward and outward man estranged, for the inward man seeks to worship God, while the outward man has only a destructive connection to the world God has made.

Remedies

The good news is that we're not stuck with all of this. We're not stuck being gluttons. At this point, it's still almost impossible to completely remove ourselves from the gluttonous system, but there are ways that we can start to distance ourselves from it, and those ways are becoming more accessible all the time. If we make even small efforts to try to change how we consume, we immediately discover that there are people out there working very hard to make it more possible for us. There are people starting small farms because they want to produce food in a way that is less burdensome for the world. There are people organizing farmers' markets to connect us with those small farmers. There are people teaching workshops about how to grow and store and cook our own food. Those people are creating opportunities for us, and if we take them up on it, even in a small way, we'll immediately experience two things. First, we'll notice that taking advantage of any of these things involves a cost for us, and that's to be expected, since responsible eating means taking the burdens that have been pushed onto the poor and bringing them back to us. Instead of paying very little for our food, we'll pay a just price that actually allows producers to avoid the ravages of efficiency, and instead to pay their workers a living wage and tend the land without chemicals that poison it. We pay a price that represents and actually allows for care of people and land. And we'll also find that we have to do more to prepare our food — we will actually have to *cook* it, instead of letting the processing plants do our cooking for us. That moves the burden away from the forests being cut down for palm oil and back into my own kitchen.

The second thing we notice is that taking those burdens back on ourselves brings a particular kind of reward. When we harvest our own broccoli, when we bake our own bread, when we go down to the farmers' market and get hold of some tomatoes grown by someone we know in a way that we respect, it's a very different experience from grabbing some crackers from who knows where. It's not just because it usually tastes a lot better, it's also a fundamentally different *spiritual* experience — it's richer, more full of gratitude. It's the satisfaction we know when we're carrying our own burdens. It's the fullness we feel when we're participating in something that, instead of degrading the community, enriches and enlivens it. It's the experience of our inner and outer man realigning. And with the proliferation of farmers' markets, with the increasing number of people courageous enough to start up sustainable farms and community gardens, we can have that experience more and more easily.

There is even more good news: not only are there people giving us practical options for better ways to consume, there are also people who are doing the work of trying to think through the questions of responsible consumption. People like Joan Gussow, Michael Pollan, Marion Nestle are trying to think about the moral realities of eating in a very complicated world. And what is remarkable, and in a sense reaffirming for us, is how these writers, although their perspectives are generally not informed by the traditions of the Church, tend to echo ideas from the gluttony tradition we've lost sight of. Pollan, who has made a career out of thinking about our industrial food problem, once set out to try to establish a set of practical rules for responsible eating. And what kinds of rules did he come up with? Here are a few examples: *Always eat with other people. Always eat at a table. Don't eat food with ingredients you can't pronounce. Eat food, not too much, mostly plants.*[22] Anything about those rules sound familiar? Here we have a twenty-first-century journalist, a man coming from a secular Jewish tradition and living in Berkeley, California, and when he devotes himself to trying to figure out how to define responsible eating, he comes up with a set of rules that sound a bit like John Cassian. Eat communally. Eat simply and moderately. Eat knowing that it's your way of being in the world.

---

22. Michael Pollan, *In Defense of Food: An Eater's Manifesto* (New York: Penguin Press, 2008), 147-201.

CHAPTER 14

Establishing an I-Thou Relationship between Creator and Creature

David Vincent Meconi, SJ

To encounter another deeply is to meet the other personally. It is the lover who sees most totally, and to the poet, even the most mundane things speak of a world filled with beautiful mystery. Tertullian (d. ca. 220) can see in the outstretched wings of birds in flight a cruciform prayer, and John Milton (d. 1674) calls out to ever-envious time.[1] This is the kind of sensitivity that enabled T. S. Eliot (d. 1965) to hold the most whimsical of conversations with cats, and what gives Louise Glück license to beg the earth to be kind to her mother, recently put to rest therein.[2] Or take the anonymous author of the alliterative seventh- or eighth-century poem *Dream of the Rood,* whose cross narrates the death of Christ itself.[3] The cross's own words draw us into the eerie realization that, not only is Jesus Christ pierced with nails, vilified, and covered with blood, but so too is this wood with which Christ has since become one. Both Christ and cross become simultaneous signs of betrayal, derision, and loss. Together they remain loyal and suffer what both

---

1. Tertullian, *De oratione,* §29; John Milton, "On Time," in *Complete Poetry and Selected Prose of Milton* (New York: Modern Library, 1950), 29-30.

2. Cf. T. S. Eliot, *Old Possum's Book of Practical Cats* (London: Faber & Faber, 1953); Louise Glück, "The Open Grave," in *Poems, 1962-2012* (New York: Farrar, Straus & Giroux, 2012), 368.

3. The most accessible study of the Rood legend is *The Dream of the Rood,* ed. Michael Swanton (Exeter: University of Exeter Press, 1996); for a more extensive examination, see Éamonn Ó Carragáin, *Ritual and the Rood: Liturgical Images and the Old English Poems of the Dream of the Rood Tradition* (London: British Library; Toronto: University of Toronto Press, 2005).

the Roman soldiers as well as all of posterity associate with them: death and the ignominy cruciformity now represents. In allowing birds to pray and crosses to speak, such theologians and poets are the ones who strive to live metaphysically large enough to elicit a "you" from otherwise inanimate and nonhuman existents, created agents of eternal beauty. In fact, the greatest lover of all reprimands fevers directly (Luke 4:39), he deems every creature (πάσῃ τῇ κτίσει) worthy to have the gospel proclaimed to it (Mark 16:15), and he promises that one day even the rocks and stones will cry out (κράξουσιν) in their recognition of him (Luke 19:40).

The Scriptures and the saints of the Christian tradition, especially, display a profound appreciation for the sacredness of all things, manifesting a deep awareness of a personal "thou" within every creature. They are blessed with an awareness that the divine is recognizable in every creature and thus worthy of personal attention. We have monks who pray for lizards and saints who preach to birds.[4] In more mundane cases, we have probably all spoken to our car as it struggled to sputter uphill, or we have shouted at our computers and phones when they refused to cooperate. Certainly all of us have talked to our pets and to our plants and think no more of it.[5] Yet to someone like Rainer Maria Rilke, "All beauty in animals and plants is a silent, enduring form of love and yearning. . . . The earth is full of this secret down to her smallest things."[6] Like Rilke, this essay aims to understand such exchanges as more than just naive anthropomorphizations of creatures.

The poetic as well as the dominical do not simply pretend to decorate things with personhood. There is something much deeper going on. We must therefore resist the temptation to discount the scriptural references of God's addressing nonperson creatures as "you" as hyperbolic jargon. We should not dismiss the Scriptures and the saints interacting with subhuman creatures in a second-person relationship as eccentric embarrassments. As such, we shall aim to ask how we might make sense of God's calling upon inanimate and nonhuman creatures as "you." By extension, how are we to understand

---

4. Isaac of Nineveh (d. ca. 700), as found in Sebastian Brock, *Heart of Compassion: Daily Readings with Isaac the Syrian*, ed. A. M. Allchin (London: Darton, Longman & Todd, 1989), 29; *The Little Flowers of Saint Francis*, §§17-18, in *Francis of Assisi: Early Documents*, vol. 3, ed. Regis Armstrong, OFMCap et al. (New York: New City Press, 2001), 594-95.

5. Rupert Sheldrake argues that this talking to nonhumans reflects our need for personal connections with our surroundings; see his *The Rebirth of Nature: The Greening of Science and God* (New York: Bantam Books, 1991), 212.

6. Rainer Maria Rilke, *Letters to a Young Poet*, trans. Joan M. Burnham (Novato, CA: New World Library, 2000), 37.

the Church's holy men and women who treat all of creation with a precious mindfulness and with personal dignity? The overall thesis I advance here is that Christian holiness and recognition of second-person relationships are coextensive; that the more like God one becomes, the more of God's own divine personhood in all things one is able to perceive and embrace.

We shall accordingly move in three main sections. The first section takes up the scriptural images where God and creatures reveal a second-person exchange. How do we understand God's calling upon inanimate and vegetative life as a personal "you"? Next comes an examination of the metaphysical discussion of *esse* and *ens:* all of creation displays not only the being and universal attributes of God but inevitably his personal presence as Trinitarian lover, beloved, and love as well. Here the insights of St. Augustine and his theology of a Logocentric creation shall serve as a foundational model before turning to St. Thomas's cosmology and his contribution of the conservation of being. This second section concludes by translating these patristic and medieval insights into Martin Buber's language of the second-person "I-Thou" relationship. We shall then, in the third and final section, raise the possible implications of this argument, centering ourselves on the Christian promise of human divinization. The incarnation of God provides a richly unique instance of the transformative encounter between others and can thus be used as a model for how we humans are likewise called to a certain condescension that might thus elicit the qualities of "you" from the animal and mineral strata of our world.

Second-Person Relationships Portrayed in Scripture

In her magisterial work on theodicy *Wandering in Darkness,* Eleonore Stump, my friend and colleague at St. Louis University, points out how God has a personal, paternal care for all his creatures. That is, God sees other existents not simply as things that he has fabricated *ex nihil,* but also as others for which he has a providential, protective, and even personal love. In his celestial solicitude, God chooses to relate to his creatures as the sort of beings who are able to listen and respond to one who cares for them. Various scriptural episodes depict the Almighty addressing his creatures as a "you," attending to them with delicately individuated regard, and being present to them in a personal attentiveness. In response, these creatures sometimes prove to be rebellious and ungrateful, wandering recklessly far from their Father; at other times, they act and assent to what their Maker asks of them.

To illustrate Stump's point, let us look at her analysis of God's first speech with Job, wherein we hear Yahweh inquire of Job: "And who shut within doors the sea, when it burst forth from the womb; when I made the clouds its garment and thick darkness its swaddling bands? When I set limits for it and fastened the bar of its door, and said: 'Thus far shall you come but no farther and here shall your proud waves be stilled!'" (Job 38:8-11). The author of Job thus portrays God as one able to enter into a second-person relationship with all creatures, animate and inanimate, rational and extra-rational. God could obviously control his creation any way he chooses, but he prefers to engage the waters as a "you" in order to bring them willingly into his divine economy.

Focusing on this first discourse in Job, we see how God treats his creatures not as a distant strongman manipulates mere "stuff" clearly well below him. While God is entitled to treat his creatures however he sees fit, he instead engages his creature in second-person discourse wherein God addresses water tenderly as a "you," as a "thou." In so doing, the divine lends the sea an identity and a dignity that it does not have apart from God. Stump therefore writes:

> The speech portrays a second-person experience (as it were) between God and the sea, in which God says "thou" to the sea. As God describes his interactions with the sea in this part of the divine speech, God addresses the sea directly, in second-person forms of speech. In fact, God talks to the sea as if the sea were a rambunctious and exuberant child of his, but nonetheless a child who can hear him, understand him, and respond to him. And so, in God's descriptions of himself in this part of the speech to Job, God brings the sea into conformity to his will by talking to the sea and explaining to the sea what it can and cannot do.[7]

Given the personifications of other ancient cosmogonies, the Jewish and Christian traditions have not thought too deeply about what Stump has here pointed out. That is, the various mythoi explaining the world's beginnings found in Israel's neighboring foes demanded the active role of animated anthropomorphizations that either carried out or stood in direct opposition to greater deities' desire to tame the world for the human race. How different is Yahweh's interaction with this water when compared, for example, with the Babylonian epos the *Enuma Elish,* where Marduk must tame the defiant

---

7. Eleonore Stump, *Wandering in Darkness: Narrative and the Problem of Suffering* (Oxford: Oxford University Press, 2010), 188.

waters Apsu and Tiamat, as well as the great winds that must be coaxed into service. Similarly, in the Egyptian Book of the Dead, we hear of Nu(n), the primordial and ambiguously male or female waters, again in need of divine constraint.[8]

Perhaps such very un-Christian cosmogonies have kept the Christian tradition from exploring more fully the possible significance of God's speaking "you" to the waters of Job. Take, for example, the Church's great commentator on Job, Pope Gregory (d. 604). He sees fit to translate the waters here into the Church's persecutors, and only then does God's interaction with this threatening mob make sense.[9] While John Chrysostom (d. 407) likewise relegates his reflections to God's power, and that by constraining such restless waters and rendering them still, the teeming sea "proclaims the power of God."[10] Contemporary commentaries are not much help here either. Most follow suit and concentrate on the power of God, who orders his creatures with his oracular strength. Marvin Pope's standard commentary on Job, for example, notices how this exchange is reminiscent of other Mesopotamian creation epics, but he skips over any possible meaning contained in God's words to the waters.[11]

We hear Yahweh's discourse here in Job echo also toward the beginning of Mark's Gospel, when the incarnate Son continues this second-person interaction with watery creation: "Jesus was in the stern, asleep on a cushion. They woke him and said to him, 'Teacher, do you not care that we are perishing?' He woke up, rebuked the wind, and said to the sea, 'Quiet! Be still!' The wind ceased and there was great calm. Then he asked them, 'Why are you terrified? Do you not yet have faith?' They were filled with great awe and said to one another, 'Who then is this whom even wind and sea obey?'" (Mark 4:38-41). Dominical might is once again manifested, not as the manipulation of an omnipotent vassal over a disposable subject, but as

8. Cf. *Babylonian Creation Myths,* ed. W. G. Lambert (Winona Lake, IN: Eisenbrauns Press, 2013).

9. Cf. Gregory the Great, *On Job,* §27 (PL 76:131).

10. John Chrysostom, *Commentary on Job* 38.11; Ursula Hagedorn and Dieter Hagedorn, eds., *Johannes Chrysostomus. Kommentar zu Hiob,* Patristische Texte und Studien 35 (Berlin: De Gruyter Verlag, 1990), 186. Isho'Dad of Merv (a ninth-century Nestorian bishop) does focus on the tenderness God sees in the waters and treats them "like a baby who gets out after being fashioned in the womb and is wrapped in clothes of wool," but he does not raise the significance of God's addressing the waters in the second person (*Commentary on Job* 38:8 [CSCO 230, 309-11]).

11. Marvin Pope, *Job: The Anchor Bible Commentary* (Garden City, NY: Doubleday, 1965), 251.

a second-person experience where the Lord speaks to his rambunctious creature as another. "Quiet! Be still" (Σιώπα, πεφίμωσο) are indeed strong imperatives, but they are signs of the Creator's personal interaction with the waters as an interlocutor able to heed divine commands.

We see this level of interaction again later in Mark's Gospel when he builds the suspense of the Christ's revelation in Jerusalem. Jesus and his disciples are leaving Bethany, and Mark unashamedly tells us that the incarnate God is hungry. This drama between God's physical emptiness and the satiety only his creation can offer next comes to the fore: "The next day as they were leaving Bethany he was hungry. Seeing from a distance a fig tree in leaf, he went over to see if he could find anything on it. When he reached it he found nothing but leaves; it was not the time for figs. And he said to it in reply, 'May no one ever eat of your fruit again!' And his disciples heard it" (Mark 11:12-14). When the Lord of all life draws near, one best bear fruit, lest one be cut down. What is intriguing here is Jesus' relating to the fig tree at the familiar level of "you." The Creator expects his creatures to recognize him and even to respond to his own needs and desires.

As Mark would have us see it, the fig tree dwells between two ways of life: to live in unison with its own natural, albeit limited, cycle of fertile and infertile times, or to live in total openness to its Maker, who seemingly assures the tree of its own unyielding fruitfulness. The call of the divine is ever greater than what appears to us to be the right or wrong season (fig trees in Israel give fruit between late May and early October, not in early April, when Christ most likely was making his way to Jerusalem for Passover). This exchange between Jesus and the fruitless tree effects a connection that appears so outside of the disciples' normal world; their overhearing of this exchange is deemed important enough for a scriptural recording ("And his disciples heard it").

Yet again, in turning to the commonly cited commentaries today, we come up empty-handed. Joel Marcus's volume on the Gospel of Mark in the Anchor Yale Bible Series is unaware of the possible importance of the incarnate Creator speaking to one of his creatures in this way. In her otherwise thorough volume on Mark in the Hermeneia commentary series, Adela Yarbro Collins cites many prominent biblical scholars to show how the fig tree represents various concerns in the first-century Jewish consciousness: the barrenness of all who turn away from God (Ernst Loymeyer), the present state of Israel (Heinz Giesen), the uselessness of the old temple cult (William Telford), and the current situation of all the nations heedlessly rejecting God

(James R. Edwards).[12] Unfortunately, no mention is made of any possible significance of the Lord's choosing to engage the tree *qua* tree in a second-person address.

Perhaps it has taken the more modern threats of ecological disaster and our growing awareness of the earth's fragility for the Church to begin to listen attentively to, what Vatican II (1962-65) named the "discourse of creatures." While God clearly initiates this dialogue, creation responds to the Lord in turn, and this interactive relationship is what gives each creature its intelligibility. Upholding the integrity of the created order, *Gaudium et spes* is careful not to isolate creatures from their Creator, accordingly teaching:

> If, however, the autonomy of earthly realities is taken to mean that created things are not dependent on God and that we can use them without reference to their Creator, then anyone who acknowledges God realizes the falsity of such opinions. For without its Creator the creature simply disappears. And all believers of whatever religion have always sensed the voice and manifestations of the Creator in the utterances of creatures [*creaturarum loquela*]. If God is ignored the creature itself is impoverished.[13]

Here Vatican II teaches that God's voice is heard in the discourse between him and his creatures. From this exchange emerges a solicitude for creatures, to see them and therefore treat them as God does. All people are hence called to foster the kind of attentiveness that allows this conversation between the Creator and all his creation to become part of their own life. Only in this exchange can the human person become fully aware of God's universal activity. For if God can say "you" to all existents, it follows that all existents can therefore say "you" to God.

The Scriptures are replete with accounts of God and nonpersonal creatures interacting at a very personal and collaborative level. Only the Lord can call all the stars by their name (Ps 147:4), he can mission his ravens to tend to the needs of his prophet Elijah (1 Kgs 17:6), and even the frightful Leviathan is cajoled into speaking "gentle words" to God alone (Job 41:3). Because God speaks all there is into existence (*Dixitque Deus: Fiat lux. Et facta est lux;* Gen 1:3) and continues this conversation with each creature,

---

12. For all these standing opinions, see Adela Yarbro Collins's commentary in the Hermeneia series: *Mark: A Critical and Historical Commentary on the Bible* (Minneapolis: Fortress Press, 2007), 523.

13. *Gaudium et spes*, §36, as found in *Decrees of the Ecumenical Councils,* ed. Norman Tanner, SJ, et al. (Washington, DC: Georgetown University Press, 1990), 1090-91.

the Scriptures are able to record how all God's creatures praise him in return.[14] That is, because God speaks to his creatures, they are then enabled to discourse with him as agents of his own glory.

This is how the sun and moon and all the shining stars can likewise call back to God in their created concord of praise. How often the psalmist depicts God caring for his creatures in very intimate ways (Pss 84:2; 104), or how the waters lift up their voices just as the floods lift up their waves (Ps 93:3), or how beautifully the prophet Daniel will record how all things offer fitting worship: "All you works of the LORD, bless the LORD . . . all you waters, sun and moon, stars of heaven . . . cold and heat . . . ice and snow . . . nights and days . . . light and darkness, bless the LORD" (Dan 3:52-81).

From this dialogical exchange throughout Scripture, let us now venture a metaphysical rendering of how this exchange might possibly take place. Here we shall focus on the two pillars of the Catholic intellectual tradition: Augustine of Hippo (354-430) and Thomas Aquinas (1225-74). While neither of these thinkers offers us direct insight into an establishing the importance of a second-person relation between God and creatures, their cosmologies do provide helpful matrices by which we can further our understanding of how God and creatures interact.

Conseruatio Amandi

Western philosophy began not only to search for the primal *arche* of all reality but also to inquire into the point of contact between that first organizing cause and the *archai* found in our daily human experience of the world around us. The pre-Socratic understanding was that things that become, must necessarily participate in that which alone is. Therefore, every existent contains a trace of the very existence that underlies the cosmos. For Thales, it was water; for Heraclitus, fire; for Anaximenes, air.[15] By the time Plato

---

14. Notice that God must create in a "third-person" manner ("Let there be . . ."), not speaking to and with a creature (for it does not yet exist), but commanding that this and that creature now be. Only thereafter is God able to engage his creatures personally. While he was in Carthage around 416, Augustine cagily picks up on this necessity (*Sermon* 169.13) when he preaches against the Pelagians' self-sufficiency: "So he who made you without you, will not save you without you" (*Qui ergo fecit te sine te, non te iustificat sine te* [PL 38:923]). That is, God must at first command all of creation into being, but he then refuses to domineer mere things but chooses, rather, to coax every creature personally.

15. There are many good surveys of the pre-Socratic search for the ultimate principle of

begins to teach, the need for contact between beings and Being remains, but now we no longer look for the source of all things in the material realm but in the immutable idea. Now all things in varying degrees participate in the ultimate idea of the Good, by which all other forms are recognizable.[16] Aristotle built upon this insight and came to see how the first and eternal *arche* is a causal divine mind connecting all things — "fishes and fowls and plants" — and in so doing, actualizing and ordering all things back to itself.[17]

The Neoplatonic tradition explained this connection between the first principle and participatory existents in terms of conversion. Terms such as στρέφω and ἐπιστρέφω signified signified a "turning back" or "the changing of direction," which resulted in the determination and formation of all contingent being. In Plotinus's worldview, all lower beings exist only by turning back to their prior and therefore superior source. Such conversion is the way by which all things come from and stay united to the One. For example, Nous comes into being qua Nous by turning back to the One: "Nous comes into being [γενόμενον] by turning back upon [ἐπεστράφη] the One to be filled, and thus becomes Nous by gazing upon the One. This turning back toward the one and gazing upon the One makes Nous what it is, Intellect and being."[18] This process of turning to the source of an existent's being continues throughout the Plotinian cosmos, thus uniting the world into a harmonious whole. In this way Plotinus's henology assures not only the existence of all things but their goodness as well, as all things that exist are really instantiations of the Good on a lower level.

When Jesus' disciples met followers of Plato and Aristotle, they too began to adopt this line of inquiry. But under the guidance of revelation, Christian thinkers had to account for the glaring difference that the ultimate principle of reality is not an abstract universal but three divine persons. Furthermore, the origin of the Christian universe is not an impersonal *eidos* or emanator; rather, it is a Trinitarian communion of persons who deliberately will to create and sustain all that is. For the Christian, then, the spatiotemporal order of being not only comes freely from God, it is held even now in

---

reality; see, for example, Robin Waterfield, *The First Philosophers: Presocratics and Sophists* (Oxford: Oxford University Press, 2009). See also Leo Sweeney, SJ, *Divine Infinity in Greek and Medieval Thought* (New York: Peter Lang, 1999).

16. Cf. Plato, *Republic* 508E.

17. Cf. Aristotle, *Metaphysics* 12.10, 1075a16-18; for more here, see Paul Blowers, *Drama of the Divine Economy: Creator and Creation in Early Christian Theology and Piety* (Oxford: Oxford University Press, 2012), 37.

18. *Enneads* 5.2.1, my translation.

a loving Father's providence. All things are therefore grounded not in some Greek ideal but in the community of persons who divinely will that there be creatures that these persons not only create but sustain in existence at every moment, thereby endowing them with various levels of beauty and form.

Gregory of Nazianzus (d. 390) explained this transition as he reflected on the star of Bethlehem. Here all astrology ceased because no longer were the stellar deities fating the movements of man; rather, the stars were moving in orbits determined by a little child below.[19] Pope Emeritus Benedict XVI refers to this image in his 2007 encyclical *Spe salvi* (§5), but earlier (as Joseph Cardinal Ratzinger), he wrote how Christianity came to root all reality in "the Trinitarian faith" of Father, Son, and Spirit because the universe "has a deeper foundation: the mind of the Creator. . . . The Logos himself is the great artist, in whom all works of art — the beauty of the universe — have their origin."[20] In contrast to the Hellenic and even the Hebraic cosmologies, then, the ultimate principle discernible in creation is persons, three divine persons, who now freely create all that is, making possible a personal relationship between causer and caused.

For the Christian, the divine is not just *esse* but also *ens* — not just the perfect universals of the pagan philosophers, but also persons defined wholly through mutual relationships. If so, there is thus a trace of personhood in every creature, a scintilla of the Father, Son, and Holy Spirit's own other-centered life and joy together. This is how creatures and God can be depicted in dialogical relationship: he speaks to them as he can, and they lift up their voices to him insofar as they are able.

Let us now briefly take up two metaphysical paradigms by which Christian thinkers have attempted an explanation for how God and his beloved creatures are united. For Augustine, the image offered is one of all creatures impersonating the Word's eternal conversion before the Father; for Thomas Aquinas, the image is instead one of all things reflecting the divine mind, which originally brought them into being.

As Augustine sees the cosmos, all creatures speak to the inquiring soul of the God whose they are. God speaks, and so creatures exist. In turn, those same creatures speak incessantly of God: "I put my question to the earth, and it replied, 'I am not he.' . . . And to all things which stood around the portals of my flesh I said, 'Tell me of my God. You are not he, but tell me something

---

19. Cf. Gregory of Nazianzen, *Dogmatic Poems*, V.53-64 (PG 37:428-29).
20. Joseph Ratzinger, *The Spirit of the Liturgy* (San Francisco: Ignatius Press, 2000), 153.

of him.' Then they lifted up their mighty voices and cried, 'He made us.' My questioning was my attentive spirit, and their reply, their beauty [*Pulchritudo eorum, confessio eorum*]."[21] In Augustine's way of imagining the cosmos, the Father creates all things in imitation of the Son's turn toward him in their mutual Spirit. This filial conversion in the Spirit is traceable in every created being, and as such, the Word's turn toward and adherence to the Father becomes the model for all creatures as well. This is how Augustine himself is able to ask:

> Or is it that when the unformed basic material, whether of spiritual or bodily being, was first being made, it was not appropriate to say God said, *Let it be made,* because it is by the Word, always adhering to the Father, that God eternally says everything, not with the sound of a voice nor with thoughts running through the time which sounds take, but with the light, co-eternal with himself, of the Wisdom he has begotten; and imperfection or incompleteness does not imitate the form of this Word, being unlike that which supremely and originally is, and tending by its very want of form toward nothing? Rather, it is when it turns, everything in the way suited to its kind, to that which truly and always is, to the creator that is to say of its own being, that it really imitates the form of the Word which always and unchangingly adheres to the Father, and receives its own form, and becomes a perfect, complete creature.[22]

Augustine sees how the ontologically lowest being is the conceptual creature, a thing so obscure and unformed, he has to invent a term to describe it: *formabilitas.*[23] Between this ability-to-be-formed to the highest creature, the *caelum caeli,* Augustine argues that all things by their very nature tend toward nonbeing. What saves them from falling into the original *nihil* from which they have been brought is their Logocentric stance toward the Father. We see this pattern consistently throughout Augustine's com-

21. Augustine, *Confessions* 10.6.9, trans. Maria Boulding, *The Confessions,* ed. David Vincent Meconi, SJ (San Francisco: Ignatius Press, 2012), 271.

22. Augustine, *Literal Meaning of Genesis* [*Gen. litt.*] 1.4 (CSEL 28.7-8), in *On Genesis,* trans. Edmund Hill, OP (Hyde Park, NY: New City Press, 2002), 171. For more here, see my *The One Christ: St. Augustine's Theology of Deification* (Washington, DC: Catholic University of America Press, 2013), 15-31.

23. Augustine coins *formabilitas* at *Gen. litt.* 5.5 (CSEL 28.147). Note that *formabilitas* in the standard Lewis and Short *Latin Dictionary* (London: Clarendon Press, 1958 [1879]), 768, is cited at *Gen. litt.* 5.4 because of a difference in textual divisions between the PL and the CSEL editions.

DAVID VINCENT MECONI, SJ

mentaries on Genesis: a creature is brought into being by God's power and stays in being by being turned back to God.[24]

In this way, Augustine discovered a way of explaining creation's need to be converted continuously toward God, as well as a way of showing how God is manifest in all of his good creation. Relying on John's Prologue, Augustine stresses how all things are created *ex nihil* and therefore are given existence and a definable nature only in the Word. Necessarily imitative of the Word, then, creation must forever adhere to the Father by imitating the Word's own turn toward and reception of the Father's very being. While never discussing the second-person relationality between Creator and creature explicitly, the great bishop of Hippo does attribute an imitative turning to all existents: everything is and is what it is because all things imitate the Word's eternal receptivity before the Father. More than anything in the Augustinian tradition, this existential turn toward and in God provides a metaphysical basis for God's addressing creatures as "you": all things exist through a filial posture before their progenitor Father, who wills them and, in his Word, calls each creature to himself in an adhering union of love.

This Logocentrism gives Augustinian cosmology its Trinitarian nature. Because all things come from this original and eternal conversation between the Father, Son, and Holy Spirit, all things exhibit a triadic ontology in which every creature (1) exists, (2) is some sort of being or nature, and (3) is ordered hierarchically within its own proper place within the cosmos. Augustine sees this created trinity scripturally in Paul's cosmology at Romans 11:36, where the apostle delineates all things as *a quo, per quem,* and *in quo.* Too, Augustine would have heard Ambrose comment on this passage in the year 386, when the great bishop of Milan translated these three distinct factors into the *principium et origo* of all things, their *continuatio,* and their *finis.* By 389 Augustine had reworked this triad consistently into the three characteristics of all created being: that it exists *(sit),* that it is of a particular nature, either this or that *(hoc uel illud),* and that it remains in the cosmos as it is able *(maneant, quantum potest).*[25] This triad of *esse, essentia,* and *manentia* would prove to be a permanent mark of an Augustinian metaphysic.

Turning to the Thomistic tradition, we see this same Trinitarian pattern in all creatures. All things "represent the Word" *(repraesentat uerbum)* by

24. *Gen. litt.* 1.3: "*eam [lucem] reuocante ad se creatore, conuersio eius facta atque inluminata intellegatur*" (CSEL 28.7).

25. *Epistula* 11.3 (PL 33:76); see *Gen. litt.* 4 on how the Creator is the one who makes every creature abide incessantly; throughout the cosmos, Augustine descried a Trinity wherever he looked.

bearing a trace of the Trinity. At *Summa theologiae* I, q. 45, art. 7, Thomas asks whether the Trinity is at all present in creatures. Of course, the triune God is present to those made in his image and likeness, but Thomas here wants to know how the Father and Son and Spirit might be said to be found in nonrational, nonpersonal creatures. Answering that, Yes, in fact the Trinity is present in every created existent, Thomas continues to elaborate on the nature of a "trace," a *vestigium* that may represent the causality of an effect but not the nature of the cause — as smoke is a trace of fire. In this way the Trinity is traceable in every creature, for every creature exhibits subsistence in being, a particular formal nature, as well as a relationship to others, but it does not *image* the Trinity because not all creatures have words conceived and love proceeding. Yet both Word and Spirit are represented by all beings because all that exists comes from the Father as a piece of work from a craftsman, and all that exists represents the Spirit insofar as it comes from the loving will of the Father. In this way, each and every creature is at least a *vestigium Trinitatis.*

From this and other related ideas, it is clear that Aquinas's cosmos is a rich constellation of beings who reflect the Trinity's attributes. If so, and while admitting that Aquinas does not make this point explicitly, we may safely contend that, since a trace of the Father's begetting the Son in Love is indeed present in every creature, divine personhood is able to be encountered in each and every existent. As for other philosophers like Plato and Aristotle, who rightly saw how all things reflect in the way proper to them the ultimate Good, Thomas can see the divine persons reflected (to various degrees) in all that is. All creatures depend on God's life to keep them in existence, as nothing apart from God has the ability to keep itself in existence: "In this manner all creatures need to be preserved by God. For the being of every creature depends on God, so that not for a moment could it subsist, but would fall into nothingness were it not kept in being by the operation."[26] This conservation of being provides the metaphysical framework by which water and trees and all else can be addressed in personal terms because all that is reflects the personhood of God, *ens,* and not just the being of God, *esse.*

This relationship between being and personhood comes into even starker relief when we turn to the opening pages of the *Summa contra gen-*

---

26. *Summa theologiae* I, q. 104, art. 1, resp.; all citations from the standard translation by the Fathers of the English Dominican Province (Westminster, MD: Christian Classics, 1948), 511.

tiles. Here this same dynamic not only provides Thomas's explanation of the existence of all things but even becomes the foundation for the fittingness of the incarnation. We again see how all things reflect God their Maker by speaking to us of God's creative wisdom, but now God sends his Son so as to reveal within the created order the very divine intellect that brought all things into original existence:

> Now, the end of each thing is that which is intended by its first author or mover. But the first author and mover of the universe is an intellect, as will be later shown. The ultimate end of the universe must, therefore, be the good of an intellect. This good is truth. Truth must consequently be the ultimate end of the whole universe, and the consideration of the wise man aims principally at truth. So it is that, according to his own statement, divine Wisdom testifies that he has assumed flesh and come into the world in order to make the truth known: "For this was I born, and for this came I into the world, that I should give testimony to the truth" (John 18:37). The Philosopher himself establishes that first philosophy is the science of truth, not of any truth, but of that truth which is the origin of all truth, namely, which belongs to the first principle whereby all things are. The truth belonging to such a principle is, clearly, the source of all truth; for things have the same disposition in truth as in being.[27]

In this rather multiplex passage from the *Summa contra gentiles,* Thomas contends that the ultimate source of the cosmos is not merely abstract being but a personal mind. Consequently, the good of the entire universe is this creative intellect. Since the final end of creatures is the divine mind or wisdom, the purpose or goal of every creature, even those on the elemental, mineral, and vegetative levels, is to enter into relationship with this divine consciousness.

For Thomas, the creatures of the cosmos are likewise loci of God's interpersonal activity. All things exist because a Trinity of love has lifted them out of nothing in order to reflect God's own majesty and thus praise him each in its own appropriate way (e.g., at *Summa theologiae* I, q. 70, art. 2). Divine persons are thus the ground and continuation of all being; consequently, there must be a trace of divine person in all that is. If so, an openness to a second-person experience is possible in all that flows from and is returning back to a personal God.

---

27. *Summa contra gentiles* I, ch. 1.2, trans. Anton C. Pegis (Notre Dame, IN: University of Notre Dame Press, 1975), 60.

From these patristic and medieval patterns explaining God's creating, sustaining, and directing all existents, the twentieth century brought a renewed insistence on even more dialogical and personalistic concepts. For example, in 1923 Martin Buber received the chair in Jewish religious history at the University of Frankfurt and soon thereafter released his *Ich und Du,* setting much of the stage for twentieth-century thought, in philosophical as well as theological circles, both Jewish and Christian. What Buber provided to generations of thinkers was a focus on the importance of how each human person interacts not only with other persons but with all of reality.

For Buber, the quality of one's own "I" is inevitably determined through one's interaction with the whole of the external world. No man, woman, or child is pure person alone, but is realized fully only through one's own quality of engagement with the other. Knowing oneself truly is thus achieved only through reaching out and relating to the other rightly. In this acknowledgment of the other, each human must choose whether to embrace the other as a "Thou" (*Ich-Du*) or as an "It" (*Ich-Es*). Nothing short of one's own humanity is at stake; at every moment either I am able to face another as a subject who makes demands on me and for whom I have a particular responsibility, or I can choose to encounter another only as an object that I can deface, manipulate, or otherwise seek to control.

Through one's volitional engagements, one realizes this twofold "I." This binary self is the ability to become a fleshy interlocutor personally invested in the other before oneself; or, conversely, to become a stony self separated from all else — to live as an engaged "I" or to distance oneself from true engagement and thereby one day discover oneself as a "separated I."[28] According to Buber, this dynamism occurs on three different levels: (1) between God and human persons, (2) between human persons, and (3) between humans and the entire world of nature. Setting the first two categories aside for now, it is significant for our purposes that Buber sees brute creation as a sphere in which we become fully human or not. For here the individual can most easily reduce the other to machines valued only for what they can do for him or her; in so doing, the individual inevitably acts as a replaceable "It" as well.[29]

28. Martin Buber, *I and Thou,* trans. Ronald Gregor Smith (New York: Scribners Classic, 1987), 65.
29. Buber, *I and Thou,* 68. Walter Kaufmann applies the very argument Buber advances when discussing how to read *I and Thou.* If it is engaged simply as a philosophic essay, Kaufmann writes, the reader misses the essential aspect of the work. "But if instead of examining the book as an object, an It, we open our hearts to it to hear what it has to say

We realize the interconnectedness of God, humanity, and nature only by genuinely engaging each as a "Thou" to whom I unreservedly give myself in attentiveness and personal presence. Nothing falls outside of this call to welcome and to be wholly aware of the reciprocity offered. For as I allow the other truly into my life, I am drawn into the life of not only addressing the other but of being addressed mutually as well. No longer can I hide in some existential asbestos; the world and the world's Maker are making demands on me to be present, aware, and engaged. This is what Buber describes as "being wakened and educated to solidarity of relation," and it is what allows us to imitate God in recognizing all things as a "Thou."[30] In so doing, we avoid the extremes of reducing all things to discriminate and disposable objects, or of wrongly deifying them into idols without which we think we cannot live. The *ewige Du*, the eternal Thou, is discernible only when we allow ourselves to be drawn rightly into the mutuality *(Mutualität)* and reciprocity *(Gegenseitigkeit)* of all that surrounds us. Only here can we be caught up into the Word's turn toward the Father in the Spirit; only here do we become aware of the divine persons' vestigial presence in all things.

Ecclesiology and the Extension of Personhood

Such a portrait of how the divine persons interact with the created realm determines the godly similitude of both the human and the nonhuman order. Stewards of the created world, those made in God's own image and likeness (cf. Gen 1:26-27), however, are called by the biblical tradition to look outward and recognize not only their own smallness but the grandeur of the cosmos they are called to serve. We catch a glimpse of how this is done in Scripture when God chooses to call and interact with even mineral and vegetative creatures as another "you." This is not to argue that God somehow renders water and trees into persons in their own right, but it is to recognize God's greatness in extending his own personhood to all that is before and because of him. Yet in addressing creatures in an "I-Thou" exchange, the Lord is showing his creatures who they are before him, thereby providing an example for those able to imitate him freely and rationally.

---

to us, can it be anything but what Buber suggests in this little book, namely *das ewige Du*?" (Walter Kauffman, "Buber's Religious Significance," in *The Philosophy of Martin Buber,* ed. P. A. Schilpp and Maurice Friedman [Cambridge: Cambridge University Press, 1967], 683).

30. Buber, *I and Thou,* 105.

Take as a schematic window the human domestication of an animal in order to see how this extension of personhood might occur. In its native state, the brute animal is instinctually impulsive and may, more often than not, be quite aggressive. When brought into a human family, however, that animal is eventually made to forfeit its ferociousness and adapt itself to the new expectations demanded of it: it will eat here and not there, this space alone (and absolutely nowhere else) will serve as the bathroom. The animal will learn the inflections of human voices and the meanings of a few particular words. In time it will come to understand what the rattling of car keys might suggest, what the big red leash means, and so on. The family pet will also learn how to sulk when corrected, hide when mischievous, and rejoice with the promise of some treat. In this process of domestication, the cat remains forever feline and the hound always canine; now, however, human personhood is extended to them, which affords the animal a life it would not have had otherwise.

In her book on calling animals by name, *Adams's Task,* the veteran trainer Vicki Hearne explores the modifications that occur when one takes an animal out of its natural world and introduces it into the world of humans. In this new society the animal is conferred with an unexpected set of demands but also dignities. Hearne is also quick to point out with myriad anecdotes of prisoners, special-needs people, the aged, and the lonely, how dog owners themselves are transformed as well: "If training is completed properly, the dog makes an intuitive leap — joins the group, as it were — and may later display degrees of ingenuity and courage in finding lost objects and lost children that astonish the uninitiated. The handler, too, changes through his acceptance of posture and responsibility. He joins the group, too, enters the moral life as well, and learns to talk to Fido."[31]

In this reciprocity, the trainer grows metaphysically larger in extending his or her own personhood to an otherwise feral beast. As handler and beast begin to contribute to a new, shared reality, both become dedicated to each other, and both begin to change. As the two begin to interact jointly in a common purpose, the benevolent handler in-personates the dog with a new identity and new set of powers that the dog itself would not naturally ever possess on its own; in turn, the dog renders its owner more humane and more like the person he or she was made to be.

Perhaps this interchange is what C. S. Lewis was drawing from when he

---

31. Vicki Hearne, *Adam's Task: Calling Animals by Name* (New York: Skyhorse Publishing, 2007), 29.

introduced the talking beasts in his *Chronicles of Narnia* tales. The normally predatory and self-seeking animals are granted the gift of speech as they grow in allegiance to ever-good Aslan. But if ever they are found treacherous, they may be struck dumb and forced to spend their days stripped of the gifts otherwise offered them. Take, for example, the turncoat cat Ginger at the Battle of Stable Hill in *The Last Battle*. After denying Aslan (and all objective reality for that matter), Ginger loses the divinely granted ability to speak. Because of the rebellious cat's disobedience, Ginger's punishment comes by way of being reduced to mere "catness," naturally unable to converse on a higher level and instantly showing evidence of this lapse back to what animals would be when choosing to live opposed to Aslan. In his betrayal before Tirian, the last King of Narnia, we see how, once empty of Aslan's deifying powers, Ginger is slowly reduced to his natural feline state:

> "Aii — Aii — Aii — Aaow — Awah," screamed the Cat.
> "Art thou not called a *Talking* Beast?" said the Captain. "Then hold thy devilish noise and talk."
> What followed was rather horrible. Tirian felt quite certain (and so did the others) that the Cat was trying to say something: but nothing came out of its mouth except the ordinary, ugly cat-noises you might hear from an angry or frightened old Tom in a backyard in England. And the longer he caterwauled the less like a Talking Beast he looked. Uneasy whimperings and little sharp squeals broke out from among the other Animals.[32]

Ginger's ability to talk lies in direct proportion to his fidelity to Aslan: the more they are one, the more he is able to enjoy the gifts that Aslan alone can give him. The greater the unity, the greater the appropriation, and thus the more felinity is transformed into personality.

Lewis includes this process of transformation of a lower into a higher being in *Mere Christianity* as well. As children offer their own games and rules to the dolls and tin soldiers with which they play, Christ likewise offers his

32. C. S. Lewis, *The Last Battle*, ch. 10, in the collected *Chronicles of Narnia* (New York: HarperCollins, 1982), 727. In *Letters to an American Lady*, ed. Clyde S. Kilby (London: Hodder & Stoughton, 1967), Lewis mentions that one of his cats was "a huge Tom called Ginger" (see letter of February 22, 1958). It is also intriguing to call to mind the particularly British phrase of something being so fine that it could "make a cat speak," said usually about an exquisite alcoholic drink. One cannot help but wonder whether this colloquialism stems from Shakespeare's line in *The Tempest* (II.ii) when Stephano seeks to force his wine upon the subhuman Caliban, thus elevating him momentarily out of his normal savagery: "Here is that which will give language to you, cat; open your mouth."

own life to those willing to be placed in his hands. This is how creatures are transformed into a perfection that is not inherently their own. Mothers and dog owners do the same, and so, in the words of Lewis, "A mother teaches her baby to talk by talking to it as if it understood long before it really does. We treat our dogs as if they were 'almost human': that is why they really become 'almost human' in the end."[33] Could it not be that, in such an exchange, one invites a creature to greater dignity, and in so doing recognizes in all the beasts of the earth a simulacrum of personhood? Perhaps this is a faint hint of what the Trinity does absolutely, perfectly, and eternally to extend and thus find one's own personhood in another.

So it is not that St. Francis preached to the birds of Umbria and rebuked the wolf of Gubbio because he saw in them rational persons whose eternal destiny would be determined by their actions; instead, he encountered creatures whose worth and dignity spoke to Francis of God's own divine personhood, and whose own mendicant mandate called him to extend his own human personhood to these beloved creatures of God. Francis recognizes the bird's ability to praise the Lord by being a bird, but he also realizes his own ability to preach the good news to all of creation as instructed by the Lord. He enters into an "I-Thou" conversation with all around him and, in so doing, renders not only them better birds, but himself a more receptive saint who now, through his preaching, experiences the gift of God at levels and in creatures not accessible to those tone-deaf to the symphony of praise played between Creator and creation.

Not all, of course, have ears to hear this "utterances of creatures [*creaturarum loquela*]," as *Gaudium et spes* describes it above, but this is precisely what good theology must provide: the space to "hear" how Creator and creatures interact incessantly. In his famous poem *The Hound of Heaven*, Francis Thompson realizes that nonpersoned creatures do not "speak" in how we understand normal human speech, but they do nonetheless communicate to those still enough to hear: "For ah! we know not what each other says, / These things and I; in sound *I* speak — / *Their* sound is but their stir, they speak by silences."[34] The more one grows in godliness, the one more is able to hear and see no longer from a purely created perspective. Grace elevates and expands the creature's ability to interact with all things the way the Creator does.

---

33. *Mere Christianity*, IV.7; for more here, see my "*Mere Christianity*: Theosis in a British Way," *Journal of Inkling Studies* 4, no. 1 (April 2014): 1-18.

34. Francis Thompson, "The Hound of Heaven," in *Complete Poems of Francis Thompson* (New York: Modern Library, 1913), 91.

The denouement of this dialogue is the divinization of the elect. When God deifies his children in his Spirit of sanctification, he elevates and transforms us into a life not naturally our own. When we are elevated and transformed by partaking of the divine life (2 Pet 1:4), we are offered in Christ a new agency, new expectations, and a new identity. Of course, we never cease to be human, but we are no longer constrained to live at the merely biological or fallen human level. Something new is underway, and in this process we are brought into a new home and expected to live a new way of life. Whereas other animals are domesticated when brought into a human *domus,* Christians are ecclesialized when brought into the divine *ecclesia.* Here we are granted a new destiny as God extends his own divine personhood, which enables us to live as new creatures, other Christs, adopted children of our heavenly Father. In the Son's incarnation, God in-personates himself into our human condition with the only desire that we in turn begin to live as full human persons, living a life never ours to possess but ours in which to partake.[35]

This point is made even more clearly by considering its contrary. What has been the first move of tyrants and dictators throughout history? When the powerful want to debase another, they do not add to the other's personhood but strip him or her of it. This is how Heinrich Himmler could justify his determination to exterminate the Jewish people: by first reducing them in the public's eyes to *Ungeziefer* ("vermin"), and how Hutu propaganda advanced the slaughter of the Tutsi *inyenzi* ("cockroaches"). The depersonalization of our enemy is primal. Sin defaces another and refuses to name the other truly and wholly. This is what Adam did when he first pointed at his beloved wife, who was just given the name Eve, and accused her of being merely *that woman,* whom he accused of leading him to fall (Gen 3:12). For when we recognize the inherent goodness of another, it also leads, to some degree, to an awareness of personhood.

Such personalizing also means protecting: the more we can imitate God's calling each creature by name, his entering into a second-person re-

---

35. Perhaps the most official and magisterial passage describing this deification is found at *Catechism of the Catholic Church,* §460: "The Word became flesh to make us '*partakers of the divine nature*' (2 Pet 1:4): 'For this is why the Word became man, and the Son of God became the Son of man: so that man, by entering into communion with the Word and thus receiving divine [adoption], might become a son [or daughter] of God' (St. Irenaeus). 'For the Son of God became man so that we might become God' (St. Athanasius). 'The only-begotten Son of God, wanting to make us sharers in his divinity, assumed our nature, so that he, made man, might make men gods' (St. Thomas Aquinas)."

lation with all that is, the more we will recognize both the inherent beauty of each creature and also our own value as persons called to protect personally all entrusted to us. This is how a rather extreme ecologist like Carolyn Merchant can now make more sense to me when she writes, "One does not readily slay a mother, dig into her entrails for gold, or mutilate her body. As long as the earth was conceptualised as alive and sensitive, it would be considered a breach of human ethical behaviour to carry out destructive acts against it."[36] Whereas I admittedly once would have dismissed such sentiment as dangerous totemism, I now see how only enemies and threats are defaced or depersonalized. When we grow in imitation of the Creator's care for every creature, however, we can begin to see how all things can be embraced as a creature where not only the being of God but the personal love of Father, Son, and Spirit is alive.

Conclusion

Between the autumn of 1965 and the late winter of the following year, two Russian literary rebels were summoned before Communist officials to defend their works. The manically suspicious KGB saw in their themes of transcendence and beauty, malignant threats to the Soviet state. The writers' promises of seeing this world differently, and maybe even the promise of a new world, cost Yuli Daniel (d. 1988) and Andrei Sinyavsky (d. 1997) years in a labor camp and subsequent deportation. Explaining the writer's role in society, Sinyavsky confessed he had to convey the themes he did because, as he looked back over the twentieth century, there had become really only two ways of life: Communism or Christianity. Whereas the former "has given us millions of corpses" and manufactured lies that cost the world so much innocence, the latter found life where only death seemed inevitable. From this fissure, Sinyavsky came to understand that there are, in the end, only two ways to communicate truth and beauty: "There is religion and there is poetry."[37] And as this essay has argued, the theologian and the poet converge

---

36. Carolyn Merchant, *Radical Ecology: The Search for a Livable World* (New York: Routledge, 1992), 43.

37. Andrei Sinyavsky, "Solitude et communication," *Recontres internationales de Genève*, 1975 (Neuchâtel 1975), 167; as found in Aelred Squire, *Summer in the Seed* (London: SPCK, 1980), 35. Dr. Hilary Finley has pointed out the many ways Russian literature establishes a second-person relationship among creatures. Take, for example, Fr. Zosima's instruction to his fellow monks in *The Brothers Karamazov:* "My brother asked the birds to forgive him;

precisely where both allow themselves to encounter others tenderly enough so as to recognize personhood therein.

Sadly, at the end of his life Charles Darwin confessed that he had wholly lost "all pleasure from poetry of any kind."[38] Since Darwin's day, the division between poetry and science has only widened, the separation between studying the earth and exploiting it has become more and more obvious. Poetry and personhood, personhood and a Father God who creates all things in his Son and unifying Spirit: perhaps this is where the poet and the theologian merge, in seeing that all reality is ultimately personal. So, while God may be the ultimate poet who alone is metaphysically large enough to elicit a "you" out of all things, those made in this Trinity's image and likeness become their truest selves as they impersonate God in his in-personation of all creatures.

Since all creation originates from the one heavenly fiat, all creatures are to be encountered as expressions from this divine cry *ad extra*. Anything other than a reverent care for all creatures leads not only to a division between creatures themselves but also to an internal fragmentation within created persons. The more alienated I become from the world in which I am called to live, the more divided I become within my own self. The less I see the three divine persons alive in each and every creature, the less I understand this world and myself. For in all things there is a trace of divine personhood, Trinitarian relationality — whether explained as a Logocentric turn or as a vestigial presence. To those who live with refined eyes and purified hearts, the desert fathers and the tender poets see in all things another worthy of our mercy and our tears, our prayers and our love.

---

that sounds senseless, but it is right. . . . It may be senseless to beg forgiveness of the birds, but birds would be happier at your side — a little happier, anyway — and children and all animals, if you yourself were a little nobler than you are now" (VI.3, "Of Prayer, of Love, and of Contact with Other Worlds").

38. *The Autobiography of Charles Darwin and Selected Letters,* ed. Francis Darwin (New York: Dover Publishing, 1958), 53.

CHAPTER 15

The Liturgical Theology of the Participation of Creation in the Sacred Triduum

Esther Mary Nickel, RSM

Jesus answered them, "The hour has come for the Son of Man to be glorified. Amen, amen, I say to you, unless a grain of wheat falls to the ground and dies, it remains just a grain of wheat; but if it dies, it produces much fruit."

JOHN 12:23-24

Behold the wood of the Cross, on which hung the salvation of the world. Come, let us adore.

FRIDAY OF HOLY WEEK

Sometimes we may find ourselves striving to understand relationships, longing to apply the fruit of our intellectual work and insights to the practice of daily life. In the cacophony of noise and increasing demands of living in a postmodern, technology-driven society, we may miss the most obvious opportunities to recognize the goodness and wonder of creation and of the cosmos. Deepening our awareness of the interrelatedness of the celebrations of the sacred liturgy and sacraments could lead to a removal of the scales from our eyes, which keep us from seeing the sacramentality of all of nature. An assertion may be made that, when we are engaged with increasing intensity, fully, actively, and consciously in the celebrations of the liturgical year,[1] the

1. *Sacrosanctum concilium,* §14, in *Vatican Council II: The Conciliar and Post-Conciliar*

more apt or prepared we are to establish a *habitus,* in the Thomistic use (not excluding freedom) of recognizing all of creation as sacred.[2] This recognition includes acknowledging with gratitude the Creator, God who is one and three, and the truth of the incarnation of the God-man: "through him all things came into being, and apart from him nothing came to be" (John 1:3). In so doing, we become more consistent in using our intellect to make acts of faith, *lex credendi;* and then we confirm in prayer the truths of our faith, *lex orandi,* which overflows into a *habitus* of generosity and a life of virtue, *lex vivendi.*[3] Reflecting on the greatest celebration of the liturgical year, the Sacred Triduum, during which we are invited to enter more profoundly into the paschal mystery of Jesus Christ, one can prepare and cultivate the soil in order to recognize and participate in these great truths of our salvation.

A discussion of the Sacred Triduum necessitates an understanding of what is implied by "liturgical theology" and participation. In some circles, liturgy is not thought of as theology per se but as prescribed rubrics or laws that govern the vestment color of the day. Some even make use of liturgical celebrations for self-expression, which diminish reverence for God and the opportunity the Church gives us to know and love more deeply the one who created all. Isolating the liturgy into the categorical disciplines of canon law or moral theology can lead to a fragmented impression of divine worship. Liturgy is public worship and is related to canon law, but one can assert that the celebration of the Eucharist preceded canon law. Also, some would categorize liturgy with the field of moral theology. It is true that we do have a moral obligation to follow the law (e.g., because of the character imparted in the sacrament of baptism, we are deputed to the worship of God),[4] and

---

Documents, ed. Austin Flannery, OP, Vatican Collection 1 (Northport, NY: Costello, 2004), 7.

2. Robert C. Miner, "Aquinas on Habitus," in *A History of Habit: From Aristotle to Bourdieu,* ed. Tom Sparrow and Adam Hutchinson (Lanham, MD: Rowman & Littlefield, 2013), 80-83.

3. "When Aquinas defines a good *habitus* (that is, a virtue) as the 'perfection of a power,' he does not mean an expansion of the capacity to decide between alternatives. The description of virtue as *perfectio potentiae* implies a very different type of expansion: the freedom to perform acts that are possible only for those in whom the power is perfected, or is growing to perfection" (Miner, "Aquinas on Habitus," 82).

4. Thomas Aquinas, *Summa theologica* III, q. 63, art. 2 (Notre Dame, IN: Christian Classics, 1981): "Respondeo dicendum quod, sicut dictum est, sacramenta novae legis characterem imprimunt inquantum per ea deputamur ad cultum Dei secundum ritum Christianae religionis" (I answer that, As stated above [art. 1], the sacraments of the New Law produce

we have an obligation to participate in the Holy Mass on Sundays.[5] If we veer away from the law, then we are susceptible to immorality, or a life un-reflective of virtue. This tendency and misinterpretation contributed to the acknowledgment in 1955 of the need for the liturgical reform of Holy Week,[6] which laid the foundation for the liturgical reform of the Second Vatican Council.

Many would agree that the theological celebration of the Mass was distanced in popular thought from any aspect of a theology of creation. In rural areas, however, persons were more likely to keep alive the relationship between the celebration of the liturgy and the sacramentality of creation. Their faith was strengthened because they knew experientially their absolute dependence upon a relationship with creation and with the Creator. When there is rain, they are grateful; in storms or droughts, they try to hold on and keep alive the hope of better times. A Minnesota farmer taught a wonderful lesson when he offered the counsel that one "hopes for the best, expects the worst, and settles for anything in-between." This philosophy suggests the reality of a lifelong pilgrimage, filled with the hope of eternal life, but realistically anticipating the obstacles that evil places along the way. While we strive for perfection and bounty, we need to be peaceful with whatever comes our way. The lesson of the farmer was not exactly "theological." yet it implied a theology that was developed through praxis, a theology that followed a trust in God who is all good, who is all merciful, and who provides and sustains us in existence. Another farmer marked his stationery with the sentence "For the promotion and diffusion of knowledge we observe and study." In addition to making each brick for his home, providing for his family with the work of his hands, he was also drawn irresistibly to the harmony of relationships in nature. He cared for his family in a paternal way and at the same time recognized husbandry as his way of relationship to his land and animals. In order to care more fittingly, he sharpened his observation skills and shared with others the insights that he gained. Those insights he attributed to his desire to cooperate with God, who gave him these gifts and whom he thanked each Sunday, many times by walking to Mass.

---

a character, in so far as by them we are deputed to the worship of God according to the rite of the Christian religion).

    5. *Catechism of the Catholic Church* (New York: Doubleday, 1997), 583, §2180, 583.

    6. Frederick R. McManus, *The Rites of Holy Week* (Paterson, NJ: St. Anthony Guild Press, 1956), v-ix.

Creation and Participation

An early philosophical work of Pope John Paul II includes his comment that "participation represents a property of the person himself, that inner and homogeneous property which determines that the person existing and acting together with others still exists and acts as a person."[7] St. Thomas Aquinas refers to being in terms of participation, which can be seen in two of his central premises: God is *esse per essentiam,* the creature is *esse per participationem.* That is, God is subsistent Being; the creature is being through participation.[8] Rhiza cites St. Thomas, noting that "creatures that more fully participate in God are more like God by being closer to the divine likeness than others."[9] There is diversity in participation in divine likeness, for although all are made in the image of God, there is a greater likeness contingent on the perfection of participation in the mystery of God, one and three, in the divine Trinity. The divine indwelling reflects this mystery, which permits participation in divinity, which makes known in concrete acts the mystery of *Deus caritas est.*

Created things, in and of themselves, do not participate in divine worship. Yet, through the mediation of humans, they are employed to enhance and also to be transformed by blessing and consecration to serve as sacramentals. The Church, in her awareness of all that is good, elevates what is of nature to serve that which is supernatural. Thus, the relationship of the participation of creation in the Sacred Triduum is the result of the harmony between humanity and all that God has created. As humanity is invited to participate in divine nature, creation serves sacramentally in this participation, and as a consequence it should be valued and reverenced.

Land and Worship

One might ask, "Is this practice of a living theology liturgical?" In Joseph Ratzinger's collected works on the theology of the liturgy, he notes a significant relationship between the land and worship. When Israel was seeking the promised land, the goal of the exodus was not only worship but also

7. Karol Wojtyla, *The Acting Person* (Dordrect: Reidel, 1979), 269.
8. Lourencino Puntel, *Encyclopedia of Theology: A Concise Sacramentum Mundi,* ed. Karl Rahner (Tunbridge Wells: Burns & Oates, 1993), 1160-63, s.v. "Participation."
9. John Rhiza, *Perfecting Human Actions: St. Thomas Aquinas on Human Participation in Eternal Law* (Washington, DC: Catholic University of America Press, 2009), 47.

land. "The land is given to the people to be a place for the worship of the true God." Land is not a possession with which one finds isolation or autonomy, but it is a way of relationship with God. Ratzinger continues, "In the Chronicles, there is a new interpretation that the land, considered in itself, is an indeterminate good. It becomes a true good, a real gift, a promise fulfilled, only when it is the place where God reigns."[10]

In reflecting on this notion of the land as an indeterminate good until its use for worship determines that is a true good, a specific good, one can see a relationship with the "matter" that is used for the sacraments. Water is an indeterminate good, yet when the sacramental words "I baptize you in the name of the Father and of the Son and of the Holy Spirit" accompanies this water while pouring or immersing,[11] the water is a specific good for baptism, and specifically for the baptism and ontological change of a unique human person. The same can be said for the oil of the infirm, or the oil and balsam for chrism, and certainly for the bread and wine that are indeterminate goods until the words of consecration determine the actual change in substance into the body and blood of the Lord.[12]

Pope Benedict continues this line of thought when he stated that "then the land will be, not just some independent state or another, but the realm of obedience, where God's will is done and the right kind of human existence is developed." What is this right kind of human existence on the land? We know that "all creation is groaning" (Rom 8:22); there is a hierarchy of creation that includes humanity. Man is to have dominion over the earth and all creatures. This dominion, which is rooted in gratitude and the desire to nurture and protect, most importantly includes relationships between communities of people and families with all of creation. Dominion as dominance and control is at the heart of what one discovers when considering the decline of rural communities. Farmers no longer need one another in the same way. With our advances in agronomic science and engineering, we actually try to be increasingly independent from one another. Typical farming practice encourages farmers to purchase and farm more acreage. Innovative devices for global positioning systems are possible to use so that the farmer no longer needs to drive the equipment but simply remains in the cab of the tractor or combine. One might consider this an ability to man-

10. Joseph Ratzinger, *Collected Works: Theology of the Liturgy* (San Francisco: Ignatius Press, 2014), 7, 8.
11. *Rite of Baptism for Children* (Collegeville, MN: Liturgical Press, 2002), §§40-41.
12. Thomas Aquinas, *Summa theologica* III, q. 75.

age "exterior land," but with a trade-off of loss of relationship with family members and neighbors. Pope Benedict has said, "Sinai gives to Israel, so to speak, its interior land, without which the exterior one would be a cheerless prospect." He continues, "Thus we can see what the foundation of existence in the Promised Land must be, the necessary condition for life in community and freedom. It is this: steadfast adherence to the law of God which orders human affairs rightly, that is, by organizing them as realities that come from God and return to God."[13] We find that in the exterior ordering, there is greater productivity, but the interior ordering of the relationship with the land and the common good suffers.

One might ask how, since all comes from God, is it possible to return anything to God, even of rightly ordered human affairs? To answer, we look to *lex credendi* and our faith that we worship one God, who is three persons in a unity of persons, and who is a communion of love. This is an act of faith, based not only on the fruit of early ecumenical councils, but also in the truth of sacred Scripture, of which we see a glimpse in the divine visitation of Abraham:

> *Abraham's Visitors.* The LORD appeared to Abraham by the oak of Mamre, as he sat in the entrance of his tent, while the day was growing hot. Looking up, he saw three men standing near him. When he saw them, he ran from the entrance of the tent to greet them; and bowing to the ground, he said: "Sir, if it please you, do not go on past your servant. Let some water be brought, that you may bathe your feet, and then rest under the tree. Now that you have come to your servant, let me bring you a little food, that you may refresh yourselves; and afterward you may go on your way." "Very well," they replied, "do as you have said." (Gen 18:1-5)

We do not attempt to prove the existence of the Trinity from this pericope; it does imply, however, a divine visitation of three persons.

In the liturgy, we celebrate this divine visitation as is evident in the concluding doxology of each Eucharistic anaphora of the Roman Rite: "Through him, and with him, and in him, O God, almighty Father, in the unity of the Holy Spirit, all glory and honor is yours, for ever and ever."[14] This unity reflects an order of communion. Creation is held in existence and harmony by this unity.

---

13. Ratzinger, *Theology of the Liturgy*, 8-10.
14. *The Roman Missal*, 3rd ed. (Washington, DC: USCCB, 2011).

Through His Son Jesus Christ God the Father creates always *(semper creas)* — as in the beginning of the world, so now also — all the products of nature. The most noble nourishing plants, that is, the material goods of wheat and grapes; for year after year he causes herbs to grow for the use of man, so that he may bring forth bread out of the earth, and wine may cheer the heart of man (Psalm 103:14-15). These created gifts of nature, the Almighty then changes through the same Jesus Christ into the heavenly sacrificial gifts of the Eucharist — a change in substance.[15]

Thus, we must acknowledge that creation is intimately related to the life of each person. There are times when we do not notice, however, and creation and created things are regarded as disposable. A disregard for creation certainly may lead to a disregard for the human person; all life is seen as disposable when it is no longer "useful." Pope Benedict states,

> We must not in our own day conceal our faith in creation: we may not conceal it, for only if it is true that the universe comes from freedom, love and reason, and that these are the real underlying powers, can we trust one another, go forward into the future, and love as human beings. God is the Lord of all things because he is their creator, and only therefore can we pray to him. For this means that freedom and love are not ineffectual ideas but rather that they are sustaining forces of reality.[16]

This thought was at the heart of the pastoral concern that motivated the reform of the liturgy of the Second Vatican Council. We have an obligation to creation, as we have an obligation to worship, but both these obligations need to include a desire for a deeper knowledge and love of God. We long for relationships, to be taken into a communion that unites, yet permits individuality. By nature we are inclined toward isolation and need to look to a union with God and neighbor in order to grow in self-knowledge. "We cannot conceal our faith in creation; we may not conceal it, knowing that the universe comes from intelligence, freedom and the beauty that is identical with love, giving us the courage to keep on living, and it empowers us, comforted thereby, to take upon ourselves the adventure of life."[17] We are

15. Nicholas Gihr, *The Holy Sacrifice of the Mass: Dogmatically, Liturgically, and Ascetically Explained* (St. Louis: Herder, 1939), 690.

16. Joseph Ratzinger, *In the Beginning . . . : A Catholic Understanding of the Story of Creation and the Fall* (Grand Rapids: Eerdmans, 1995), 18.

17. Joseph Murphy, *Christ Our Joy: The Theological Vision of Pope Benedict XVI* (San Francisco: Ignatius Press, 2008), 102.

ESTHER MARY NICKEL, RSM

invited more deeply into this adventure of life, of communion, each time we participate in the celebration of the Eucharist. Father Cipriano Vagaggini was a prominent liturgical scholar during the Second Vatican Council. He comments, "The Father is considered as the source of all good things, because it is He who creates, sanctifies, blesses all these things, and then gives them to us; and as the end of all things, all honor goes to Him. Christ our Lord is considered as the great Mediator through whom the Father accomplishes everything."[18] Through Christ, we offer everything — all of creation and ourselves — back to the Father. He it is who creates, sanctifies, vivifies, and blesses every good thing and gives it to men; it is Christ through whom, together with whom, and in union with whom, as our Head (and here we have the concept of Christ the High Priest) we return all glory to the Father.

We have access to the communion of the persons of the Trinity through the incarnation of the Son, who took our flesh and redeemed us. In his treatise on the theology of the body, Father Vagaggini also asserts that it is difficult for us to understand in our time the importance of matter and of created things because of the influence of Cartesian dualism on our contemporary anthropology. We have shifted to a spiritualism that skews the truth that God wills our salvation to come about through the physical body of his Son. He comments that the "physical body of Christ possesses a function that is always active and permanent, and even eternal. Consequently we no longer see the function of the resurrection of Christ — and therefore that of the paschal mystery and of our own resurrection — nor the function of the Eucharistic mystery. Actually, we can understand both of these notions and therefore the true nature of the liturgy only when we realize the ever active and permanent part willed by God that is played by the physical body of Christ in the accomplishment of salvation in us."[19]

Since Christ assumed our flesh by taking his flesh from the Virgin Mary, his mother, not only can we call his Father our Father, but we may participate and cooperate in the representation of the sacrifice of Christ for our salvation. We find this opportunity for participation in a particular way as an expression of the "evolving theology of creation" within the prayers of the Offertory Rite of the Mass of the Roman Rite. The following prayers are taken from *The Roman Missal*:[20]

18. Cipriano Vagaggini, *Theological Dimensions of the Liturgy* (Collegeville, MN: Liturgical Press, 1976), 223.
19. Cipriano Vagaggini, *The Flesh, Instrument of Salvation: A Theology of the Human Body* (Staten Island, NY: Pauline Press, 1969), 16.
20. *The Roman Missal* (2011 ed.).

> Blessed are you, Lord God of all creation, for through your goodness we have received the bread we offer you: fruit of the earth and work of human hands, it will become for us the bread of life.

This prayer conveys a realization that everything we have comes from God and thus is to be revered as such. With the "work of human hands," it is offered to God, with the prayer that this bread is transubstantiated into the very flesh of Christ.

> By the mystery of this water and wine may we come to share in the divinity of Christ who humbled himself to share in our humanity.

> Blessed are you Lord God of all creation, for through your goodness we have received the wine we offer you: fruit of the vine and work of human hands, it will become for us our spiritual drink.

Similarly, this prayer for the mixing of two elements from creation, water and the wine from grapes, incorporates the goods that are given for our use and are offered back to God.

> Pray brethren, that my sacrifice and yours may be acceptable to God the almighty Father. May the Lord accept the sacrifice at your hand for the praise and glory of his name, for our good and the good of all his holy Church.

All pray together that these offerings from creation may be acceptable to God, in gratitude for all that he has given to humanity. This wording conveys a distinct conviction that there is a collaboration with creation in order to offer back to the Creator the very goods that we have been given. Pope Benedict XVI reflects this thought in stating, "It is only when man's relationship with God is right that all of his other relationships — his relationships with his fellow men, his dealings with the rest of creation — can be in good order."[21] Worship gives us a share in heaven's mode of existence, in the world of God; it allows light to fall from that divine world into ours.

Creation and Sacred Triduum

The liturgical movement preceded the reform of Holy Week in 1955. Actually, this work began in 1948. Over the centuries the celebrations of Holy Week

---

21. Ratzinger, *Theology of the Liturgy*, 10.

had crept into the morning hours and thus had lost the necessary connection between the symbolism of the celebrations with the cosmos. For example, the Easter Vigil was celebrated at 10 a.m., and very few (mostly nuns in convents) participated in the most solemn celebration of the paschal mystery. This diminishment of an actual, intentional relationship with creation is also evident in other liturgical celebrations. For example, during the Second Vatican Council, in discussing the need to order the liturgical celebrations in light of the cosmos, it was necessary to assign a new title to the Divine Office. To underline the relationship to the rising and setting of the sun, these prayers of the Church are now called the Liturgy of the Hours. Some clerics, who were bound by obligation to pray the "breviary," were accustomed to praying the hours of one day late in the day (e.g., at 11:00 p.m.), and then shortly thereafter (e.g., at 12:05 a.m.) following them with all of the hours of prayer for the following day. There was no relation to the *veritas horae*, the "truth of the hour," which the prayers of the office take into consideration and correspond with in accord with the cosmos. The new name "Liturgy of the Hours" intends to realign the prayers to the actual hours of the day, acknowledging morning, midday, evening, and night.

The determination of major celebrations in the liturgical calendar also takes into account the cosmos. The celebration of Christmas is set after the winter equinox, when the day length begins to increase. It gives a cosmic interpretation to the words of St. John the Baptist, "I must decrease and he must increase" (John 3:30), said in reference to Jesus. Correspondingly, the liturgical celebration of the birth of John the Baptist is June 24, a few days after the summer equinox, when day length begins to decline. Likewise, the setting of the date for the celebration of the resurrection of the Lord takes into consideration the lunar cycle and the spring equinox. It is a so-called movable feast, with its date being determined by the Sunday that follows the first full moon following the spring equinox. Once the date of Easter is set, then the accompanying celebrations are set, including Ash Wednesday, which marks the beginning of Lent, and Pentecost, which concludes the Easter season.

The liturgical celebrations include creation in order to help us grasp more fully the mysteries that we celebrate. We depend upon what we know and what is visible in creation to symbolize that which is invisible. "The symbolism of the liturgy is based primarily on nature, which, coming from God, bears upon itself the stamp of its Creator. In nature, the most resplendent, most beautiful object is light, and for us it is the natural light of the sun, which is also the source of power for growth in life. Hence, in the liturgy, the sun is the symbol of Christ and of his light-giving mission, just as darkness represents the power of darkness and evil."[22]

Holy Thursday

The institution of the Most Holy Eucharist and the priesthood is celebrated on Holy Thursday. In the morning liturgy there is a celebration of the priesthood and the sacramental life of the Church. A significant role of creation is the blessing of olive oil for the sacramental oils to be used for the sacraments of baptism, confirmation, holy orders, and the anointing of the sick, as well as of the sacramental oil for the anointing of catechumens. The olive oil is mixed with balsam resin and is referred to as chrism, thus the name of the liturgical celebration is the Chrism Mass. Each of these plant extractions would remain indeterminate, but with the prayers of the Church they are set aside for a determinate participation in the life-changing sacraments of the Church.

In the evening, the Sacred Triduum begins with the celebration of the Lord's Supper. This liturgy begins what is a three-day celebration of one "continuous liturgy." The daily Mass begins with the sign of the cross, and there is a dismissal. On Holy Thursday the Mass begins with the sign of the cross, but there is no dismissal. The Eucharist is reserved for adoration, and all are invited to participate in the opportunity to wait with the Lord, to go with him into the Garden of Gethsemane, and to stay with him. This time of prayer lasts into the night, until midnight, once again taking into consideration the relationship between the liturgy and the cosmos.

The Sacred Triduum is celebrated in this continuum of three days once during the liturgical year, yet there are devotional feasts that recall the particular mystery. For Holy Thursday we celebrate the Solemnity of the Body and Blood of Christ. This devotional feast has a particular relationship with St. Thomas Aquinas. The history of its establishment includes an account of a priest celebrating Mass in Bolseno, a village south of Orvieto in Italy. This priest lacked faith in the actual change in substance of bread and wine into the body and blood of Christ. At the words of consecration, drops of blood fell from the consecrated bread — the body of Christ onto the corporal. This liturgical linen cloth remains in a reliquary in the cathedral at

22. Virgil Michel, *The Liturgy of the Church according to the Roman Rite* (New York: Macmillan, 1938), 76.

Orvieto. The Eucharistic miracle was the occasion for Pope Urban IV to call upon St. Thomas to transform the texts of his theology of the Eucharist into the formulary for the Mass and Liturgy of the Hours for the liturgical celebration of Corpus Christi, the Body and Blood of Christ. These celebrations include processions with the Blessed Sacrament, the faithful walking in pilgrimage. This liturgical action symbolizes a deep relationship between creation and the Creator and provides evidence of how the liturgy contributes to the organic development of the theology of creation. As one might anticipate, this connection is more readily understood by those who live in rural communities.

A summary of the mystery of Holy Thursday and the devotional celebration of the body and blood of Christ can be found in the following prayer for Corpus Christi from *The Rural Life Prayer Book:*[23]

A PRAYER FOR THE WHEAT
(Feast of Corpus Christi)

DEAR Lord, in many broad fields of this vast country of ours, the wheat is growing now. Some is still young and green, some is headed out, and all, before very long, will be golden ripe.

Most of it, dear Lord Jesus, will go to feed the hungry. In countless loaves of bread and in cereals, it will find its way to tables in city and country almost all over the world.

Some of it will be used at another table. It will be ground into fine flour and used to make the hosts, the altar-breads for Holy Mass. Priests will take it into their anointed hands and pronounce over it the words of consecration, and it will cease to be ordinary bread, and will become the Bread of angels. It will look as it did before, but we know and believe that it will be the Body and Blood, the Soul and Divinity of You, Lord Jesus Christ, there really present, under the appearances of bread.

O Jesus, bless the broad, rich fields of wheat in our whole land. Protect them from hail and beating rains, from blight and rust, from windstorms and drought. Let them be full and rich, so that the hungry may be fed, and may praise You and thank You as You deserve. And may all the Holy Masses that will be said with hosts made of this wheat hasten the day when at last there will be enough reapers working in Your harvest, which is ripe and ready now, waiting only to be gathered home. Amen.

23. Alban Dachauer, *The Rural Life Prayer Book* (Des Moines, IA: National Catholic Rural Life Conference, 1956), 84-85.

Good Friday

The liturgy of Good Friday (the Passion of the Lord) does not begin with the sign of the cross but continues the celebration of Holy Thursday. The symbolism is poignant; the celebrant enters in silence. He makes a profound act of humiliation with the gesture of prostration. All kneel in silence. The significance of this gesture is that, when realizing the cost of our redemption, words are inadequate to express our love and gratitude. Humility is from the Latin word *humus,* which pertains to soil. This meaning is also recalled at the initiation of the liturgical season of Lent with the reception of ashes on Ash Wednesday, accompanied with the words, "Remember that you are dust, and to dust you shall return."[24] The Passion according to St. John is proclaimed. There is an implied mention of Jesus, the innocent lamb who suffered, died, and offered no resistance. This lamb, Jesus, invites us to his wedding feast with his *consummatum est.* Pope Benedict sees this as a *reditus,* a return of the Son to the Father. He includes how we participate in this act of worship: "If sacrifice in its essence is simply returning love and therefore divinization, worship now has a new aspect: the healing of wounded freedom, atonement, purification, deliverance from estrangement: the Fathers saw this in the return of the lost sheep — the metaphor for man, he cannot get out of the thicket and find his way back to God — he takes the sheep on his shoulders, he assumes human nature, and as the God-Man he carries the man the creature home to God."[25] In the mystery of the celebration of Good Friday, we see how this *reditus* becomes possible through the cross of Christ. "This sacrifice has nothing to do with destruction. It is an act of a new creation, the restoration of creation to its true identity. All worship is now participation in the Pasch of Christ — this passing over from divine to human, from death to life, to the unity of the God-man."[26]

The cross is wood and is a paradox. In the mystery of the wood of the cross, we see both the tree of death and the tree of life. The liturgy of Good Friday includes the adoration of the wood of the cross, which begins with the prayerful words: "Behold the wood of the Cross, on which hung the salvation of the world. Come let us adore."[27] Our life comes from the Lord's death, a tremendous mystery. All depart in silence, prayerful fasting, and

---

24. *The Roman Missal.*
25. Ratzinger, *Theology of the Liturgy,* 18.
26. Ratzinger, *Theology of the Liturgy,* 14.
27. *The Roman Missal.*

awaiting the fruit of his salvific death: the celebration of our baptism at the Easter Vigil.

Holy Saturday

The Easter Vigil continues the one celebration of the Sacred Triduum. In this celebration we are united with the Lord in his resurrection; it is the culmination of the paschal mystery, during which we pass with him from death to life. It is at the heart of Christianity. Why do we gather? Why was so much effort put forward by servant of God Pope Pius XII, St. Pope John XXIII, and Blessed Pope Paul VI to restore the celebration of the Easter Vigil? In the account of the celebration in Jerusalem, we find that the vigil was quite extensive, during which the Christians gathered and anticipated the actual return of the Lord. In a sermon from the Easter Vigil, St. Augustine clarifies that "we need not wait for the Lord to arise, for Christ's resurrection was centuries ago. And yet, our annual celebration is not simply a commemoration of a past event; it implies a present action on our part, which we accomplish by our life of faith and of which this vigil is a symbol. The entire course of time is in fact one long night during which the Church keeps watch, waiting for the return of the Lord, waiting until he comes."[28]

The liturgy of the Easter Vigil begins, not with the sign of the cross, but with the blessing of the Easter fire: "A prayer for the blessing of the fire uplifts our mind from the human level to the divine, from the thought of man's elementary need of fire and light for warmth and vision to the thought of God in His infinite being, the light of all truth and the fire of love, who through Christ deigns to give Himself to us and to make us sharers in His own Beatitude."[29]

From the recent English translation of the third edition of the 1970 *Roman Missal*, we find the following rubric and prayer:

Then the Priest blesses the fire, saying with hands extended:
Let us pray:
O God, who through your Son bestowed upon the faithful the fire of your glory, sanctify + this new fire, we pray; and grant that, by these

28. Jean Gaillard, *Holy Week and Easter: A Liturgical Commentary* (Collegeville, MN: Liturgical Press, 1957), 102.
29. Gallaird, *Holy Week and Easter,* 107.

paschal celebrations, we may be so inflamed with heavenly desires, that with minds made pure we may attain festivities of unending splendor.

The priest lights the paschal candle from the new fire, saying: "May the light of Christ rising in glory dispel the darkness of our hearts and minds."

Those in the Church wait in darkness, with candles ready to be lit as they participate in the dialogue *Lumen Christi* (Light of Christ), responding with *Deo gratias* (thanks be to God), which is repeated three times. The chanting of the *Exultet,* the proclamation of the resurrection of Christ, follows. A portion of the celebration is rooted in the synagogue celebration of the *Lucernarium,* the lighting of the evening lamp. In the third century this lamp was replaced with the lighting of the candle in order to read from the ambo. The liturgical texts most likely originated as early as the fifth century, although not later than the seventh century. The language, rhythm, and ideas show a Pauline influence. The chanting of the *Exultet* is the beginning of Easter; it is a proclamation that invites a celebration of the paschal mysteries. This proclamation is a blessing of light; it includes a vivid theology of creation.[30]

> Exult, let them exult, the hosts of heaven, exult, let Angel ministers of God exult, let the trumpet of salvation sound aloud our mighty King's triumph! Be glad, let earth be glad, as glory floods her, ablaze with light from her eternal King, let all corners of the earth be glad, knowing an end to gloom and darkness.

And then to continue the hierarchy and order of praise:

> Rejoice, let Mother Church also rejoice, arrayed with the lightning of his glory, let this holy building shake with joy, filled with the mighty voices of the peoples. (Therefore, dearest friends, standing in the awesome glory of this holy light, invoke with me, I ask you, the mercy of God almighty, that he, who has been pleased to number me, though unworthy, among the Levites, may pour into me his light unshadowed, that I may sing this candle's perfect praises.)

The dialogue and response, which has the same form of the preface of the Mass, begins the anaphora. This is an invitation for all to participate in this great prayer.

---

30. The text of the *Exultet* is taken from *The Roman Missal.*

The Lord be with you. And with your spirit.
Lift up your hearts. We lift them up to the Lord.
Let us give thanks to the Lord our God. It is right and just.
It is truly right and just, with ardent love of mind and heart, and with devoted service of our voice, to acclaim our God invisible, the almighty Father, and Jesus Christ, our Lord, his Son, his Only Begotten. Who for our sake paid Adam's debt to the eternal Father, and, pouring out his own dear Blood, wiped clean the record of our ancient sinfulness.

The *Exultet* is filled with imagery of creation, of light overcoming darkness, or creation in relationship to the Creator, and of creation in relationship to man. Virgil Michel comments, "All creation, in a sense, fell with man and was again redeemed with him unto the glory of God. It is through man, and through him alone on earth, that the material creation can achieve its proper function of serving unto the glory of its Creator. Therefore does man make use of all creation in his liturgical worship, all of nature, so that nature may join him in the more perfect rendering of his due worship of God."[31] The *Exultet* continues in a poetic recognition of the meaning of "this night":

These, then, are the feasts of *Passover,* in which is slain the Lamb, the one true Lamb, whose Blood anoints the doorposts of believers.

This is the night, when once you led our forebears, Israel's children, from slavery in Egypt and made them pass dry-shod through the Red Sea.

This is the night that with a pillar of fire banished the darkness of sin.

This is the night, that even now, throughout the world, sets Christian believers apart from worldly vices and from the gloom of sin, leading them to grace and joining them to his holy ones.

This is the night, when Christ broke the prison-bars of death and rose victorious from the underworld. Our birth would have been no gain, had we not been redeemed.

In a most significant way regarding the evolving liturgical theology of creation, there is a beautiful homage to bees.

31. Michel, *Liturgy of the Church,* 69.

On this night of grace, O holy Father, accept this candle, a solemn offering, the work of bees and of your servants' hands, an evening sacrifice of praise, this gift from your most holy Church.

In the first English translation (1970) of the *Exultet,* according to the translation theory of dynamic equivalence, all references to bees were omitted. The reason given was that the faithful would not understand such a reference, since they were so distant from apiculture, and thus from the relationship with creation that is so important for liturgical symbolism. However, one could find an explanation of bees and the significance of beeswax in candle boxes, for example: "True to the traditions of early Christian ages, the light that these 51% beeswax candles bring to a church signifies the presence of Christ. The human nature of Christ is symbolized by the purest forms of beeswax produced from the bodies of virgin bees and used to nourish each candle's flame. The candles expend themselves during burning as Christ expended Himself in His love for mankind. The lighting of them expresses the spiritual meaning: 'Your light comes, and the splendor of the Lord goes over you.'"[32]

The *Exultet* continues:

But now we know the praises of this pillar, which glowing fire ignites for God's honor, a fire into many flames divided, yet never dimmed by sharing of its light, for it is fed by melting wax, drawn out by mother bees to build a torch so precious.

This verse of the proclamation underlines the truth of participation, that the gift of our participation in divine nature does not exhaust the Creator but invites us to a greater sharing in participation. Each in its own way, specific to its type of being, contributes to the continuity and perfection of the universe. Each receives light from the Creator, a flame is divided, but never dimmed. God diffuses goodness and cannot be exhausted.

Man is made in the image of God, but all creatures have a trace, or vestige, of God. Thus, the universe continues to reveal God, and all of creation should be esteemed in its own right, in its own way of being. "Since God both creates and guides creatures to their proper perfection on account of the same end, each creature acts in accord with its particular mode. Hence, the variety of modes of substantial participation in God causes a variety of actions (secondary perfections) which are also participations in

32. Cathedral Candle Company, Syracuse, NY.

God, who is all perfection essentially."[33] The *Exultet* concludes with the following verse:

O truly blessed night, when things of heaven are wed to those of earth, and divine to human. Therefore, O Lord, we pray you that this candle, hallowed to the honor of your name, may persevere undimmed, to over- come the darkness of this night. Receive it as a pleasing fragrance, and let it mingle with the lights of heaven. May this flame be found still burning by the Morning Star who never sets, Christ your Son, who, coming back from death's domain, has shed his peaceful light on humanity, and lives and reigns for ever and ever. Amen.

What is the meaning of these celebrations each year, and what signifi- cance might we find for a theology of creation? God has marked all of cre- ation for a purpose that he knows, and little by little we come into an aware- ness of that purpose. Our tendency is to use creation for ourselves without recognizing the long-term consequences of our short-sighted gains. Man is to have communion with the Trinity, and this communion should also enlighten an ever-new appreciation of recognizing the trace of God in every creature. We need to cultivate and consume plants and animals. We drink water and breathe air. In order to embrace a greater appreciation, we need to approach all of creation with gratitude, with thanksgiving to the one who creates and continues to sustain all in existence. "Of every creature created, from the immortal angels to 'every brute and plant on earth,' man alone is the one whose life God personally informs and 'immediately inspires,' mak- ing us to love himself and kindling us 'to fresh desires' (Dante, Anselm). Man alone is permitted to penetrate the perichoretic spheres of the one whom Dante himself, in his final canto, dares to address, the Trinitarian one."[34]

St. John Paul II concluded his encyclical *Ecclesia de Eucharistia* with a poignant summary of the theology of creation:

When I think of the Eucharist, and look at my life as a priest, as a Bishop and as the Successor of Peter, I naturally recall the many times and places in which I was able to celebrate it. I remember the parish church of Nie- gowić, where I had my first pastoral assignment, the collegiate church of Saint Florian in Krakow, Wawel Cathedral, Saint Peter's Basilica and so many basilicas and churches in Rome and throughout the world. I have

33. Rhiza, *Perfecting Human Actions*, 54.
34. Douglas Farrow, *Ascension Theology* (London: T&T Clark, 2011), 150.

been able to celebrate Holy Mass in chapels built along mountain paths, on lakeshores and seacoasts; I have celebrated it on altars built in stadiums and in city squares. . . . This varied scenario of celebrations of the Eucharist has given me a powerful experience of its universal and, so to speak, cosmic character. Yes, cosmic! Because even when it is celebrated on the humble altar of a country church, the Eucharist is always in some way celebrated *on the altar of the world.* It unites heaven and earth. It embraces and permeates all creation. The Son of God became man in order to restore all creation, in one supreme act of praise, to the One who made it from nothing. He, the Eternal High Priest who by the blood of his Cross entered the eternal sanctuary, thus gives back to the Creator and Father all creation redeemed. He does so through the priestly ministry of the Church, to the glory of the Most Holy Trinity. Truly this is the *mysterium fidei* which is accomplished in the Eucharist: the world which came forth from the hands of God the Creator now returns to him redeemed by Christ.[35]

May this little bit of exposure to the theology of creation found in the liturgical prayers of the Church inspire many to a greater appreciation and understanding of the paschal mystery, and of the participation of all of creation in liturgical prayer as divine worship. Christ humbled himself and became flesh in the womb of the Virgin so that he might exalt and redeem all of creation. In the Eucharist, his humanity is veiled, but his divinity is revealed to those with faith. The wheat from the fields awaits its service to the Creator through the work of human hands. We need to develop a deeper understanding of the goodness of creation, and thus we may discover a greater receptivity to acknowledge the Creator, seeking communion with one another and all of creation. This is the meaning of the grain of wheat: to die and bear much fruit, so that it does not remain just a grain of wheat.

35. John Paul II, *On the Eucharist: Ecclesia de Eucharistia,* §8.

Contributors

PAUL M. BLOWERS, Emmanuel Christian Seminary, Johnson City, TN

JOHN A. CUDDEBACK, Christendom College, Front Royal, VA

CHRISTOPHER A. FRANKS, High Point University, High Point, NC

MARIE GEORGE, St. John's University, New York, NY

PAIGE E. HOCHSCHILD, Mount St. Mary's University, Emmitsburg, MA

CHRIS KILLHEFFER, Yale University, New Haven, CT

MATTHEW LEVERING, Mundelein Seminary, Chicago, IL

STEVEN A. LONG, Ave Maria University, Ave Maria, FL

DAVID VINCENT MECONI, SJ, St. Louis University, St. Louis, MO

ESTHER MARY NICKEL, RSM, St. John Vianney Theological Seminary, Denver, CO

DAWN M. NOTHWEHR, OSF, Catholic Theological Union, Chicago, IL

FAITH PAWL, University of St. Thomas, St. Paul, MN

JONATHAN J. SANFORD, University of Dallas, TX

CHRISTOPHER J. THOMPSON, Saint Paul Seminary School of Divinity, St. Paul, MN

ROBERT LOUIS WILKEN, University of Virginia, Charlottesville, VA

Index of Names and Subjects

Index of Scripture References